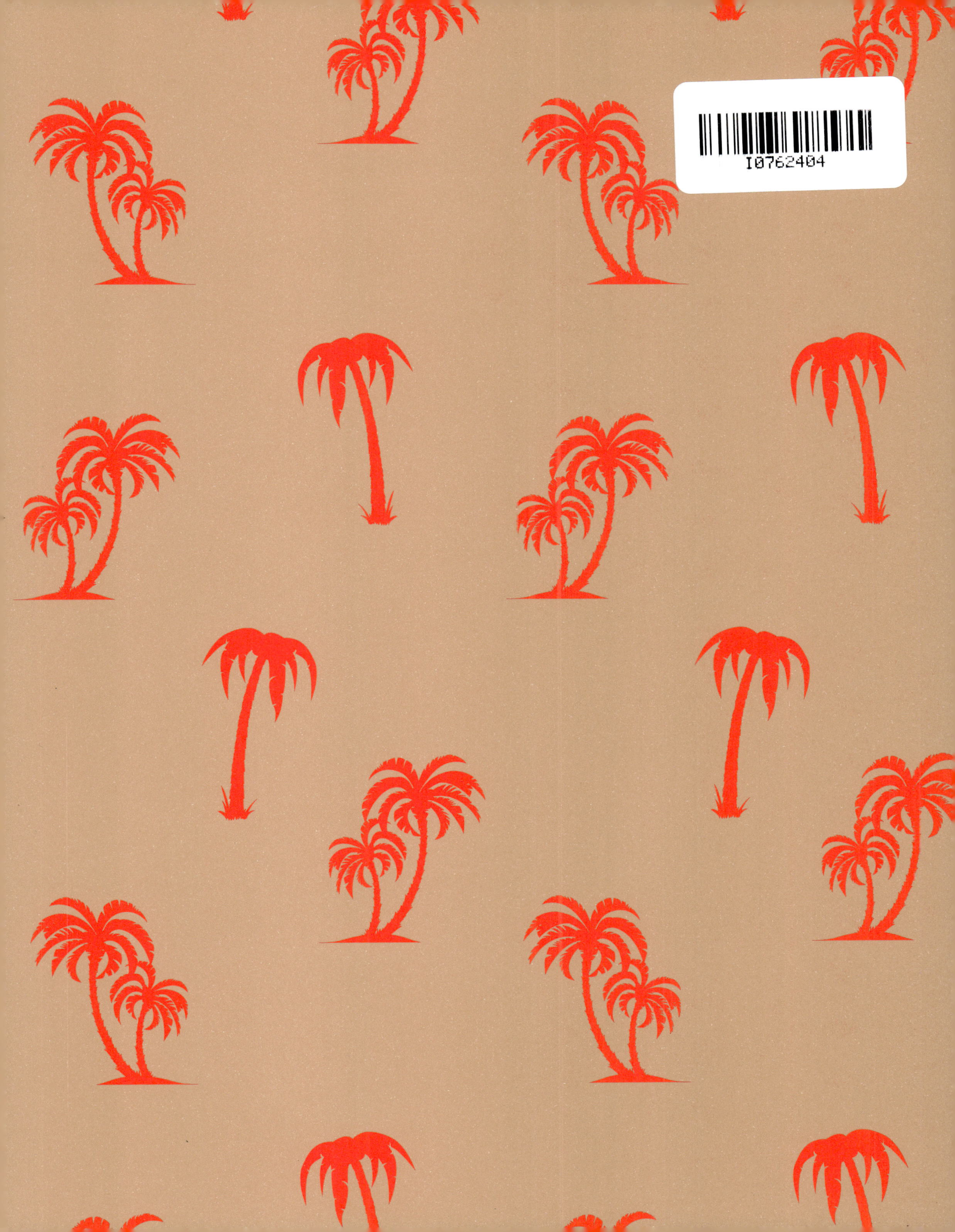
I0762404

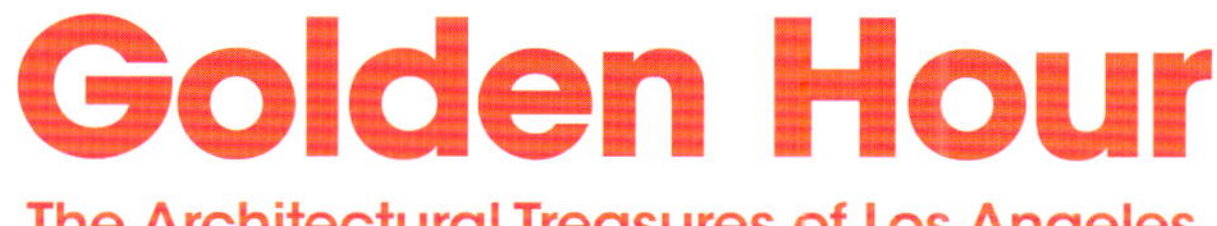
Golden Hour
The Architectural Treasures of Los Angeles

# Golden Hour

## The Architectural Treasures of Los Angeles

by **George Townley**

*Foreword by* Discover Los Angeles

PARAGON BOOKS

**Golden Hour:**
The Architectural Treasures of Los Angeles
by George Townley

First Printing
April 2025
ISBN: 978-1-952251-39-9



**Paragon Books**
929 Camelia Street
Berkeley, CA 94710-1419
paragon-books.com

**Publisher:** Ken Harman Hashimoto

**Design & Layout:** Shaun Roberts

The text was composed using Avant Garde Gothic Std. designed by Herb Lubalin, Tom Carnase, and Ed Benguiat.

Designed in Oakland, California
Printed in China

ISBN 978-1-952251-39-9
90000>
9 781952 251399

# CONTENTS

# POSTCARDS FROM AN ACCIDENTAL TOURIST

**George Townley's Los Angeles is a movie.** Dreaming of Googie starbursts and Birds of Paradise from his studio in Northern England, he has created an extensive storyboard of images depicting the City of Angels in its most magic hour—twice a day.



There's a reason that movies are made in LA. The term or terms, "Golden Hour" or "Magic Hour" were borrowed from the film industry, indicating a time of day when there's naturally dramatic light, thus, being a perfect time to shoot film. The irreplicable blue of our sunny skies and the dynamic glow of the skyline at night has attracted film directors and artist-types for decades. Correspondingly, Townley's portraits of chosen LA landmarks are always captured in pairs, during both of LA's magic hours, night and day. Offered together, they exhibit a passage of time, still frames of the city at its most effervescent. At once the Nuart Theater wakes up with a *Blade Runner* matinee on its marquee—its companion piece is alive at midnight for an audience at *Rocky Horror Picture Show*.

Yet, separately, these works reflect a nuanced personality of the architecture and possibly their viewer, depending on which depiction they favor. The daytime portrait of Union Station burns with the intensity of director Paul Schrader's *American Gigolo*, while night at the Griffith Observatory snaps with the electricity and lushness of auteur David Lynch's film, *Blue Velvet*.

In contrast to moving pictures, Townley's super-flat style of illustration is a retro-modern confluence of color, line and shape, derived from the mind and machine that creates them. The only irony exists in the fact that many of these landscapes were created before he was able to experience them in real life. Although extensively researched, these pieces are crafted with the obsessive love of a superfan, touched with just enough necessary fantasy and reverence that even locals are inspired to collect them.



Together these images form an Illustrated map of the American dream, one specific to Los Angeles. While dense with plants and palm trees, case-study modernism and vintage cars, Townley's work is simplified to the bare essence of California cool, stripped of everyday grit. Case in point, Townley's LAX theme building at sunset is a warm, gradient-infused love letter to architect Paul Revere Williams, and like all his works, is deliberately void of people. This is so you, the audience, can easily see yourself in them, as the artist does, while he creates.

And with George Townley's help, we arrive at the mix of what makes LA like no other place in the world. Colors, shapes, dreams, and the people who embody them. Thank you, George, for showing Los Angeles in such a beautiful, dramatic, light—Golden Hour and beyond.

**Shelley Leopold**
**Discover Los Angeles**

# Iconic Landmarks I

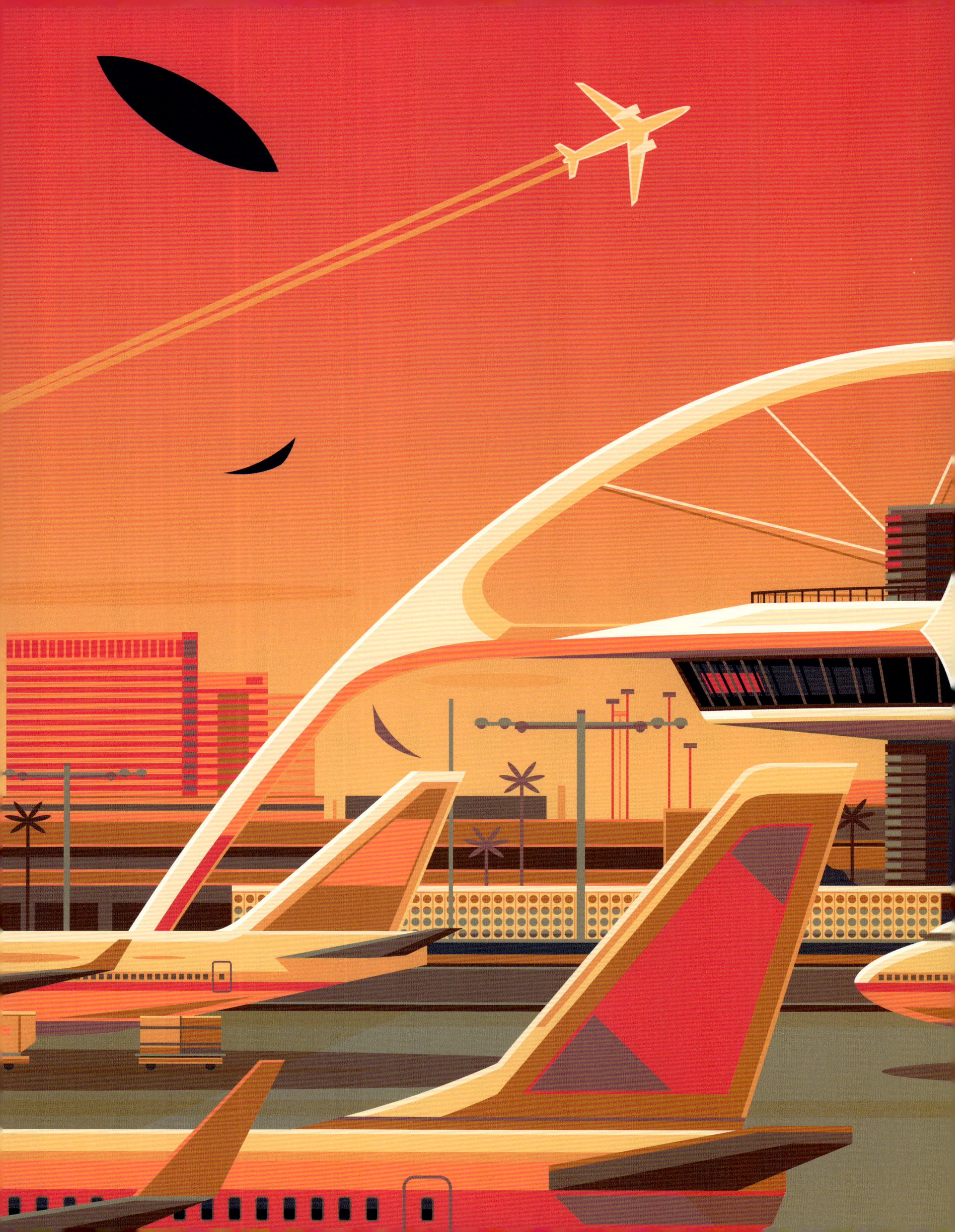

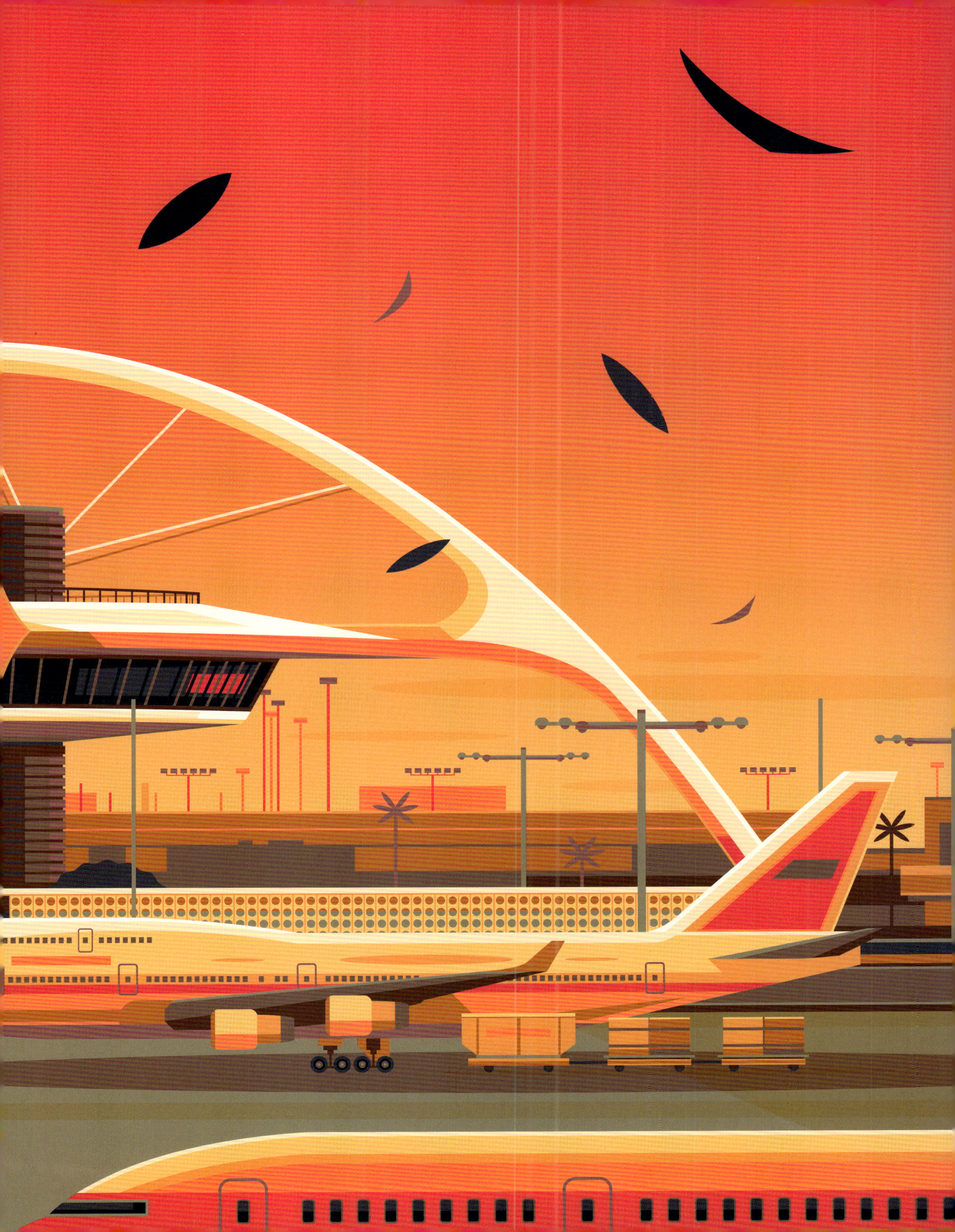

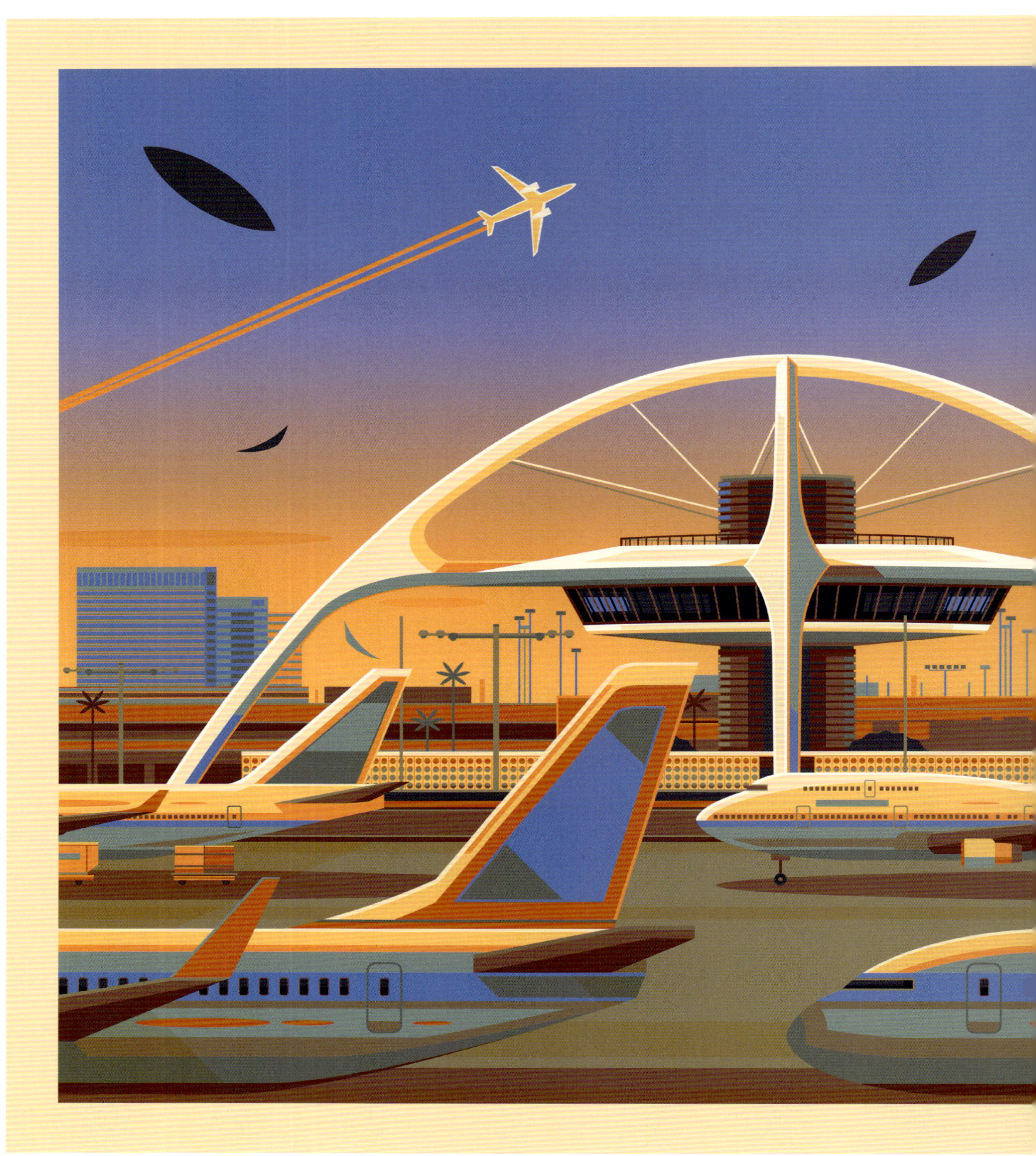

PREVIEW SPREAD

*Theme Building (Sunset)*
Limited Edition
2023

ABOVE

*Theme Building*
Open Edition
2023

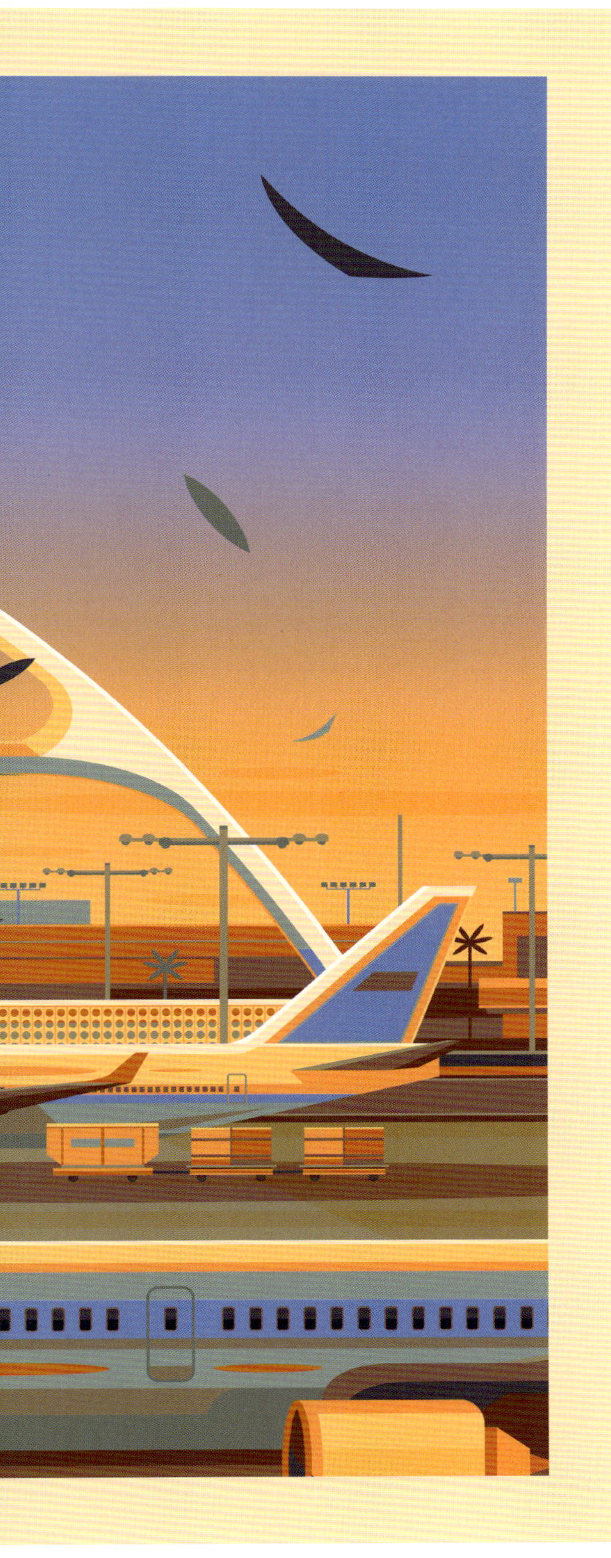

# THEME BUILDING (LAX)

| ADDRESS | ARCHITECT(S) | YEAR |
|---|---|---|
| 209 World Way<br>Los Angeles, CA<br>90045 | Pereira & Luckman,<br>Paul R. Williams &<br>Welton Becket | 1961 |



**The Theme Building is an iconic space-age structure** at LAX, it's a Googie style building which is one of my favourite styles of architecture as it's so reminiscent of the 1950s, it's very retro futuristic and feels like something straight out of *The Jetsons* or *Futurama*.

It's also a very bittersweet building for me: the Theme Building is the first thing you see as you fly into LA, as well as the last thing you glimpse before you leave. It's either marking the beginning of a new adventure or the end of a journey. So every time I see it I'm flooded with mixed emotions.

# L.A. UNION STATION

| ADDRESS | ARCHITECT(S) | YEAR |
|---|---|---|
| 800 N. Alameda St.<br>Los Angeles, CA<br>90012 | John Parkinson,<br>Donald B. Parkinson | 1939 |



**The first time I ever set foot in Los Angeles** was when I arrived into Union Station during a weekend trip I took whilst staying in San Diego. Little did I know that this moment would mark the beginning of countless visits to a city that would come to mean so much to me.

Although stepping out into Downtown Los Angeles isn't the most glamorous introduction to the city, I still knew that something about it was special. That trip would go on to cement my love for LA which led me to the journey I'm on today.

ACROSS

*Union Station*
Open Edition
2023

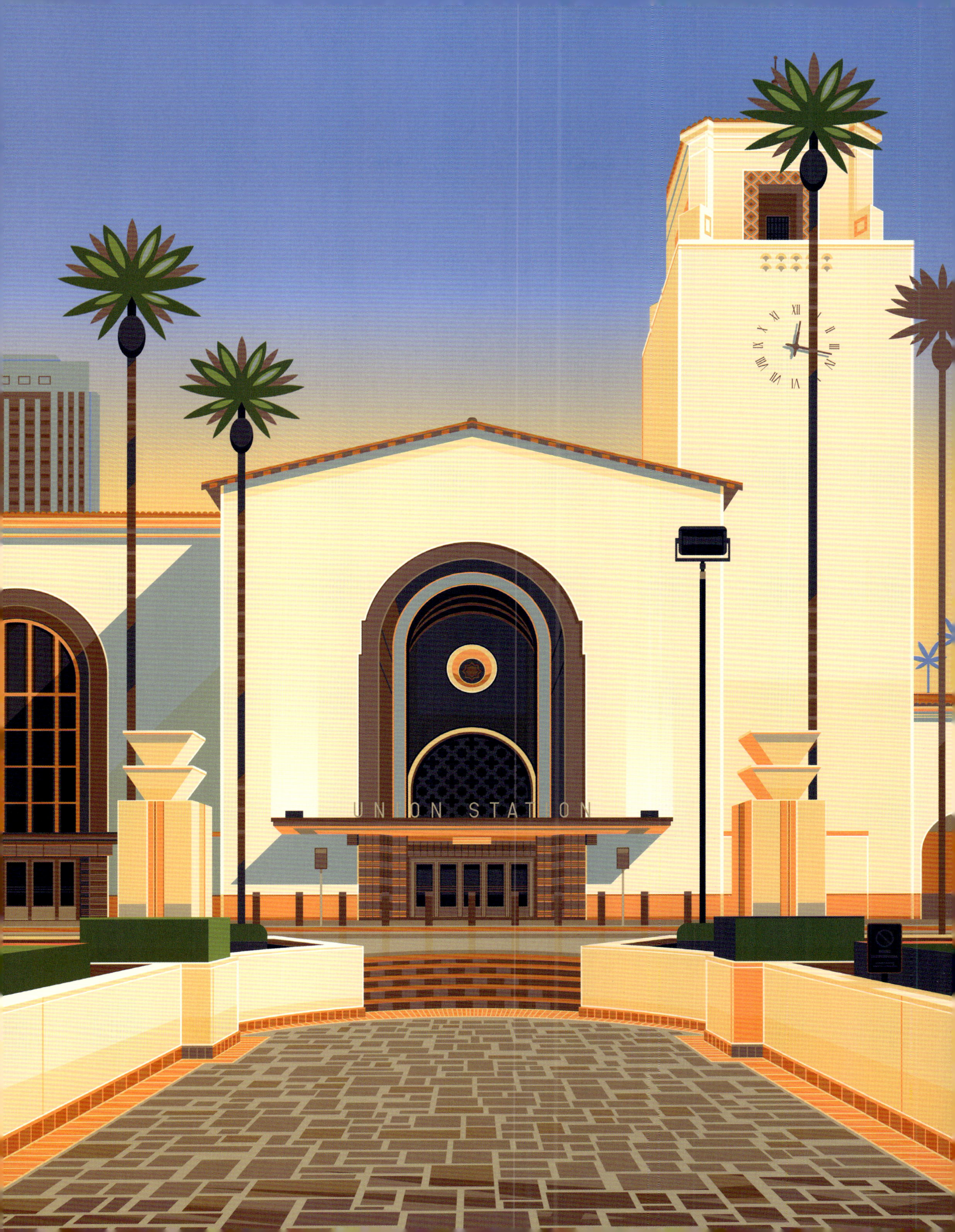
UNI ON STAT ON

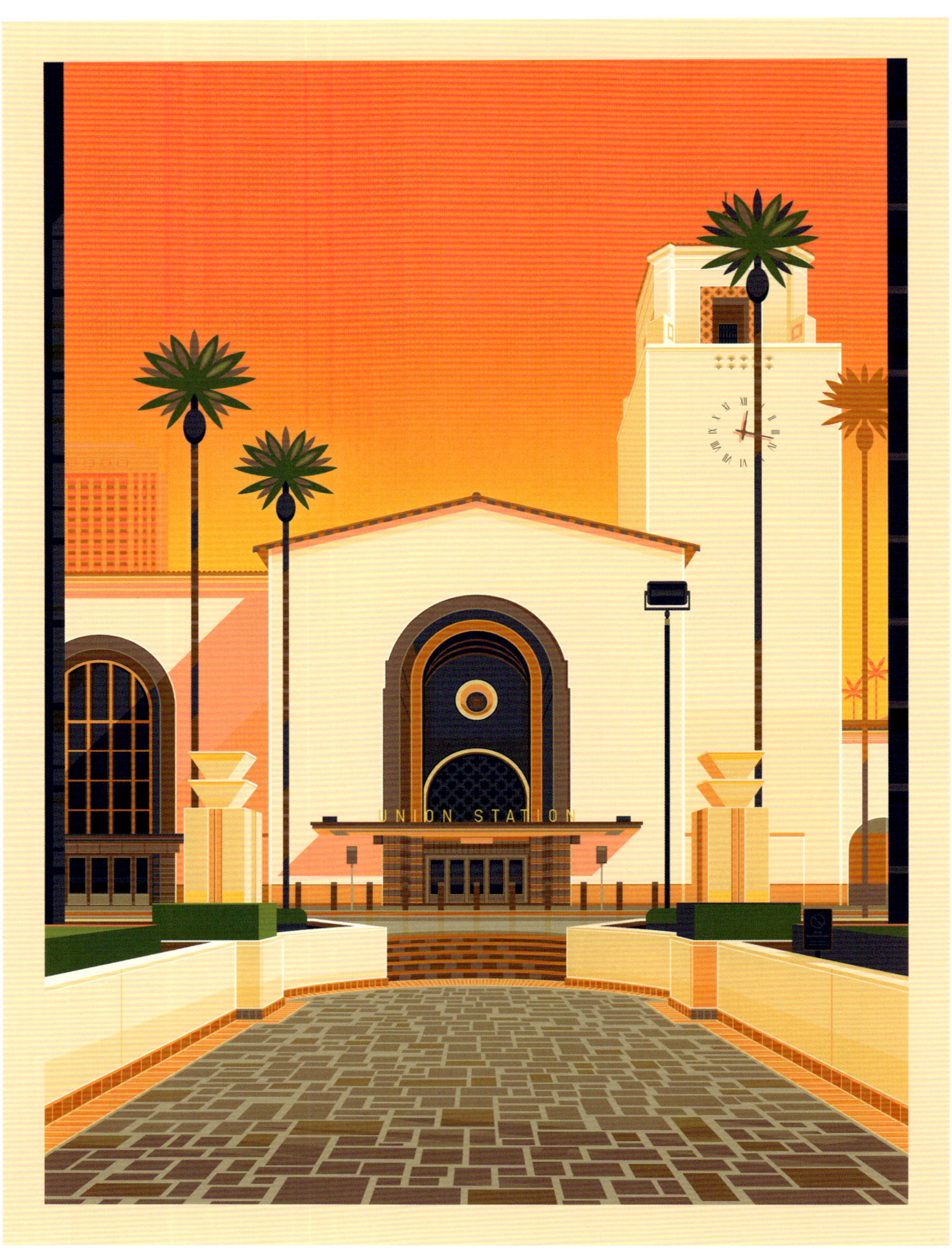


ABOVE

*Union Station (Sunset)*
Limited Edition
2023

ACROSS

*Union Station (Night)*
Limited Edition
2023

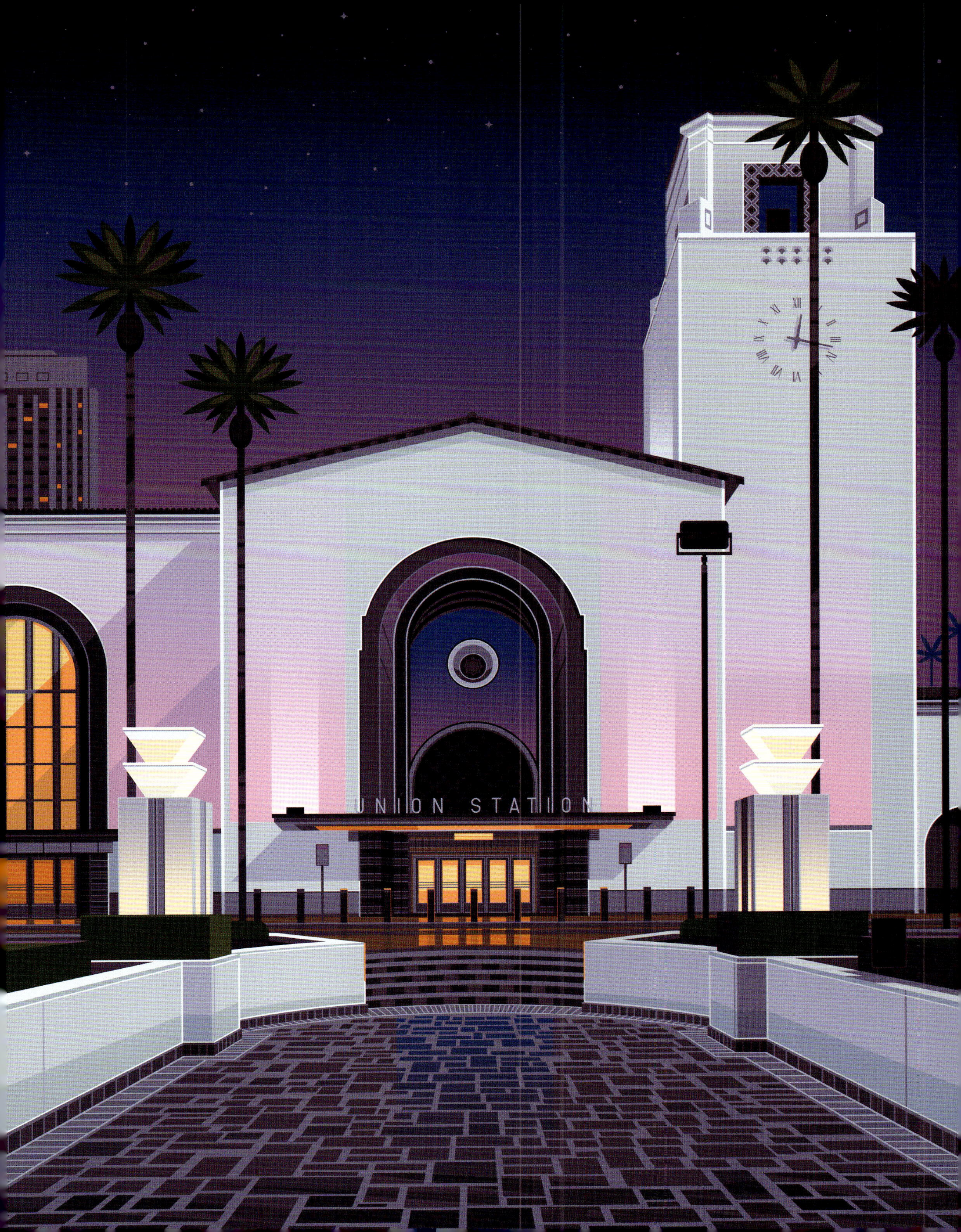
UNION STATION

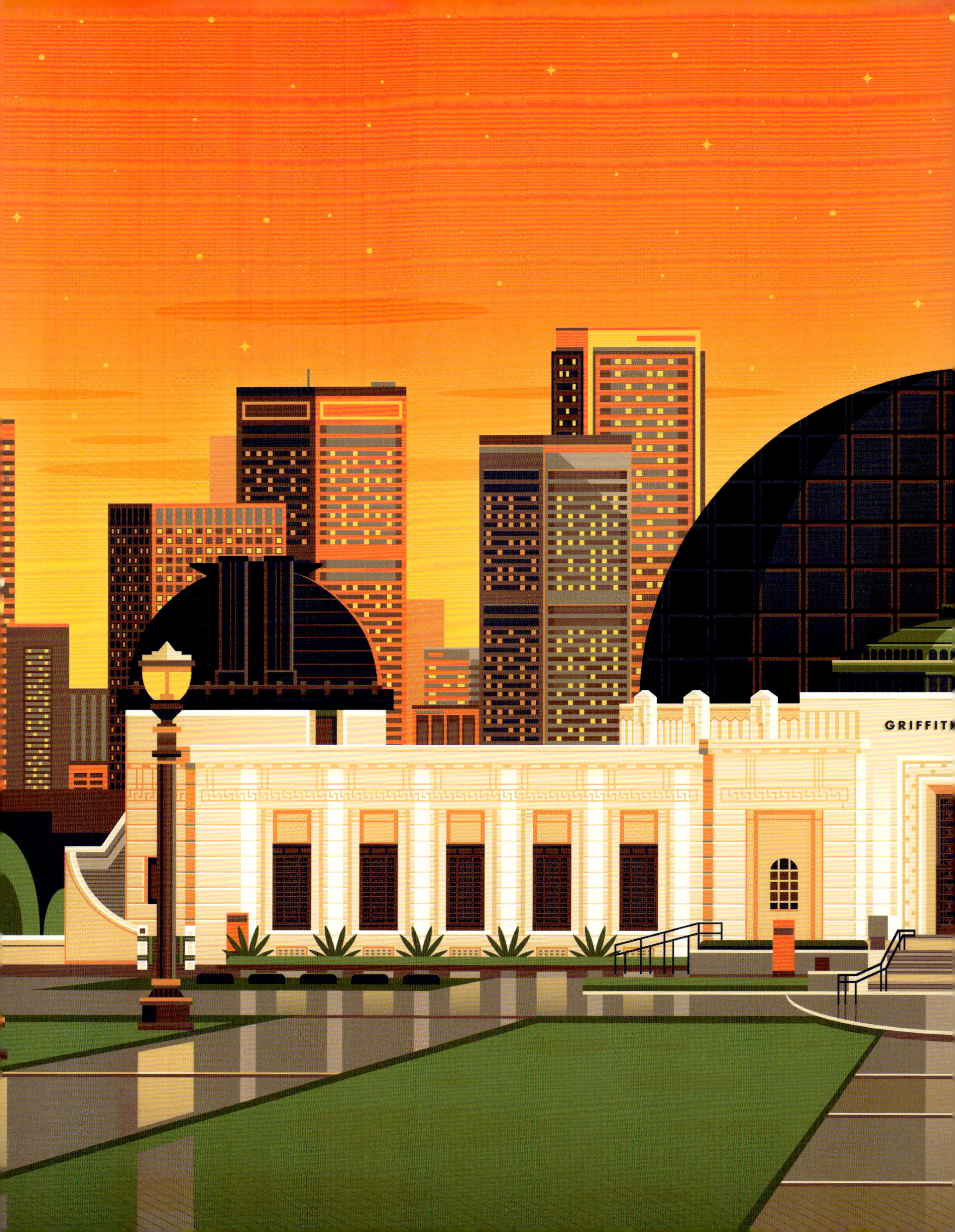
GRIFFIT

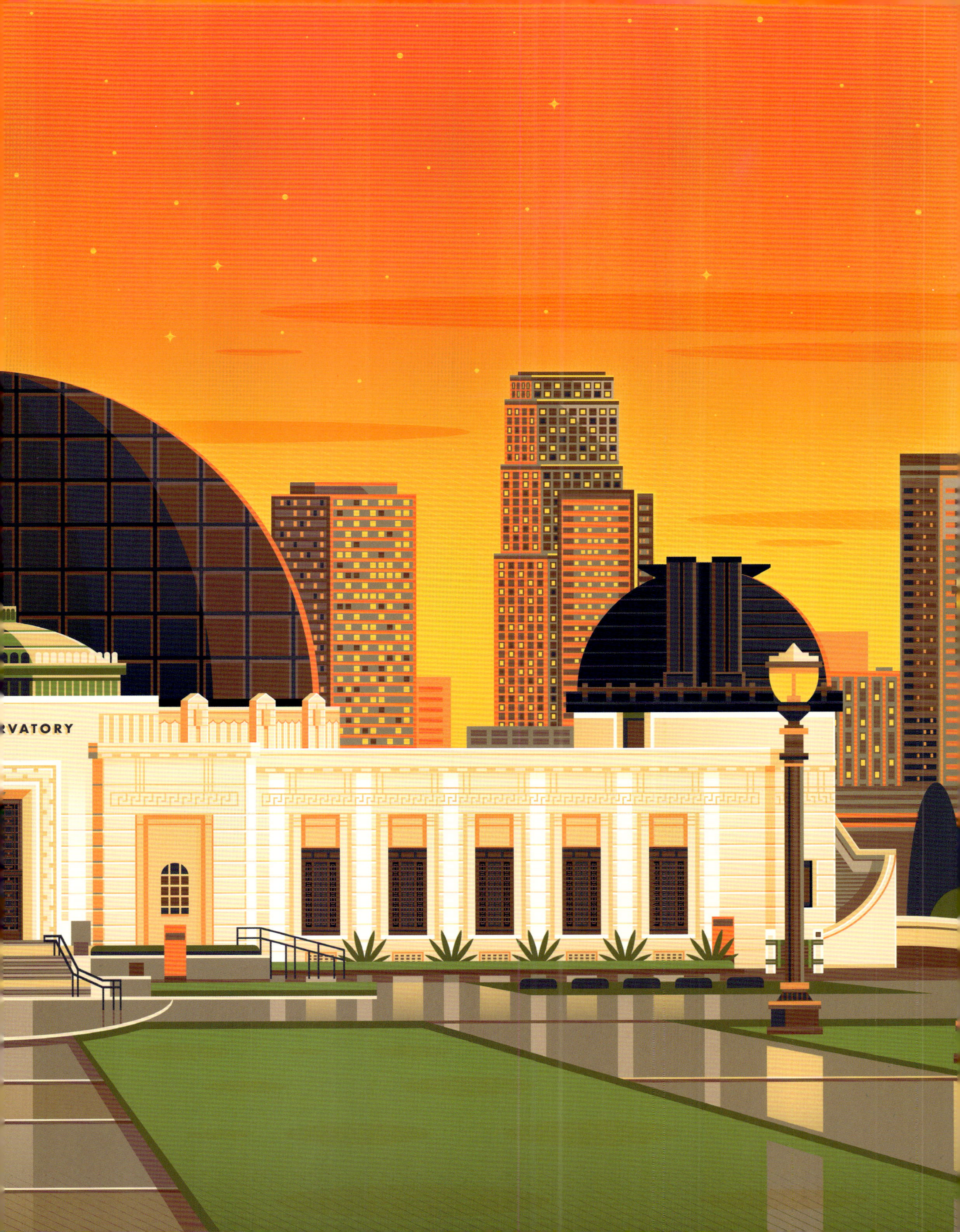
RVATORY

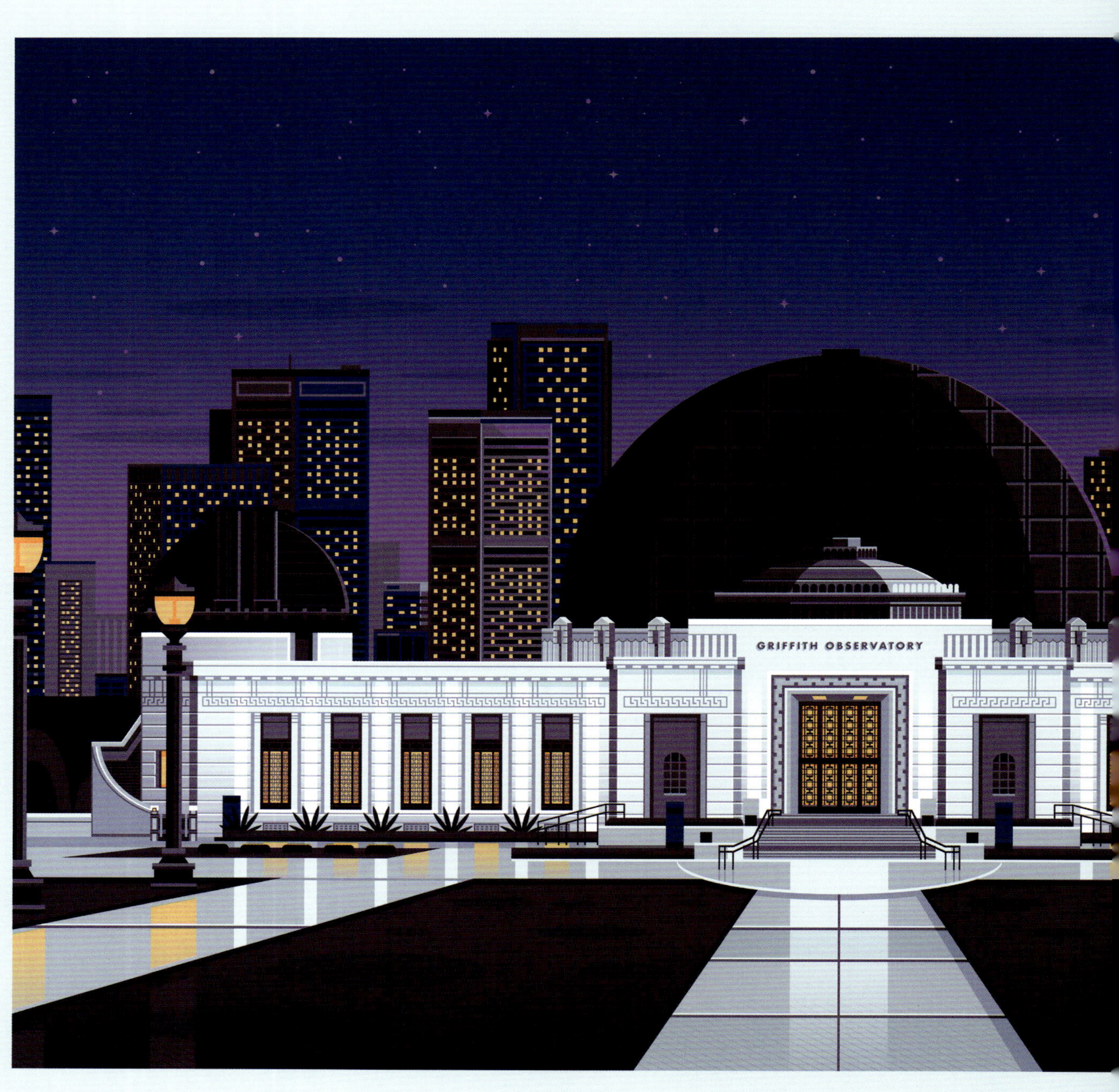


PREVIOUS SPREAD

*Griffith Observatory (Orange Sunset)*
Limited Edition
2023

ABOVE

*Griffith Observatory (Night)*
Limited Edition
2023

NEXT SPREAD

*Griffith Observatory at Sunrise*
Timed Edition
2021

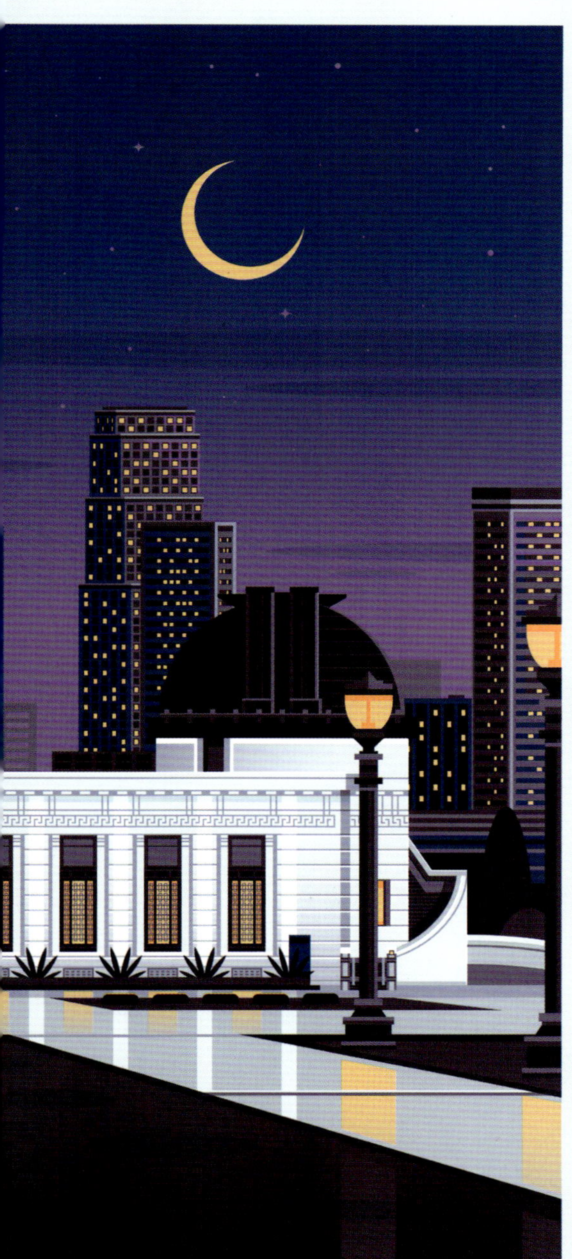

# GRIFFITH OBSERVATORY

| ADDRESS | ARCHITECT(S) | YEAR |
|---|---|---|
| 2800 East Observatory Rd.<br>Los Angeles, CA<br>90027 | John C. Austin,<br>Frederic Morse Ashley | 1935 |

**The Griffith Observatory is the entire reason** I got into drawing Los Angeles architecture in the first place. I've been obsessed long before I even knew I wanted to be an illustrator. I first saw it in the 1955 film *Rebel Without a Cause* when I was younger and immediately knew it was special.

I finally got to visit during a study abroad trip in my second year of university. Standing in the exact spot James Dean did in the film sparked something inside me—it showed me that there was more to Hollywood than just the actors. I was starstruck by a building.

Fast forward to today, and I'm lucky enough to have a great relationship with the Griffith Observatory Foundation, who are big supporters of my work. It's surreal to me, as I'm still in awe every time I go up there. I feel incredibly fortunate that they're fans of what I do, and I'll continue to support them in any way I can.

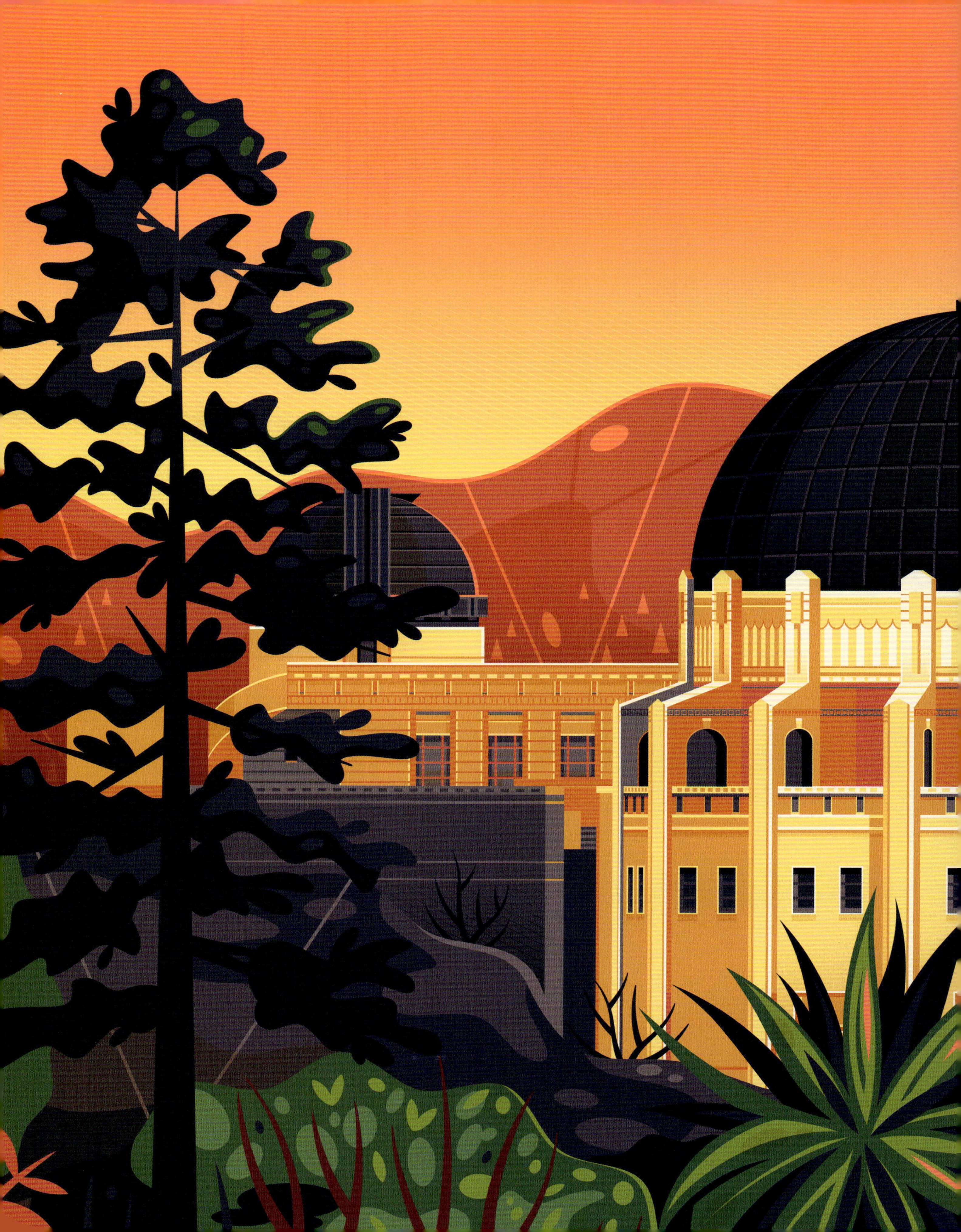

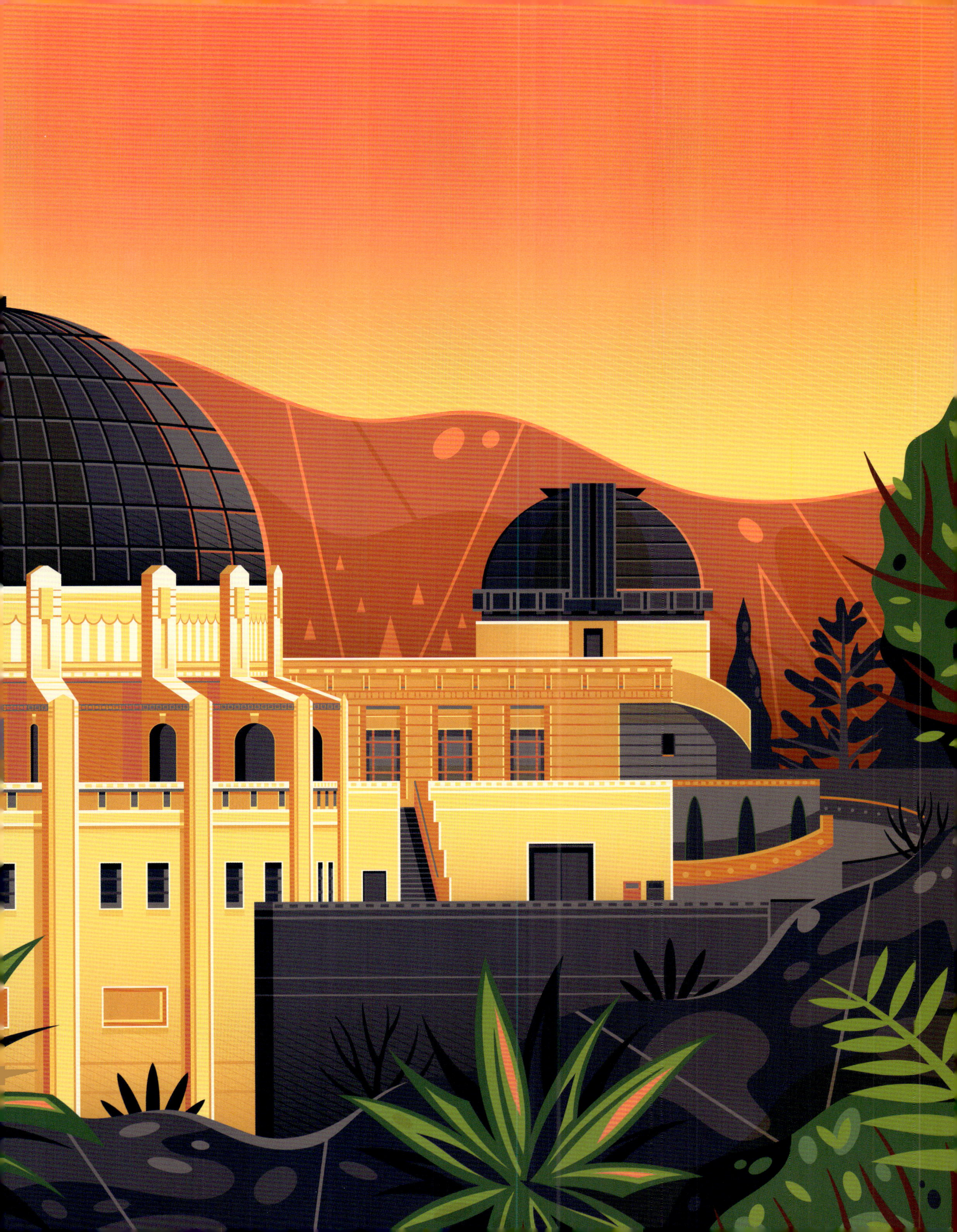

# LOS ANGELES CITY HALL

| ADDRESS | ARCHITECT(S) | YEAR |
|---|---|---|
| 200 N. Spring St.<br>Los Angeles, CA<br>90012 | John Parkinson,<br>John C. Austin | 1928 |



ACROSS

*Los Angeles City Hall*
Open Edition
2019

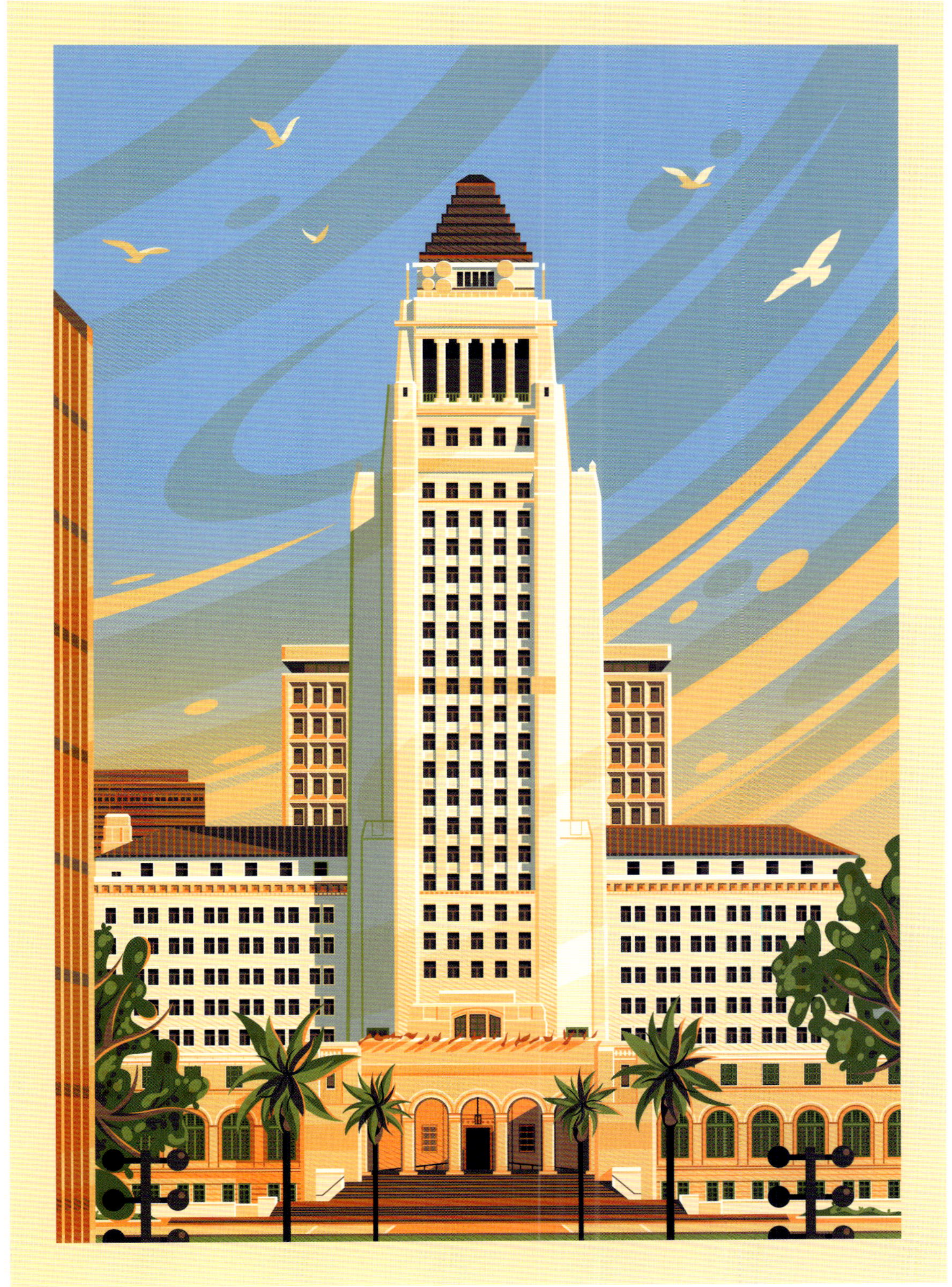

# CHATEAU MARMONT

| ADDRESS | ARCHITECT(S) | YEAR |
|---|---|---|
| 8221 Sunset Blvd.<br>Los Angeles, CA<br>90046 | Arnold A. Weitzman,<br>William Douglas Lee | 1929 |



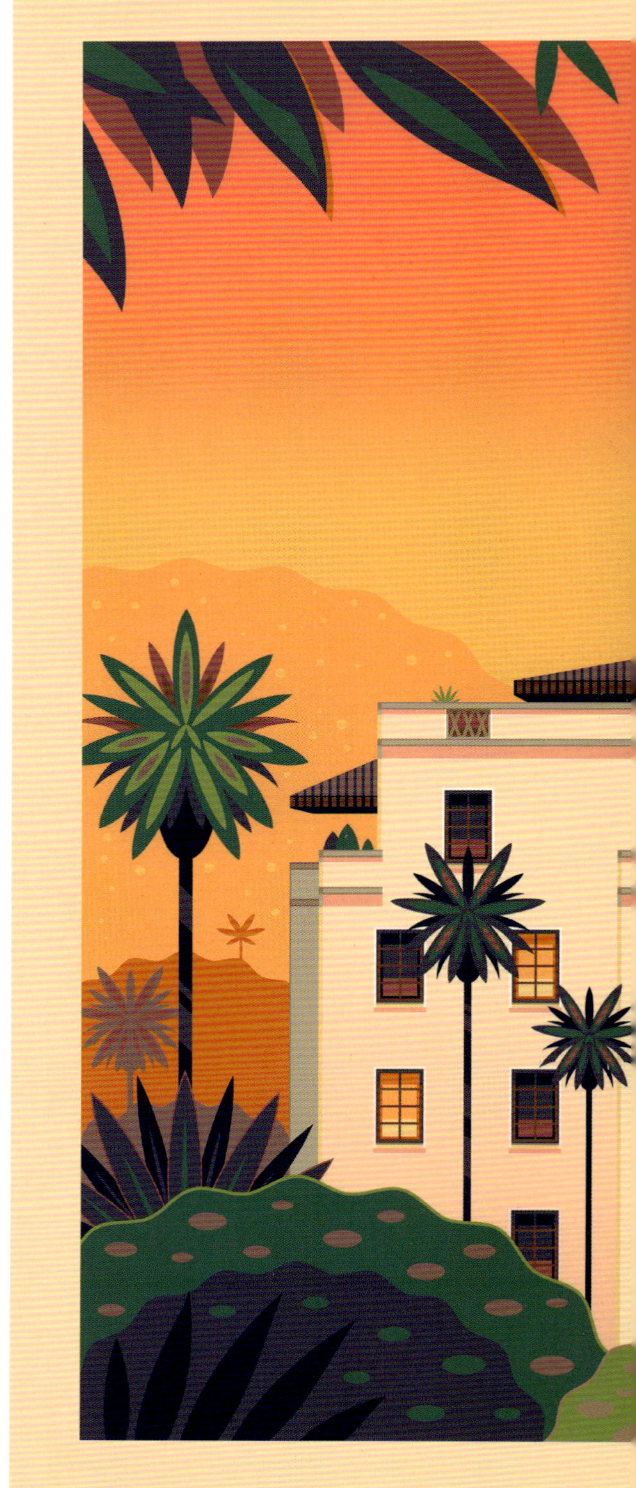

**The Chateau Marmont is my favourite hotel** in Los Angeles. I'm fascinated by the mystery, allure, and legend surrounding this building. There's something so striking about seeing a French-style château perched on a hill overlooking LA, a castle that feels completely out of place in the best way.

I was lucky enough to be invited there by someone in my audience to listen to his friend play piano in the main lobby. It was such a beautiful experience, and I couldn't help but imagine the stories those walls must hold. I just wish the drinks were a little more affordable...

ACROSS

*Chateau Marmont (Sunset)*
Limited Edition
2024

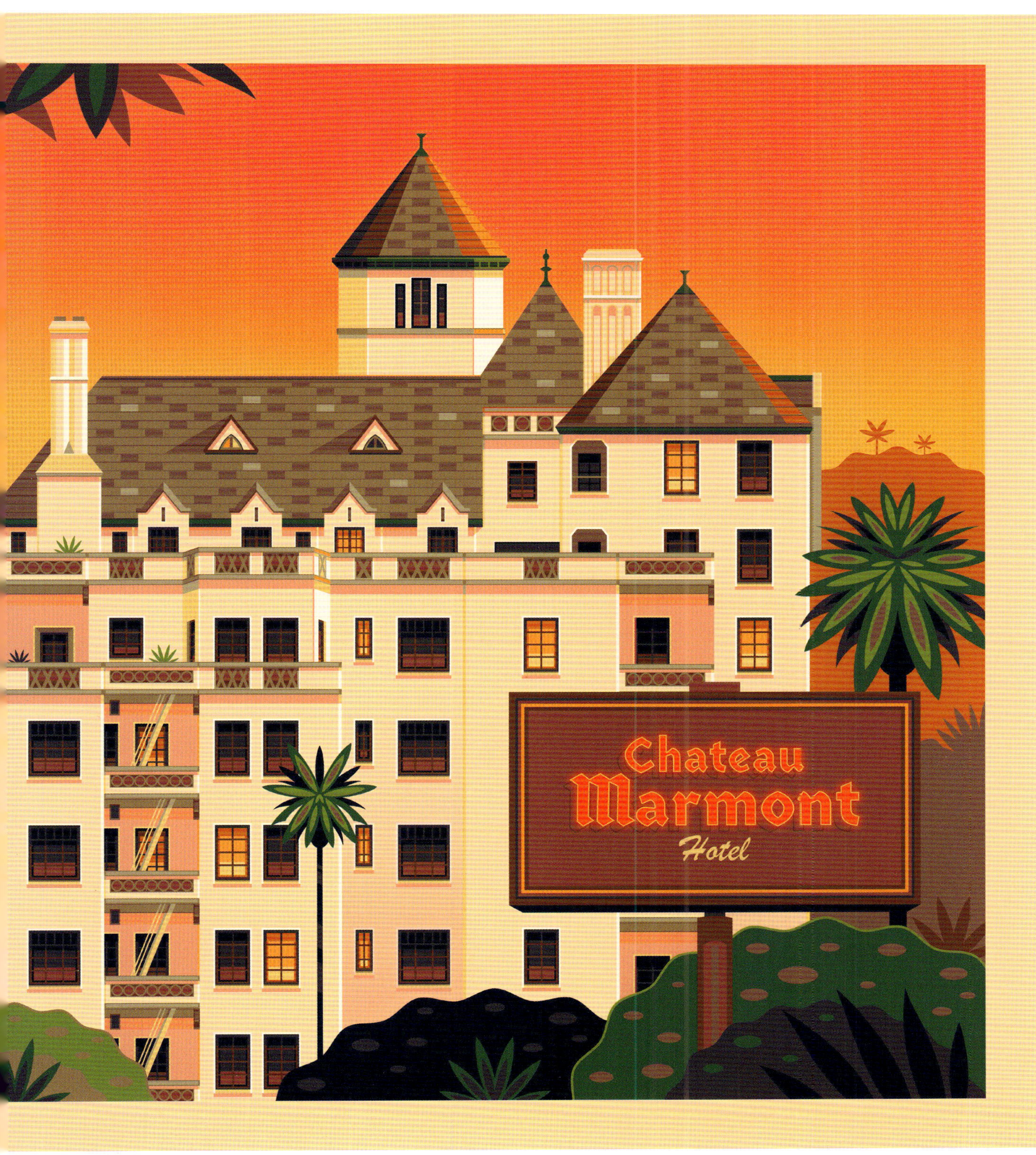
Chateau
Marmont
Hotel

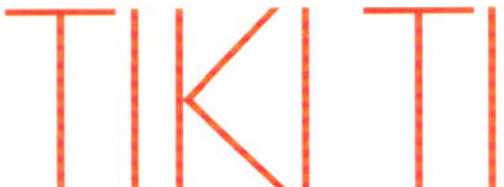

# TIKI TI

| ADDRESS | ARCHITECT(S) | YEAR |
| --- | --- | --- |
| 4427 Sunset Blvd.<br>Los Angeles, CA<br>90027 | N/A | 1961 |



**Tiki Ti has remained a family-run treasure** for over six decades. It's one of the last authentic tiki bars left, making it a beloved institution for enthusiasts and a true slice of Los Angeles history.

This was another instance where I wasn't sure whether a landmark would resonate or not. A few people had recommended the Tiki Ti to me, and I thought it looked really interesting, so I decided to draw it. Back then, that's how most of my work came about as I hadn't taken enough trips yet to truly think like a local.

To my surprise, this print absolutely exploded when it was released. It became one of my fastest sell-outs ever. While the tiki community is small, it's incredibly passionate, and capturing such an iconic place in their history seemed to really resonate with them. I'm much more in the know these days and I've also developed a newfound love for tiki drinks.

ACROSS

*Tiki Ti*
Limited Edition
2021

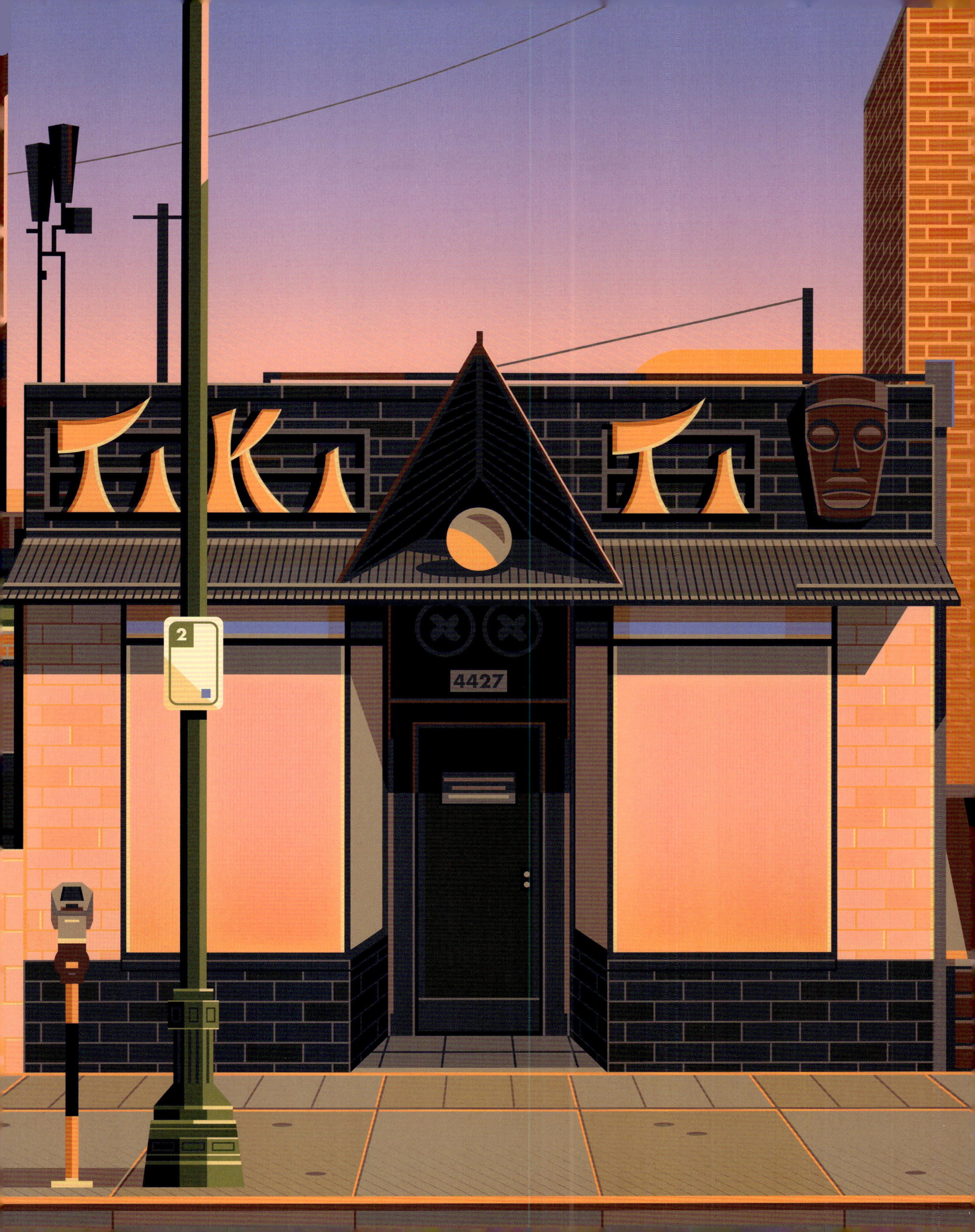
TIKI TI
4427
2

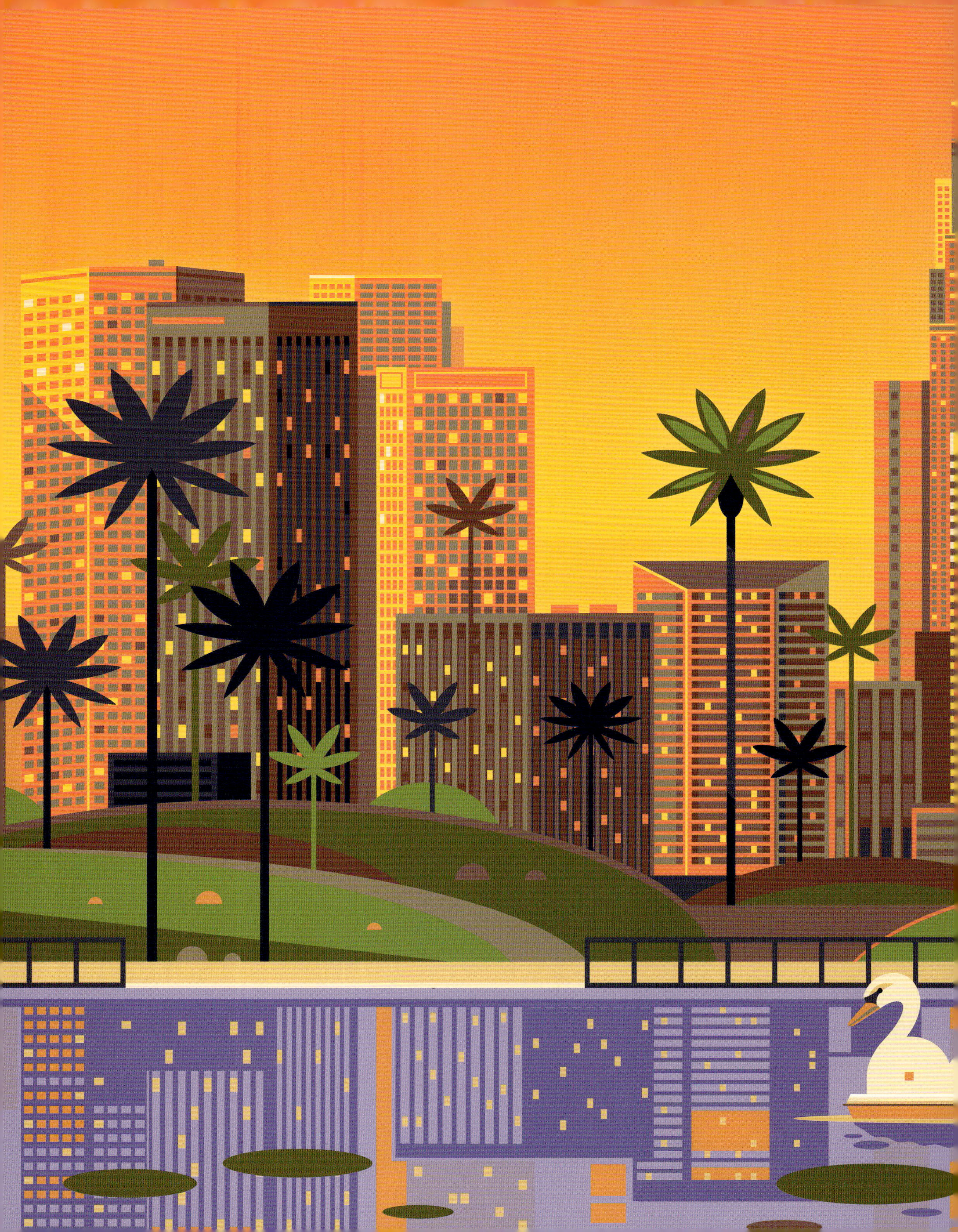

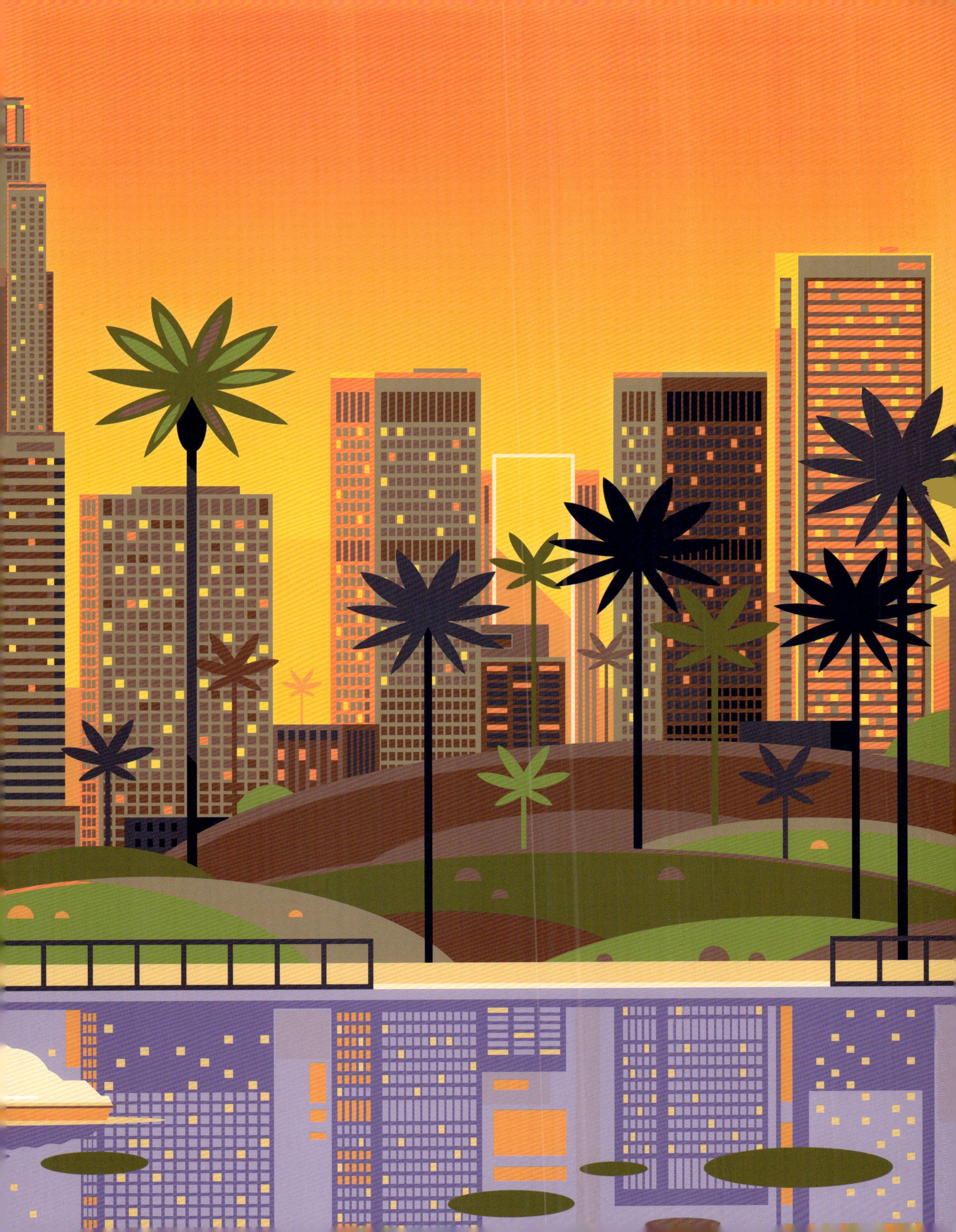

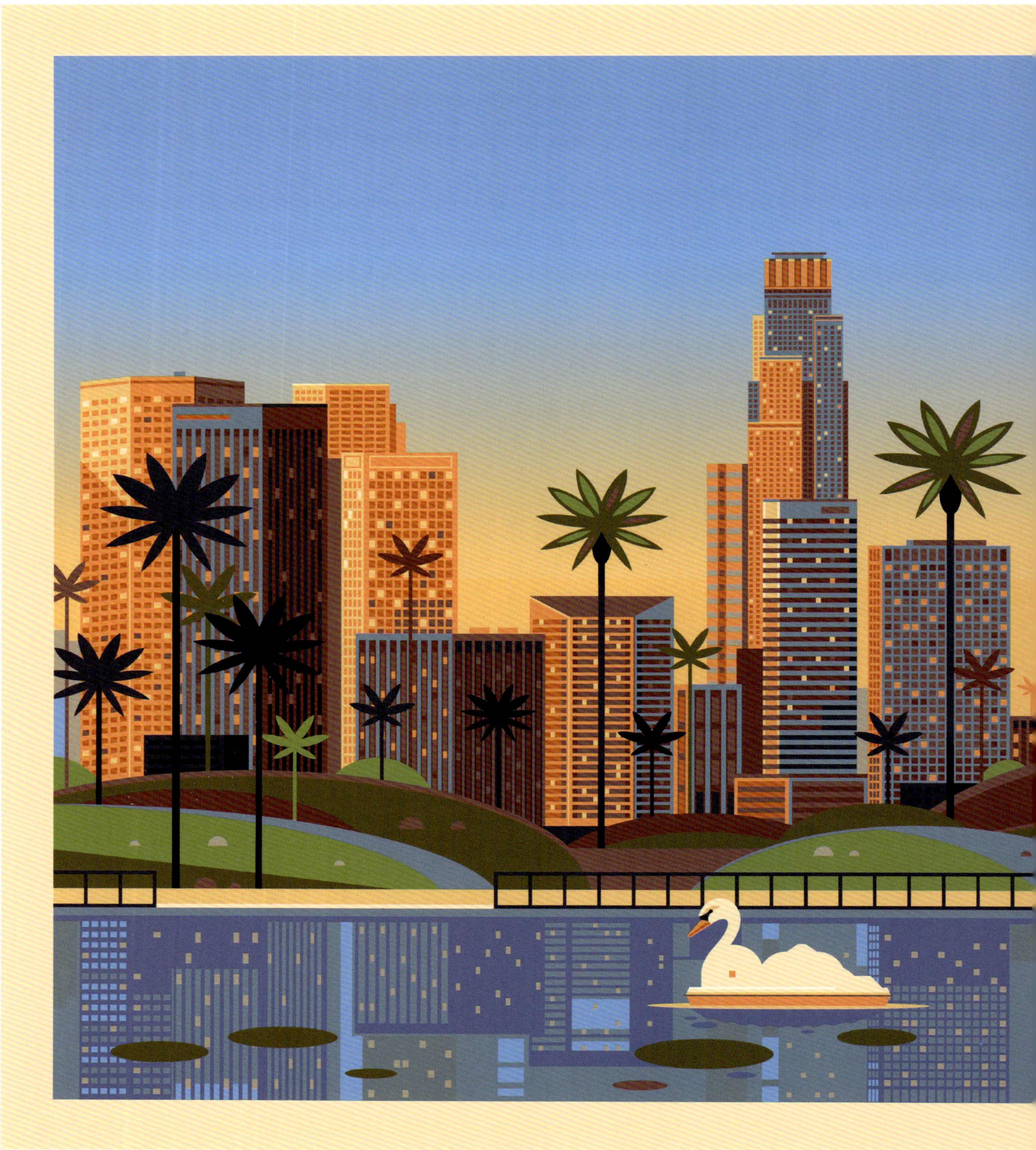

PREVIOUS SPREAD

*Echo Park (Sunset)*
Limited Edition
2022

ABOVE

*Echo Park*
Open Edition
2022

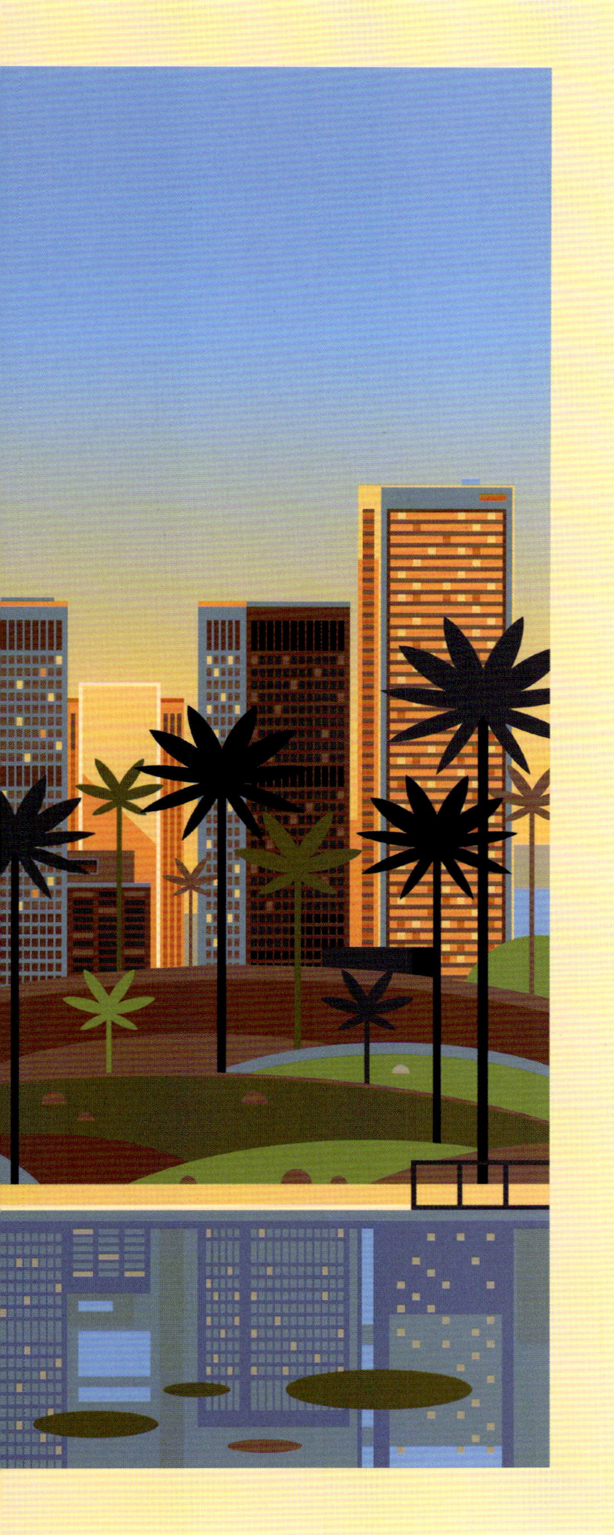

# ECHO PARK

| ADDRESS | ARCHITECT(S) | YEAR |
|---|---|---|
| 751 Echo Park Ave.<br>Los Angeles, CA<br>90026 | Joseph Henry<br>Tomlinson | 1868 |



**This is my favourite park in all of Los Angeles.** Maybe it's because I haven't had the chance to explore as many of them as I'd like, but I've just always been drawn to green spaces framed by urban backdrops, the contrast is just so interesting to me.

There's something magical about seeing a city's skyline while you're surrounded by a little bubble of nature. It feels like an escape from the chaos. I think it's one of the things that originally drew me to London.

Oh and those swan boats are just so iconic.

# DODGER STADIUM

ADDRESS
1000 Vin Scully Ave.
Los Angeles, CA
90026

ARCHITECT(S)
Praeger-Kavanagh-Waterbury,
Engineers-Architects

YEAR
1962



**I'd always wanted to see the famous Dodger Stadium** in person, and I'll never forget the day I set off walking up that hill. It was the moment I realised just how dependent LA is on cars. Reaching the stadium on foot was so challenging that I started to question whether walking there was even allowed. I still remember passing the first guard booth and seeing the confusion on their faces.

Eventually, I made it to the top and celebrated by buying a Dodgers hat, something I still wear proudly to this day. Later that year, on my first visit to San Francisco, I brought my favourite hat along, completely unaware of how deeply rooted the rivalry was. I was teased about it before I'd even stepped off the plane, with someone joking that I should take it off if I wanted to make it through border control.

GATEFOLD

*Dodger Stadium*
Open Edition
2021

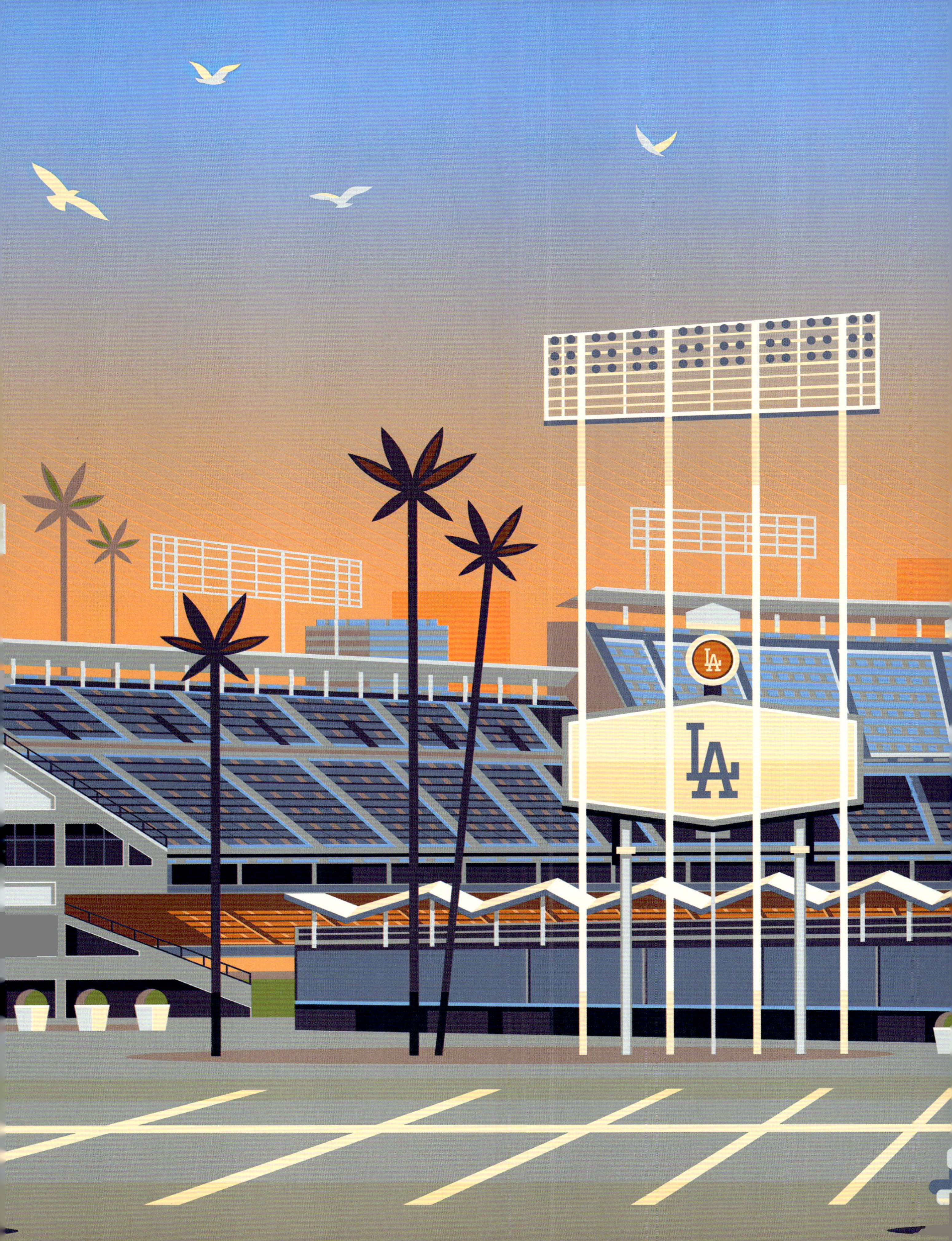
LA
LA

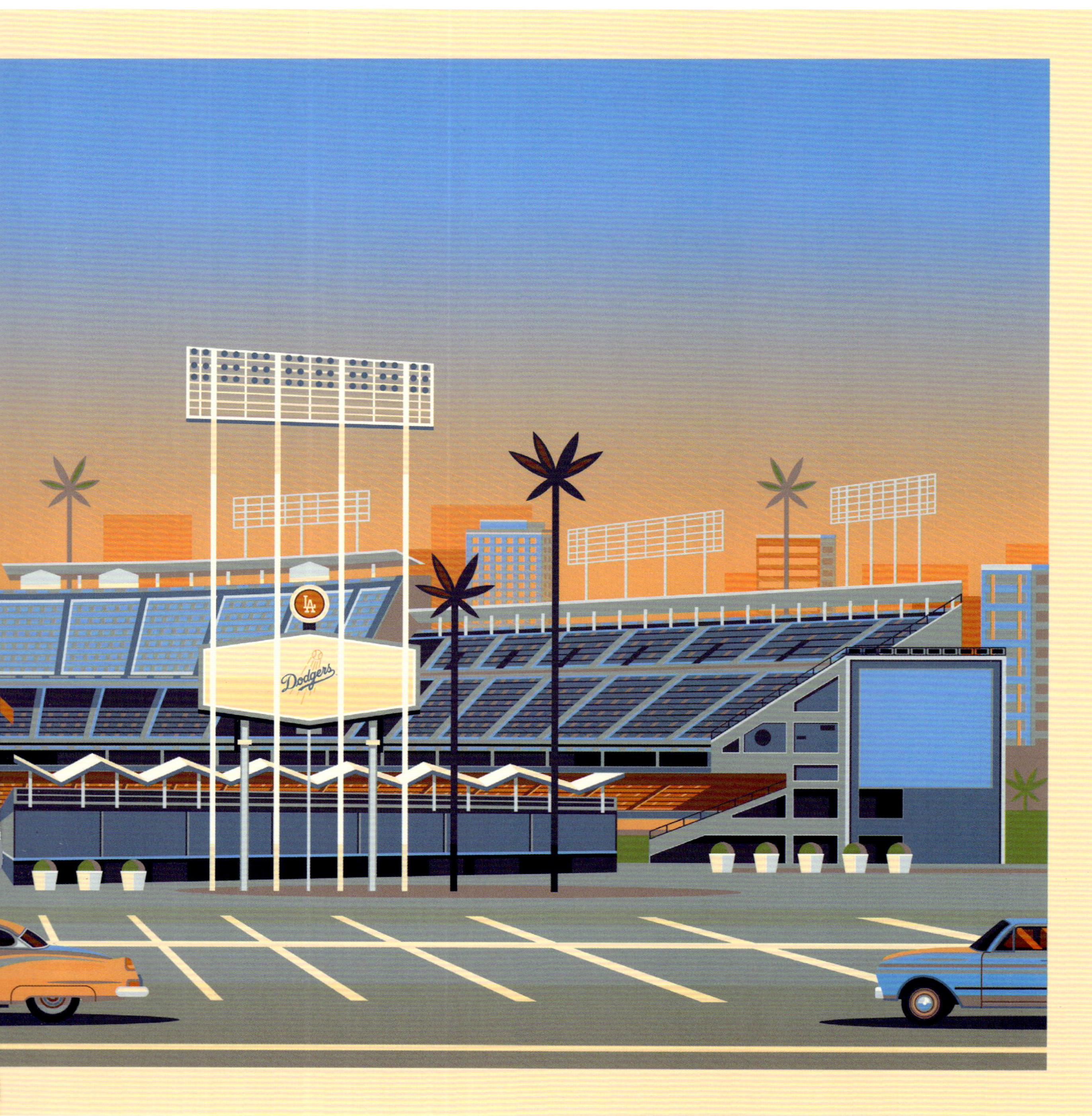
LA
Dodgers

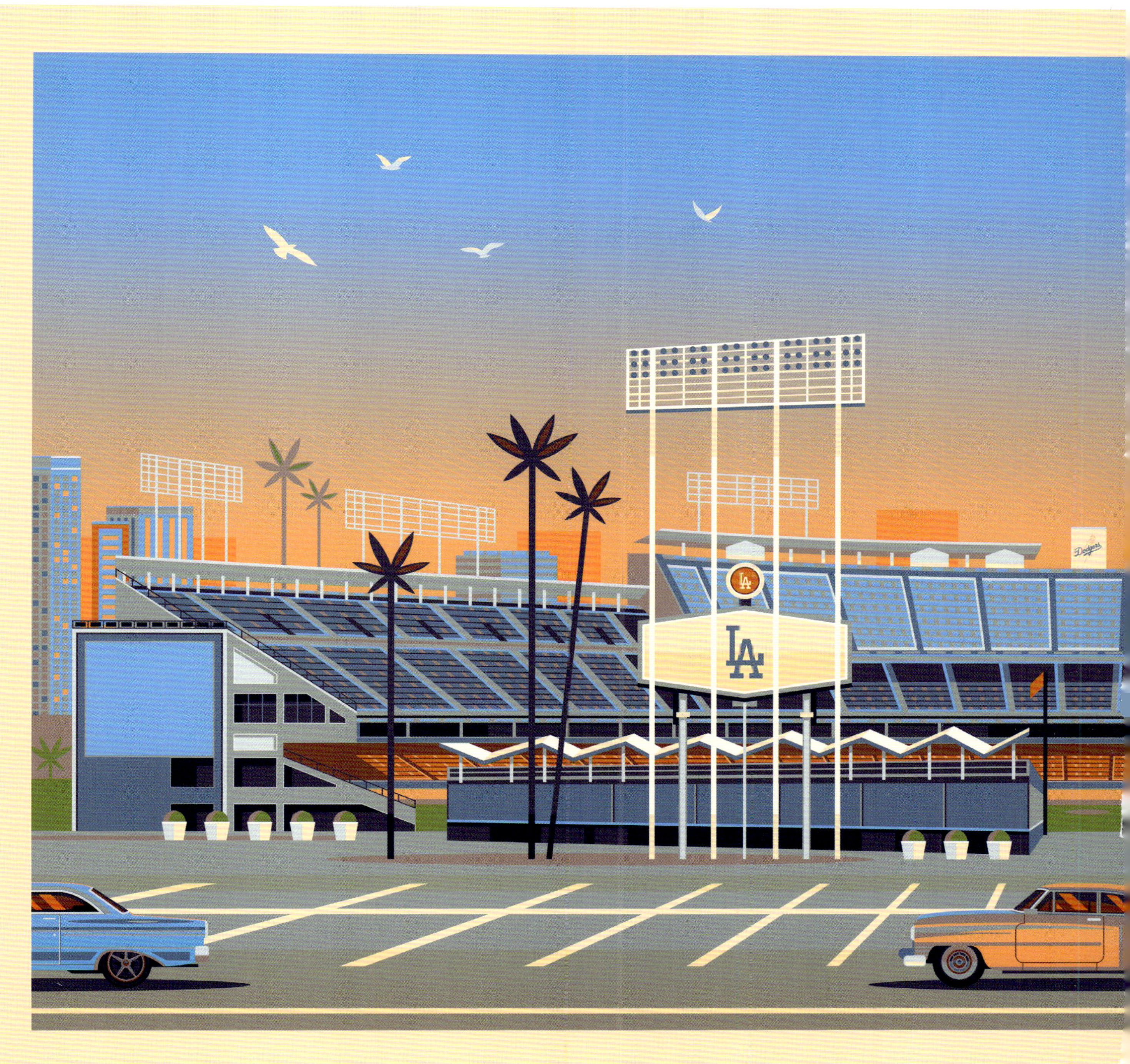
LA

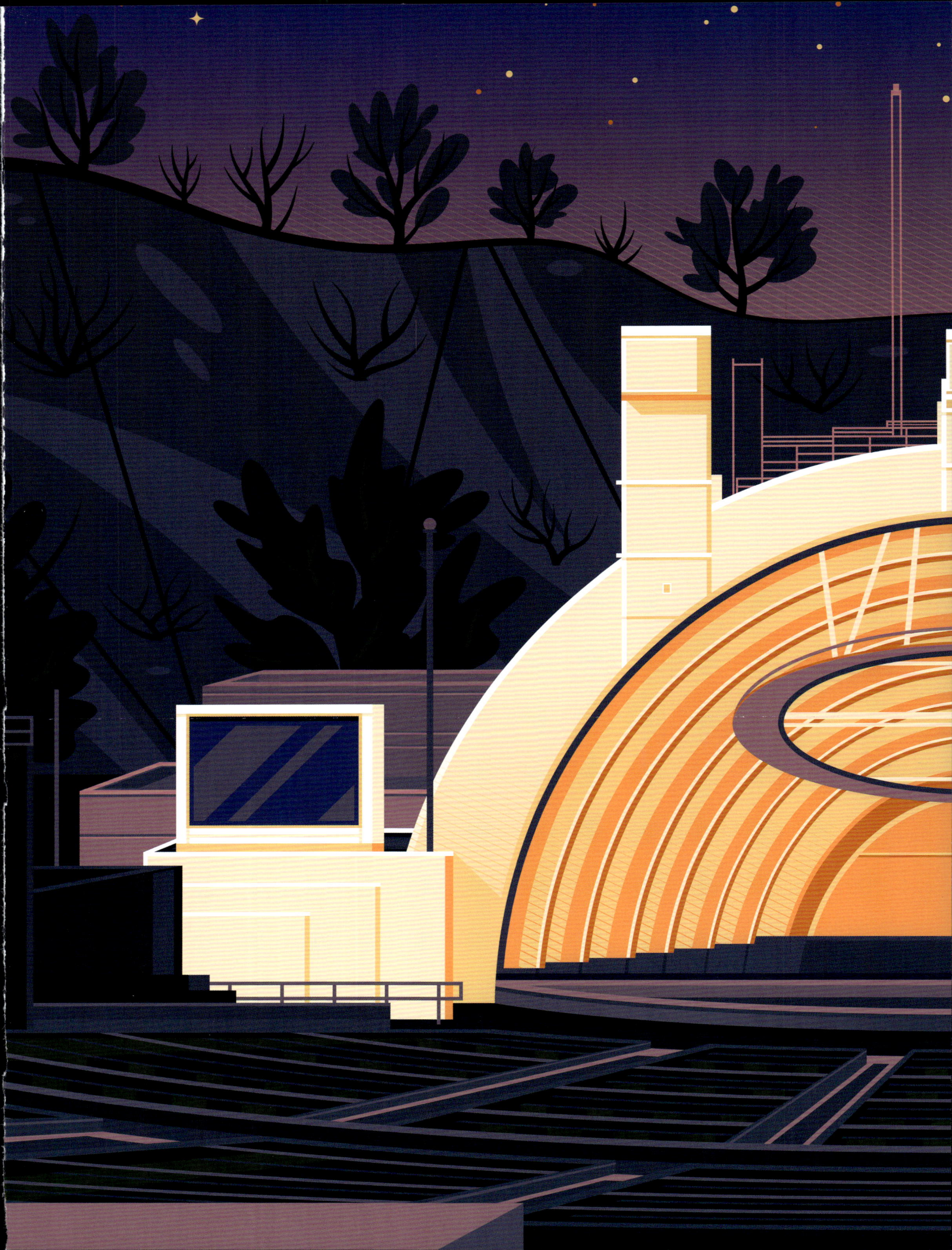

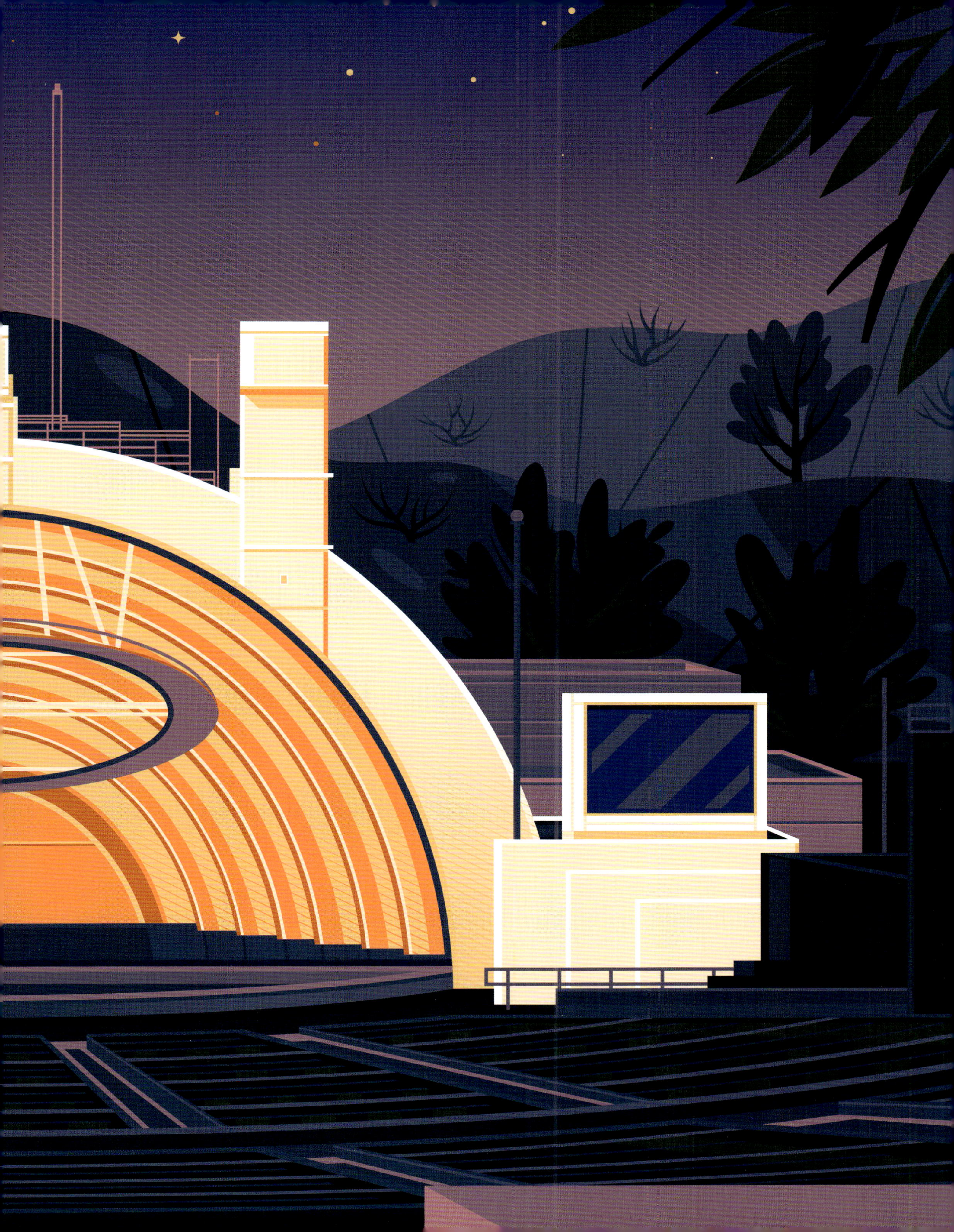

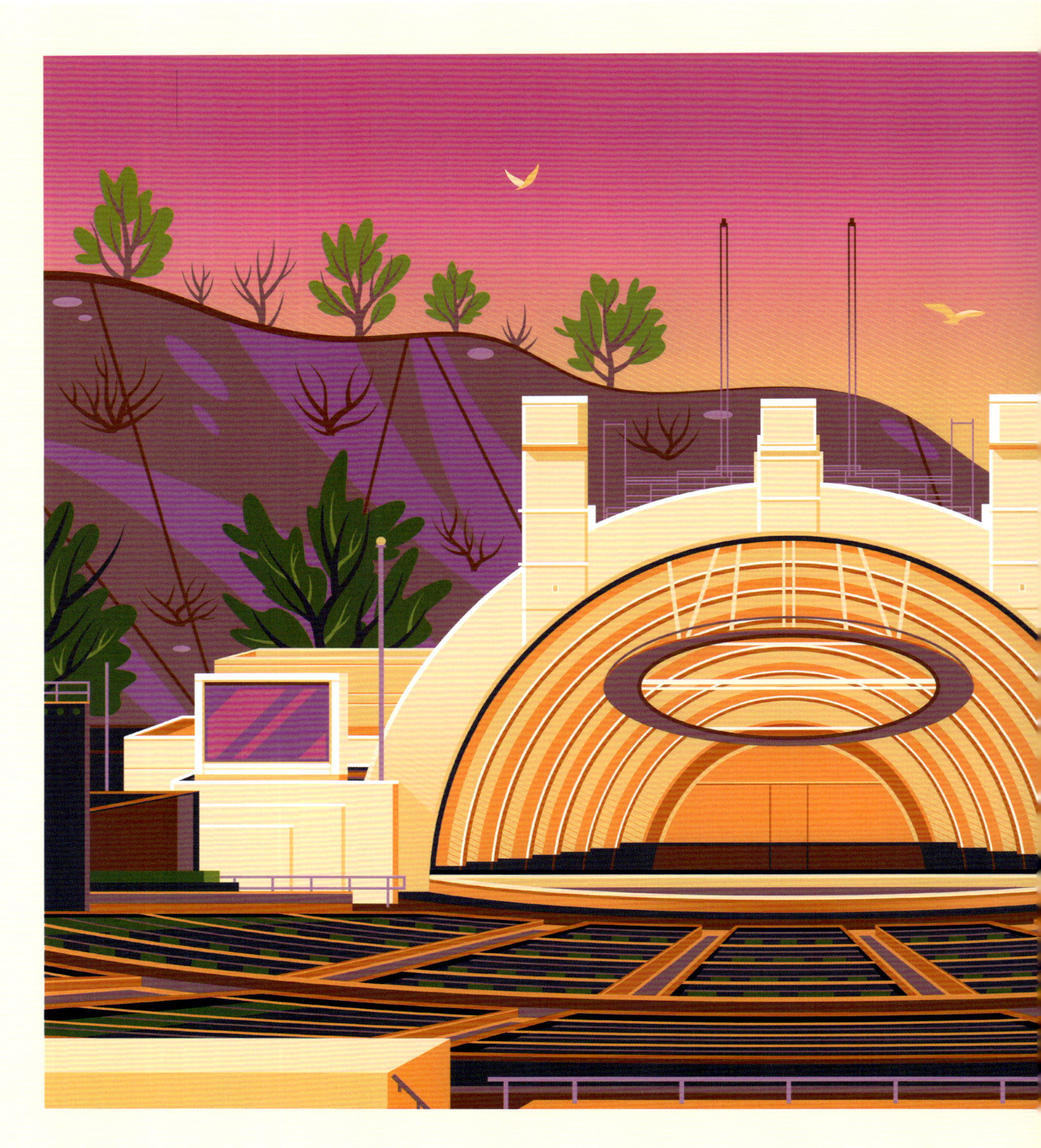

PREVIOUS SPREAD

*Hollywood Bowl (Night)*
Limited Edition
2021

ABOVE

*Hollywood Bowl (Sunset)*
Limited Edition
2021

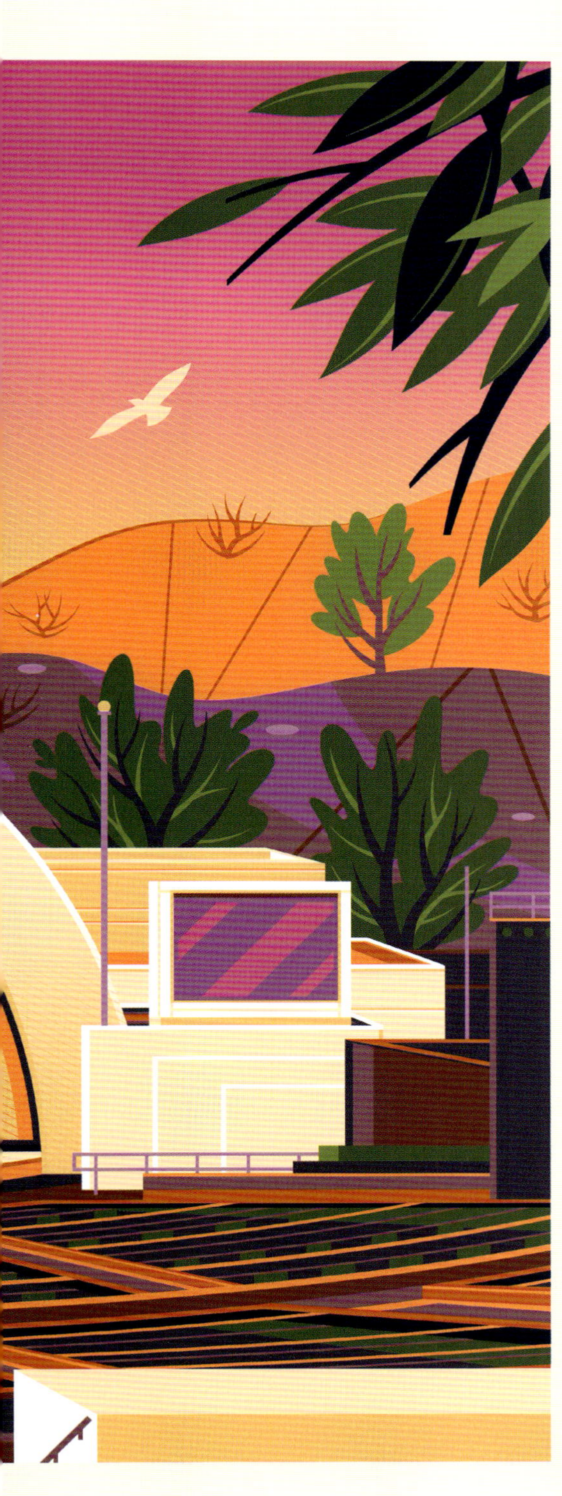

# HOLLYWOOD BOWL

| ADDRESS | ARCHITECT(S) | YEAR |
|---|---|---|
| 2301 North Highland Ave.<br>Los Angeles, CA<br>90068 | Frank Gehry,<br>Myron Hunt,<br>Lloyd Wright | 1922 |



**Something not many people know** about the Hollywood Bowl is that it's actually a national park, and you can just walk around the grounds during the off-season. I discovered this by chance after driving there and striking up a conversation with one of the security guards, hoping I could bribe my way in. Turns out it was completely free anyway.

Funny enough, I mentioned to the same guard that I'd done some design work for the Bowl, but he could not have cared less, which is what I deserved for trying to brag.

That evening, I had the entire venue to myself. It was surreal to be surrounded by rows of empty seats steeped in so much talent and history, watching the sun set behind the iconic amphitheatre. This artwork was inspired by a photo I took in that exact moment.

# VENICE BEACH CANALS

| ADDRESS | ARCHITECT(S) | YEAR |
|---|---|---|
| Venice Canals,<br>Los Angeles, CA<br>90291 | Moses Sherman,<br>Eli Clark | 1905 |



**I could spend hours just walking the winding paths** of the Venice Beach Canals, taking in the unique houses and the peaceful atmosphere. It's such a perfect escape from the city, yet somehow you're still surrounded by it.

It's also a reminder of one of my favourite aspects of Los Angeles: how each neighbourhood has its own unique identity, offering something new to discover. One moment, I'm strolling through a quiet, Italian-inspired canal, and the next, I can head across the city to somewhere lively like West Hollywood, where the energy is completely different. The way these diverse communities and cultures blend together is what gives LA its sense of endless possibilities.

ACROSS

*Venice Canals (Sunset)*
Limited Edition
2022

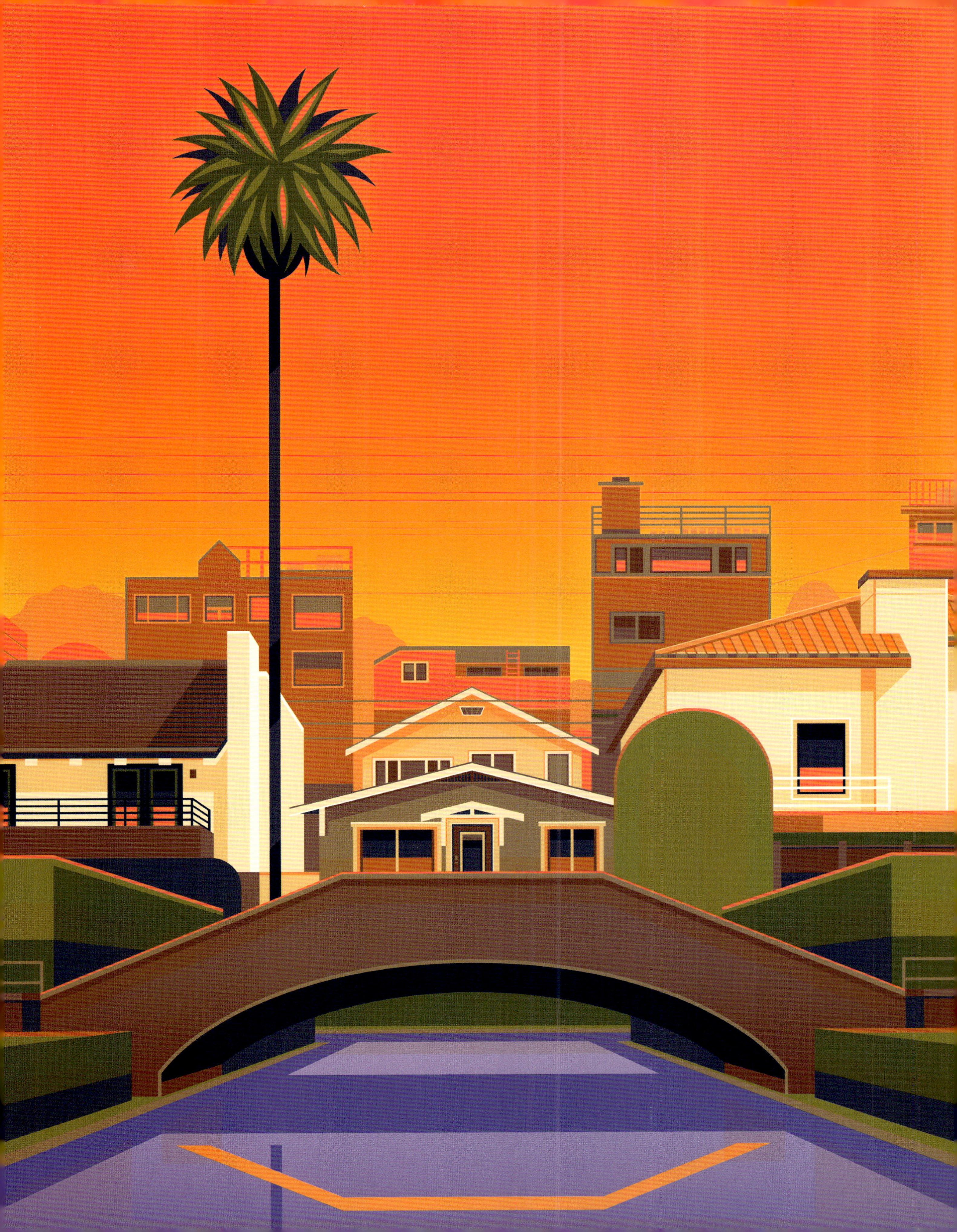

ACROSS

*Venice Canals*
Open Edition
2022

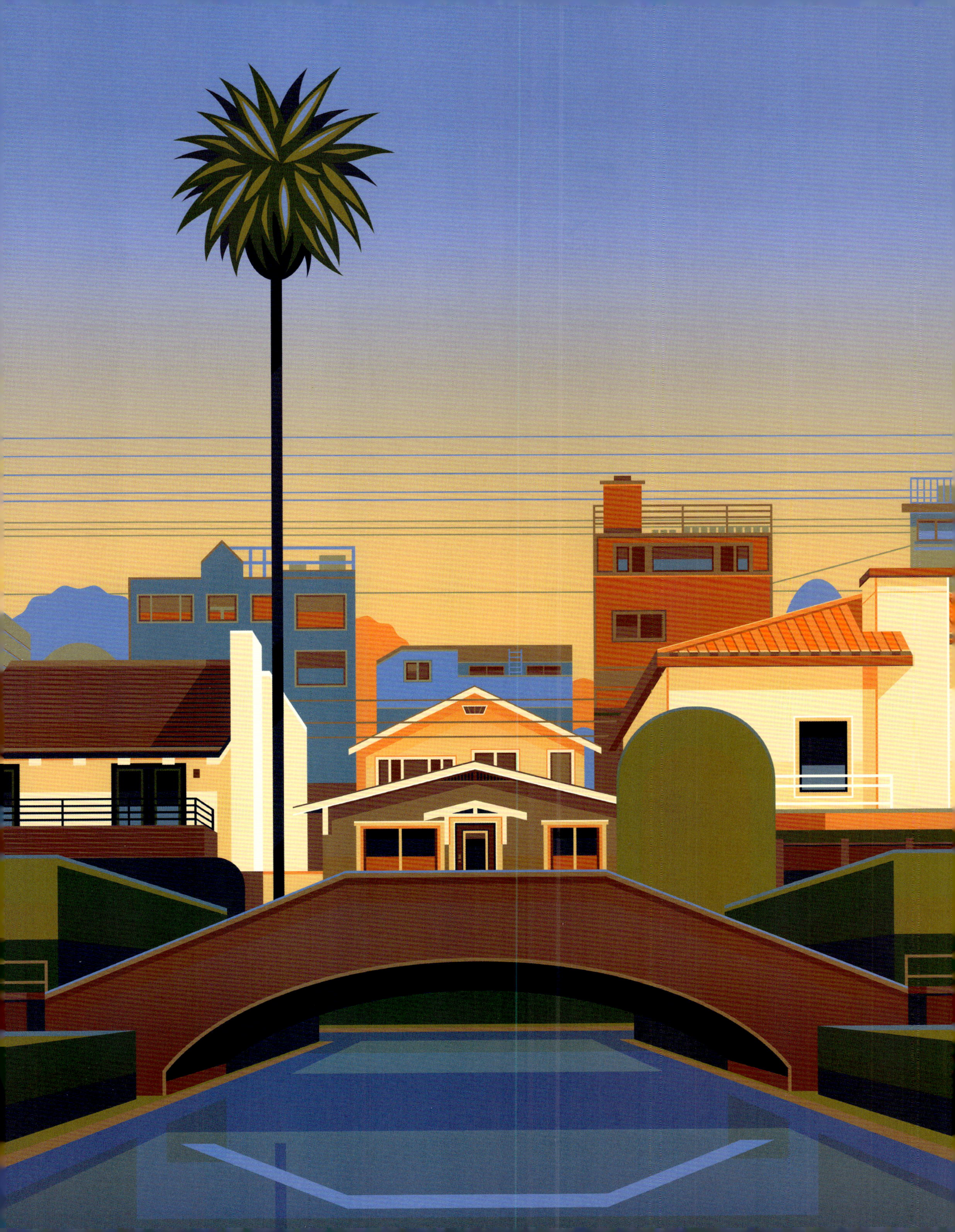

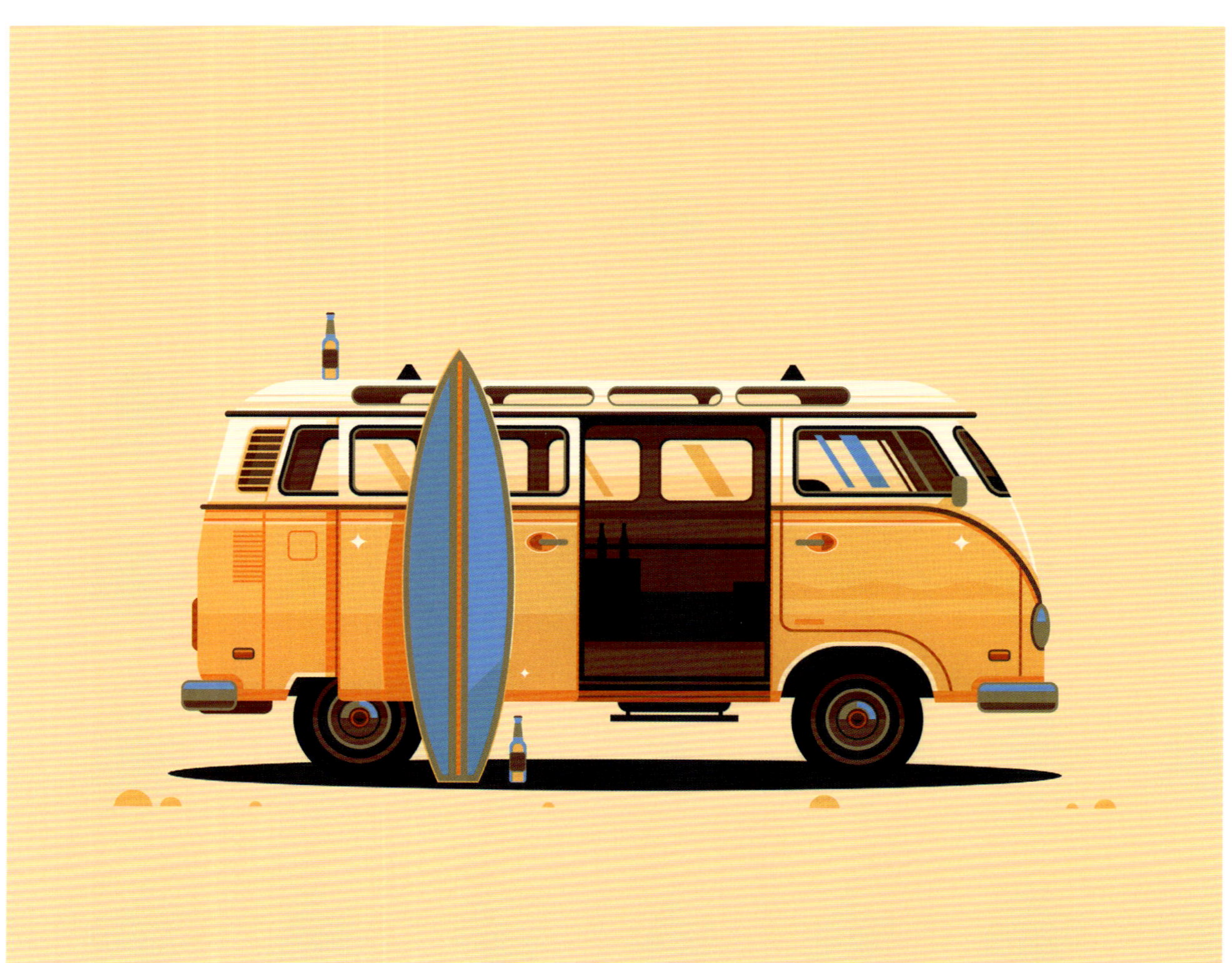

ABOVE

*Campervan*
Open Edition
2023

ACROSS

*Mail Truck*
Open Edition
2023

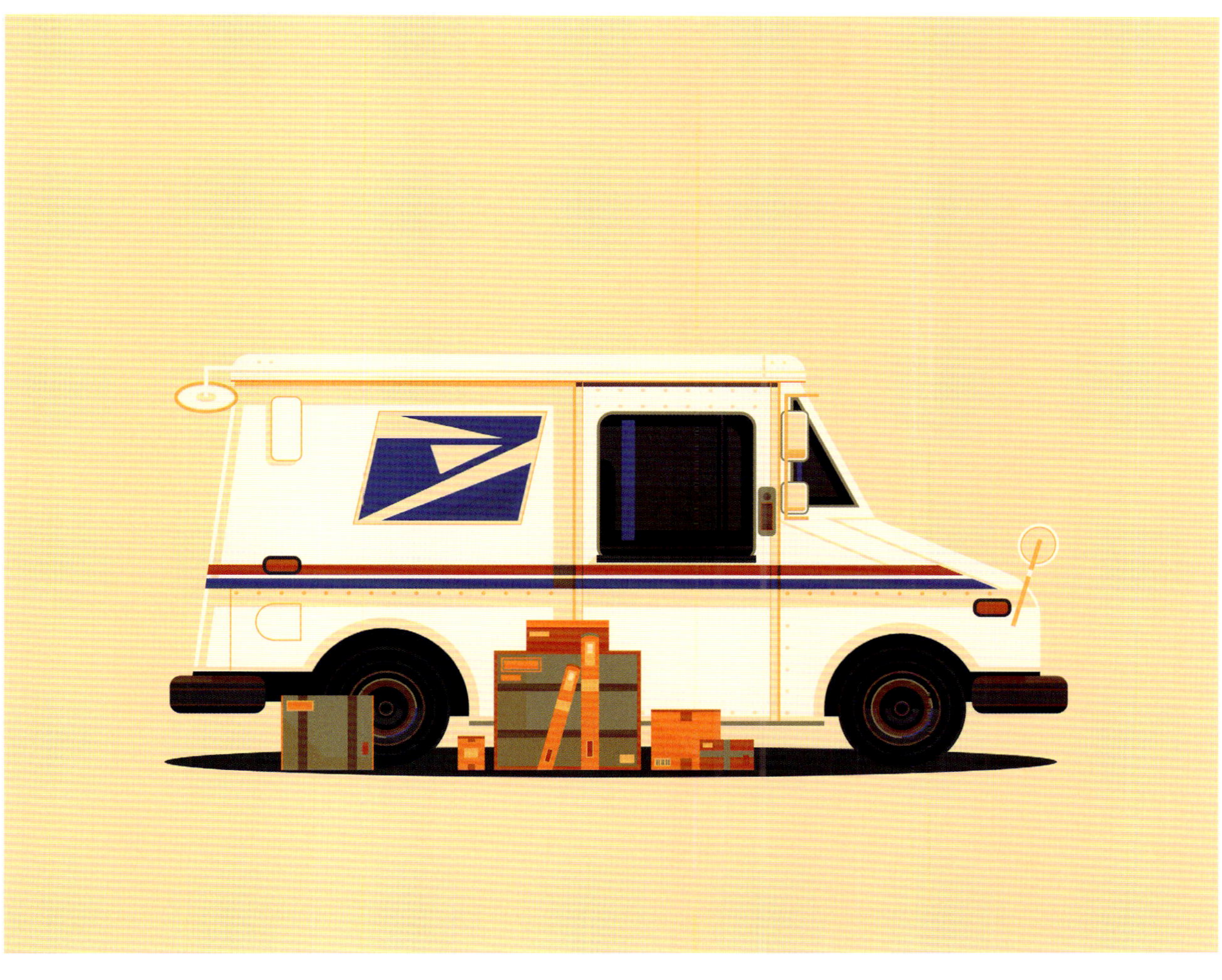

# OCEAN FRONT WALK

ADDRESS
Ocean Front Walk
Venice, CA
90292

ARCHITECT(S)
Abbot Kinney

YEAR
1905



**Venice Beach is my go-to spot** to stay when I visit Los Angeles. Not only is it a fun, chill, vibrant area with a wonderful community, but it's also conveniently close to LAX. Every time I pass by the rows of houses lining the iconic front, I can't help but imagine how lucky it would be to live in such a prime location, waking up to the Pacific Ocean right on your doorstep.

One of my favourite memories happened shortly after we arrived in LA one time. Jet-lagged after an 11-hour flight, we wanted to stay awake to adjust to the time zone, so we headed to a bar in Venice Beach to pass the time and avoid going to bed too early. As we sat there drinking and chatting, everyone in the bar suddenly jumped up and rushed outside. We followed suit, and to our surprise, caught a SpaceX launch over the ocean, framed perfectly by the sunset. It was such a surreal sight.

GATEFOLD

*Ocean Front Walk*
Limited Edition
2022

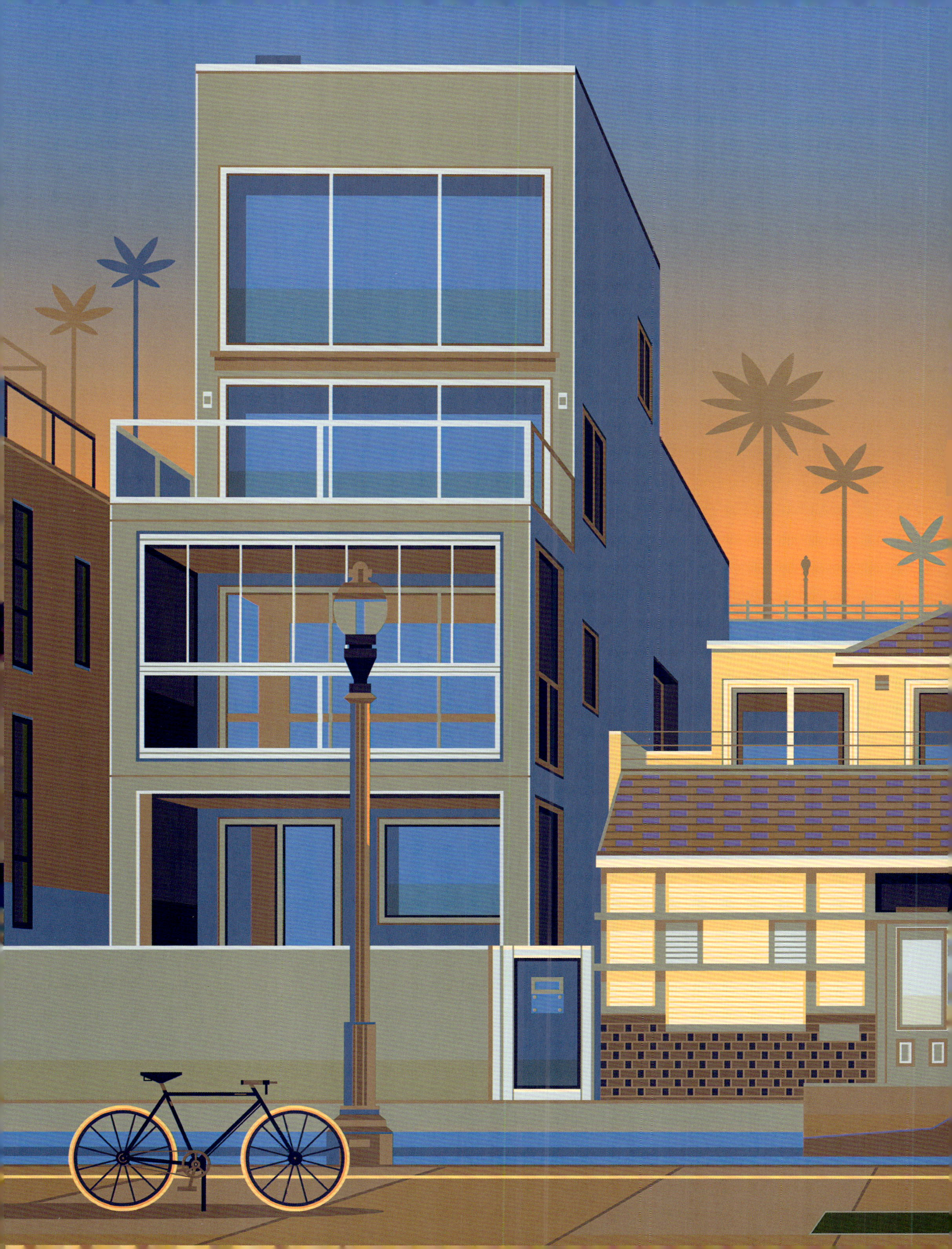

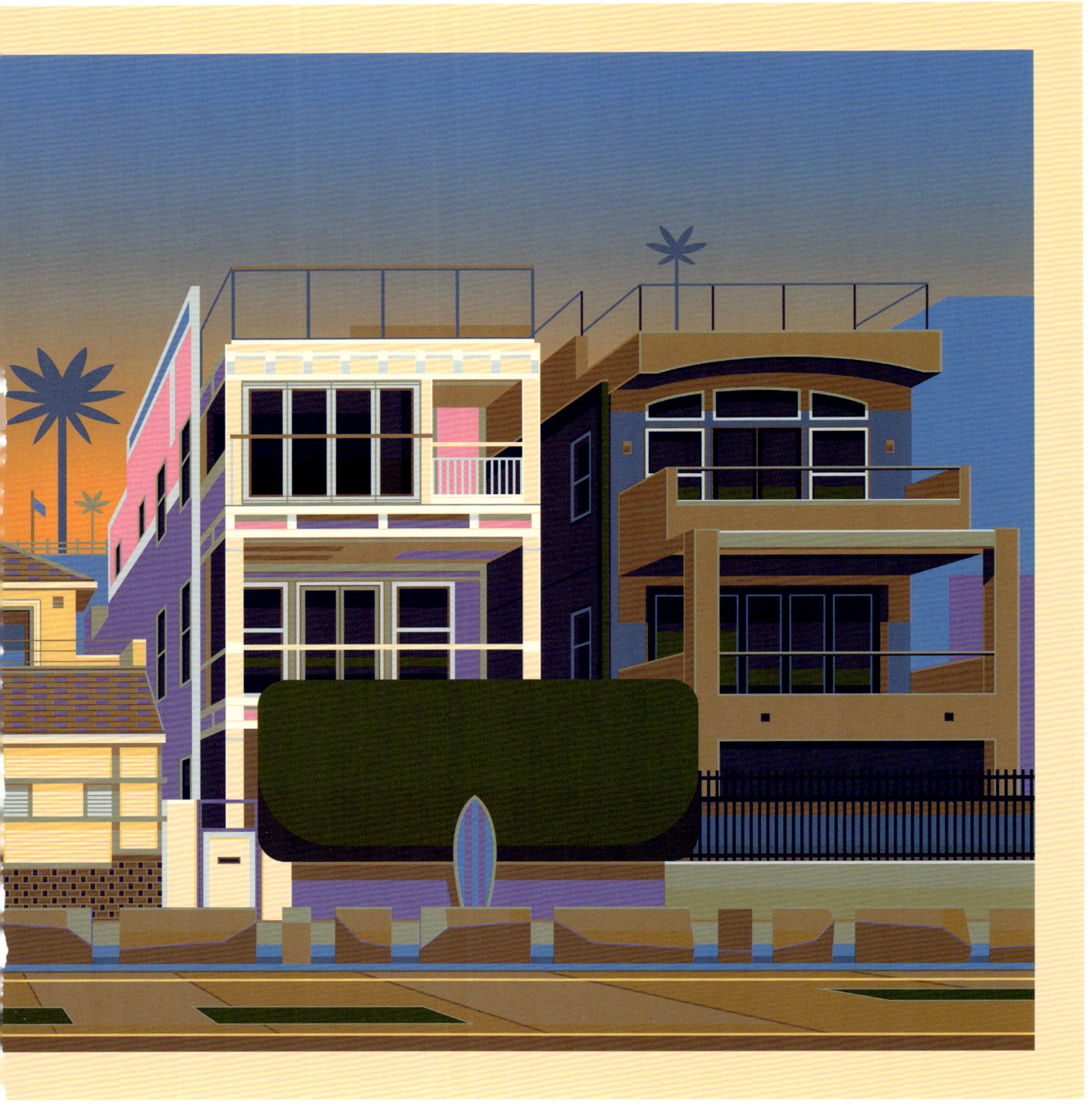

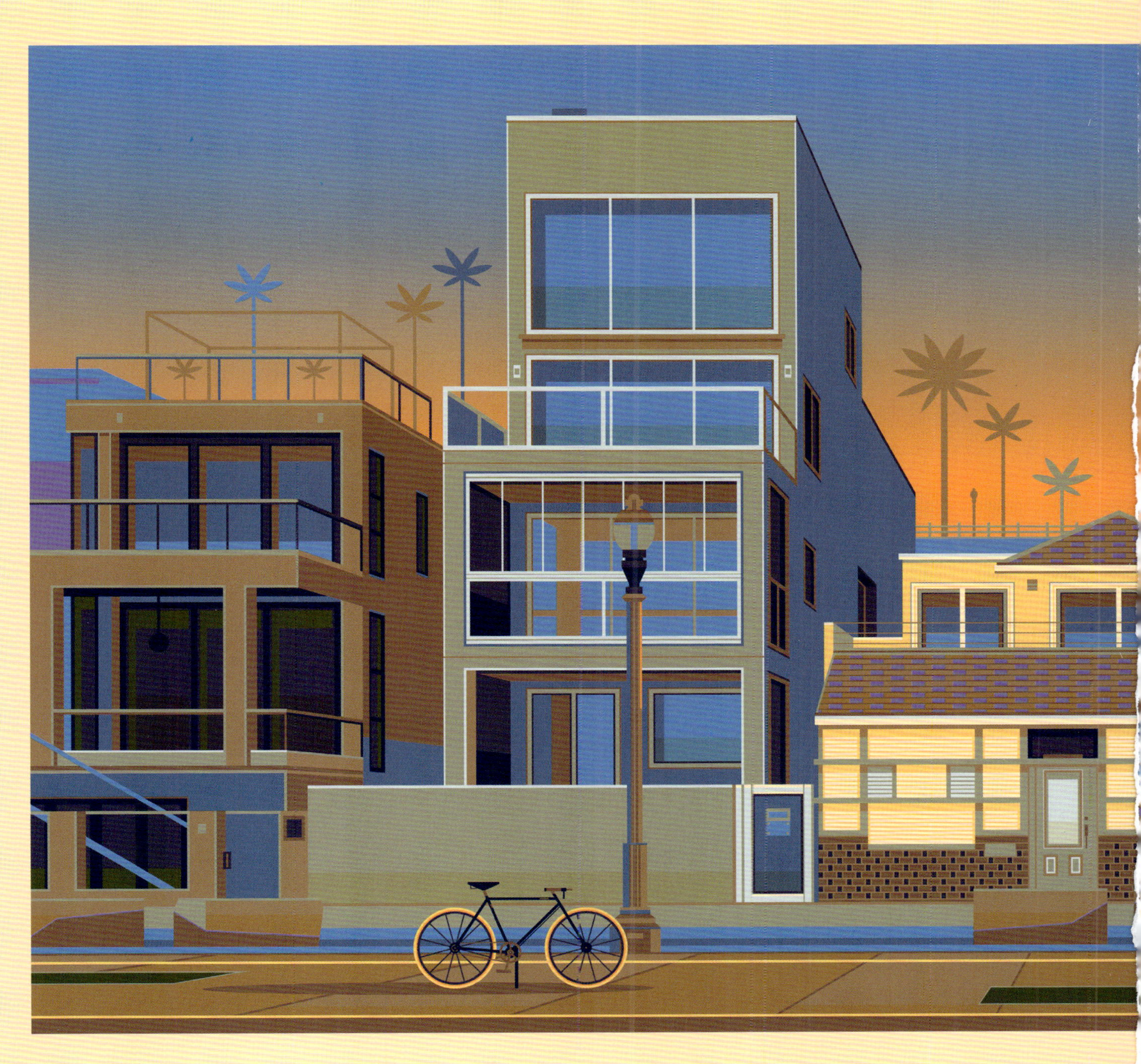

# Iconic Eateries

# RANDY'S DONUTS

| ADDRESS | ARCHITECT(S) | YEAR |
|---|---|---|
| 805 West Manchester Blvd.<br>Inglewood, CA<br>90301 | Henry Goodwin | 1953 |



**I think I first saw Randy's Donuts in *Iron Man 2*** and thought it was such a fun, over-the-top landmark, exactly the kind of thing you'd expect in LA. Seeing it in real life for the first time felt very familiar, a common occurrence when your first encounter with so many of these landmarks is through a screen.

I put extra effort into making every written detail of this illustration as accurate as possible, spending far more time than usual researching and carefully recreating the menu. It may be outdated now, but at the time, I loved the idea that someone could glance at their print and decide what they wanted to order ahead of time.

I've only had one glazed donut from here, but I can confirm it lives up to the hype, at least as far as donuts go.

ACROSS

*Randy's Donuts (Sunset)*
Limited Edition
2019

NEXT SPREAD

*Randy's Donuts (Detail)*
Open Edition
2019

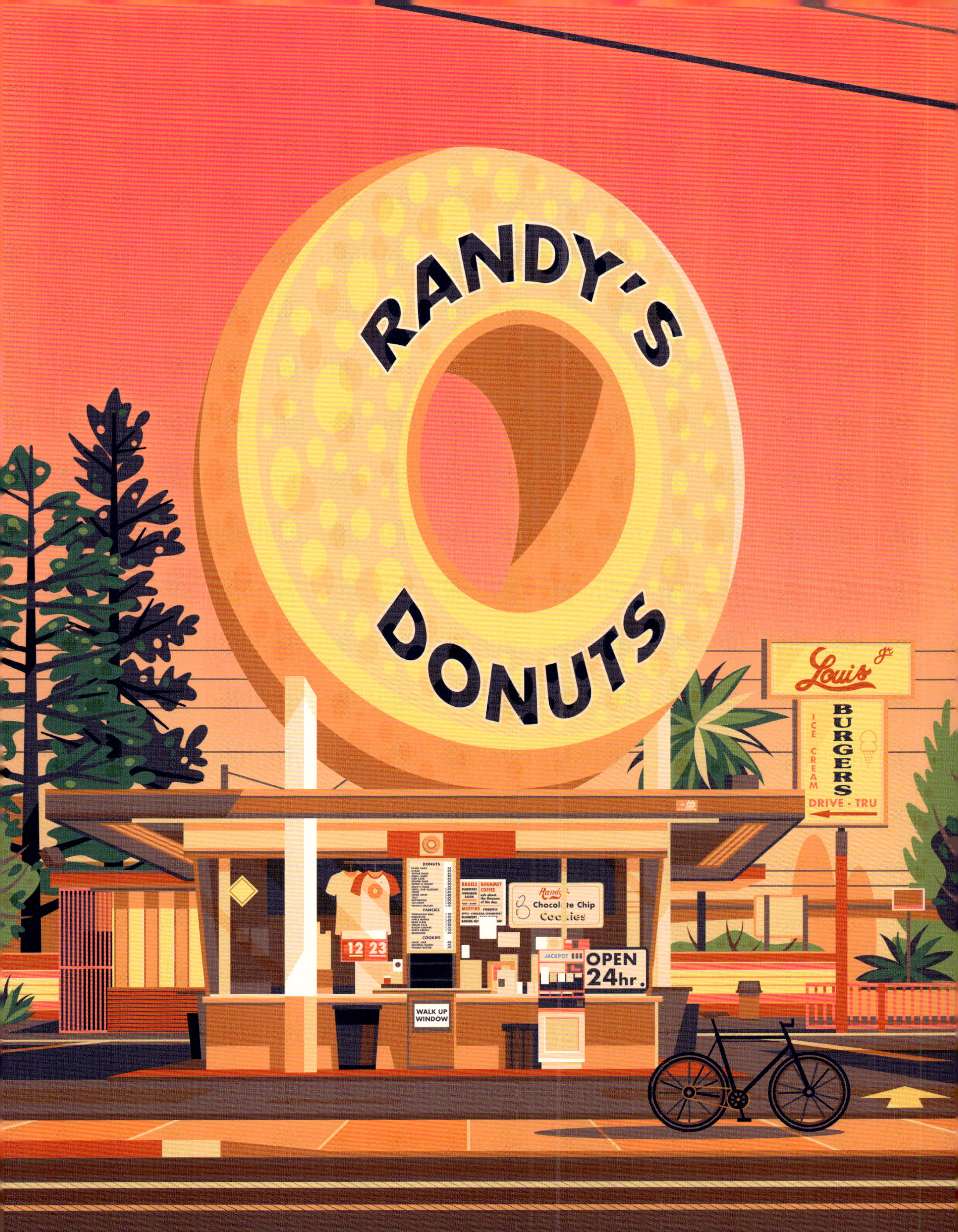
RANDY'S
DONUTS
Louis Jr.
BURGERS
ICE CREAM
DRIVE - TRU
DONUTS
FANCIES
COOKIES
BAGELS
GOURMET COFFEE
MUFFINS
Randy's Chocolate Chip Cookies
12 23
JACKPOT
OPEN 24hr.
WALK UP WINDOW

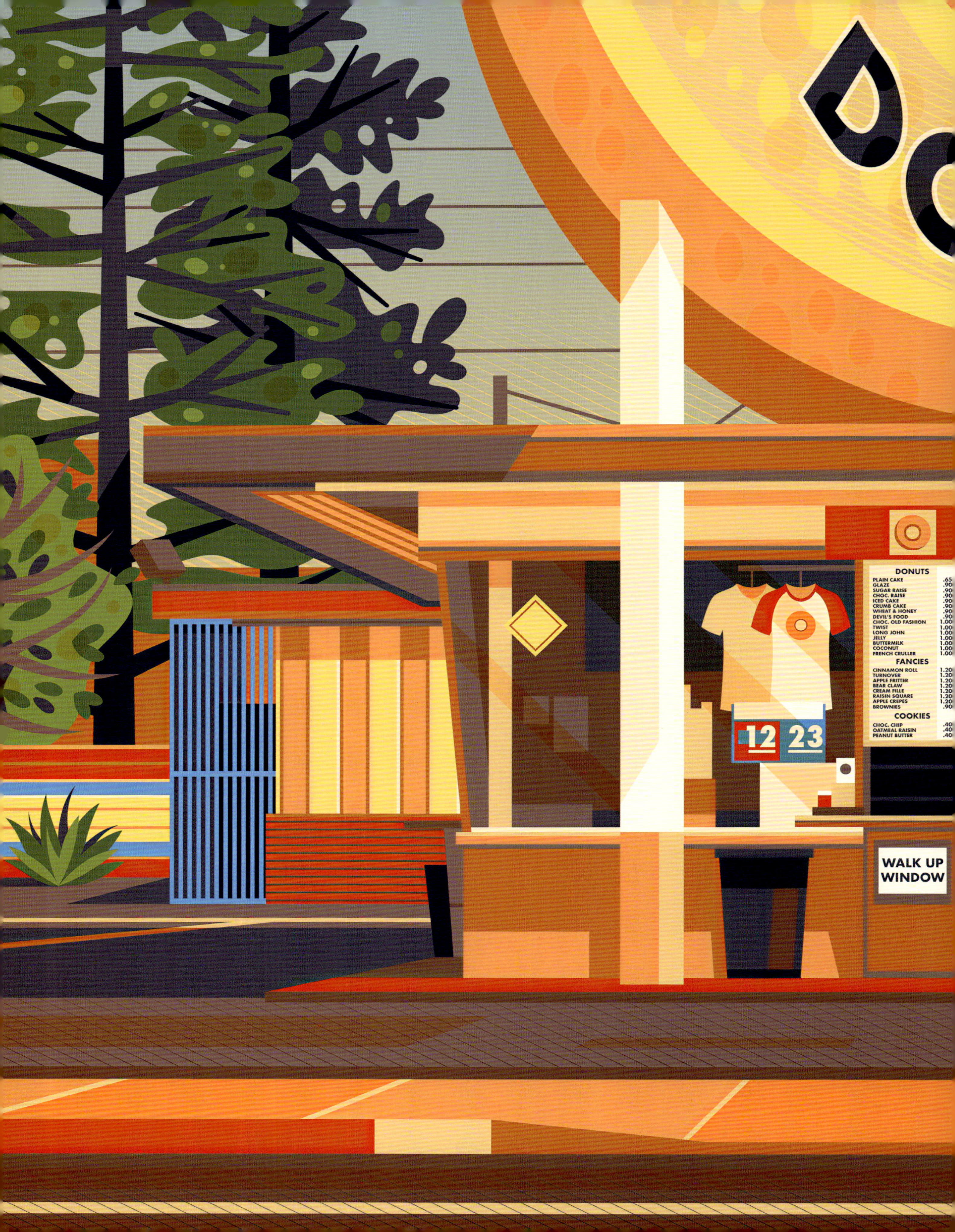
DONUTS
PLAIN CAKE .65
GLAZE .90
SUGAR RAISE .90
CHOC. RAISE .90
ICED CAKE .90
CRUMB CAKE .90
WHEAT & HONEY .90
DEVIL'S FOOD .90
CHOC. OLD FASHION 1.00
TWIST 1.00
LONG JOHN 1.00
JELLY 1.00
BUTTERMILK 1.00
COCONUT 1.00
FRENCH CRULLER 1.00
FANCIES
CINNAMON ROLL 1.20
TURNOVER 1.20
APPLE FRITTER 1.20
BEAR CLAW 1.20
CREAM FILLE 1.20
RAISIN SQUARE 1.20
APPLE CREPES 1.20
BROWNIES .90
COOKIES
CHOC. CHIP .40
OATMEAL RAISIN .40
PEANUT BUTTER .40
12 23
WALK UP WINDOW

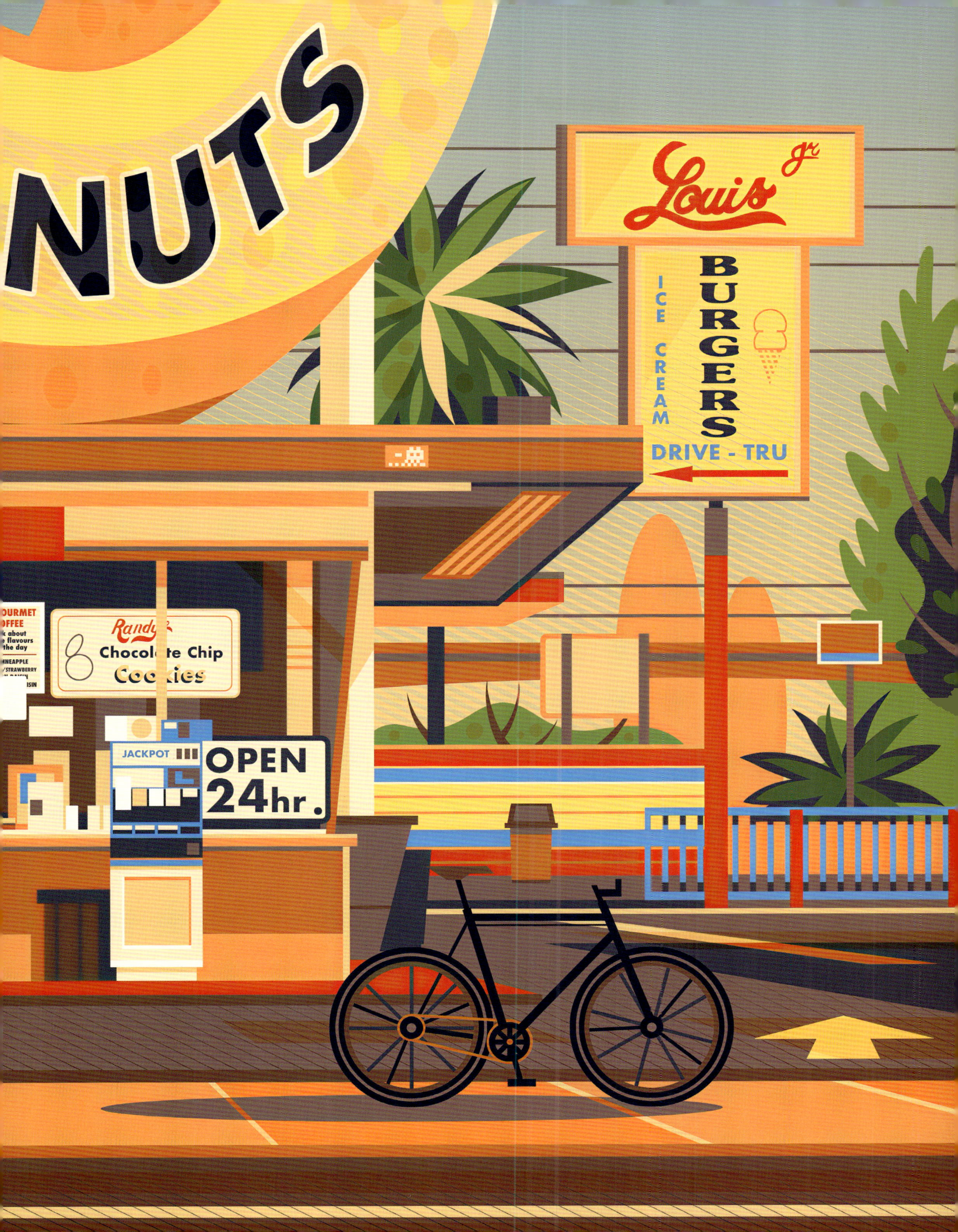
NUTS
Louis jr
BURGERS
ICE CREAM
DRIVE - TRU
JACKPOT
OPEN 24hr.

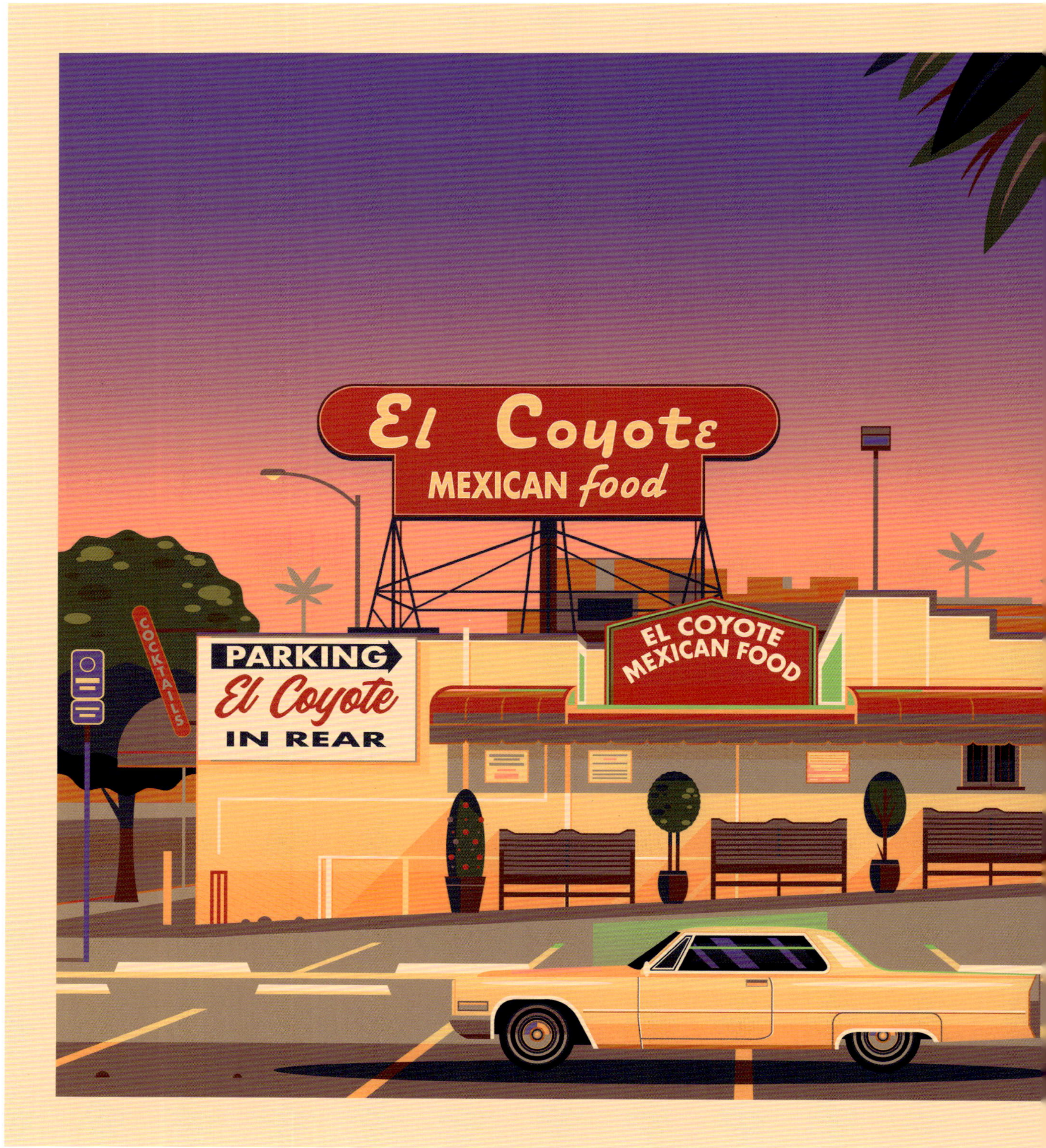


ABOVE

*El Coyote Cafe (Sunset)*
Limited Edition
2023

NEXT TWO SPREADS

*El Coyote Cafe (Night)*
Timed Edition
2023

*El Coyote Cafe*
Open Edition
2023

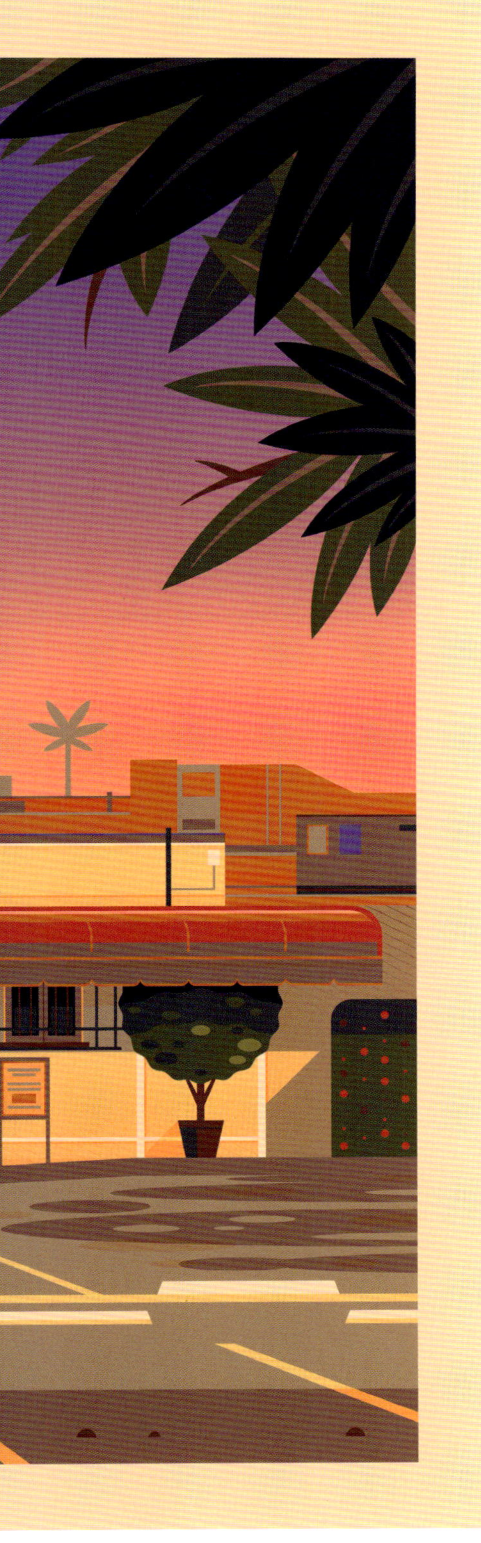

# EL COYOTE CAFE

| ADDRESS | ARCHITECT(S) | YEAR |
|---|---|---|
| 7312 Beverly Blvd.<br>Los Angeles, CA<br>90036 | N/A | 1951 |



**As a huge fan of Mexican food,** El Coyote Cafe was a must-visit for me. I first learned about the restaurant after seeing it featured in *Once Upon a Time in Hollywood*. It's well known as the last place Sharon Tate dined before that infamous night in 1969.

The food is, of course, fantastic, but I have to give a special shoutout to their margaritas, they're easily some of my favourites in the city. It's one of those rare spots where the food, the drinks, and the history all come together in the perfect experience.

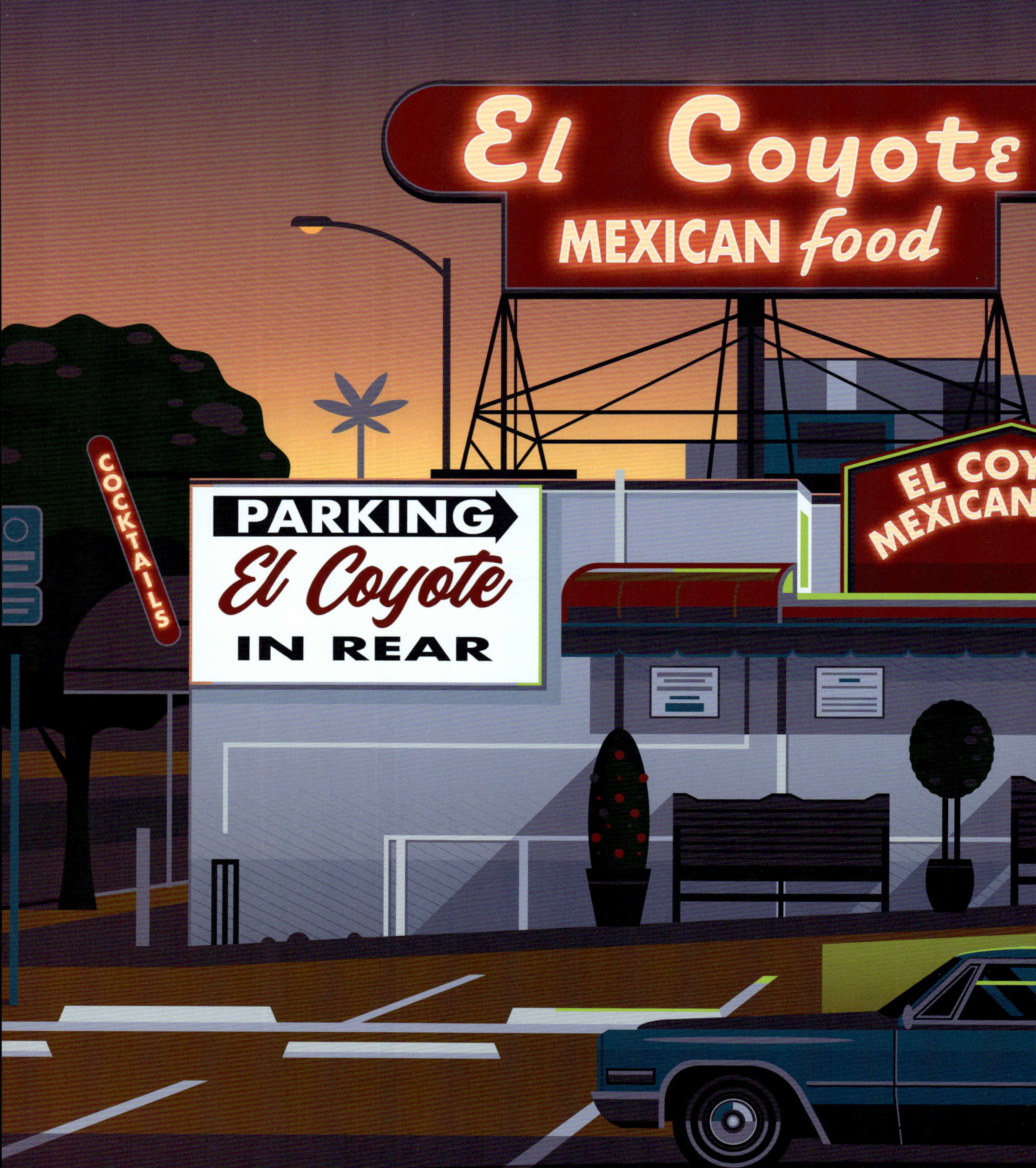
El Coyote
MEXICAN food
COCKTAILS
PARKING
El Coyote
IN REAR
EL COY
MEXICAN

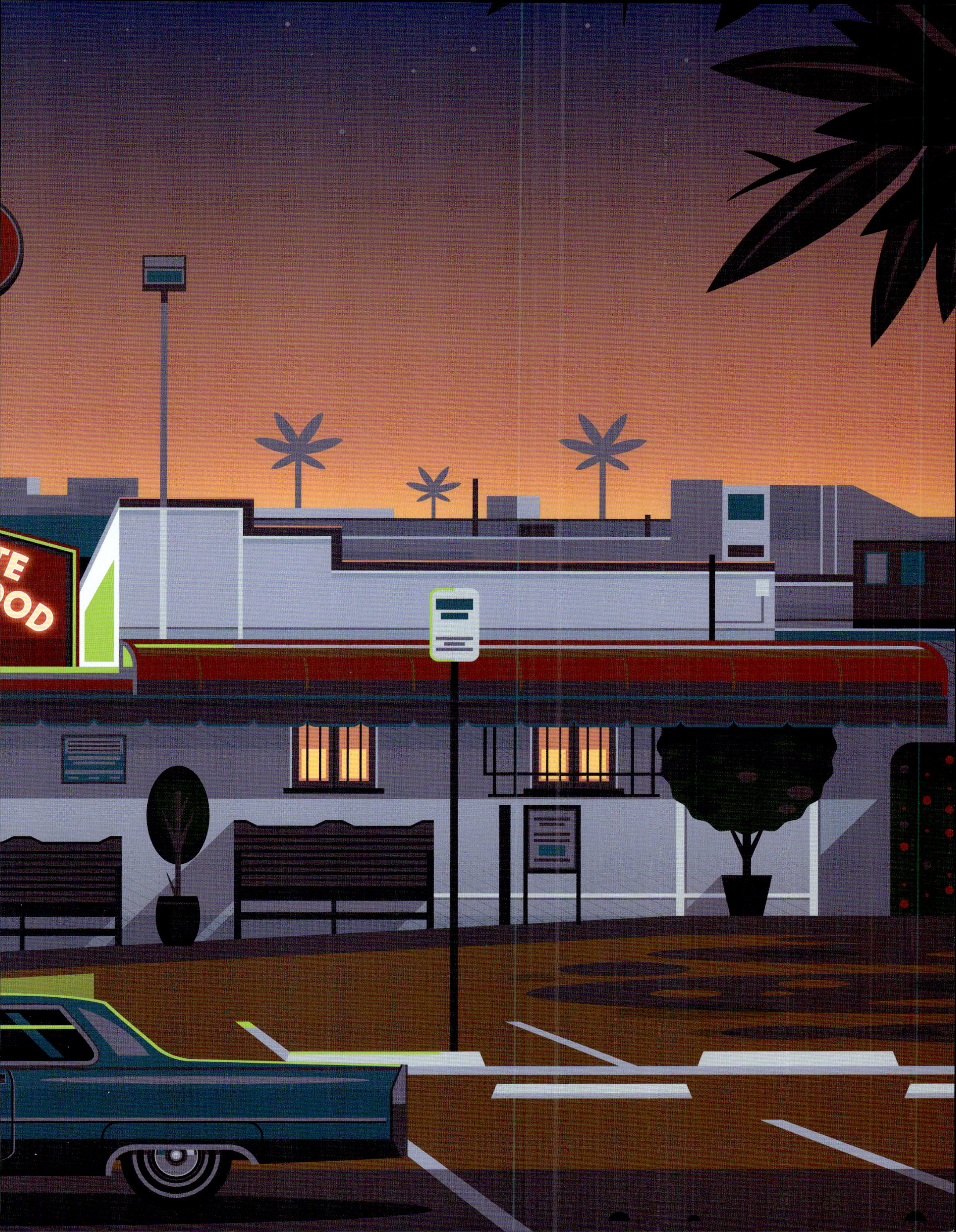

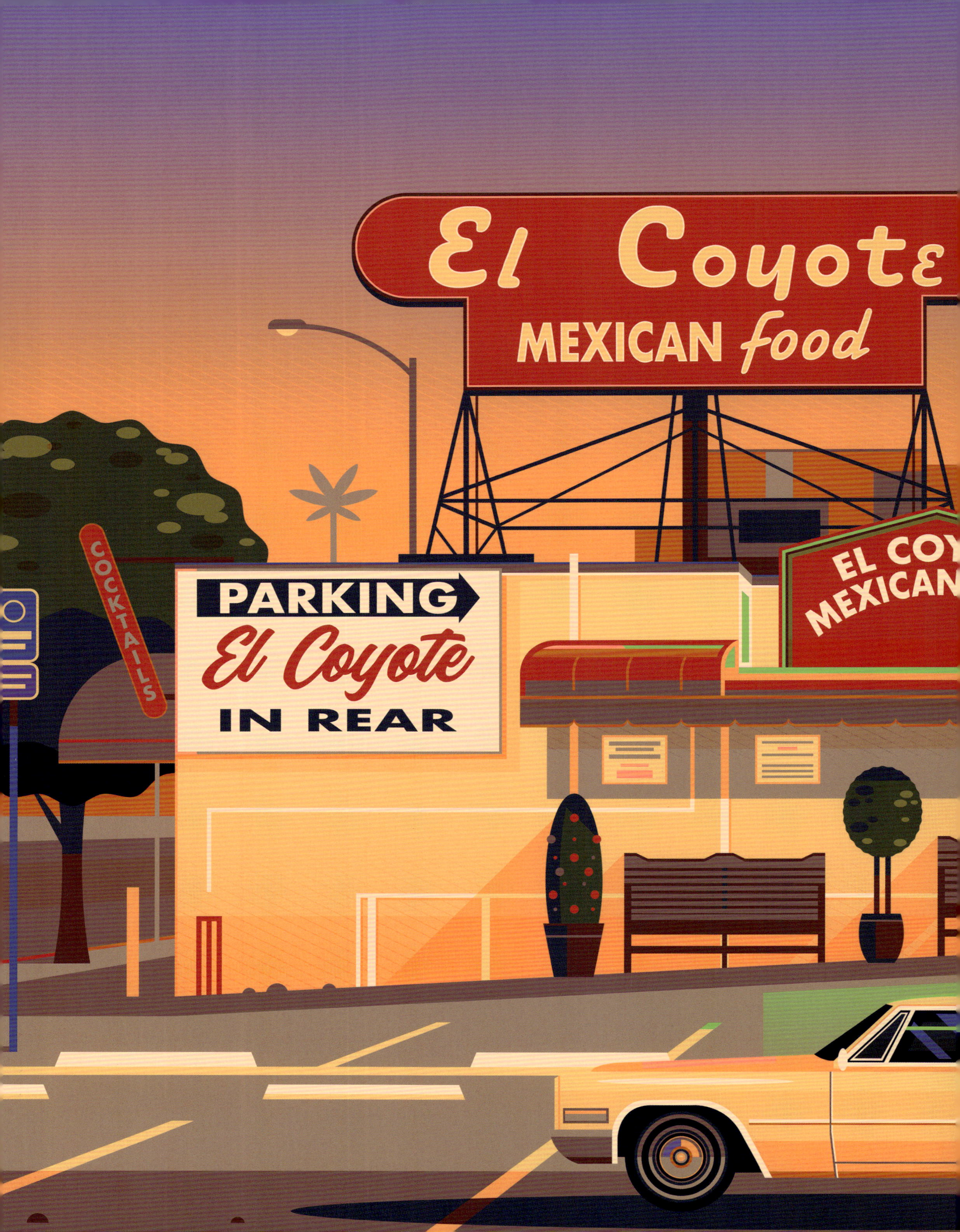

El Coyote
MEXICAN food
COCKTAILS
PARKING
El Coyote
IN REAR
EL COY
MEXICAN

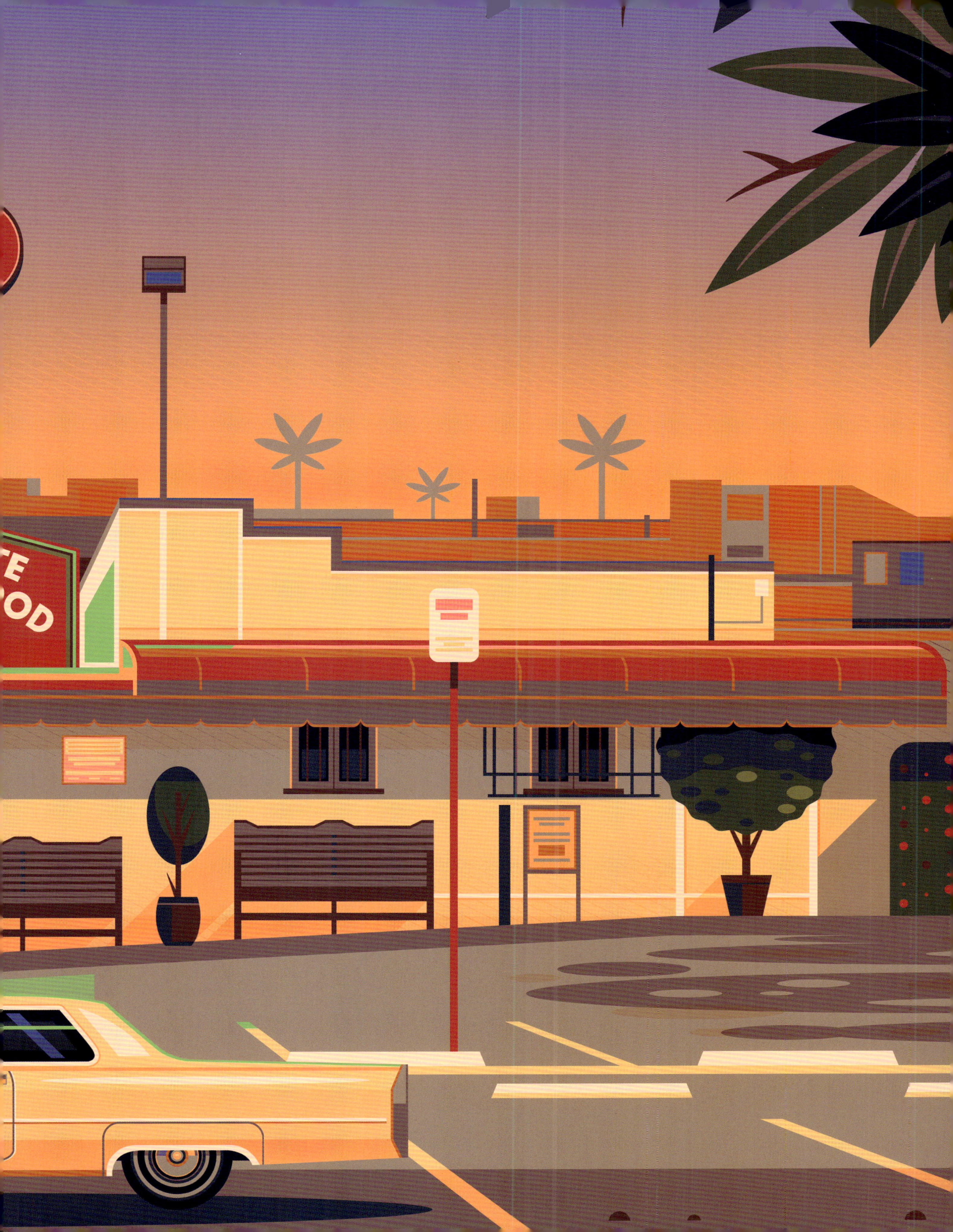

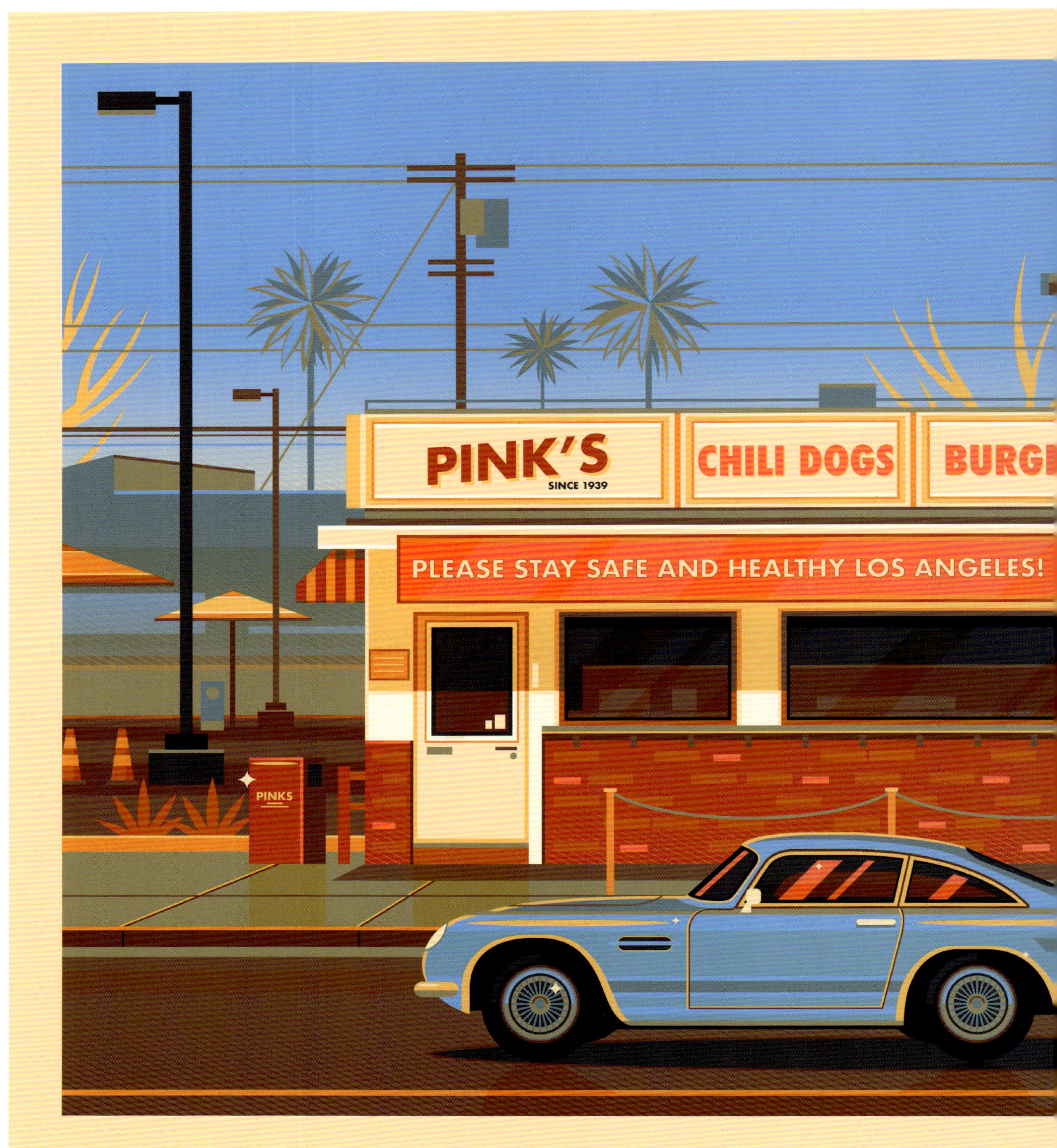
PINK'S
SINCE 1939
CHILI DOGS
PLEASE STAY SAFE AND HEALTHY LOS ANGELES!
PINKS

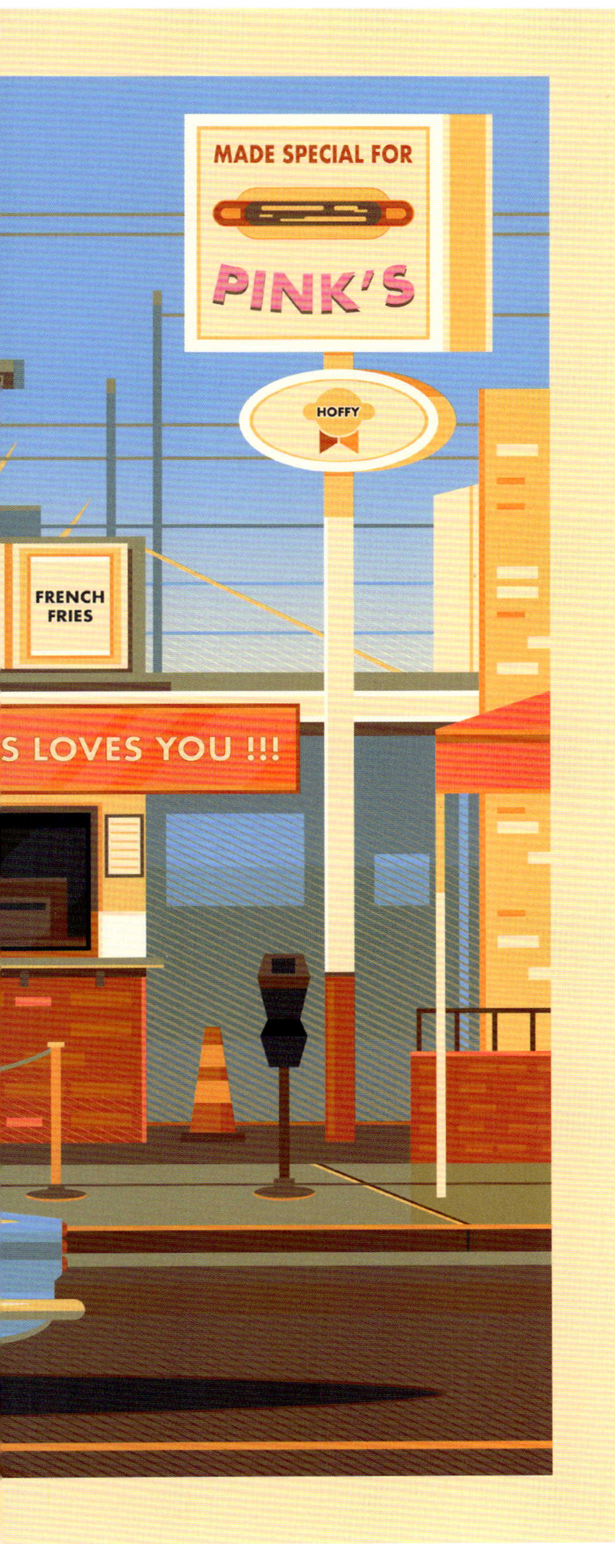


# PINK'S HOT DOGS

| ADDRESS | ARCHITECT(S) | YEAR |
|---|---|---|
| 709 N. La Brea Ave.<br>Los Angeles, CA<br>90038 | N/A | 1939 |



ACROSS

*Pink's Hot Dogs*
Limited Edition
2020

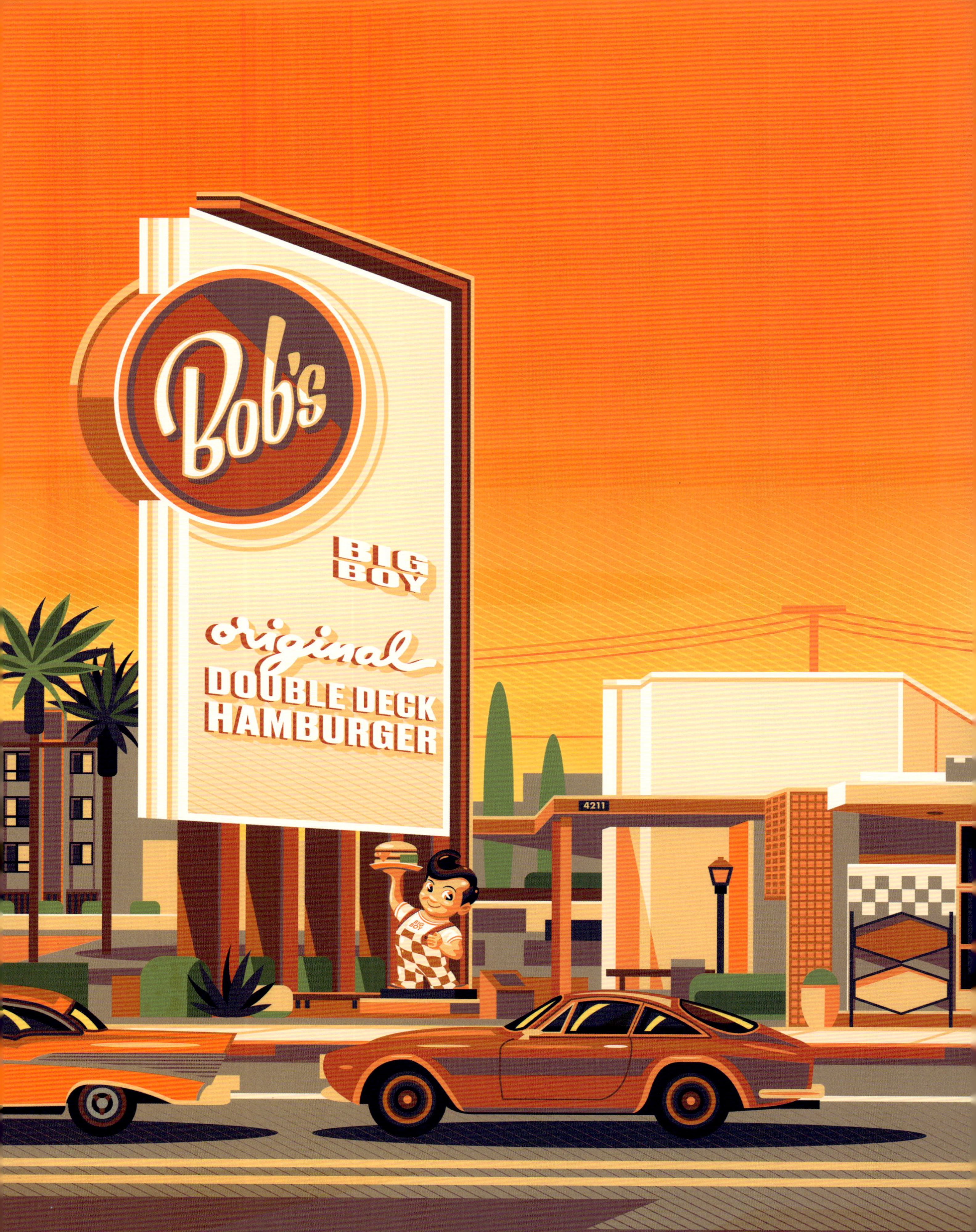
Bob's
BIG
BOY
original
DOUBLE DECK
HAMBURGER
4211
BIG
BOY

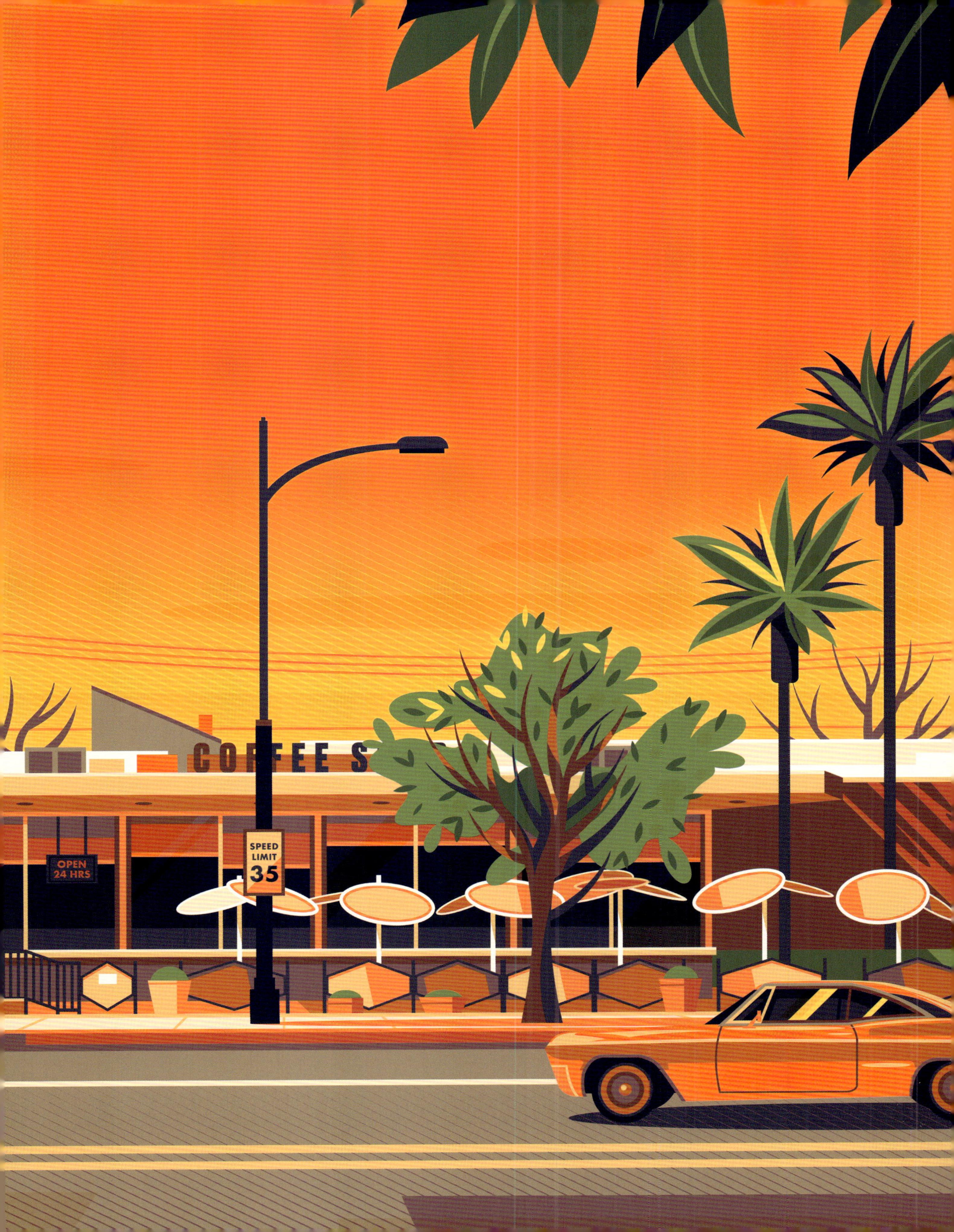
OPEN
24 HRS
SPEED
LIMIT
35

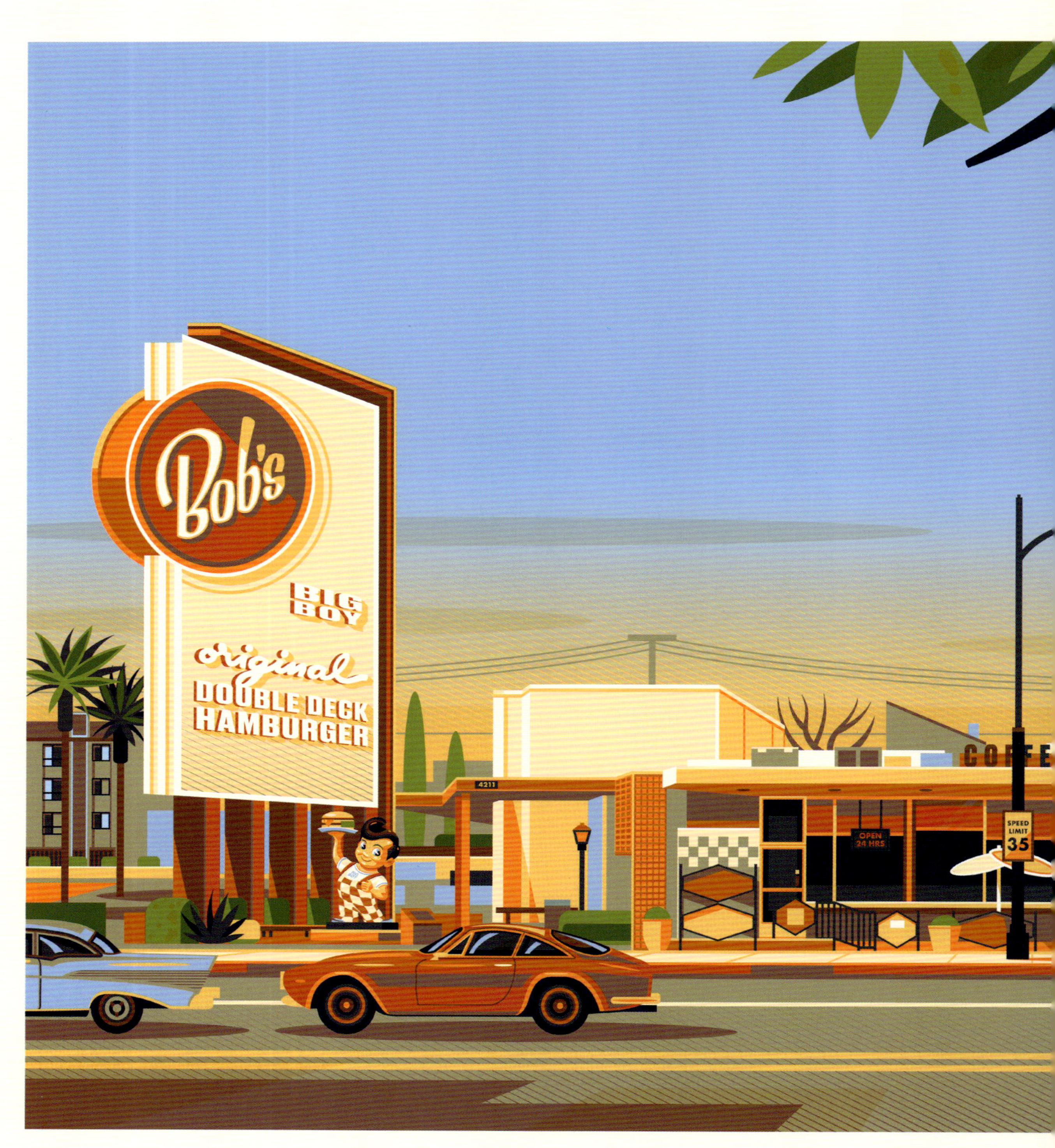




PREVIOUS SPREAD

*Bob's Big Boy (Sunset)*
Limited Edition
2020

ABOVE

*Bob's Big Boy*
Limited Edition
2020

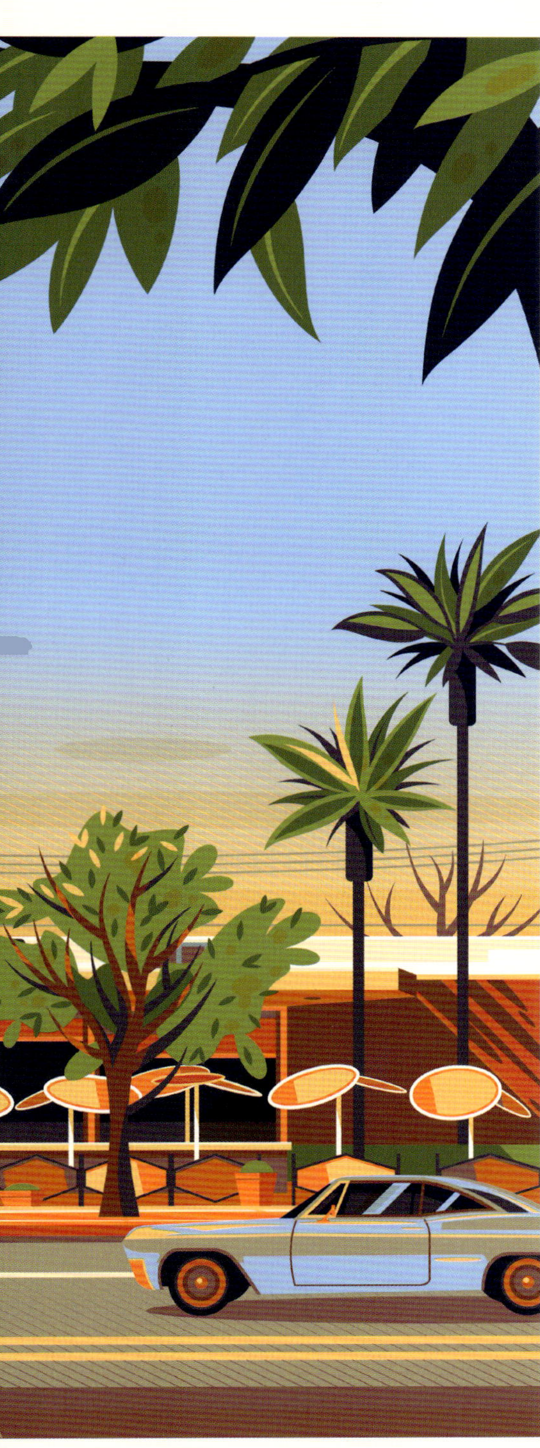

# BOB'S BIG BOY

| ADDRESS | ARCHITECT(S) | YEAR |
| --- | --- | --- |
| 4211 West Riverside Dr.<br>Burbank, CA<br>91505 | Wayne McAllister | 1949 |



**Bob's Big Boy offers that classic diner food** that's so hard to find in England, the kind you'd see on TV as a kid. I remember being amazed the first time I saw a cherry placed on top of my milkshake, it's such a small detail, but it felt so quintessentially American to me. It was quite literally the cherry on top.

I'm also lucky enough to be featured on one of the postcards you can buy at the front desk, as well as having my artwork hanging above one of the tables inside. Because of this, I've had the privilege of eating for free every time I've visited. (I knew that getting into the art business would pay off eventually). If you visit, I'd recommend the double-decker burger they're so well known for, it's the only thing I ever order.

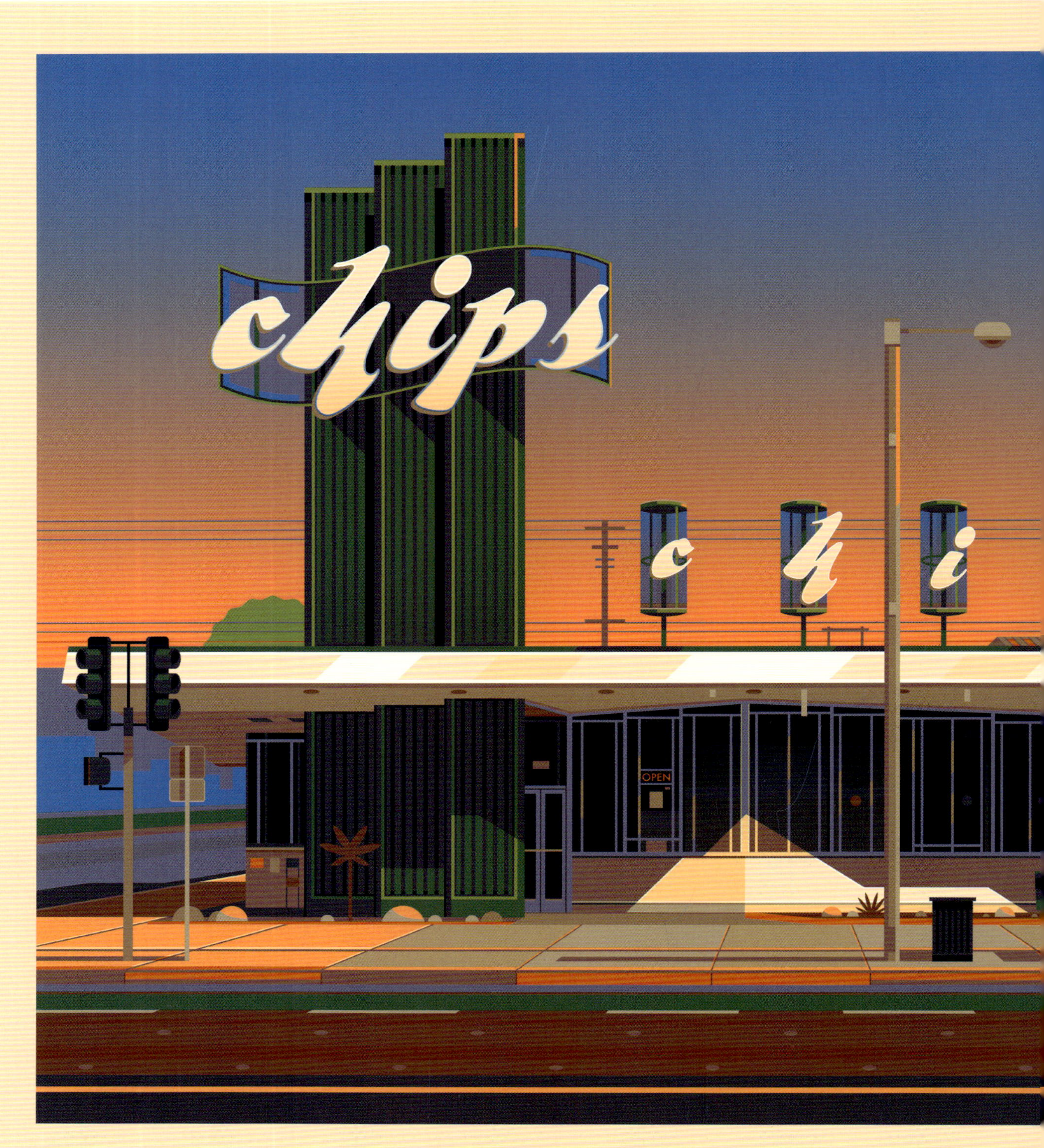
chips
c h i
OPEN

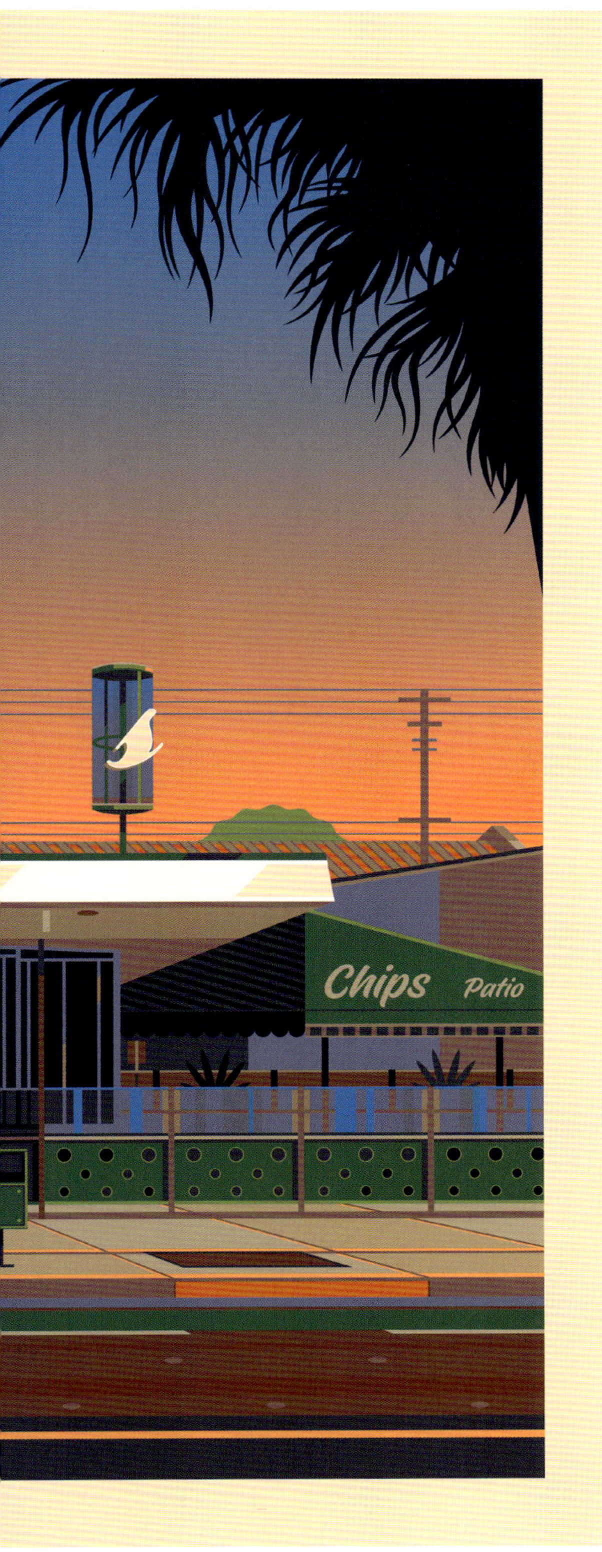


# CHIPS RESTAURANT

| ADDRESS | ARCHITECT(S) | YEAR |
| --- | --- | --- |
| 11908 Hawthorne Blvd.<br>Hawthorne, CA<br>90250 | Harry Harrison | 1957 |



ACROSS

*Chips Restaurant*
Open Edition
2023

# CANTER'S DELI

| ADDRESS | ARCHITECT(S) | YEAR |
|---|---|---|
| 419 North Fairfax Ave.<br>Los Angeles, CA<br>90036 | N/A | 1931 |



**Canter's Deli was just a few doors down** from the gallery where I held my fourth annual art show. After a long morning of signing prints and setting up, we decided to grab something to eat. Once I got over the excitement of being in such an iconic eatery, I was quickly brought back to reality when my food arrived and reminded me just how large American portions are. Despite my best efforts, I barely made a dent in my sandwich before I had to surrender and ask for a to-go box.

Fun fact: the counter inside Canter's Deli was featured on HAIM's 2021 album *Women In Music Pt. III*. As a fan of both the deli and the band, it was fun to see my two favourites come together like that.

ACROSS

*Canter's Deli*
Limited Edition
2019

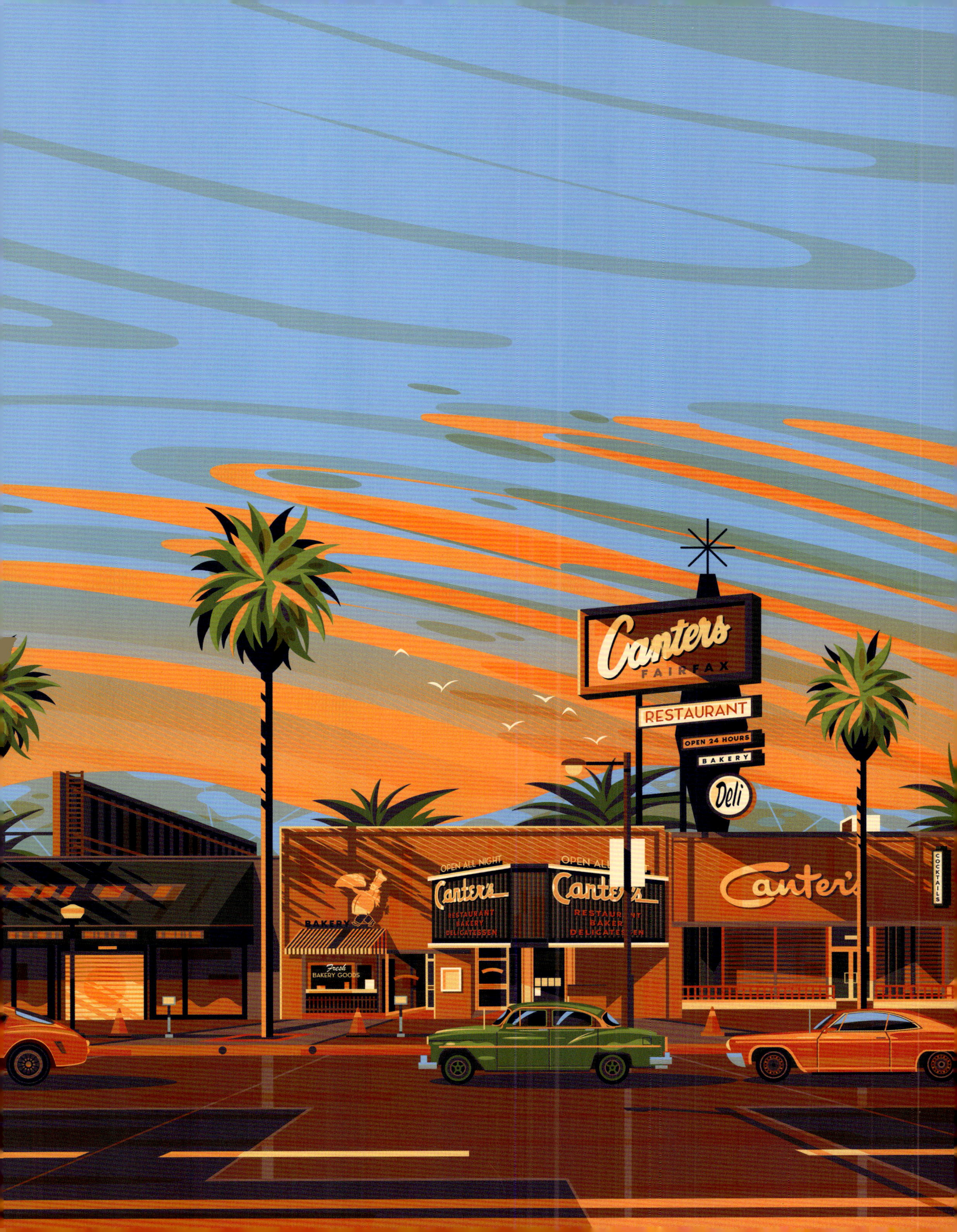

Canters
FAIRFAX
RESTAURANT
OPEN 24 HOURS
BAKERY
Deli
BAKERY
Fresh
BAKERY GOODS
OPEN ALL NIGHT
Canter's
RESTAURANT
BAKERY
DELICATESSEN
Canter's
COCKTAILS

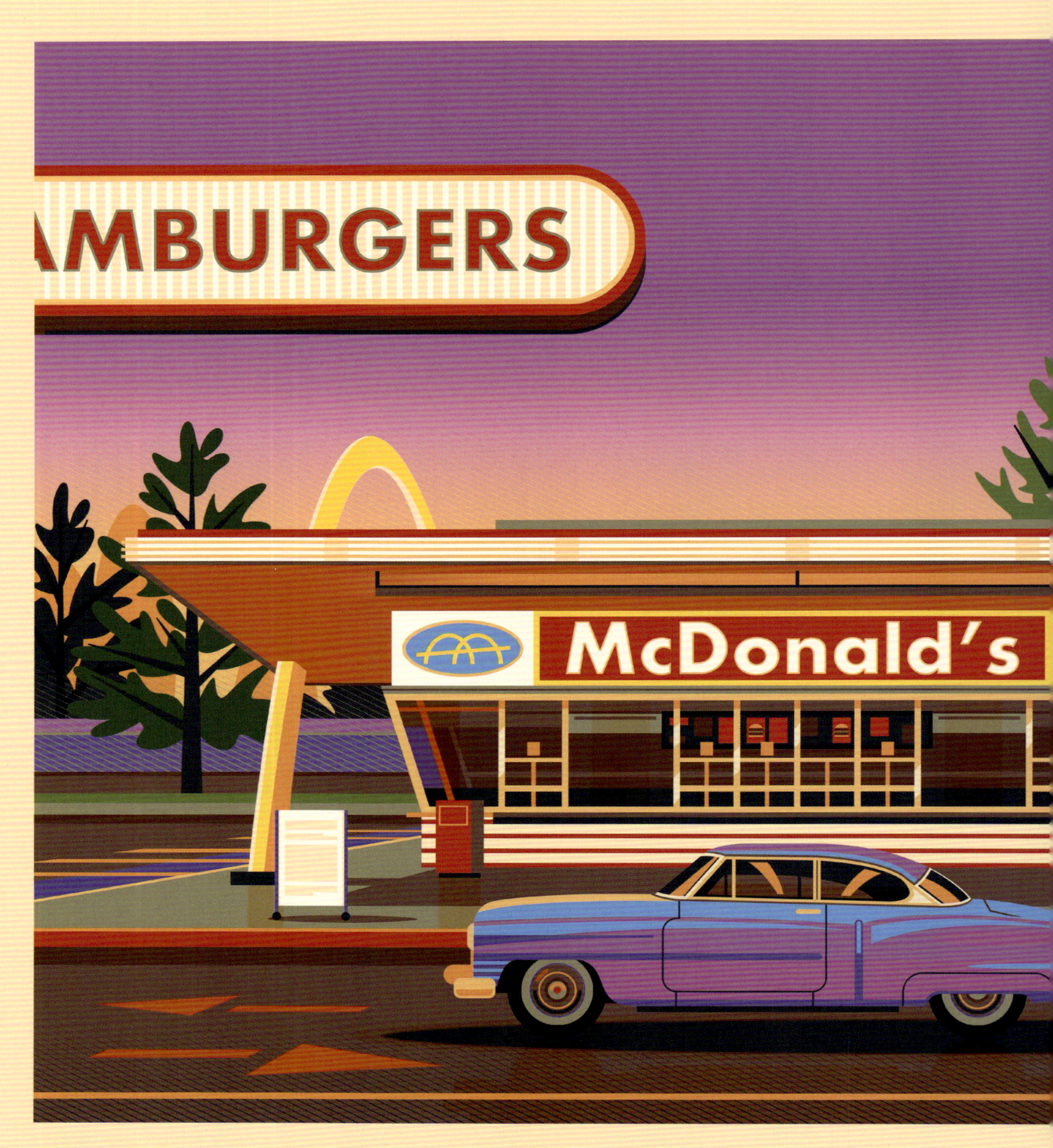
AMBURGERS
McDonald's

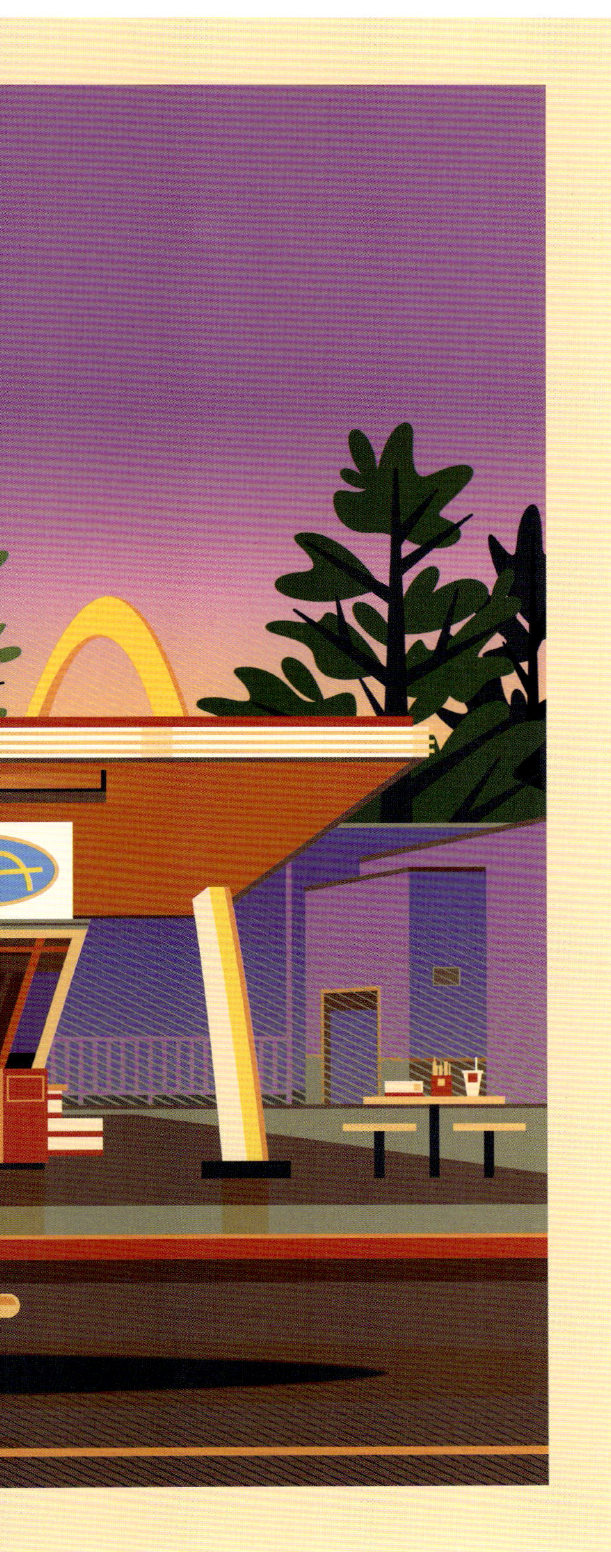

# McDONALD'S DOWNEY

| ADDRESS | ARCHITECT(S) | YEAR |
|---|---|---|
| 10207 Lakewood Blvd.<br>Downey, California<br>90241 | Stanley Clark Meston | 1953 |



ACROSS

*McDonald's Downey*
Limited Edition
2020

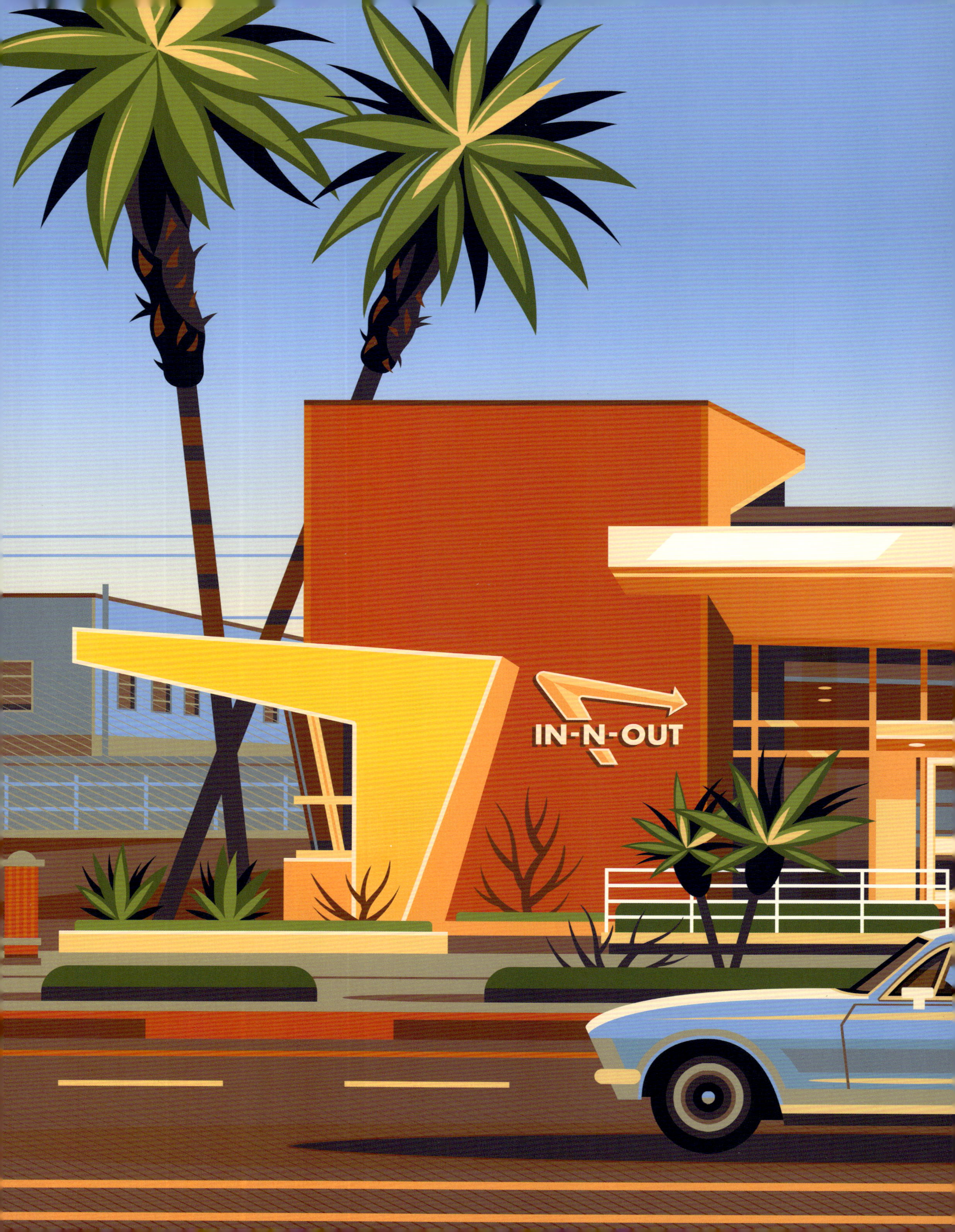
IN-N-OUT

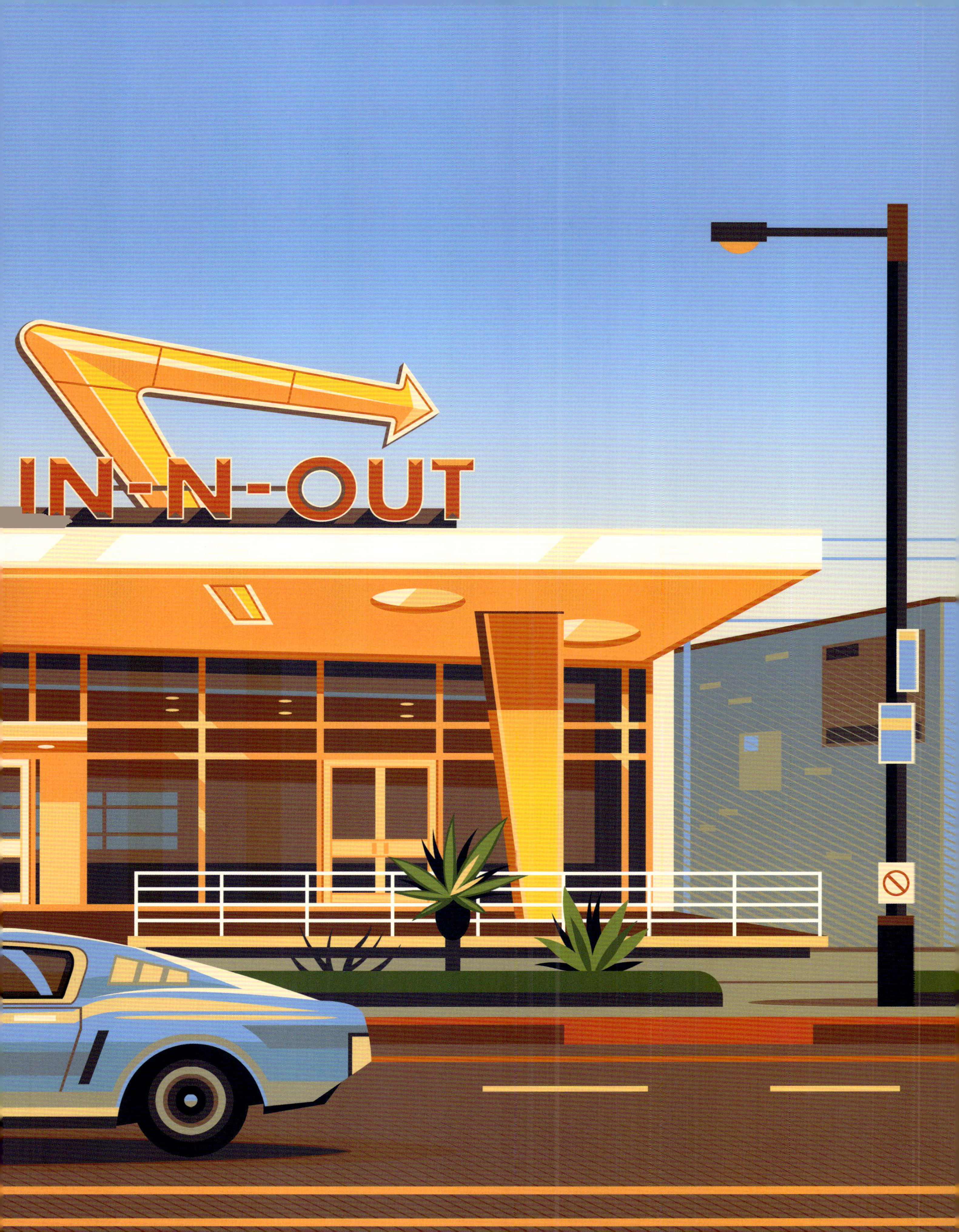
IN-N-OUT

# IN-N-OUT WESTWOOD

| ADDRESS | ARCHITECT(S) | YEAR |
|---|---|---|
| 922 Gayley Ave.<br>Los Angeles, CA<br>90024 | Stephen Kanner<br>Architects | 1997 |



**Although some people call In-N-Out overrated** (I strongly disagree), I make it a point to try and visit at least once every time I'm in LA. I'm not sure if it's just because I actually like the burgers or because it feels like a uniquely Californian experience that I can't miss out on.

This was the first In-N-Out piece I ever worked on, and at the time, I didn't know too much about the chain. I later learned that this particular location is near UCLA, which made it especially meaningful to a lot of people in my audience. Hearing their stories and fond memories tied to this spot was incredible. It reminded me why I do all this in the first place, to capture moments and places that spark a sense of nostalgia and personal connection.

Also the print did much better than I expected, it was a powerful reminder that I truly am an outsider and will never fully know what will resonate with people.

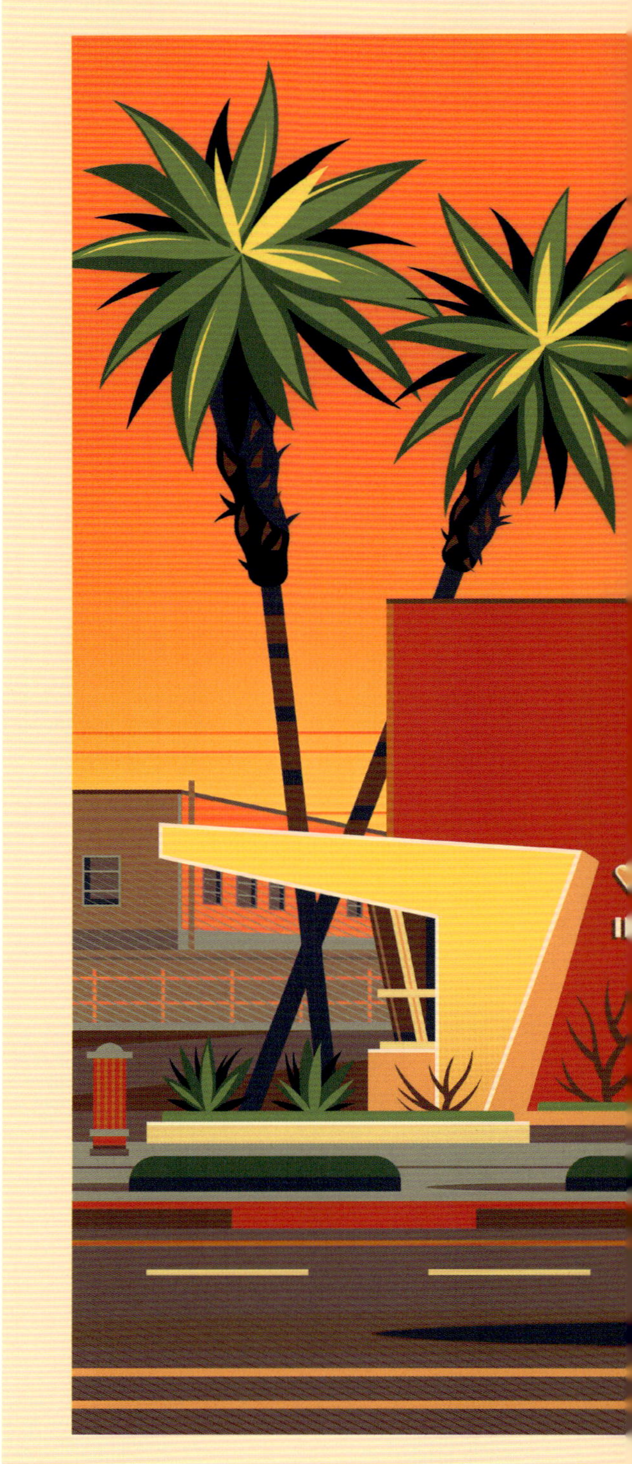

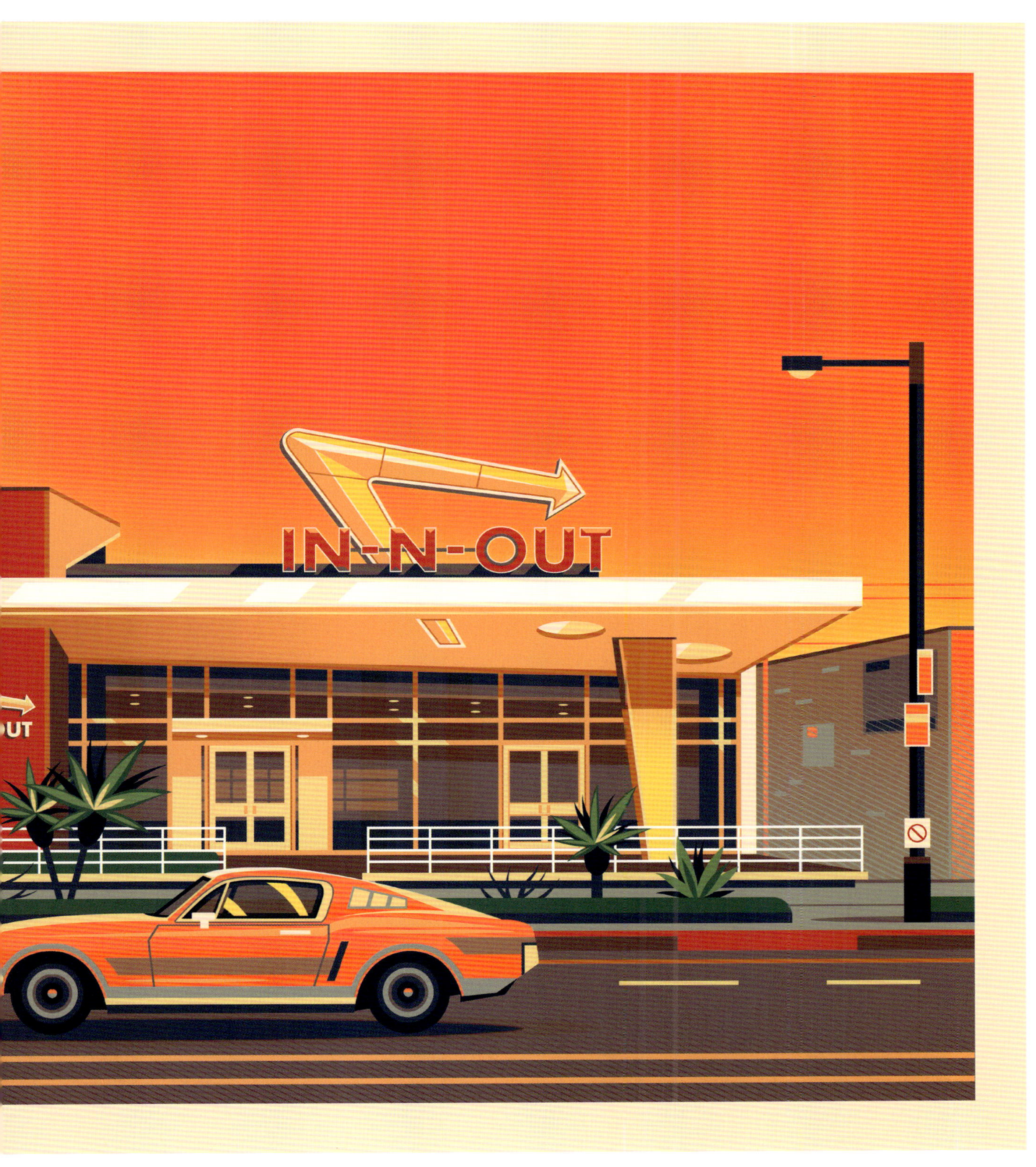




PREVIOUS SPREAD

*In-N-Out Westwood*

Open Edition
2020

ABOVE

*In-N-Out Westwood (Sunset)*

Limited Edition
2020

NEXT SPREAD

*In-N-Out Westwood (Night)*

Open Edition
2020

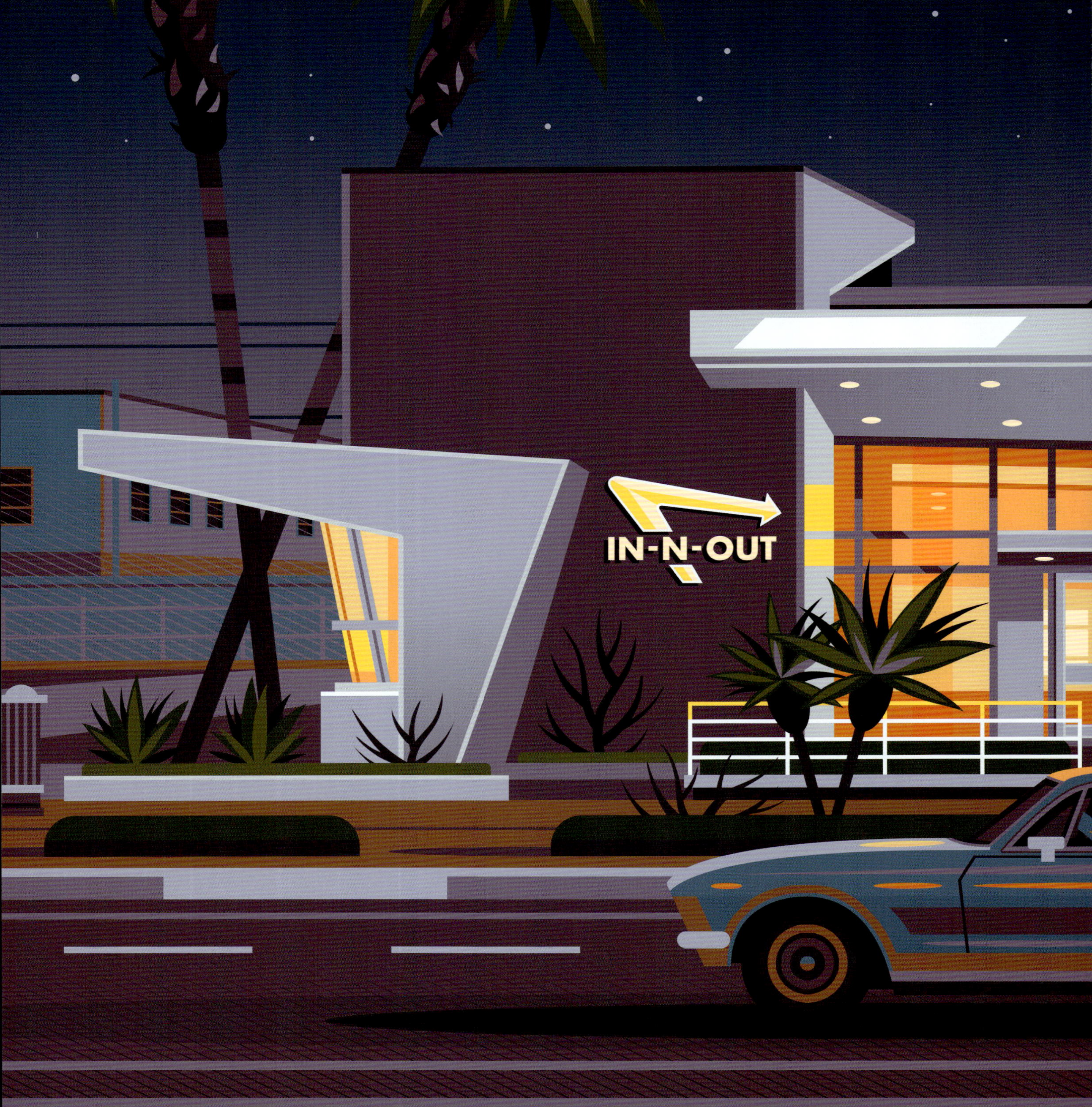
IN-N-OUT

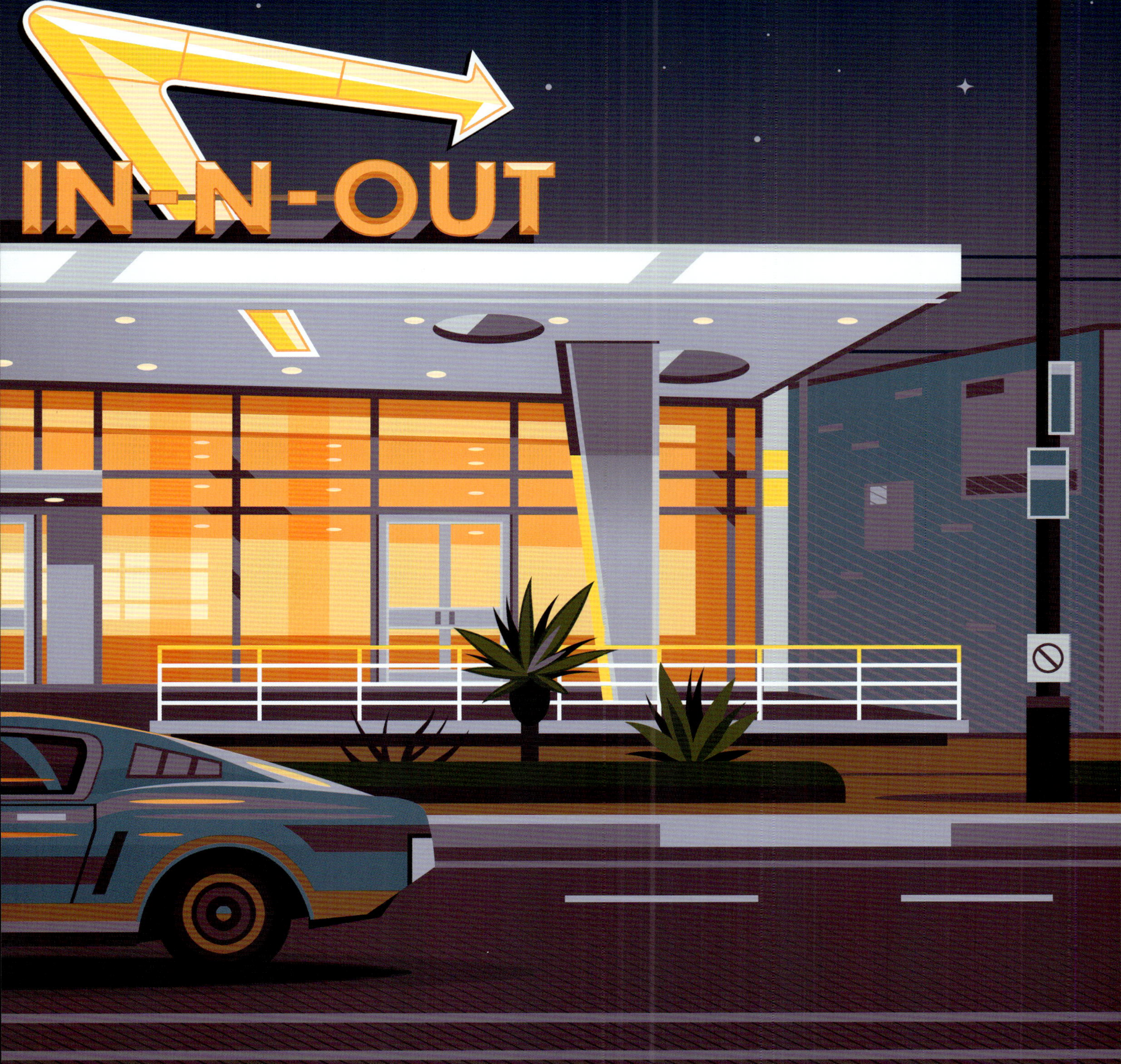
IN-N-OUT

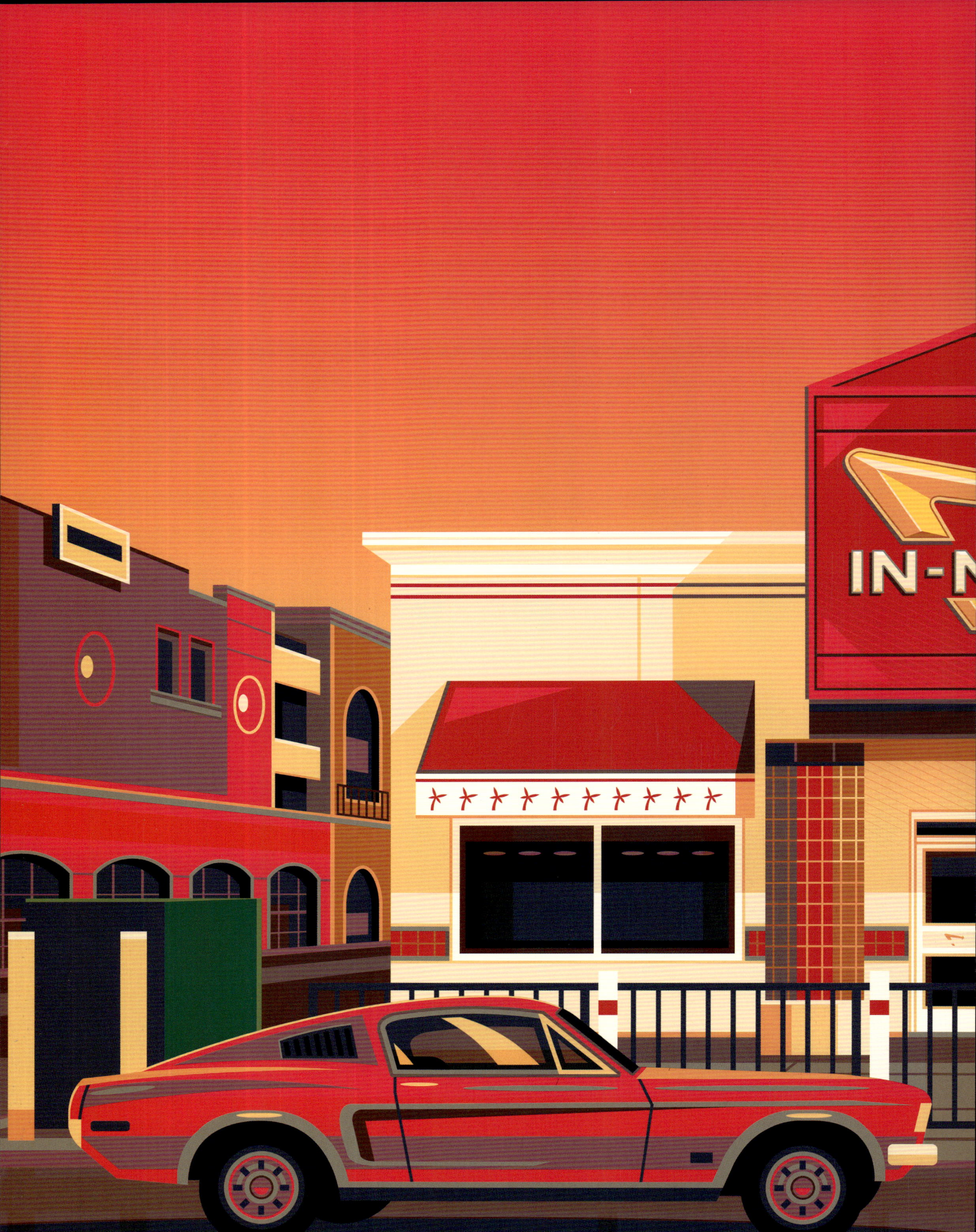

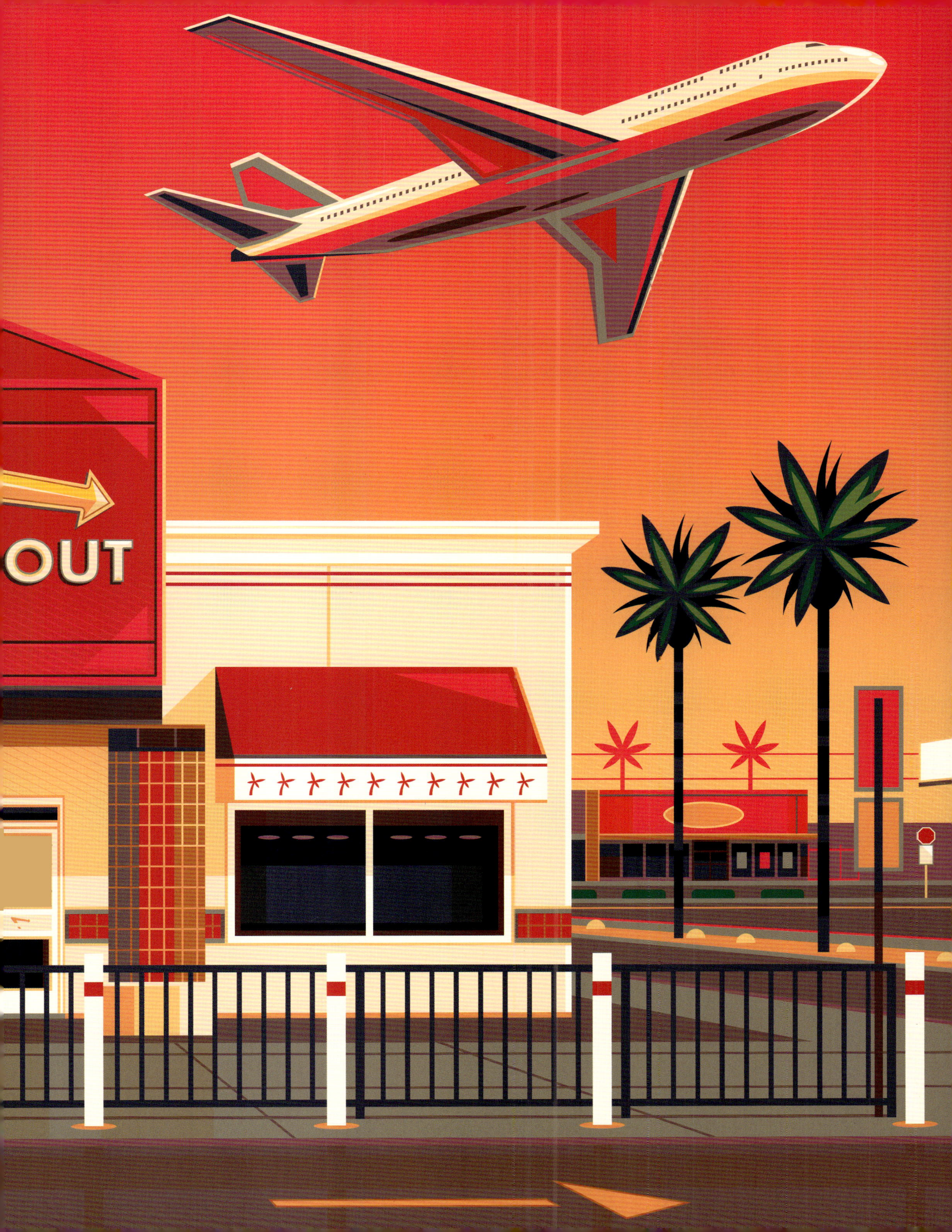
OUT

# IN-N-OUT LAX

| ADDRESS | ARCHITECT(S) | YEAR |
|---|---|---|
| 9149 S. Sepulveda Blvd.<br>Westchester, CA<br>90045 | N/A | N/A |



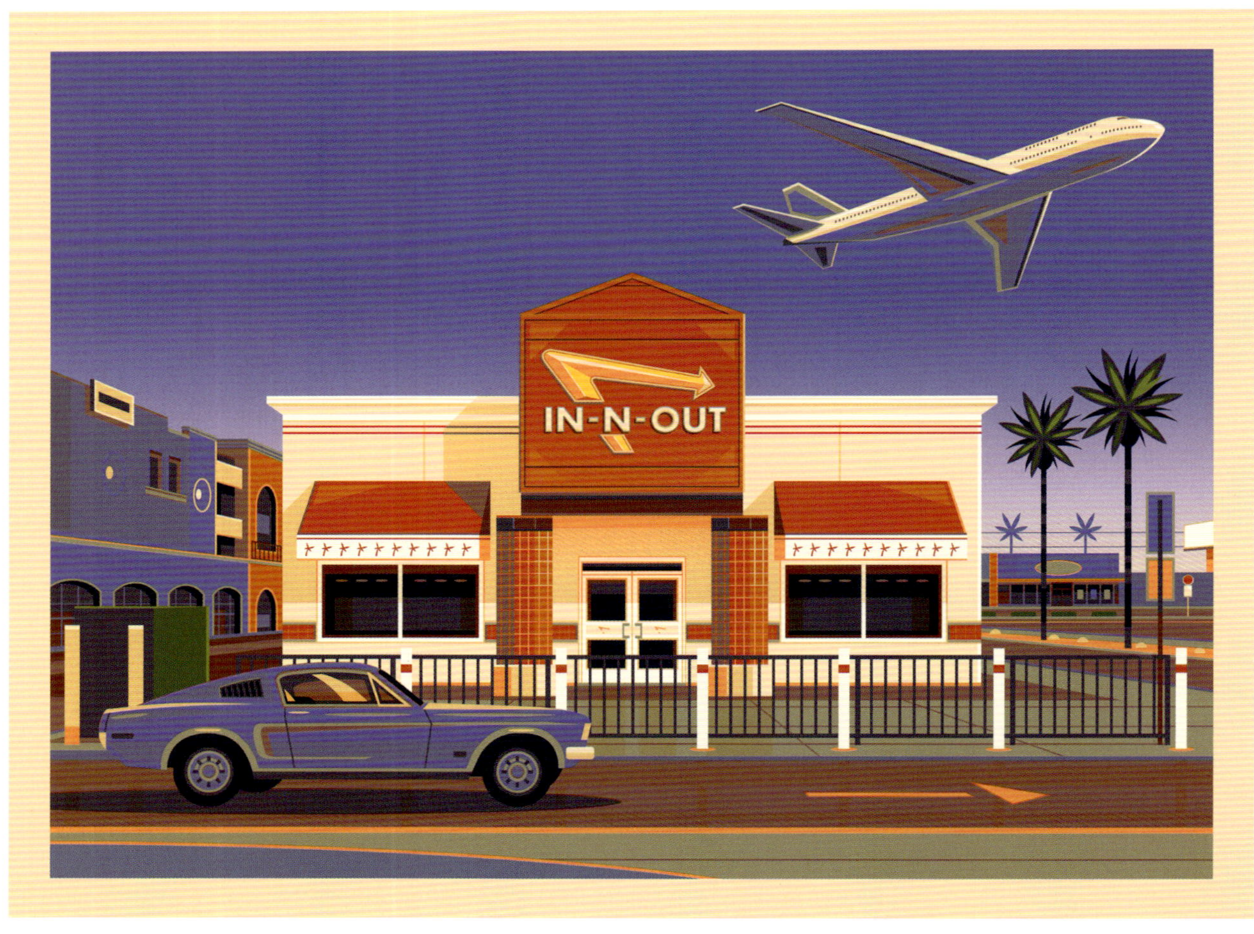


| PREVIOUS SPREAD | ABOVE | ACROSS |
|---|---|---|
| *In-N-Out LAX (Sunset)*<br>Limited Edition<br>2021 | *In-N-Out LAX*<br>Timed Edition<br>2021 | *In-N-Out LAX (Night)*<br>Limited Edition<br>2021 |

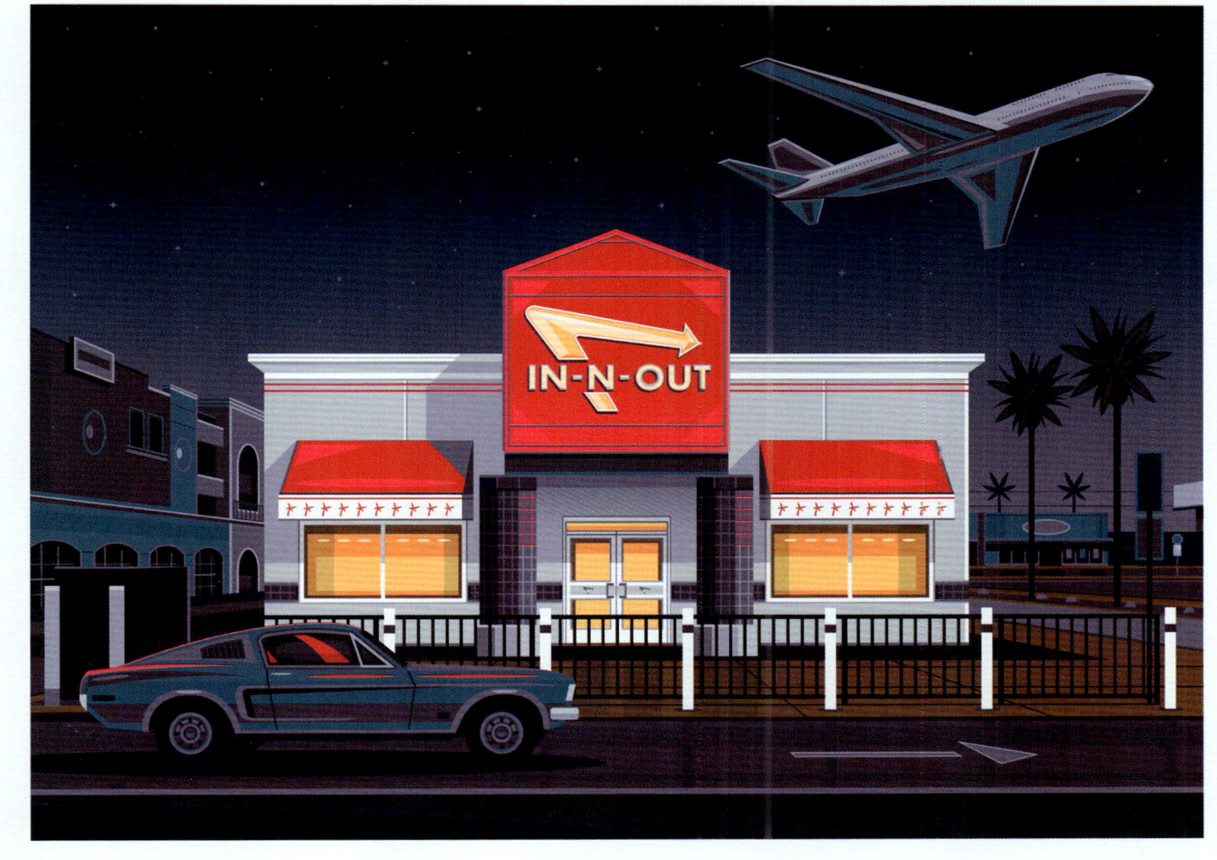
IN-N-OUT

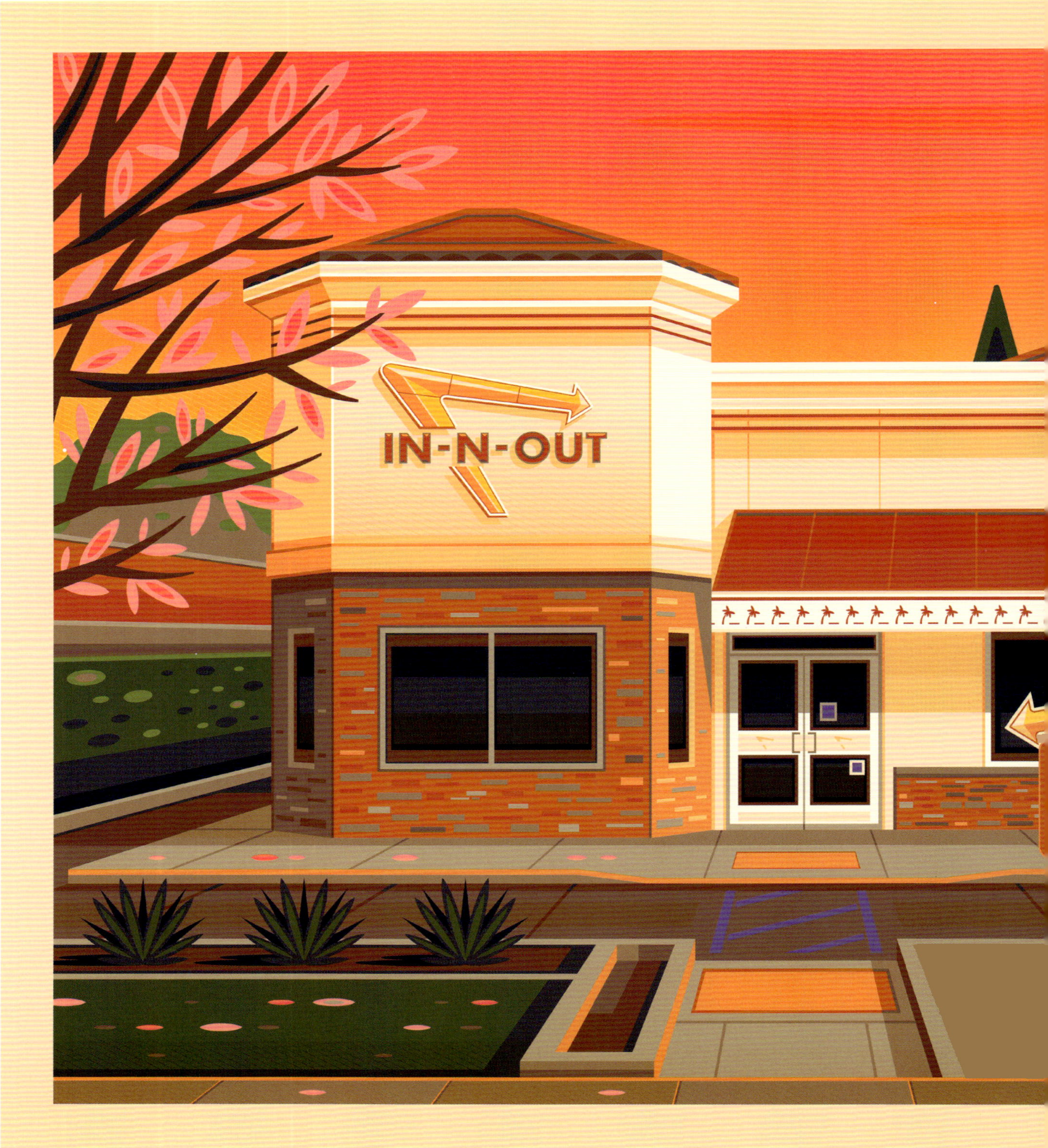

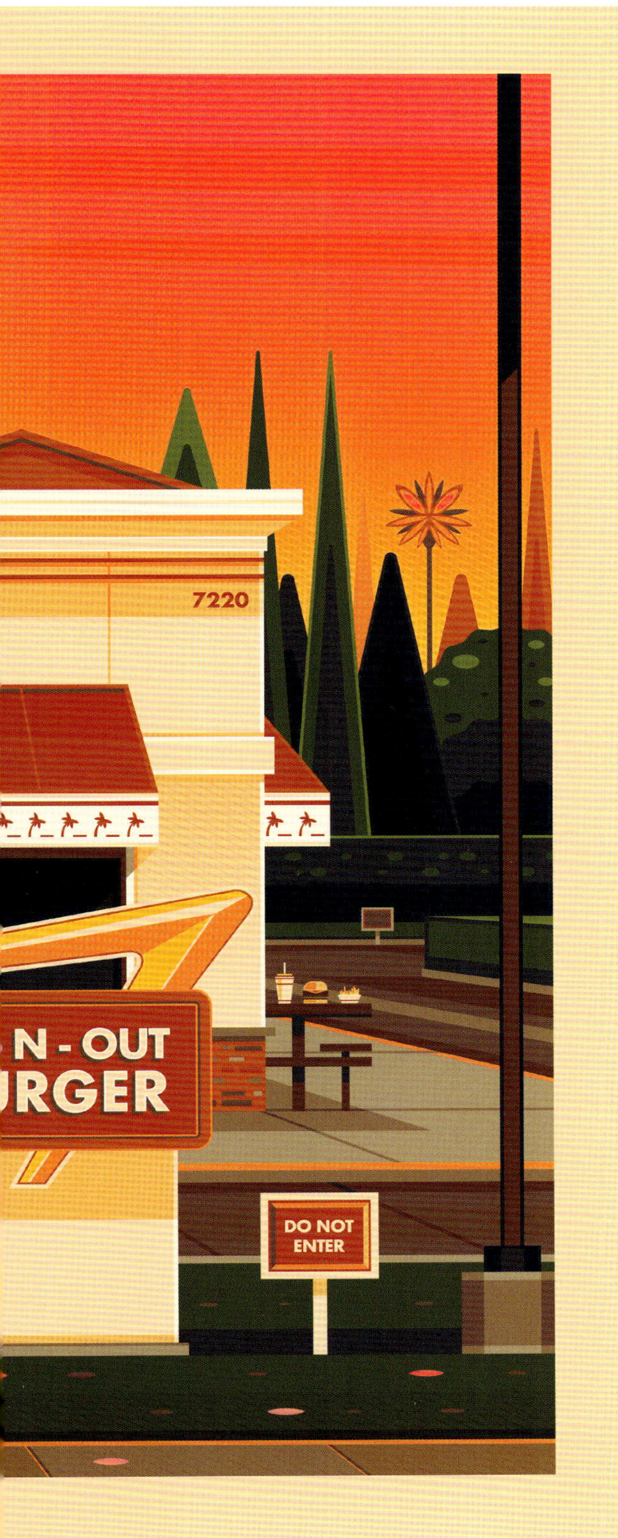


# IN-N-OUT VAN NUYS

| ADDRESS | ARCHITECT(S) | YEAR |
| --- | --- | --- |
| 7220 N. Balboa<br>Van Nuys, CA<br>91406 | N/A | N/A |



ACROSS

*In-N-Out Van Nuys*
Open Edition
2024

# IN-N-OUT HOLLYWOOD

| ADDRESS | ARCHITECT(S) | YEAR |
|---|---|---|
| 7009 Sunset Blvd<br>Hollywood, CA<br>91607 | N/A | N/A |

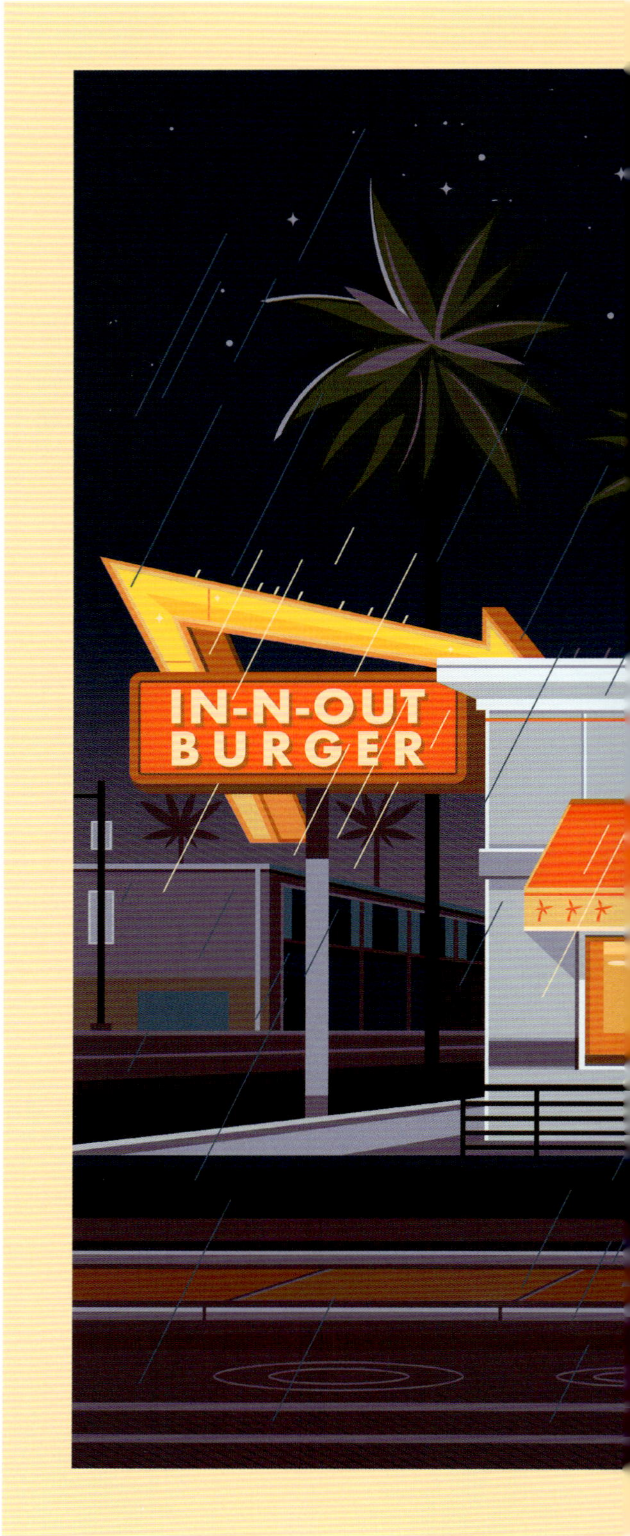

ACROSS

*In-N-Out Hollywood*
Limited Edition
2020

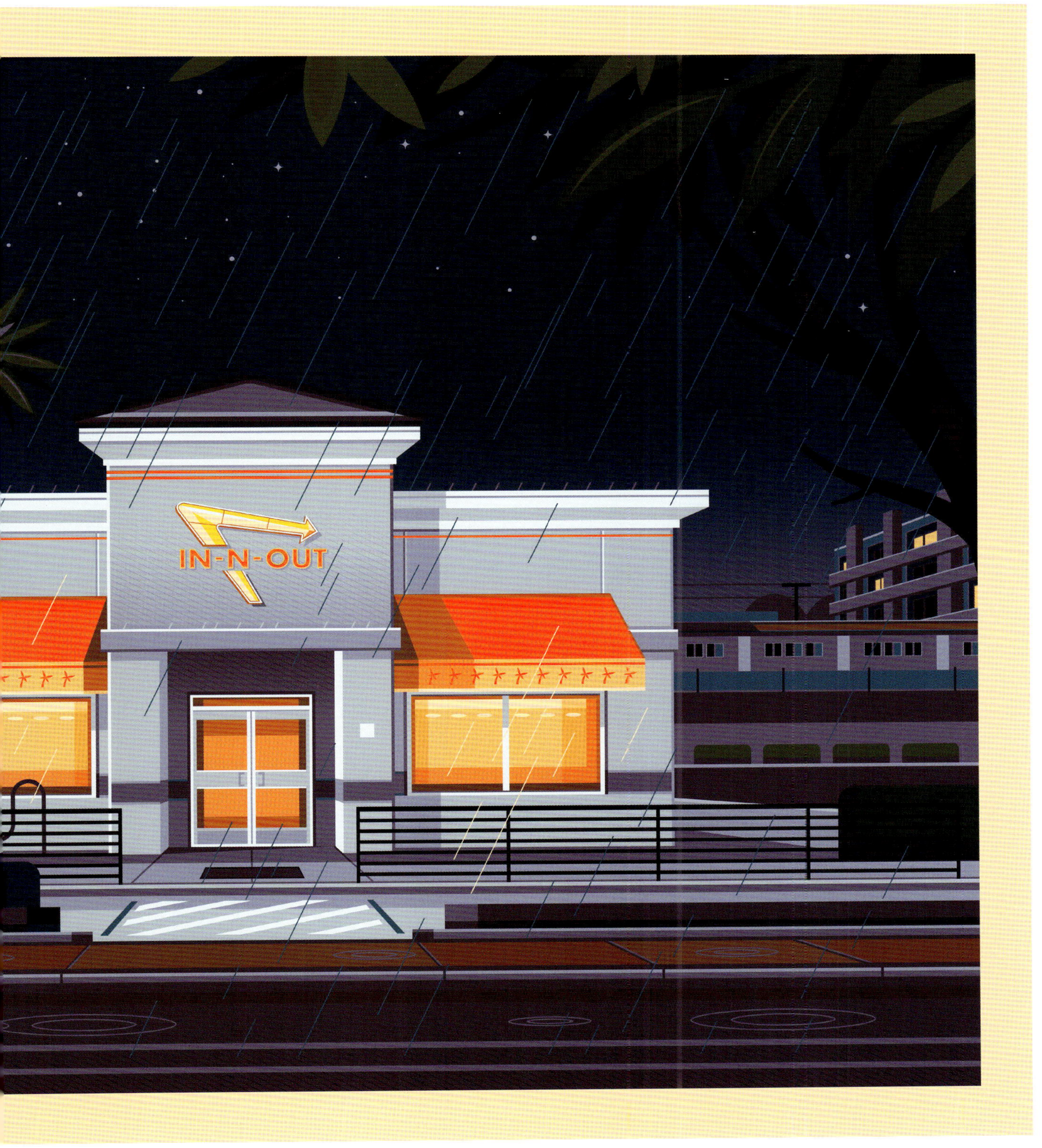
IN-N-OUT

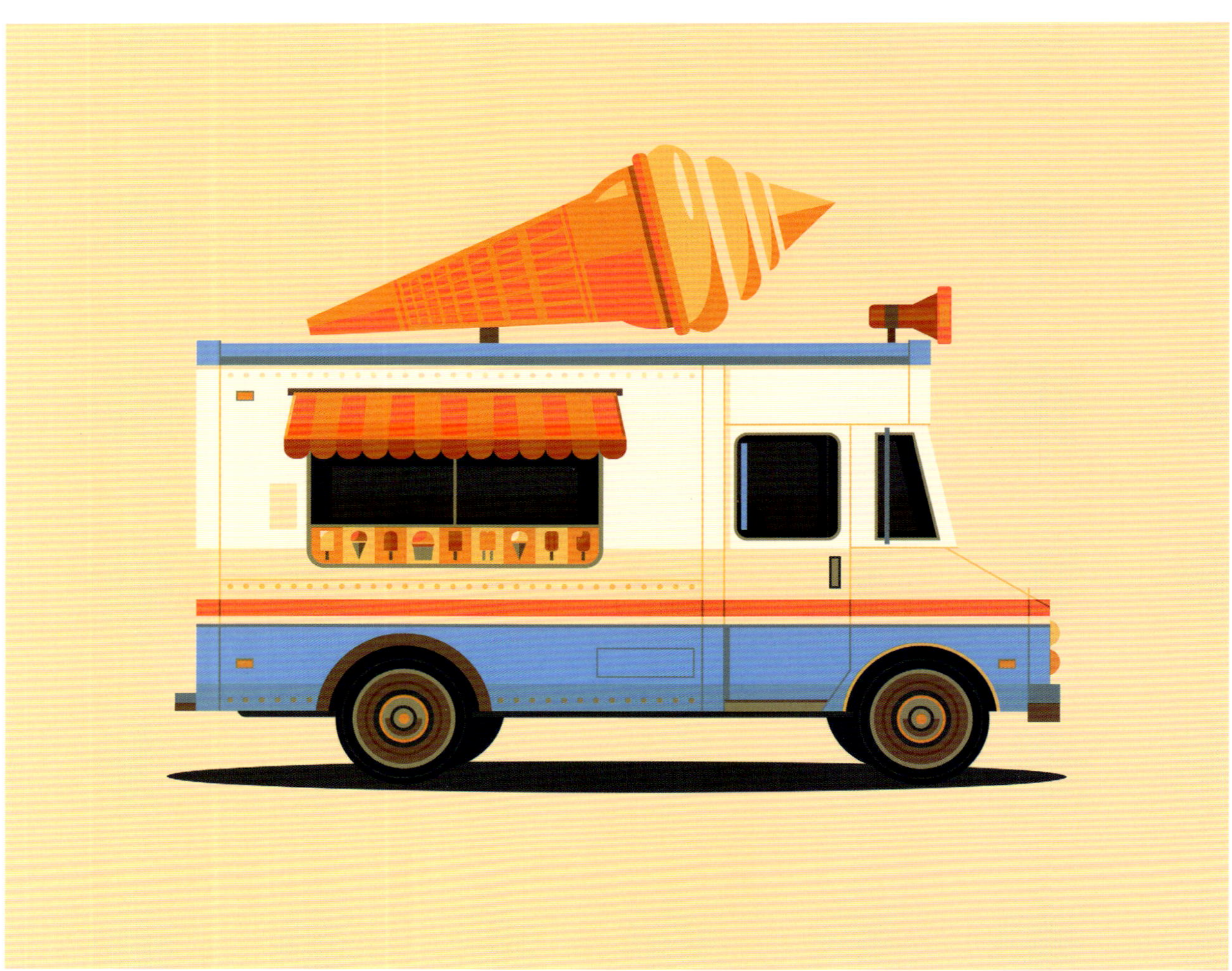

ABOVE

*Taco Truck*
Open Edition
2022

ACROSS

*Ice Cream Truck*
Open Edition
2022

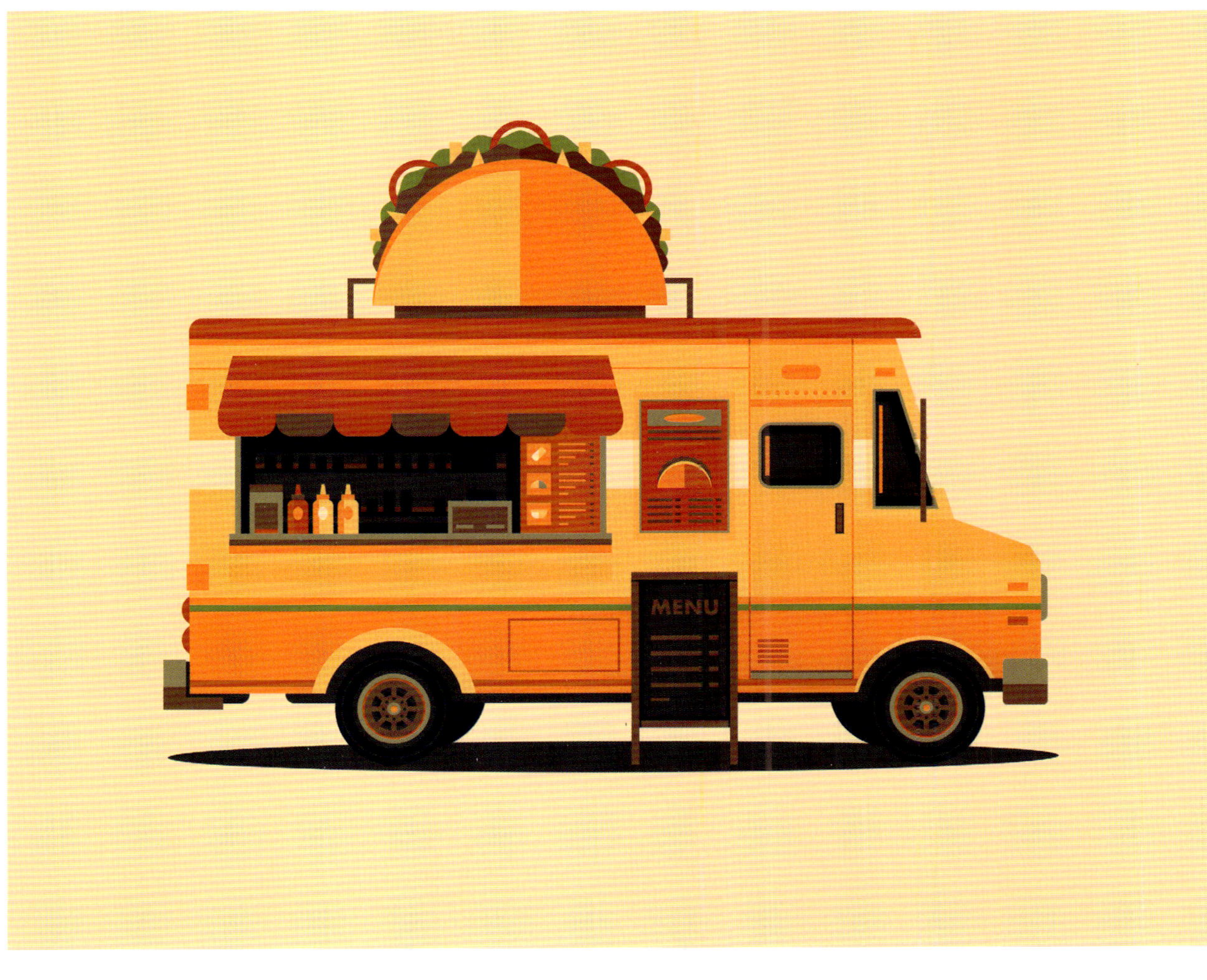
MENU

# Iconic Residences

# ENNIS HOUSE

ADDRESS
2655 Glendower Ave.
Los Angeles, CA
90027

ARCHITECT(S)
Frank Lloyd Wright

YEAR
1924



**The Ennis House is my favourite Frank Lloyd Wright** design in Los Angeles, and that's saying something, considering how many great ones there are. Filmmakers seem to share this sentiment, as the building has made countless appearances in iconic films and shows, with *Blade Runner* being the most famous example. Its bold, geometric design, inspired by ancient Mayan temples, gives it a cinematic quality that feels both timeless and otherworldly, perfect for the big screen.

I had a lot of fun drawing this house and enjoyed using a longer aspect ratio to capture its impressive scale and intricate details.

GATEFOLD

*Ennis House*
Limited Edition
2021

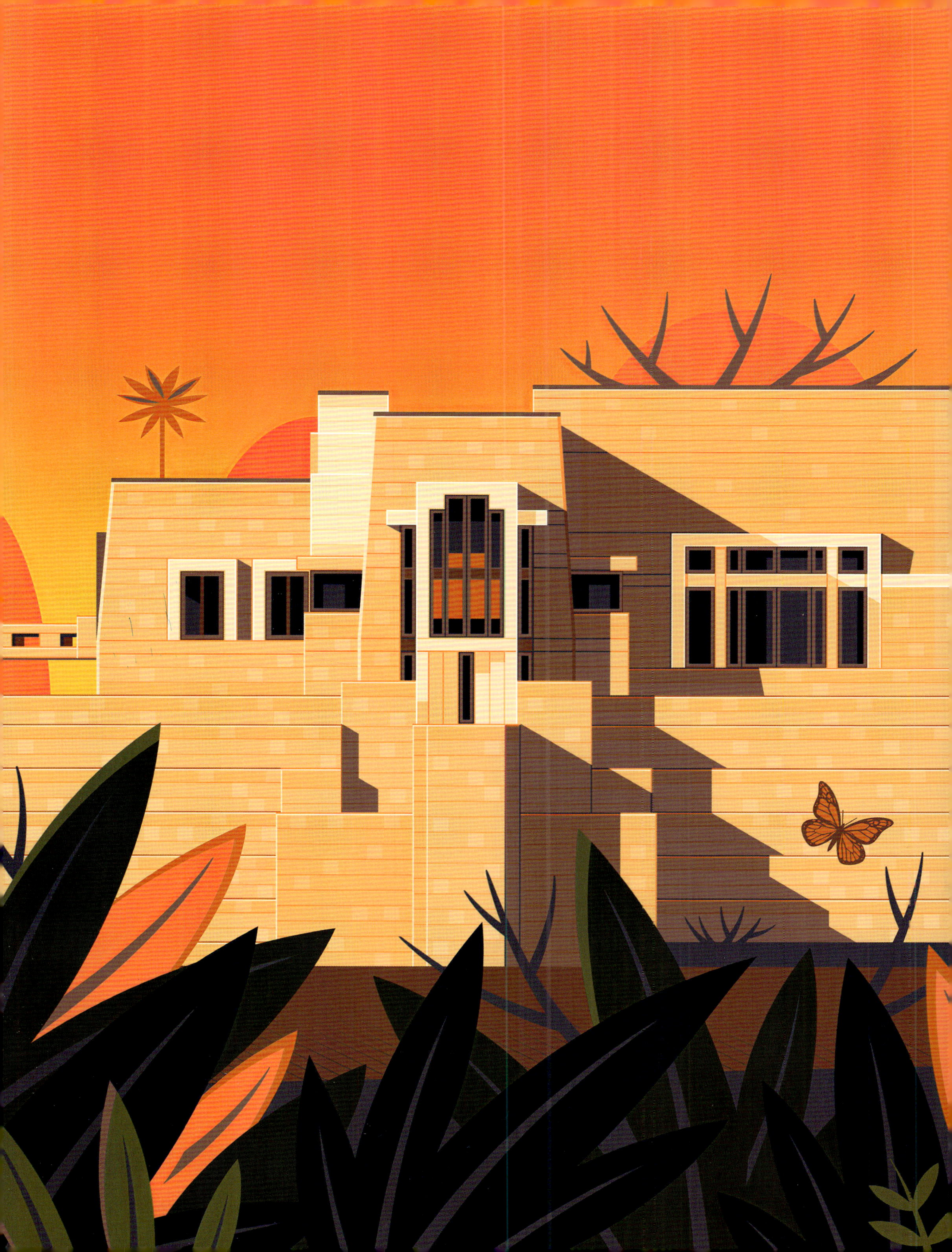

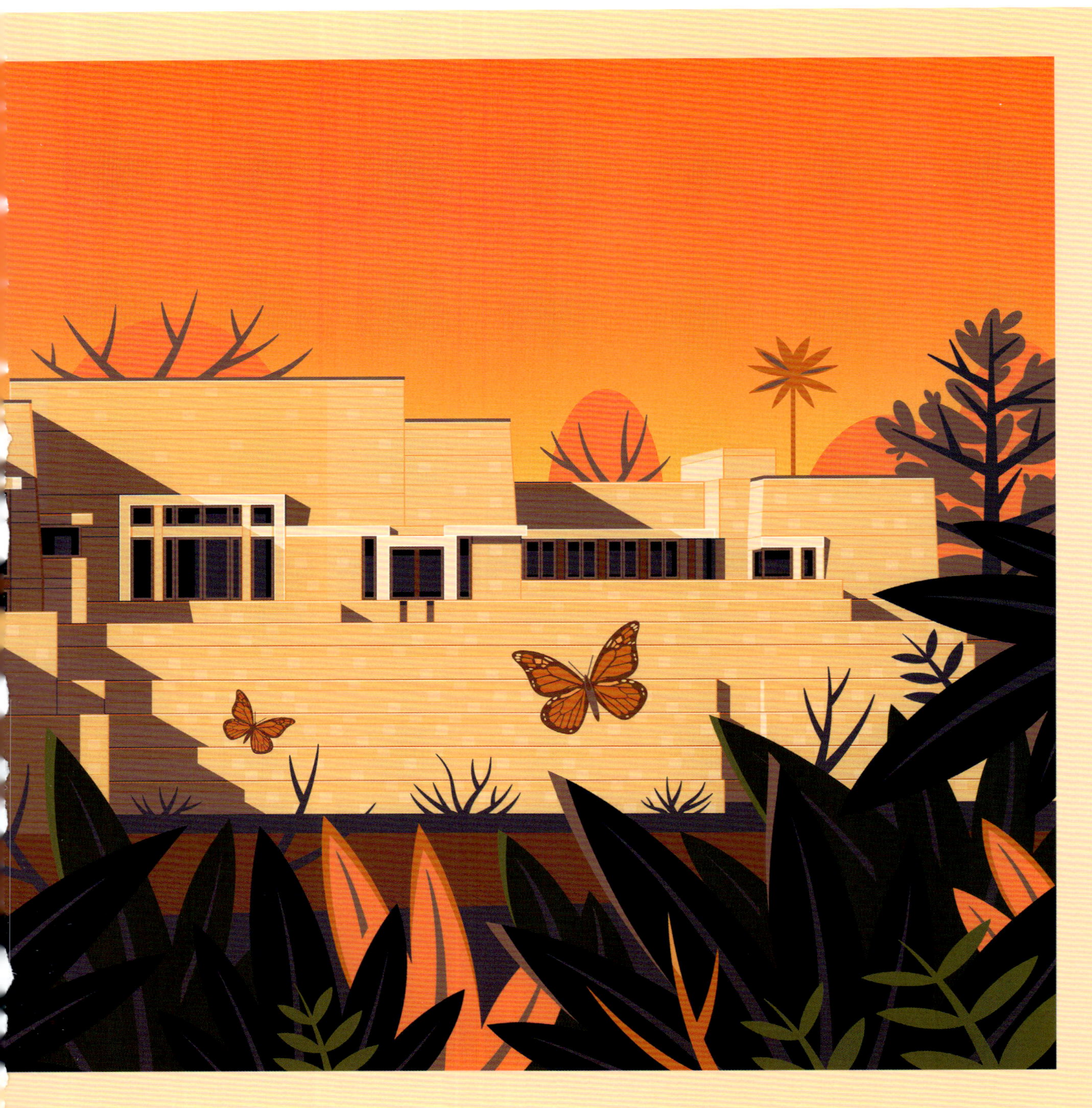

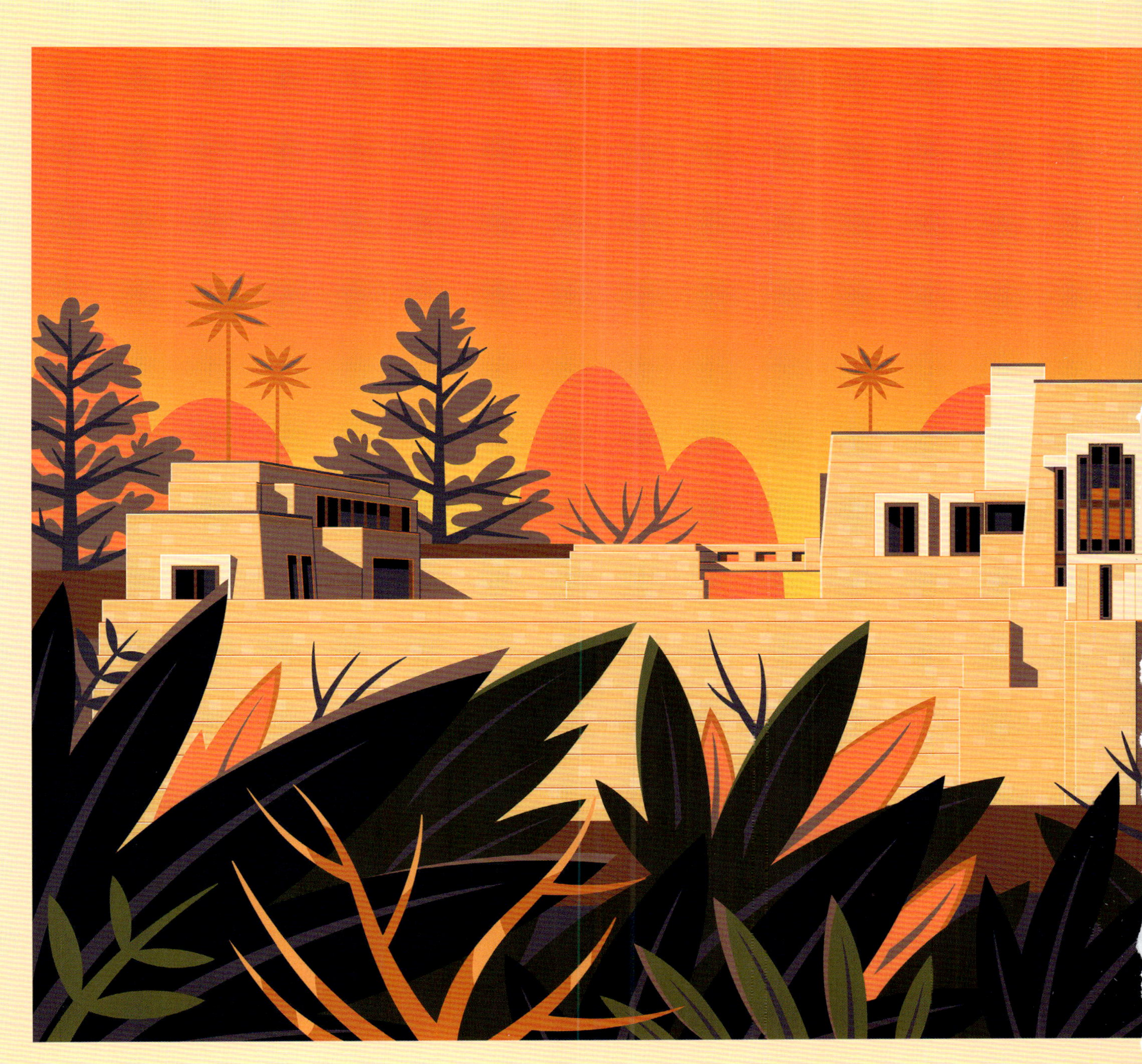

# JOHN SOWDEN HOUSE

| ADDRESS | ARCHITECT(S) | YEAR |
|---|---|---|
| 5121 Franklin Ave.<br>Los Angeles, CA<br>90027 | Lloyd Wright | 1926 |



**The John Sowden House is most famously rumoured** to be the potential site of the infamous "Black Dahlia" murders. While this is all speculation, there's definitely an unnerving atmosphere as you pass by it on the street.

I actually had the chance to visit in-person after being commissioned by the couple who live there. They'd seen my rendition of the front of the house and requested a custom illustration of their courtyard, which became my first-ever "sequel" print. Exploring the house felt like stepping into a villain's lair. The dramatic architecture and the many cats roaming around only added to the feeling.

Fun fact: the house was designed by Lloyd Wright, the son of Frank Lloyd Wright. Because their names are so similar, it's often mistakenly attributed to Frank Lloyd Wright, I remember being fooled the first time I read about it too.

ACROSS

*John Sowden House*

Open Edition
2018

NEXT SPREAD

*John Sowden House Courtyard*
Private Comission
2019

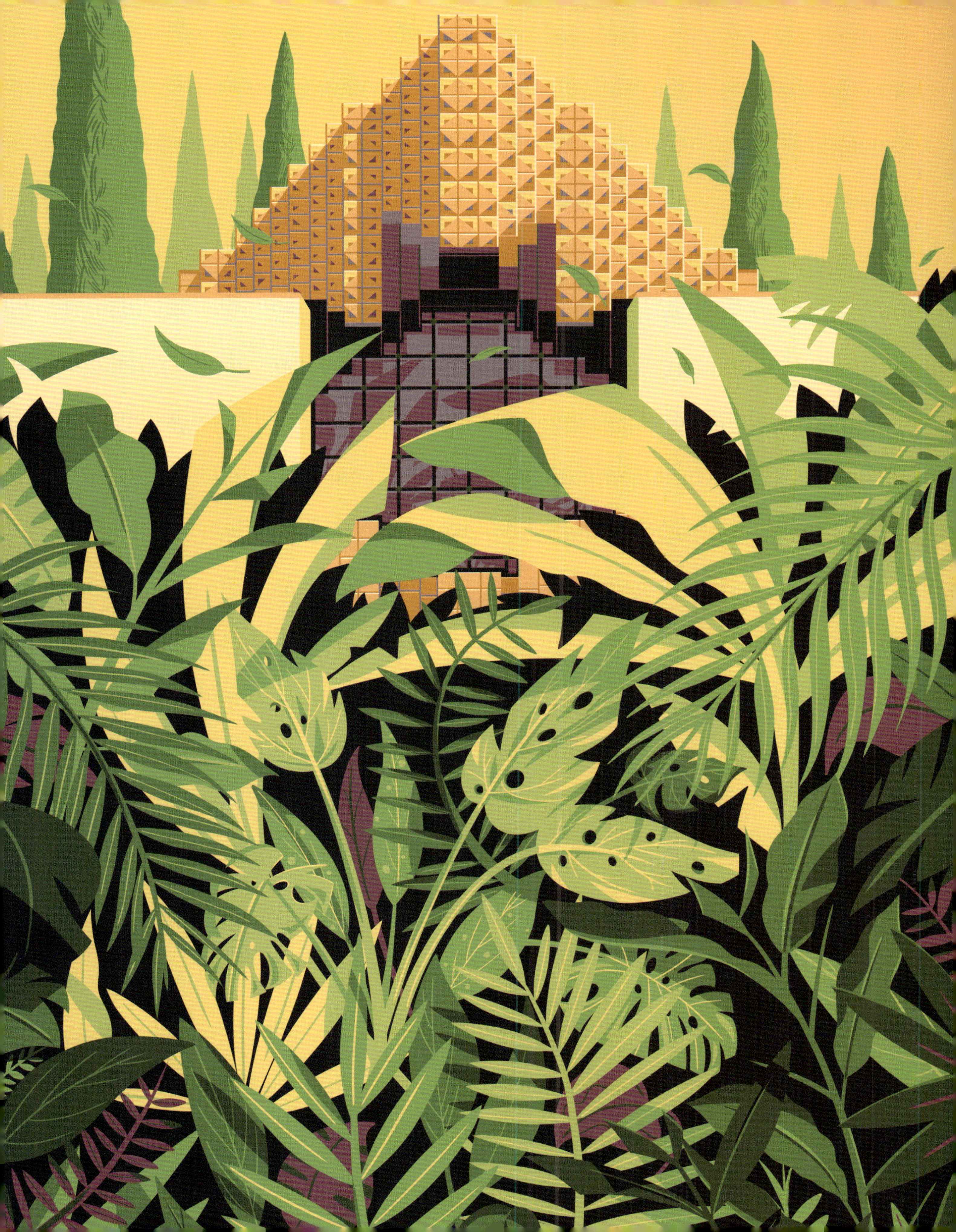

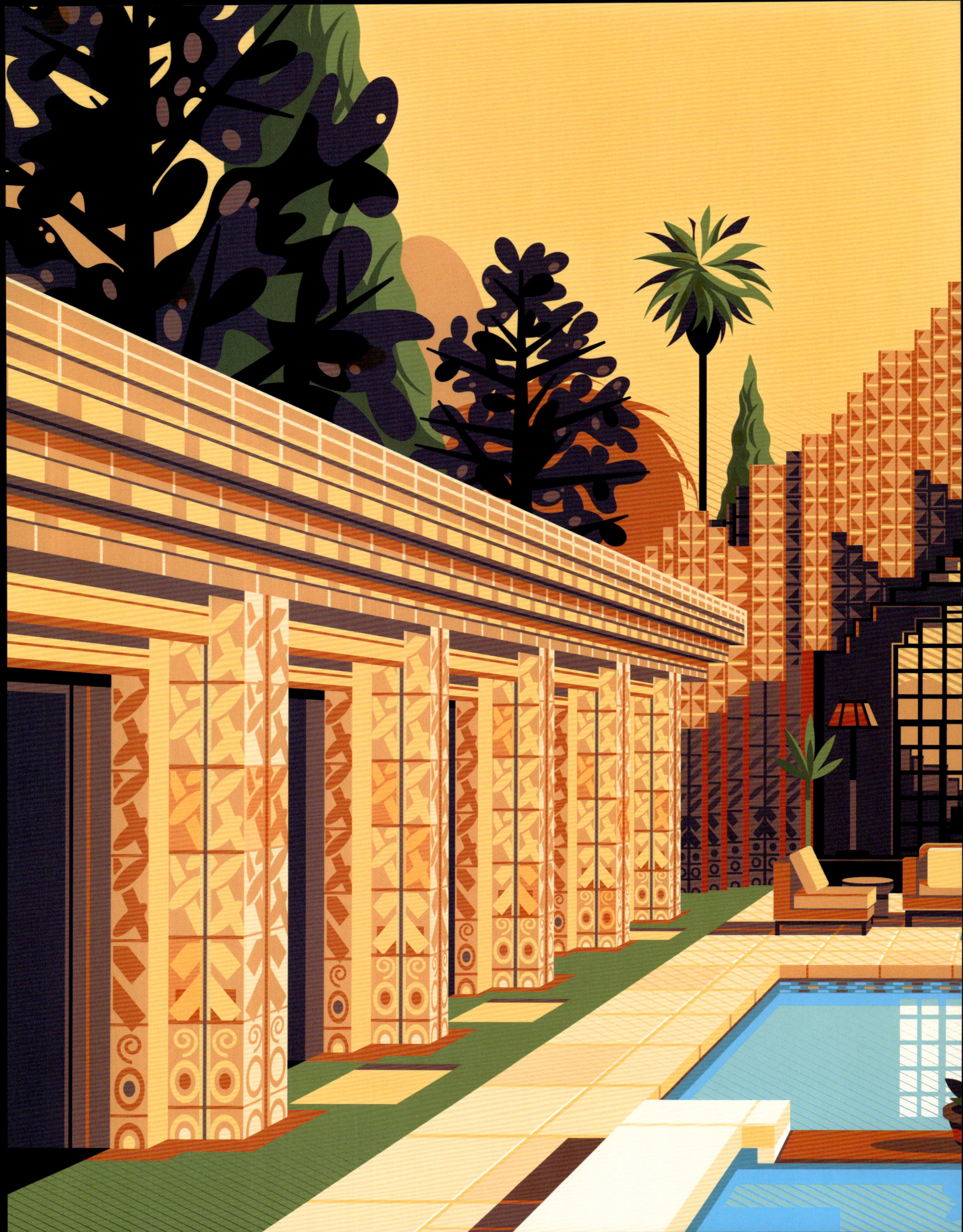

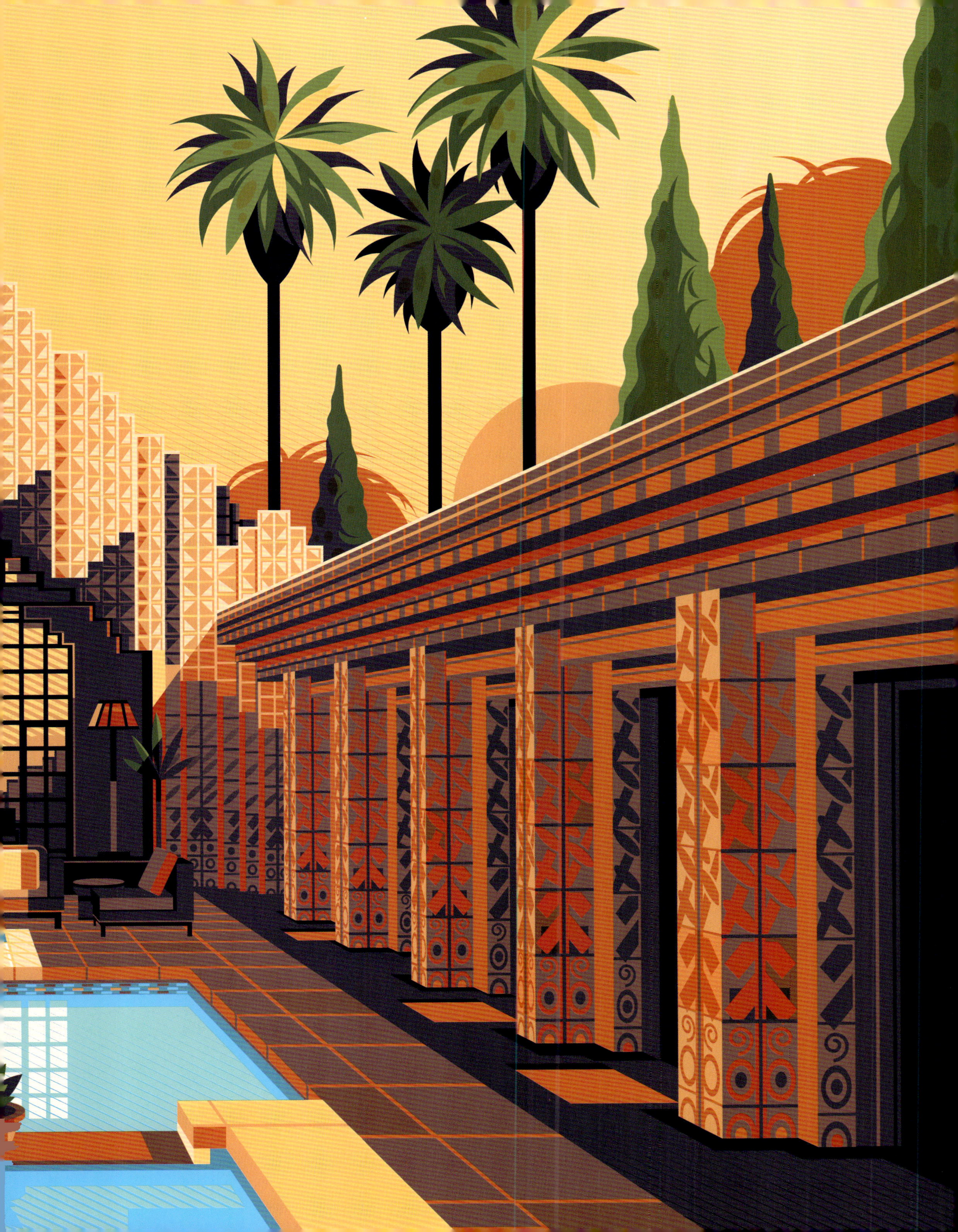

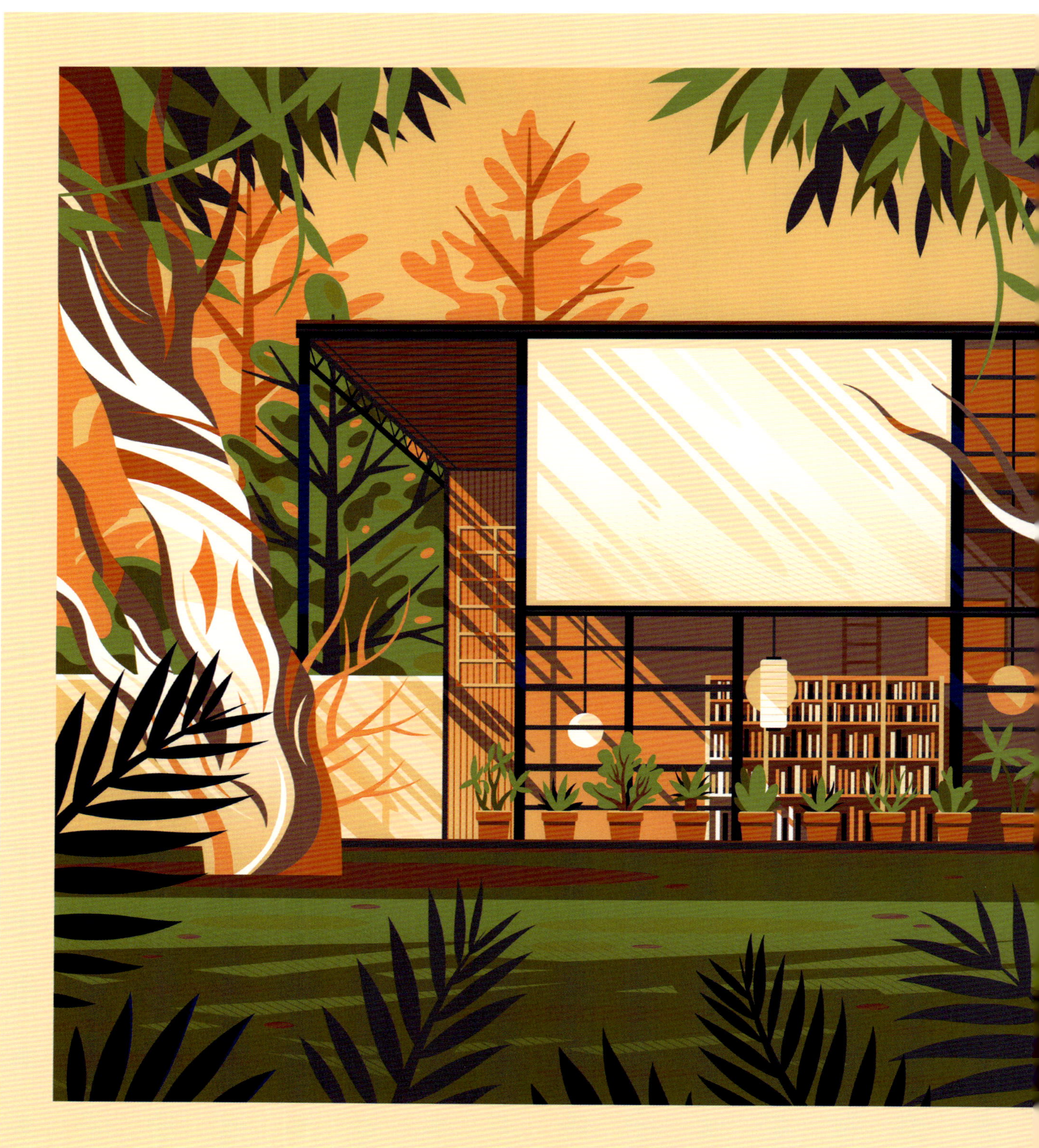

ABOVE

*Eames House*
Limited Edition
2020

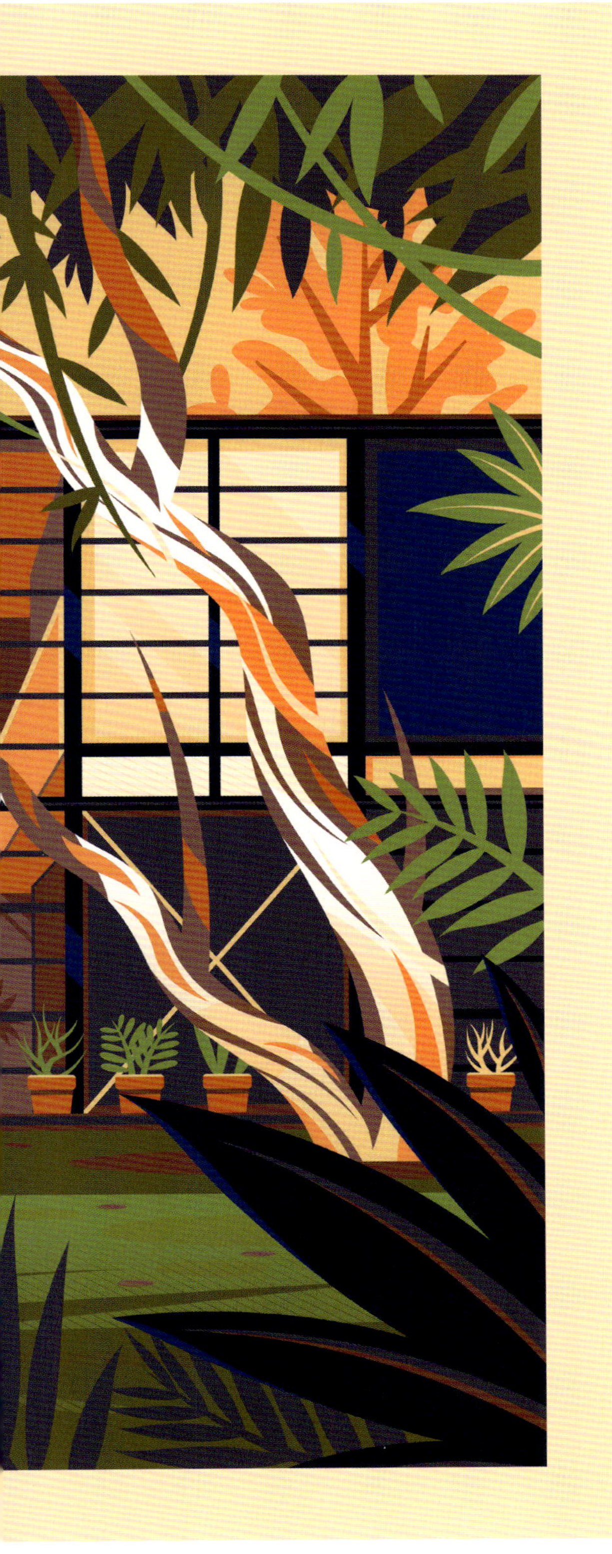

# EAMES HOUSE

| ADDRESS | ARCHITECT(S) | YEAR |
|---|---|---|
| 203 N. Chautauqua Blvd.<br>Pacific Palisades, CA<br>90272 | Ray Eames,<br>Charles Eames | 1949 |



**While the Eames House is a marvel** of architectural design on its own, its true charm comes from the fact that the Eameses themselves lived here until their deaths. It wasn't just a house, it was a home, filled with gifts from friends, family, and colleagues. It's one of those rare cases where the interior is just as celebrated as the exterior, if not more so. Every detail inside tells a story, making it feel like a living, breathing testament to their vision and lifestyle.

Also, the way the house blends so seamlessly into its natural surroundings is another reason it's so special. Nestled among the trees on a quiet hillside, it's a peaceful little retreat from the chaos of the city, despite being a short drive away.

# ADAMSON HOUSE

| ADDRESS | ARCHITECT(S) | YEAR |
|---|---|---|
| 23200 Pacific Coast Hwy.<br>Malibu, CA<br>90265 | Stiles O. Clements | 1929 |



ACROSS

*Adamson House*
Open Edition
2024

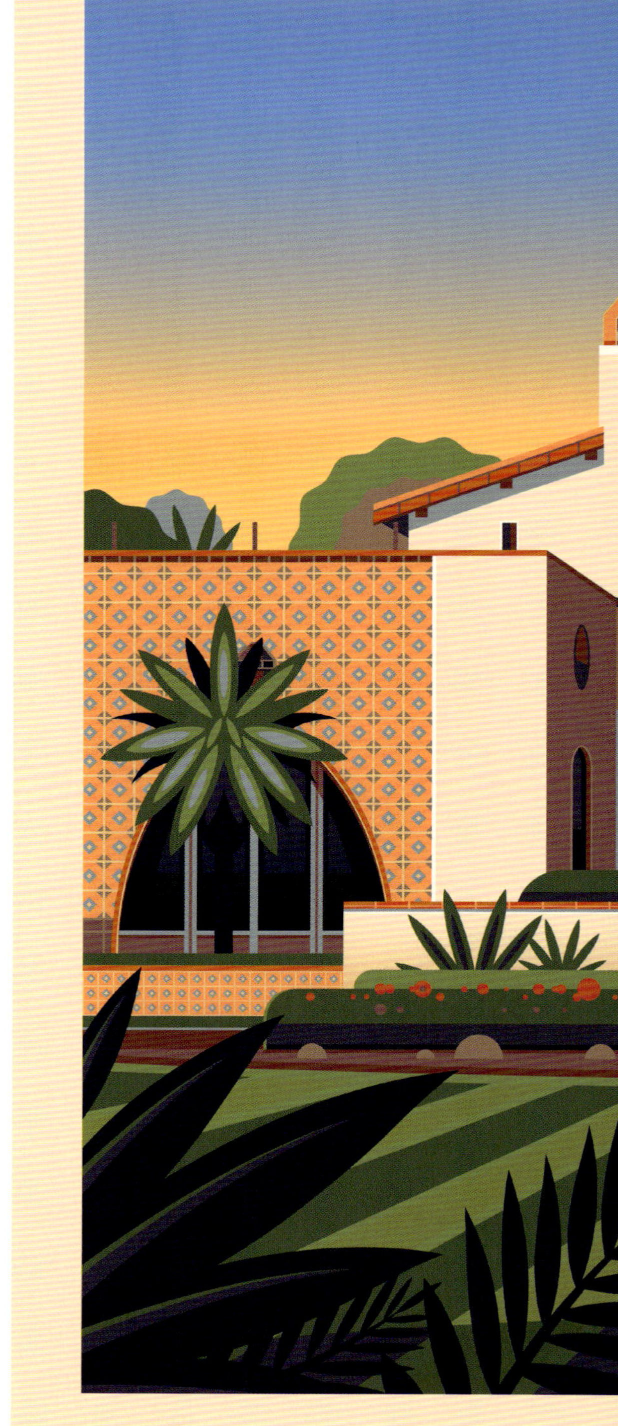

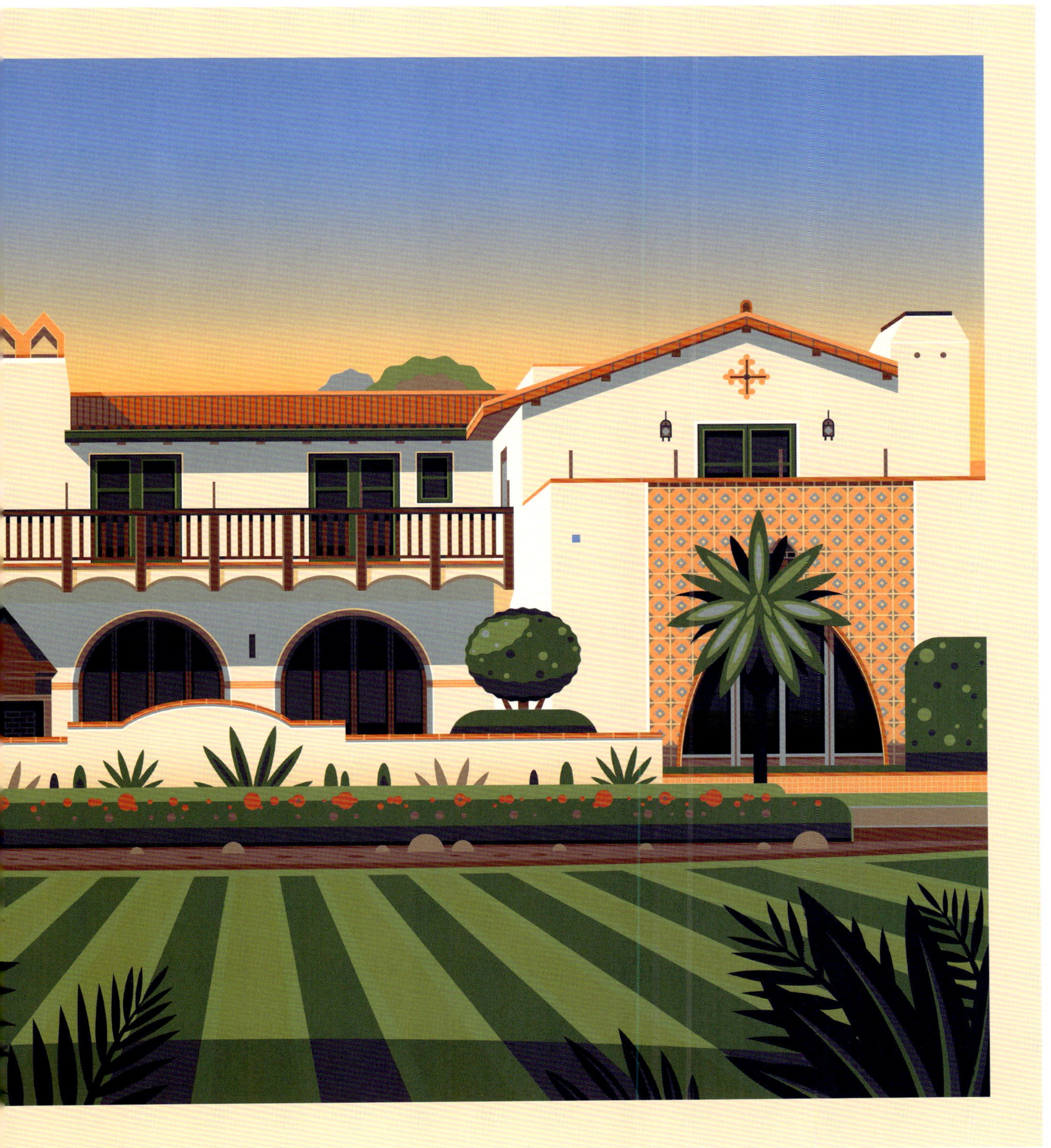

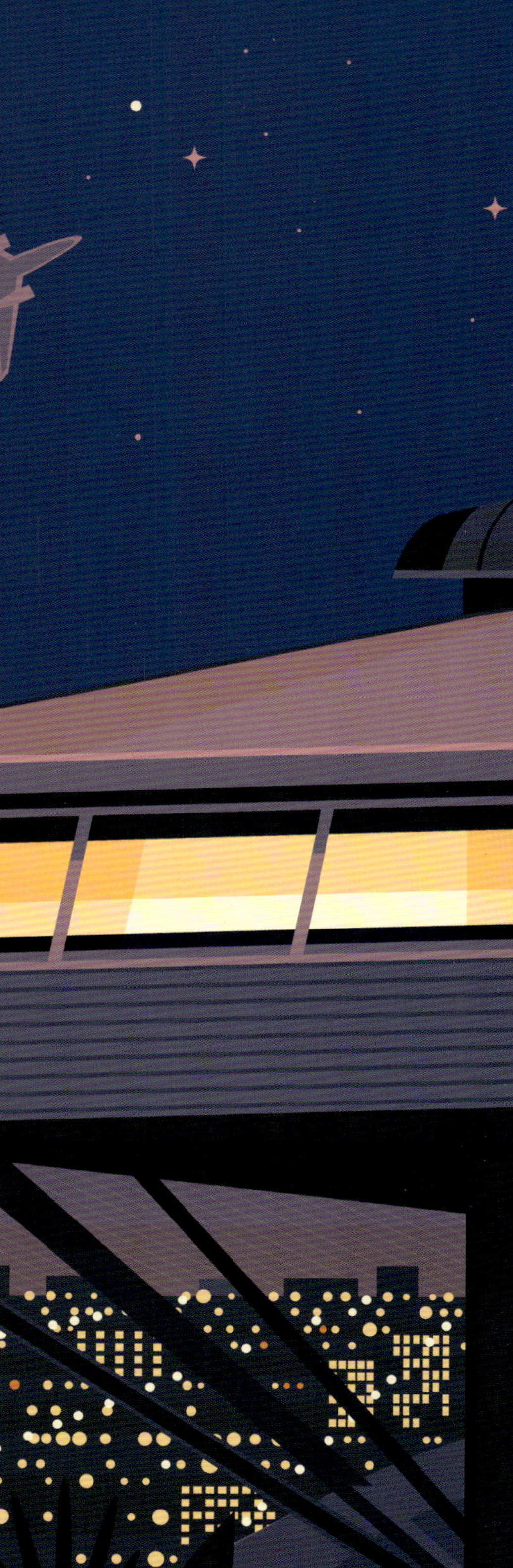

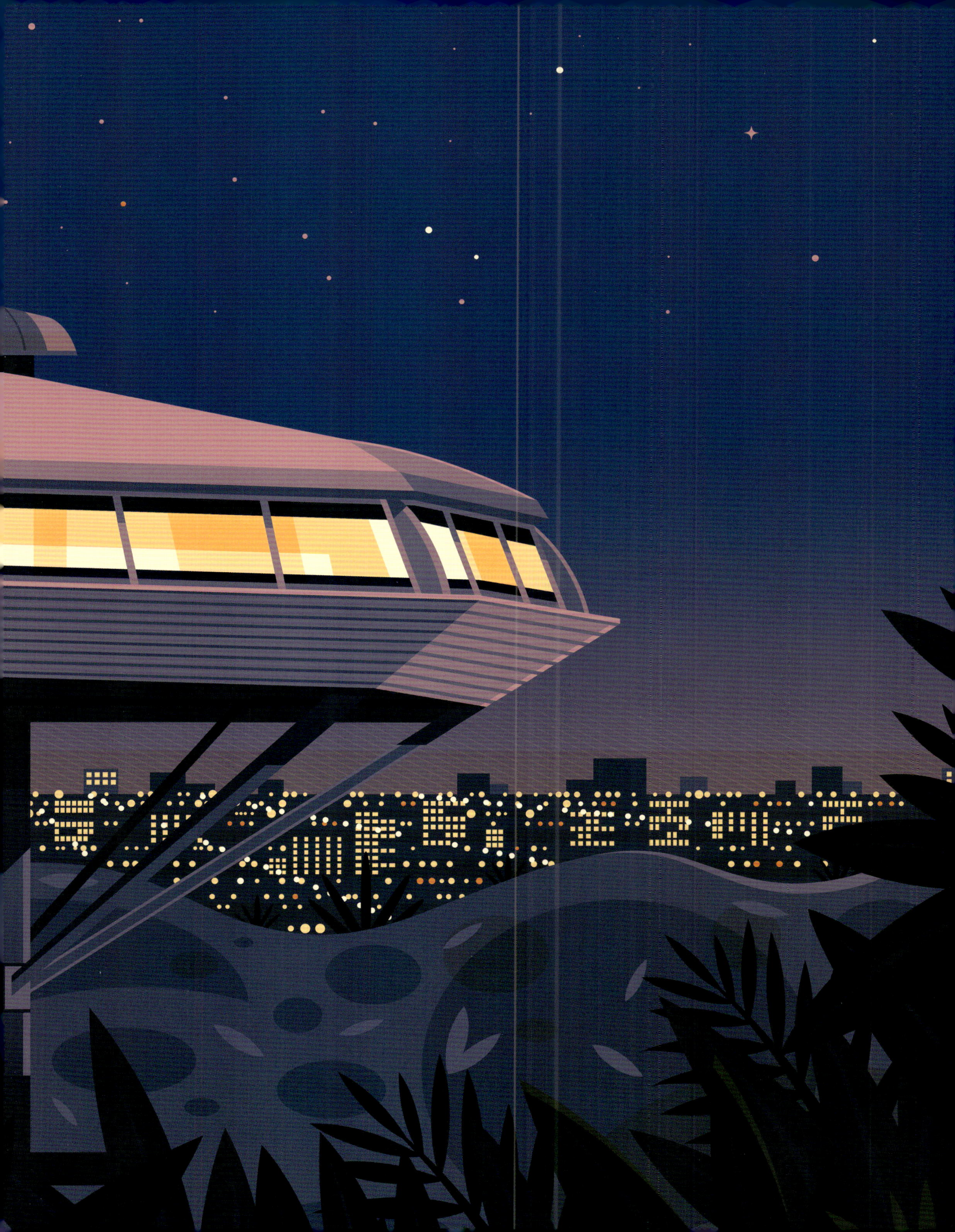

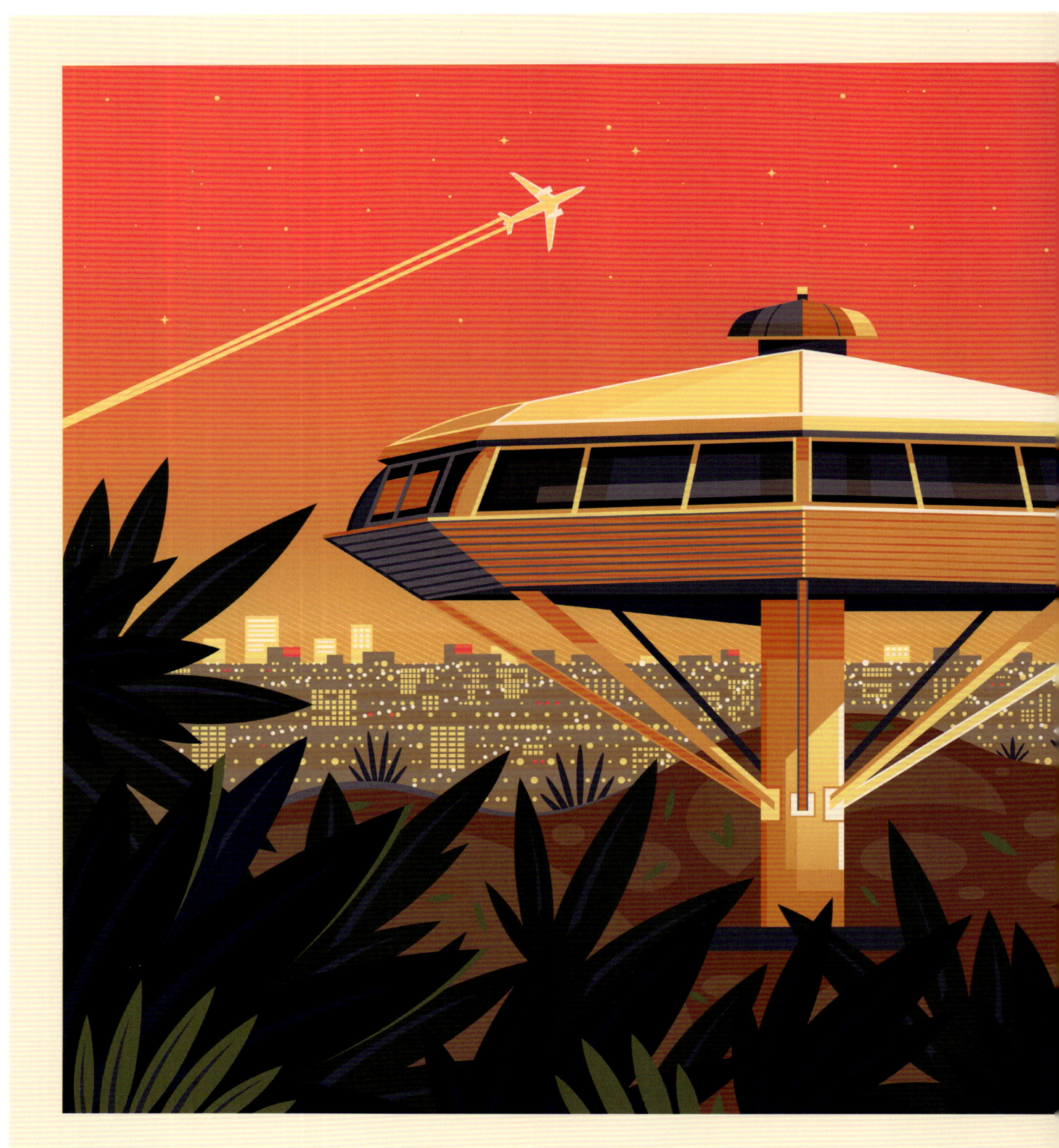

PREVIOUS SPREAD

*Chemosphere (Night)*
Limited Edition
2021

ABOVE

*Chemosphere (Sunset)*
Limited Edition
2021

NEXT SPREAD

*Chemosphere*

Open Edition
2021

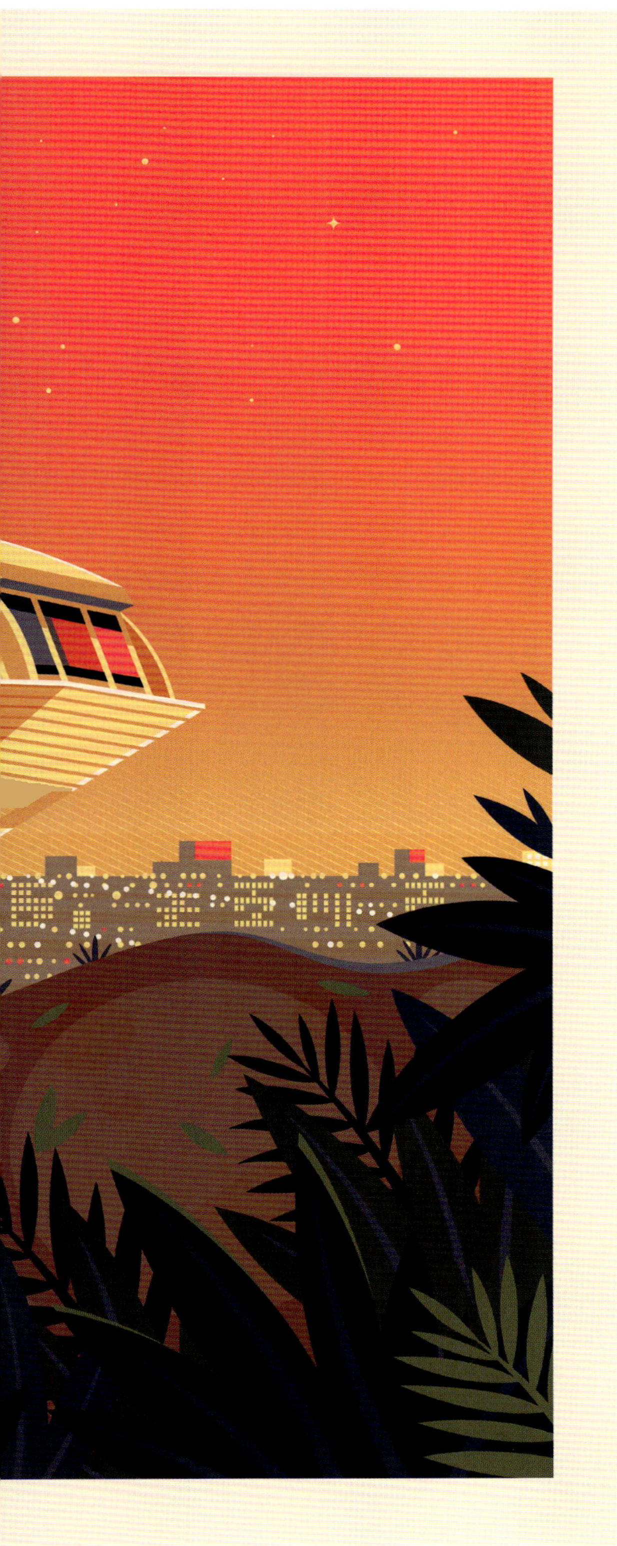

# CHEMOSPHERE

| ADDRESS | ARCHITECT(S) | YEAR |
|---|---|---|
| 7776 Torreyson Dr.<br>Los Angeles, CA<br>90046 | John Lautner | 1960 |



**The Chemosphere is often referred to as** "the most modern house in the world," and it's easy to see why. It's futuristic design and octagonal structure give its lucky owner a breathtaking 360-degree view of Los Angeles, making it truly one of a kind.

There are plenty of movies and shows that feature the Chemosphere, but let's be honest, most people either know it as the sleek lair from *Charlie's Angels* or as Troy McClure's house from *The Simpsons*. Both equally deserving of their pop culture fame.

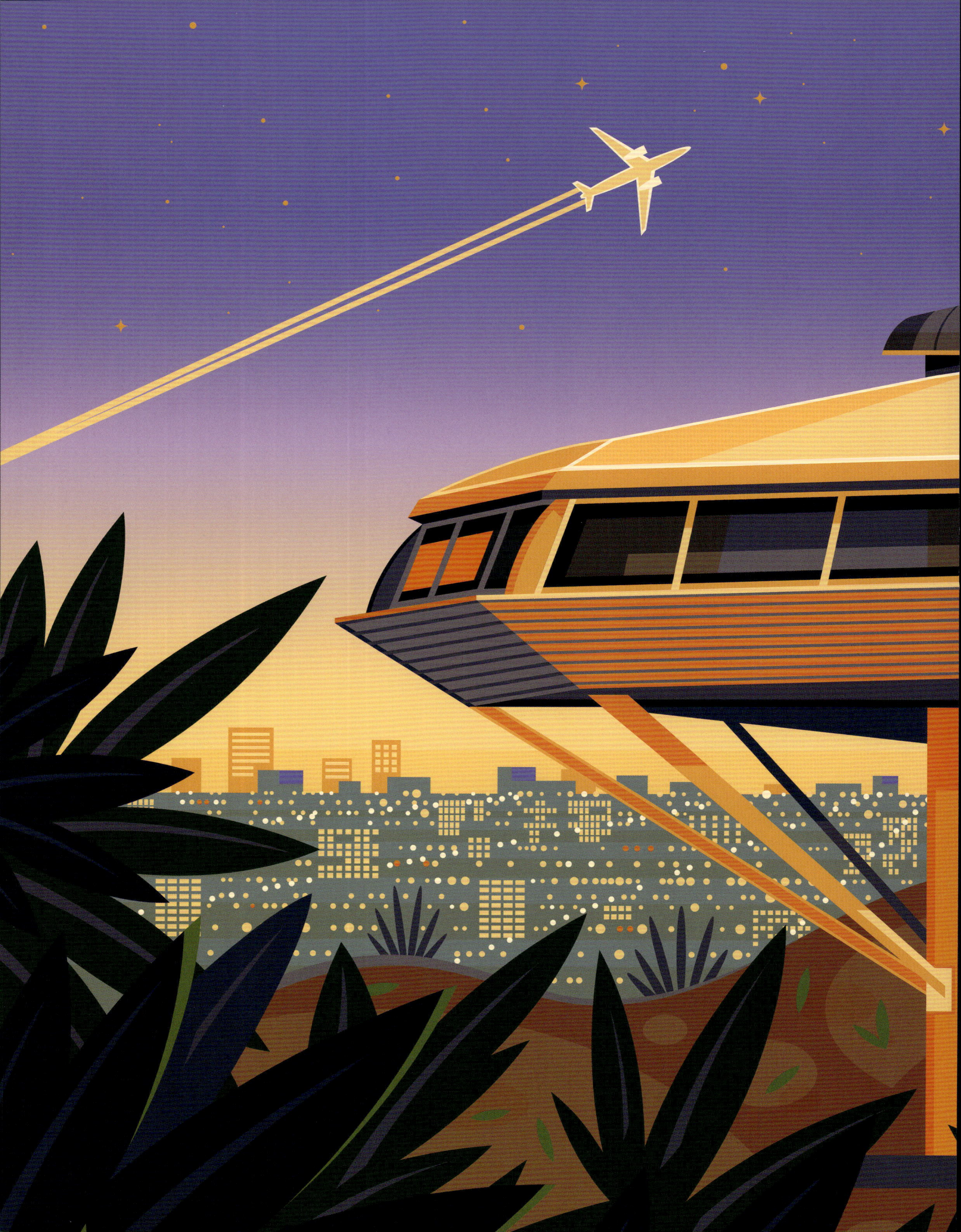

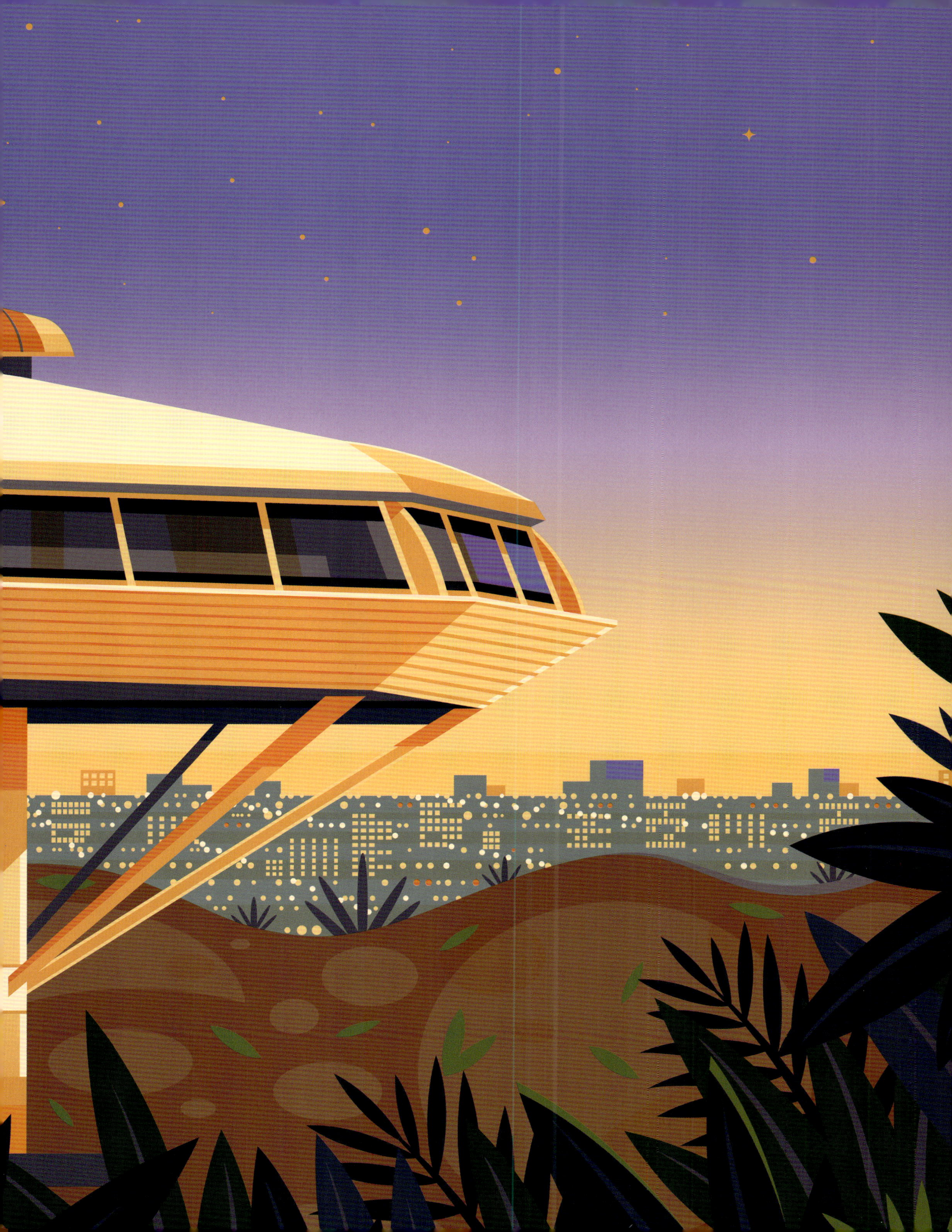

# HOLLYHOCK HOUSE

| ADDRESS | ARCHITECT(S) | YEAR |
| --- | --- | --- |
| 4800 Hollywood Blvd.<br>Los Angeles, CA<br>90227 | Frank Lloyd Wright | 1921 |



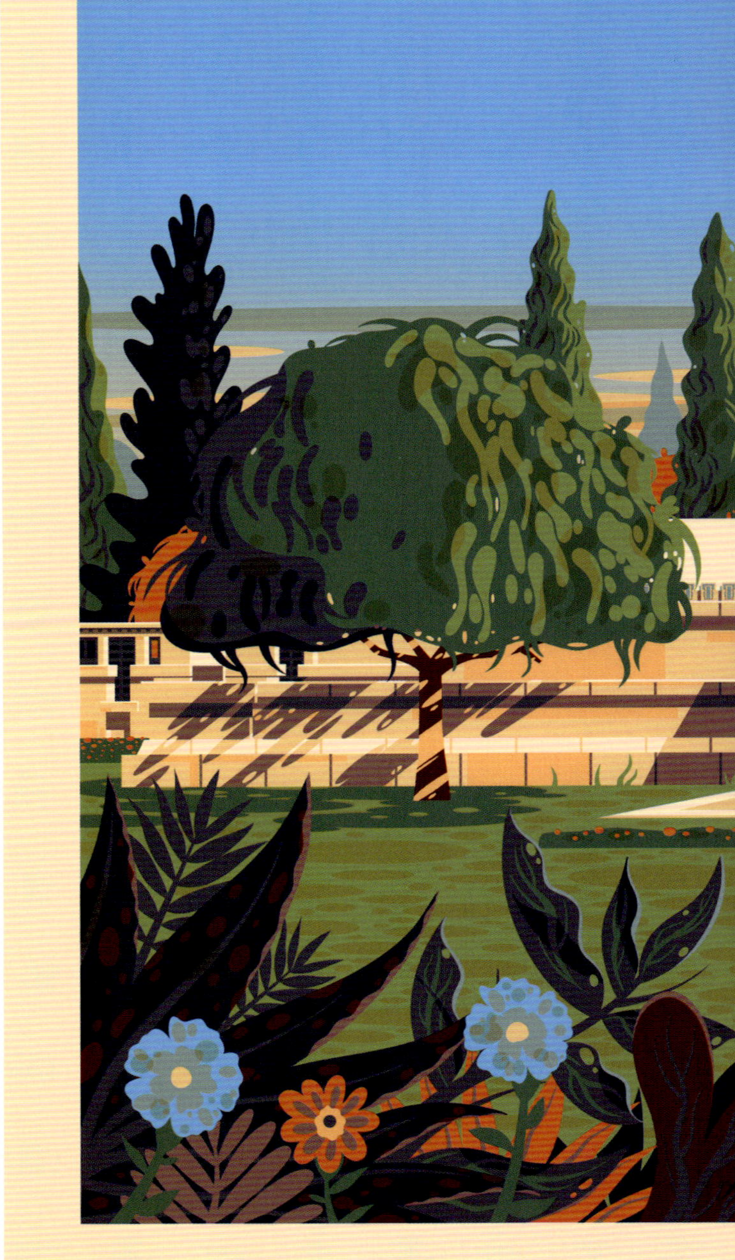

ACROSS

*Hollyhock House*

Limited Edition
2018

NEXT SPREAD

*Hollyhock House (Sunset)*

Open Edition
2018

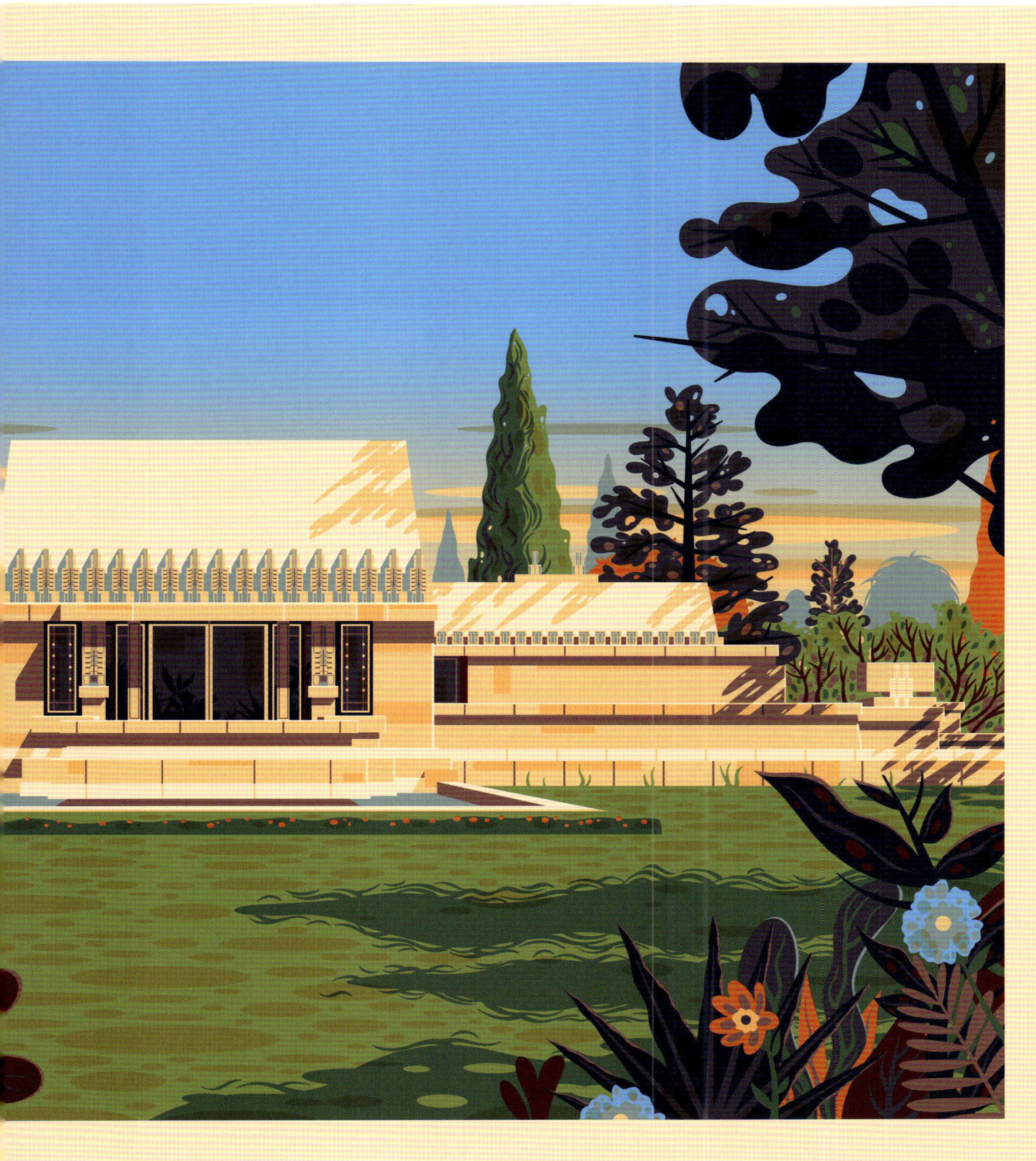

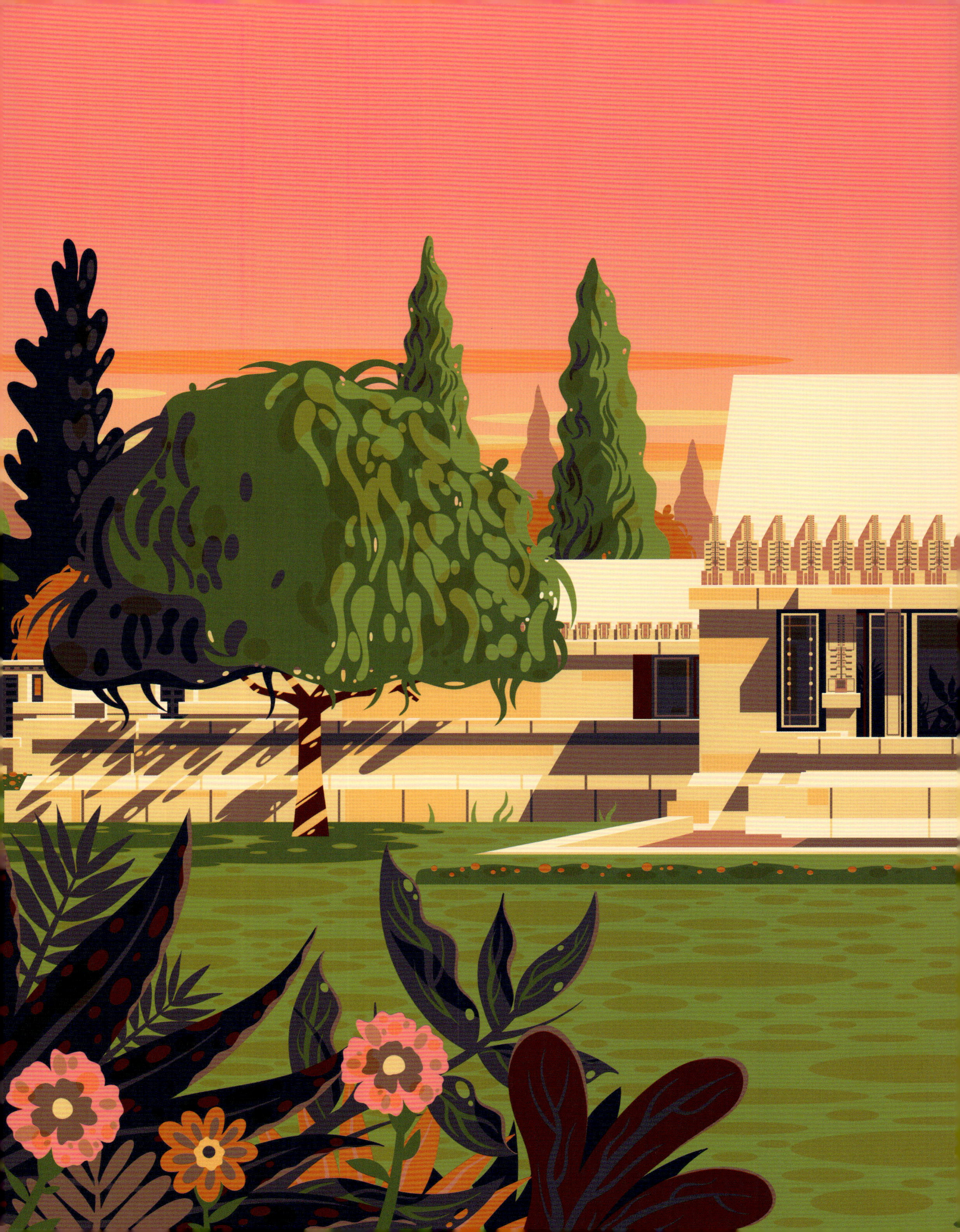

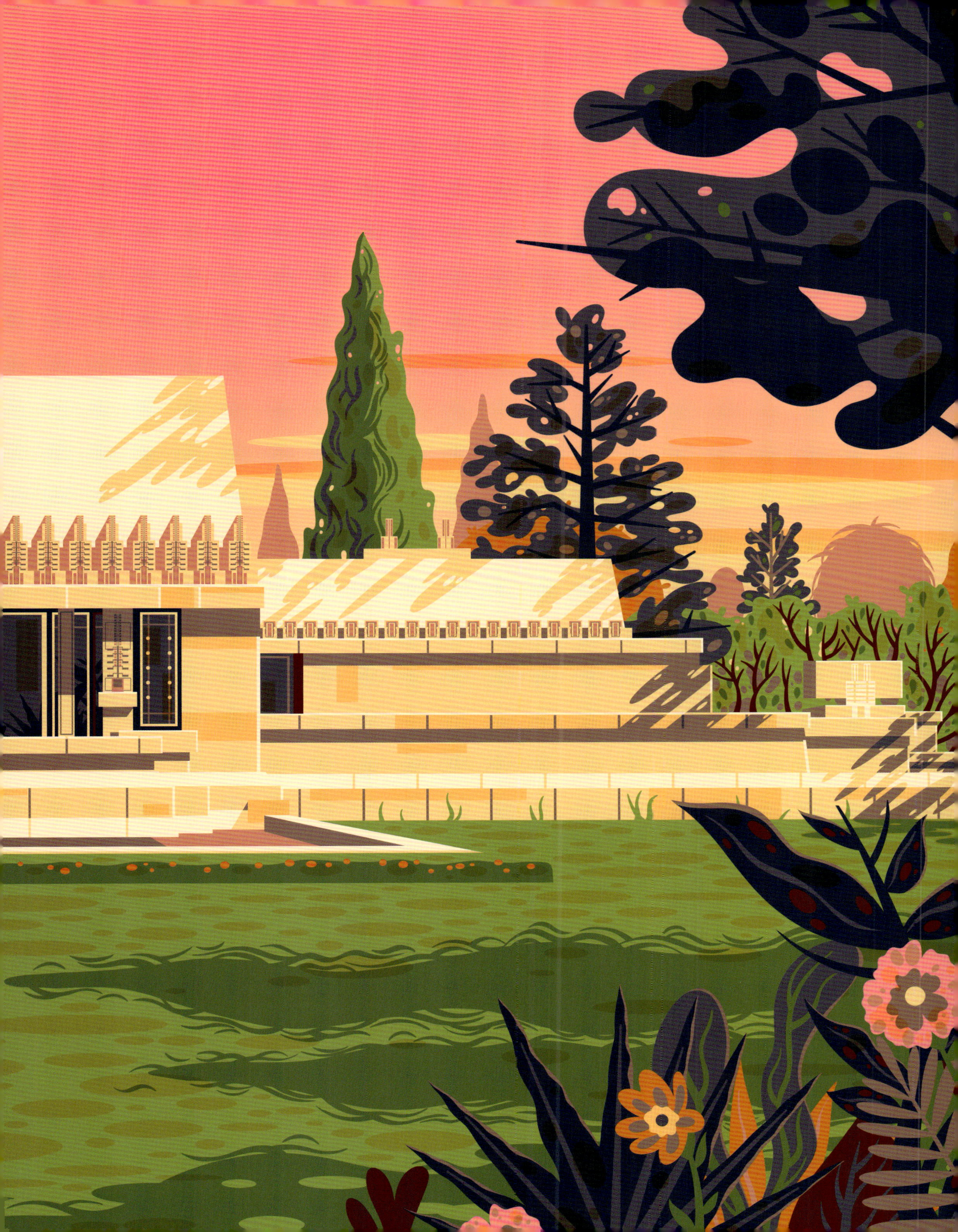

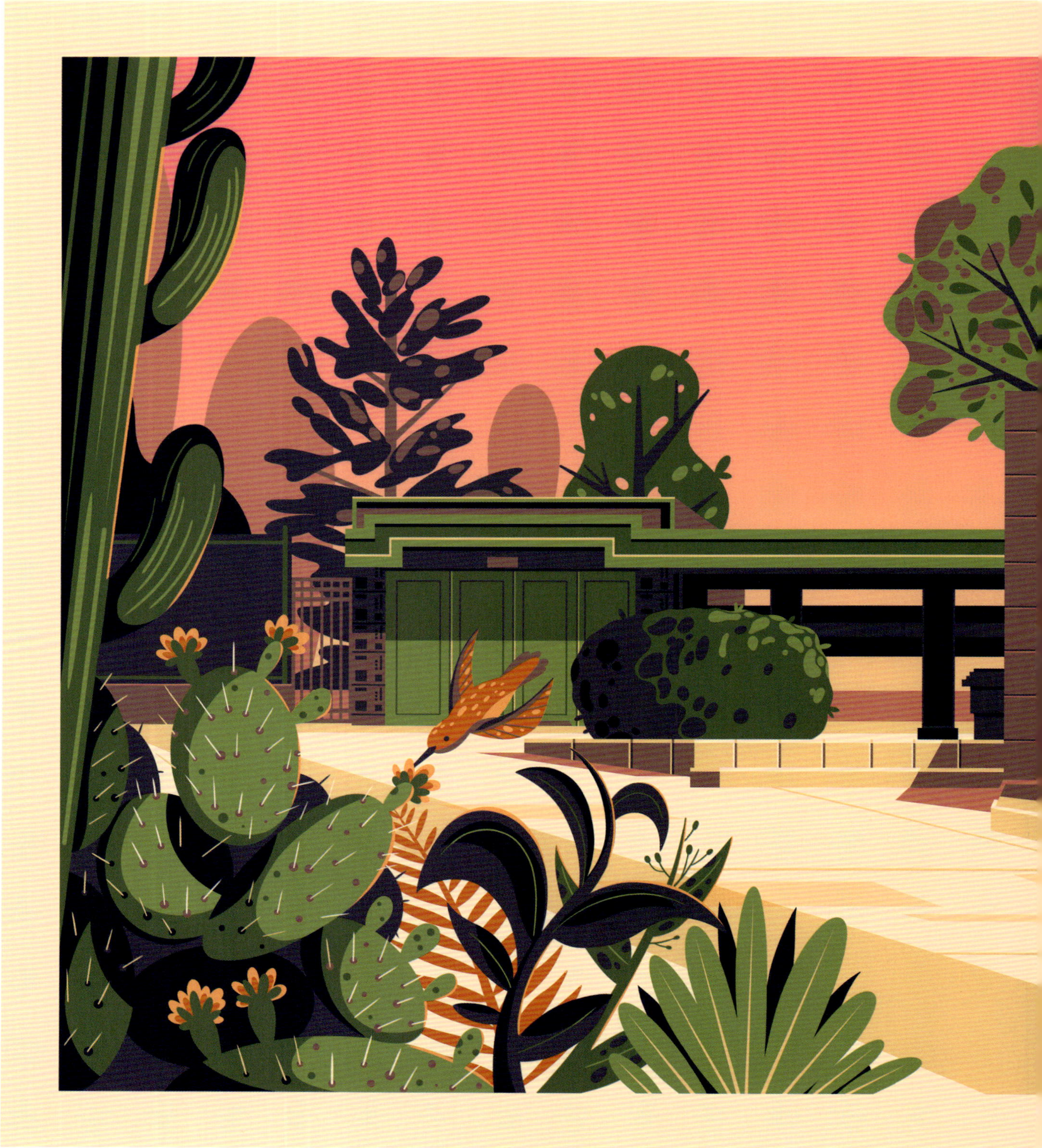

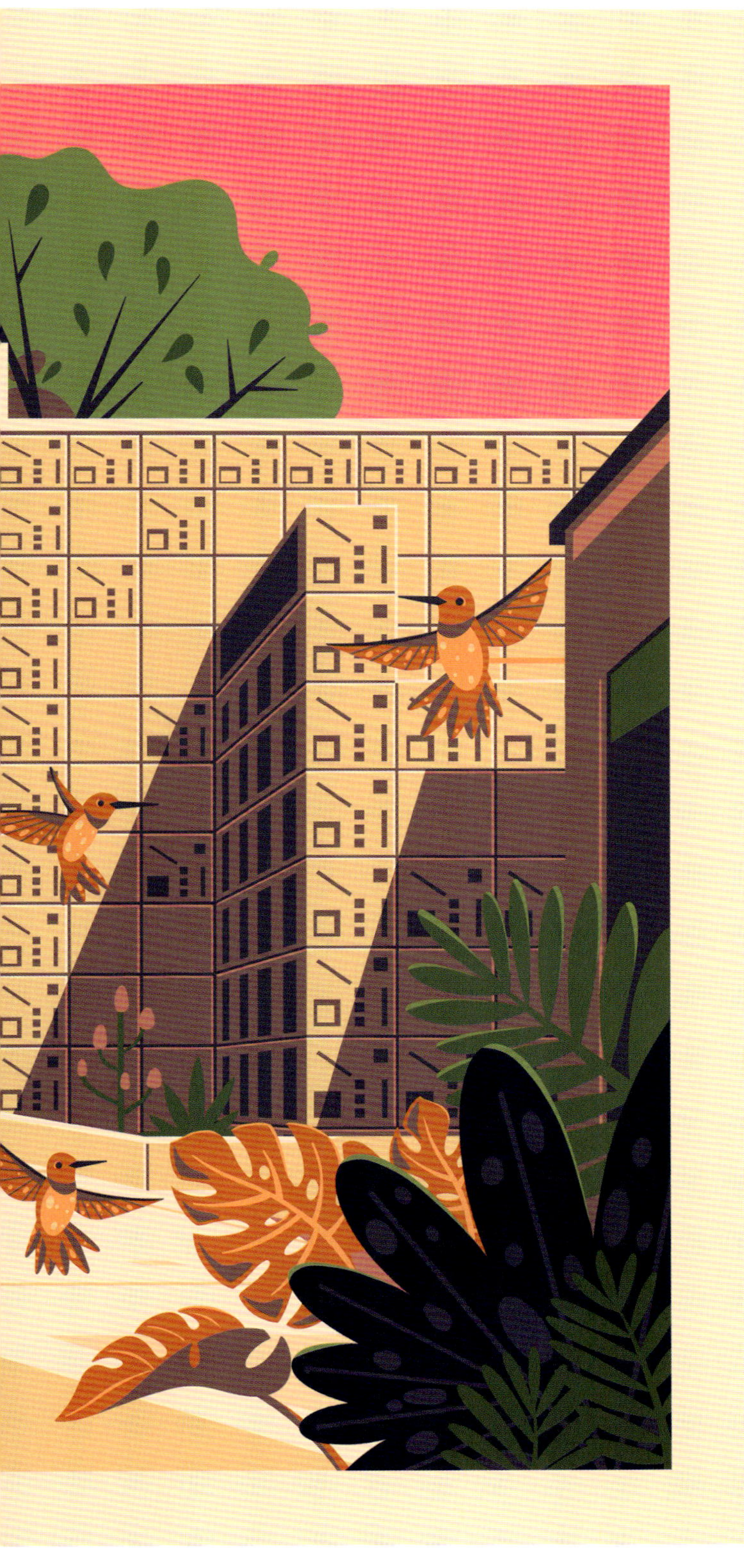

# SAMUEL FREEMAN HOUSE

| ADDRESS | ARCHITECT(S) | YEAR |
| --- | --- | --- |
| 1962 Glencoe Way<br>Los Angeles, CA<br>90068 | Frank Lloyd Wright | 1922 |



ACROSS

*Samuel Freeman House*
Open Edition
2018

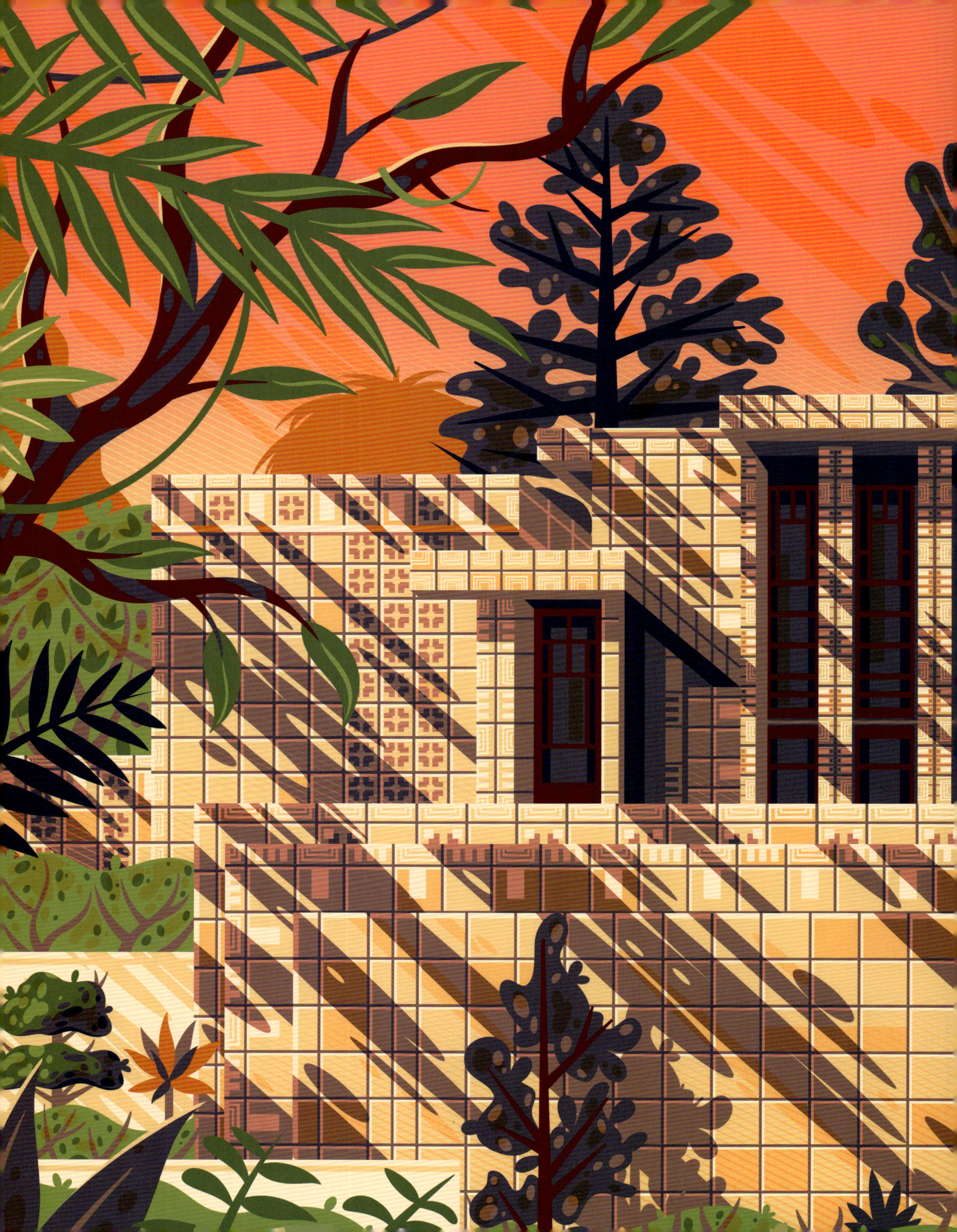

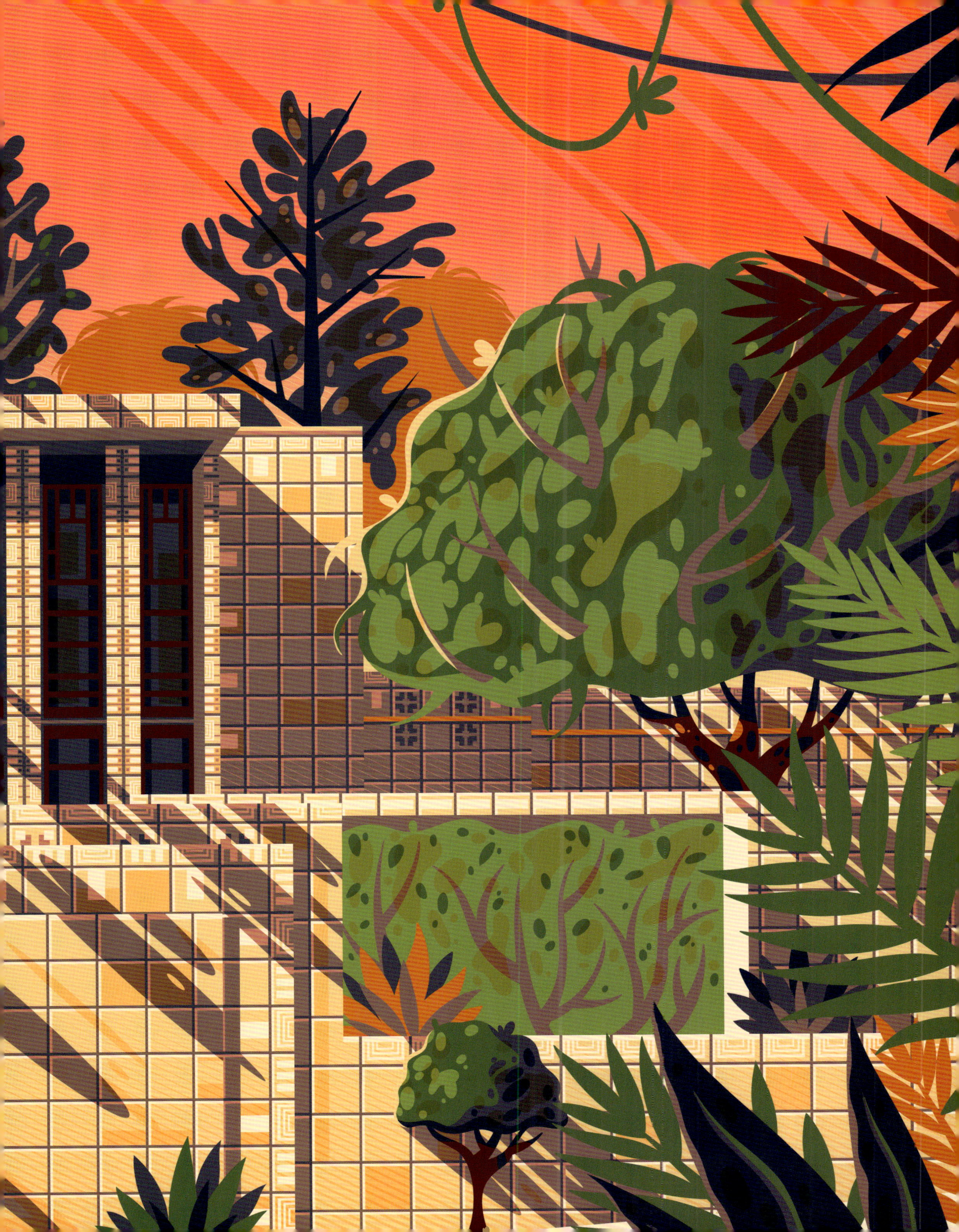

# STORER HOUSE

| ADDRESS | ARCHITECT(S) | YEAR |
|---|---|---|
| 8161 Hollywood Blvd.<br>Los Angeles, CA<br>90069 | Frank Lloyd Wright | 1923 |



PREVIOUS SPREAD

*Storer House (Detail)*
Limited Edition
2019

ACROSS

*Storer House*
Limited Edition
2019

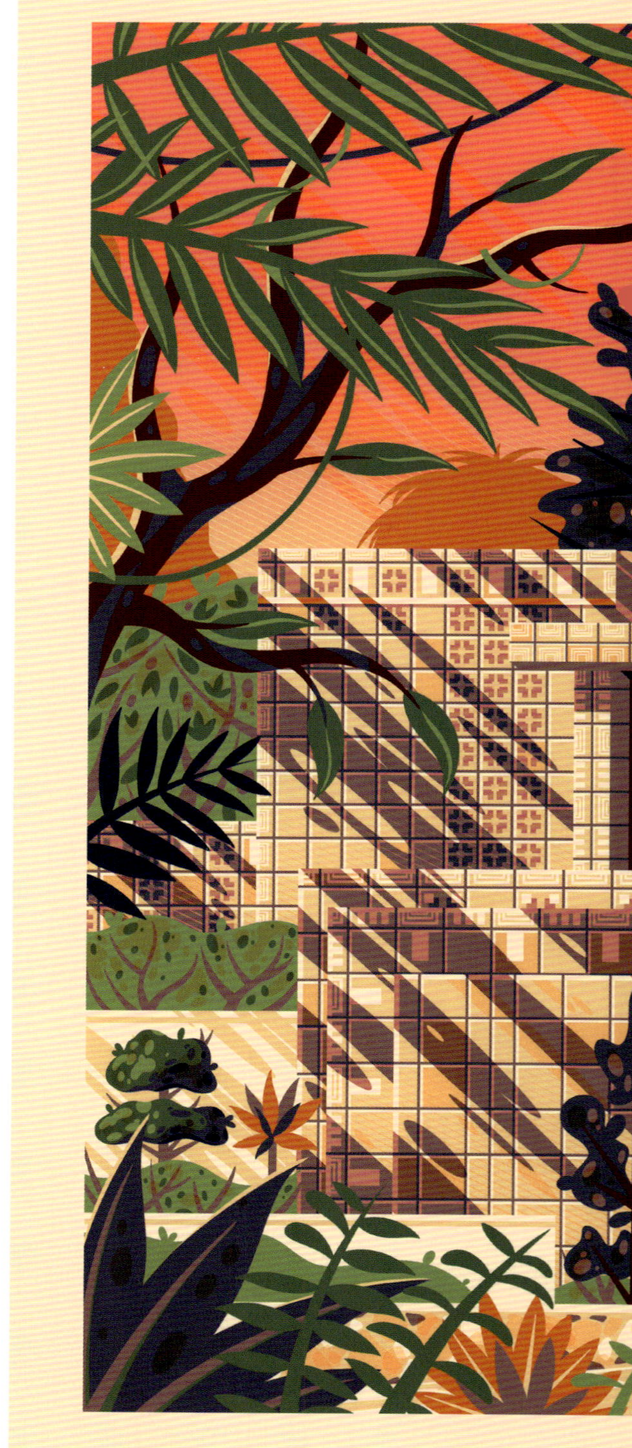

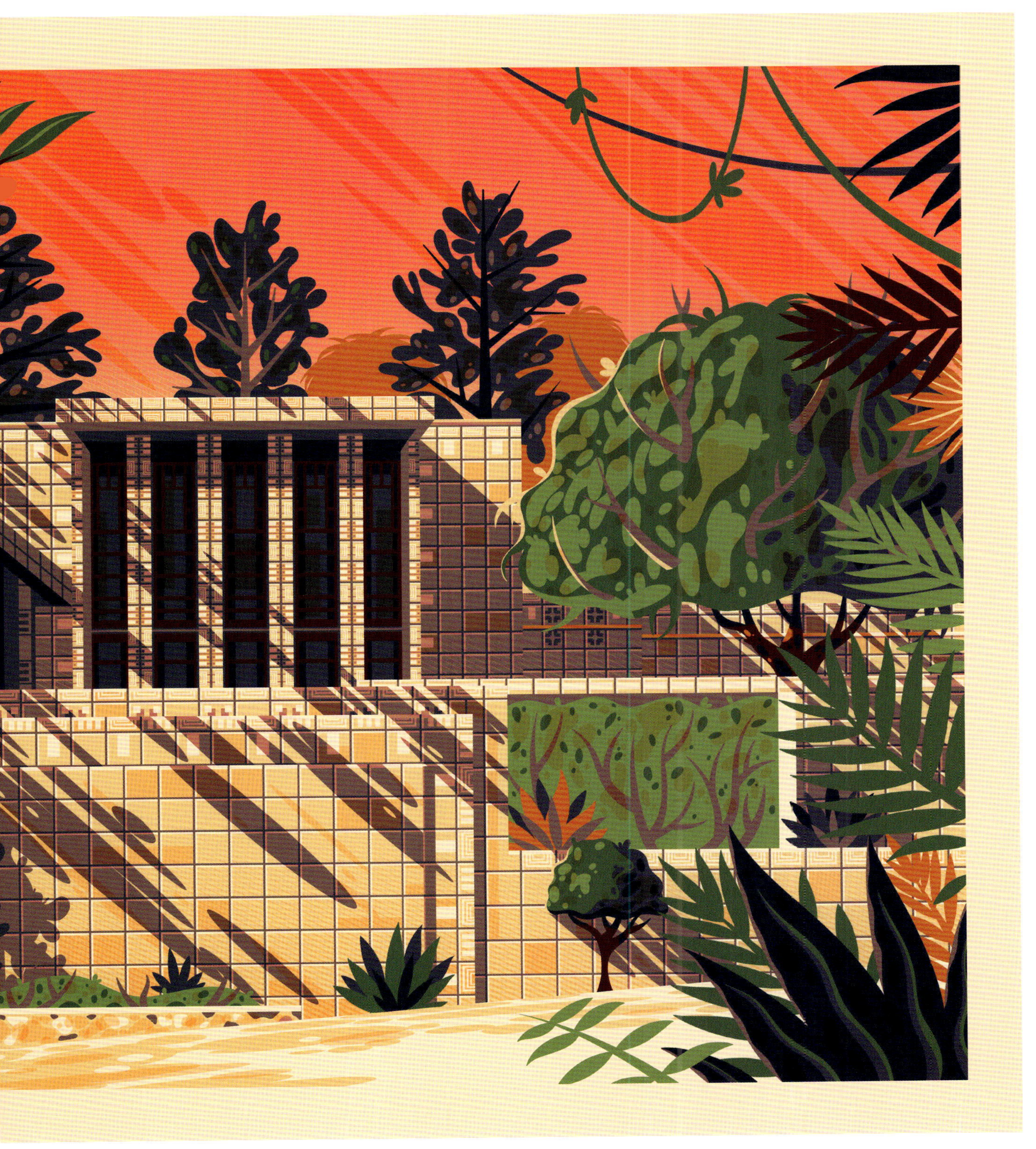

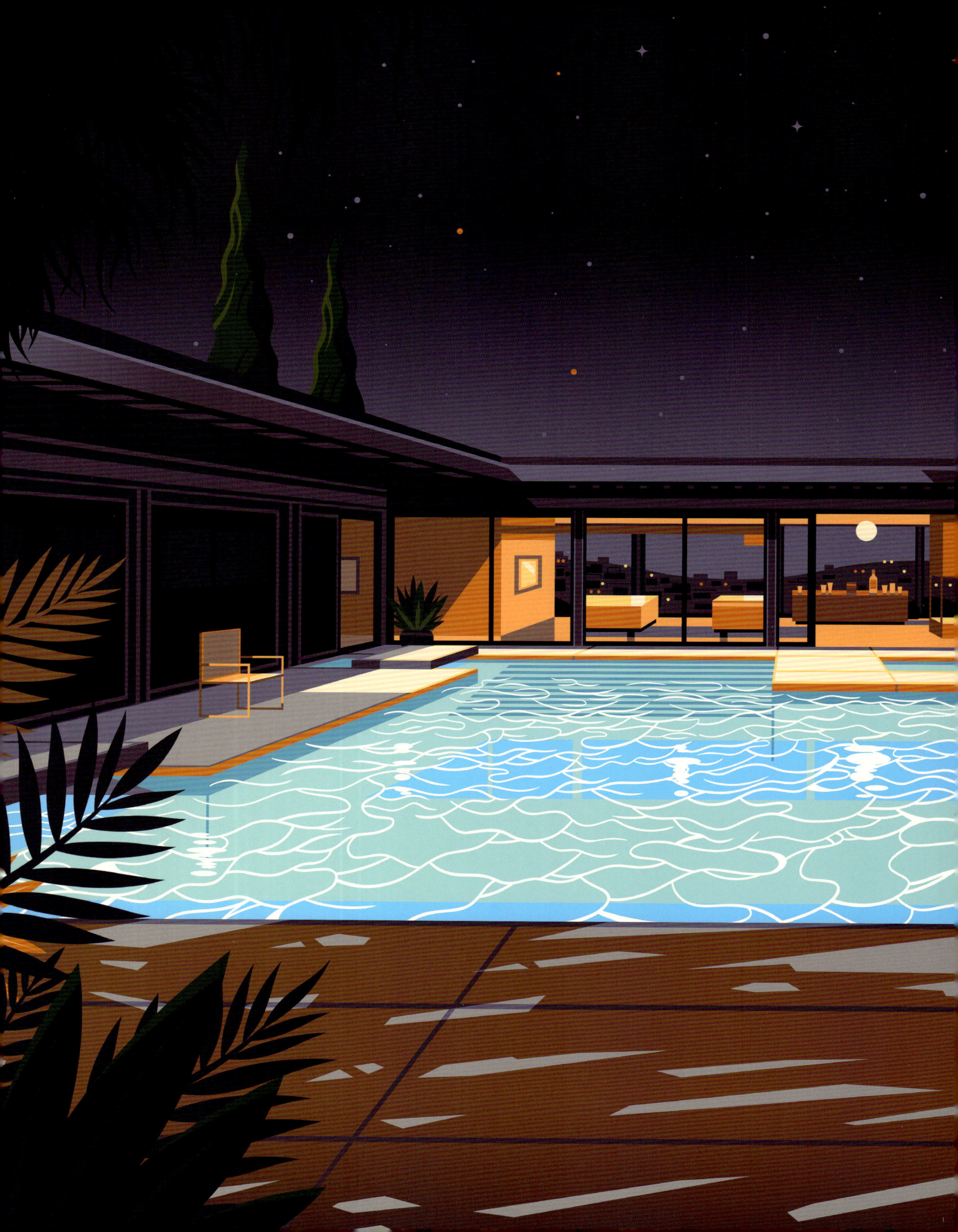

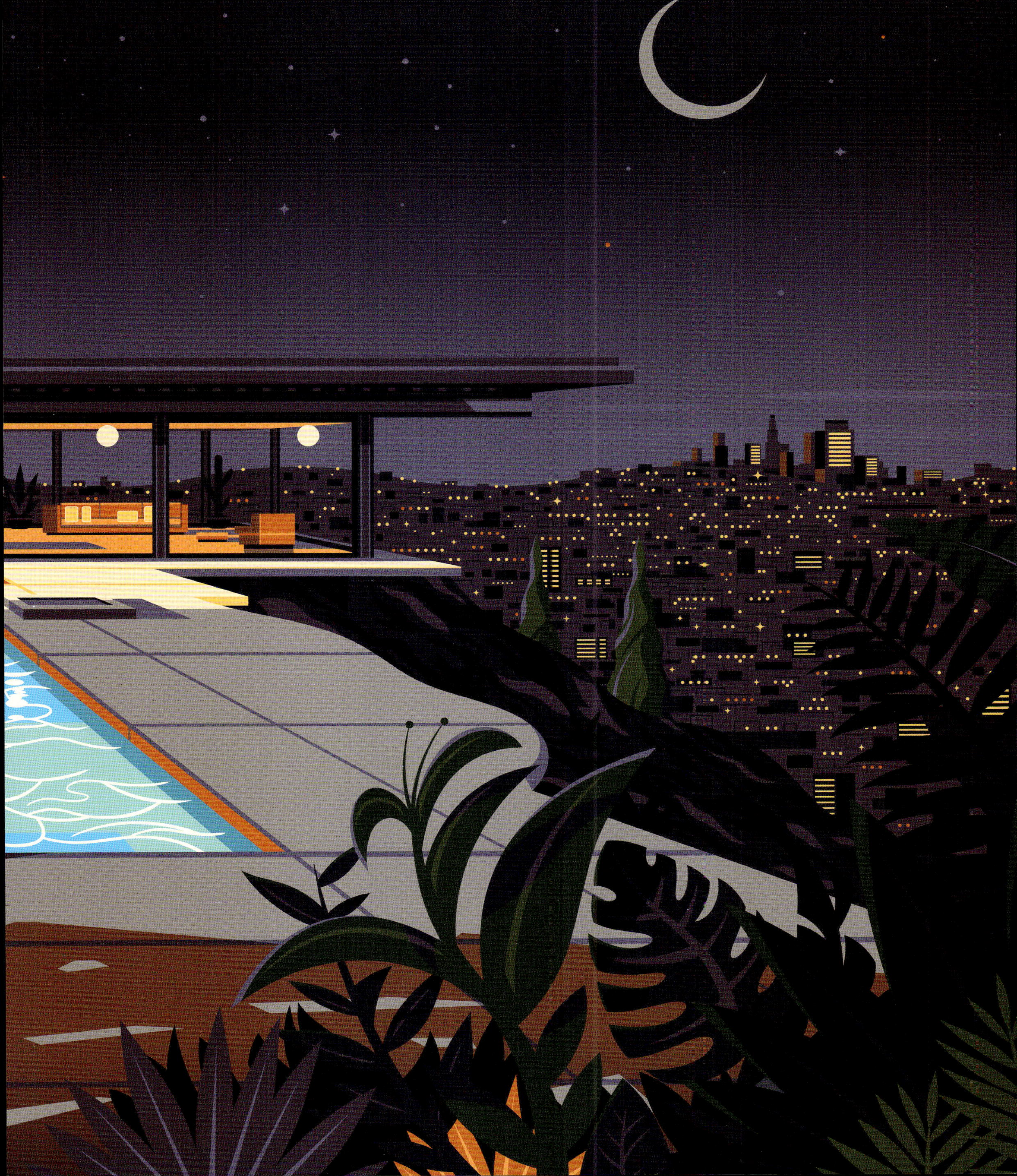

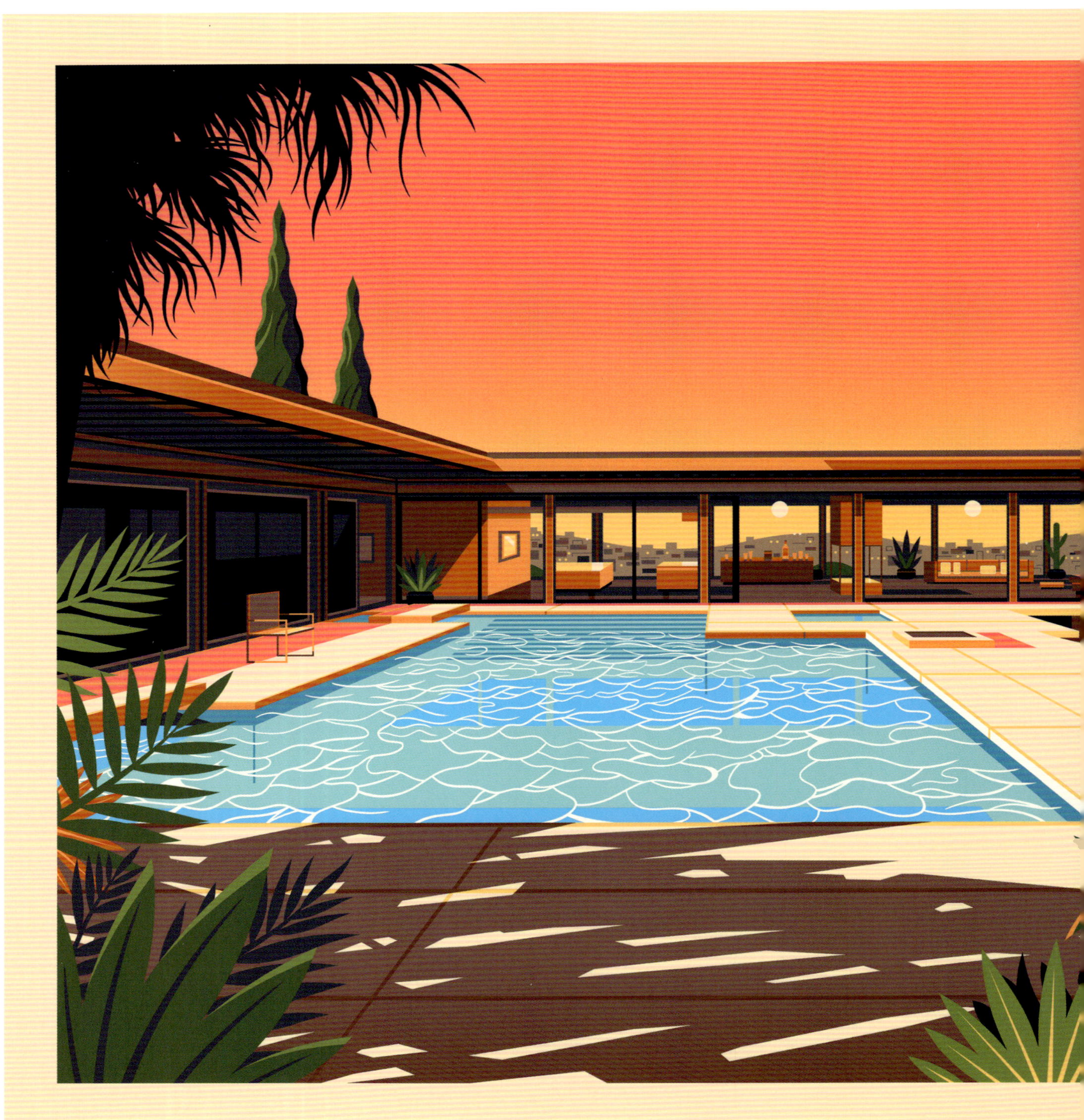

PREVIOUS SPREAD

*Stahl House (Night)*
Open Edition
2021

ABOVE

*Stahl House (Sunset)*
Limited Edition
2021

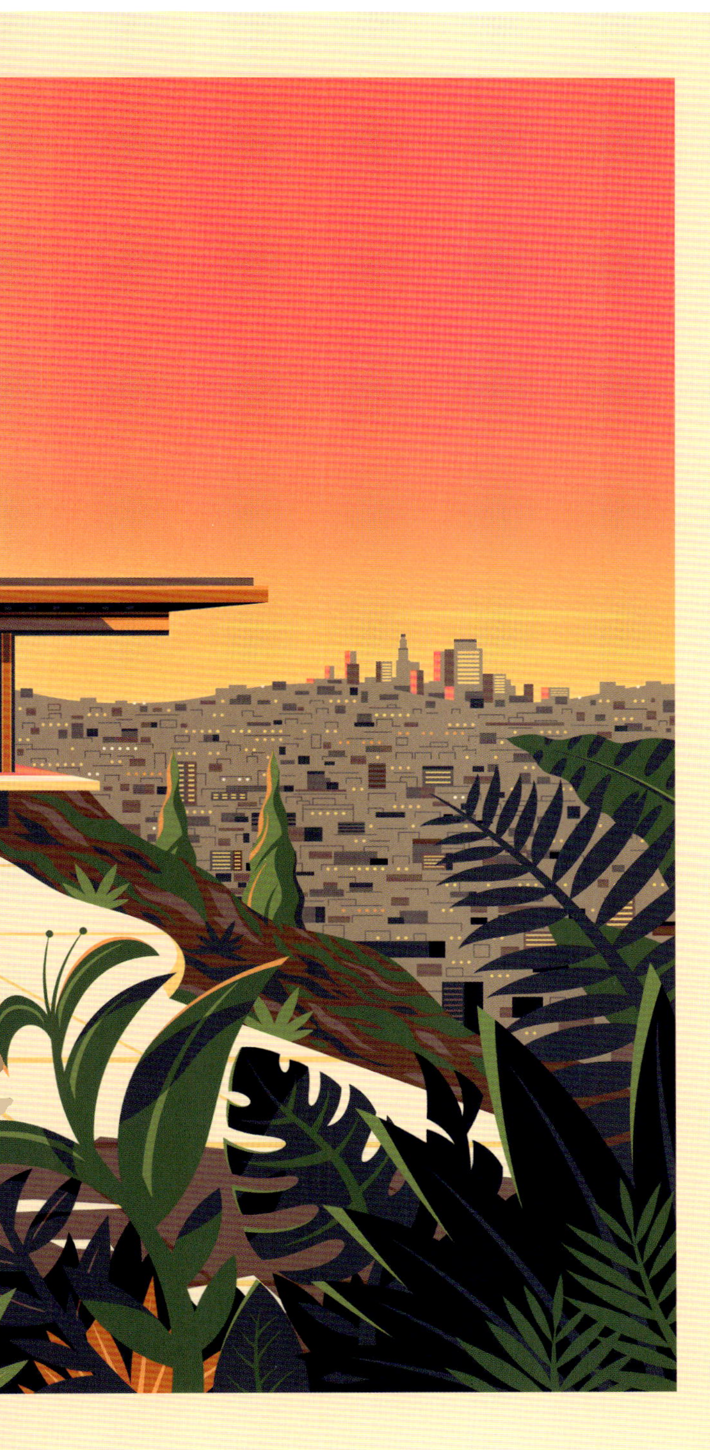

# STAHL HOUSE

| ADDRESS | ARCHITECT(S) | YEAR |
|---|---|---|
| 1635 Woods Dr.<br>West Hollywood, CA<br>90069 | Pierre Koenig | 1960 |



**The Stahl House sums up everything I love** about Los Angeles, all wrapped up in one neat, mid-century modern package. The architecture, the bright blue pool, the sun-soaked pavements, and the iconic city views, it's all there. Every time I visit LA, it's a tradition of mine to take the sunset tour.

This was the second print I created in this long running series, and I credit it as the one that truly put me on the map and started getting people's attention. I originally illustrated the Stahl House as a way to escape my own dreary surroundings, and I think that's why so many people are drawn to it too. It's not just a print to hang on the wall, but a little escape to somewhere warmer and full of possibilities. You look at a house like that and think "That's what I'm working towards".

# DINGBAT HOUSES

ADDRESS
The Greater Los Angeles Area

ARCHITECT(S)
Arthur C. Munson, & Others

YEAR
1956–1965



**I've been obsessed with these iconic yet controversial** apartment buildings for as long as I can remember. They're so uniquely Californian, and you can easily spend hours driving around the city, spotting the playful cursive typography often featured on the facade. Once you notice one, you can't unsee them.

What makes them even more interesting is the controversy surrounding them. These buildings were originally built as affordable housing, and the overhangs were designed to allow residents to park underneath, maximising space in a dense urban environment. However, the overhangs aren't very earthquake-friendly, especially in a seismic hotspot like Los Angeles. So you've got one half of the city wanting them torn down due to the risks they pose, while the other half fights to preserve them, appreciating their historical significance and the unique 1950s and '60s architecture.

ACROSS

*Dingbat House*
Limited Edition
2019

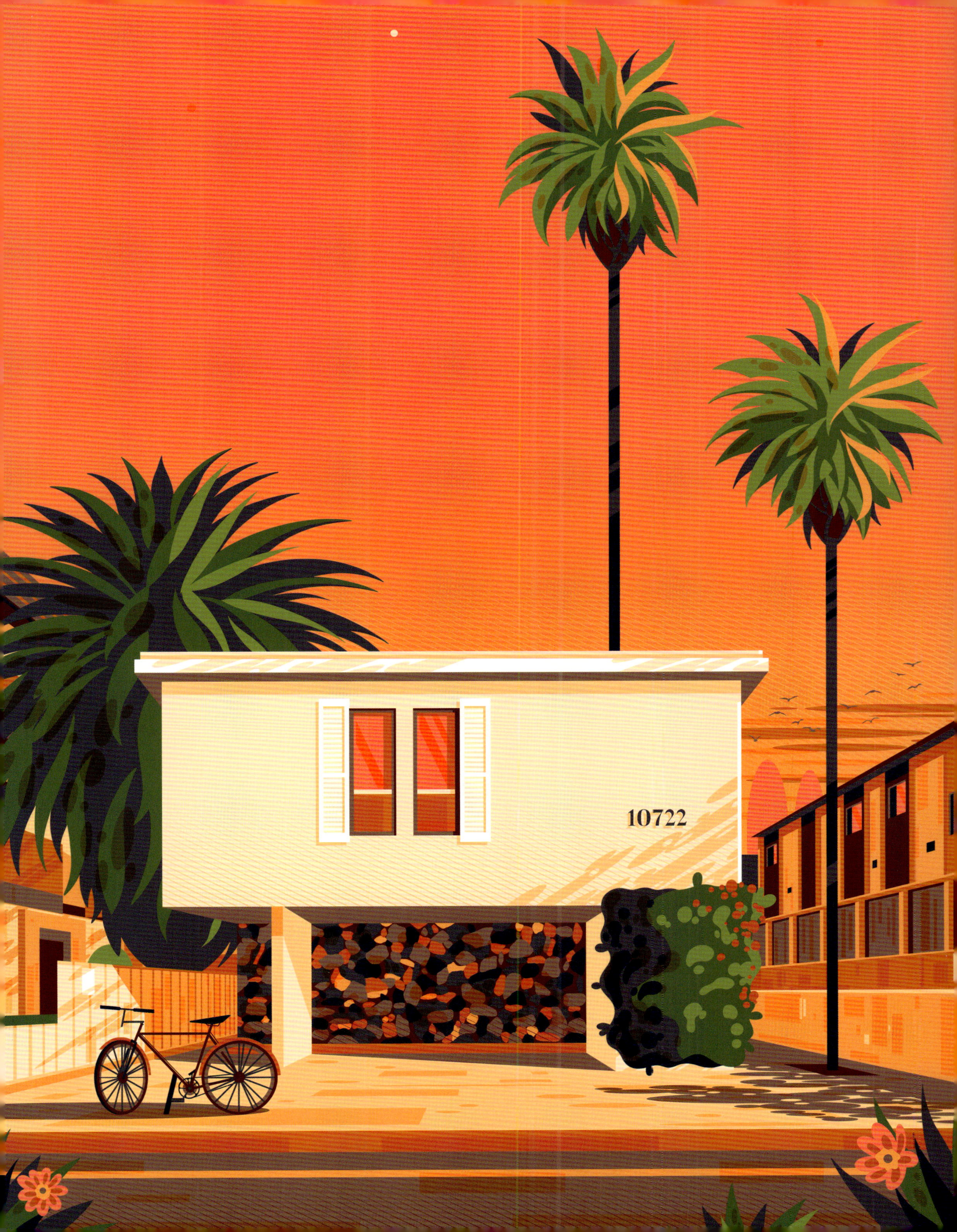
10722

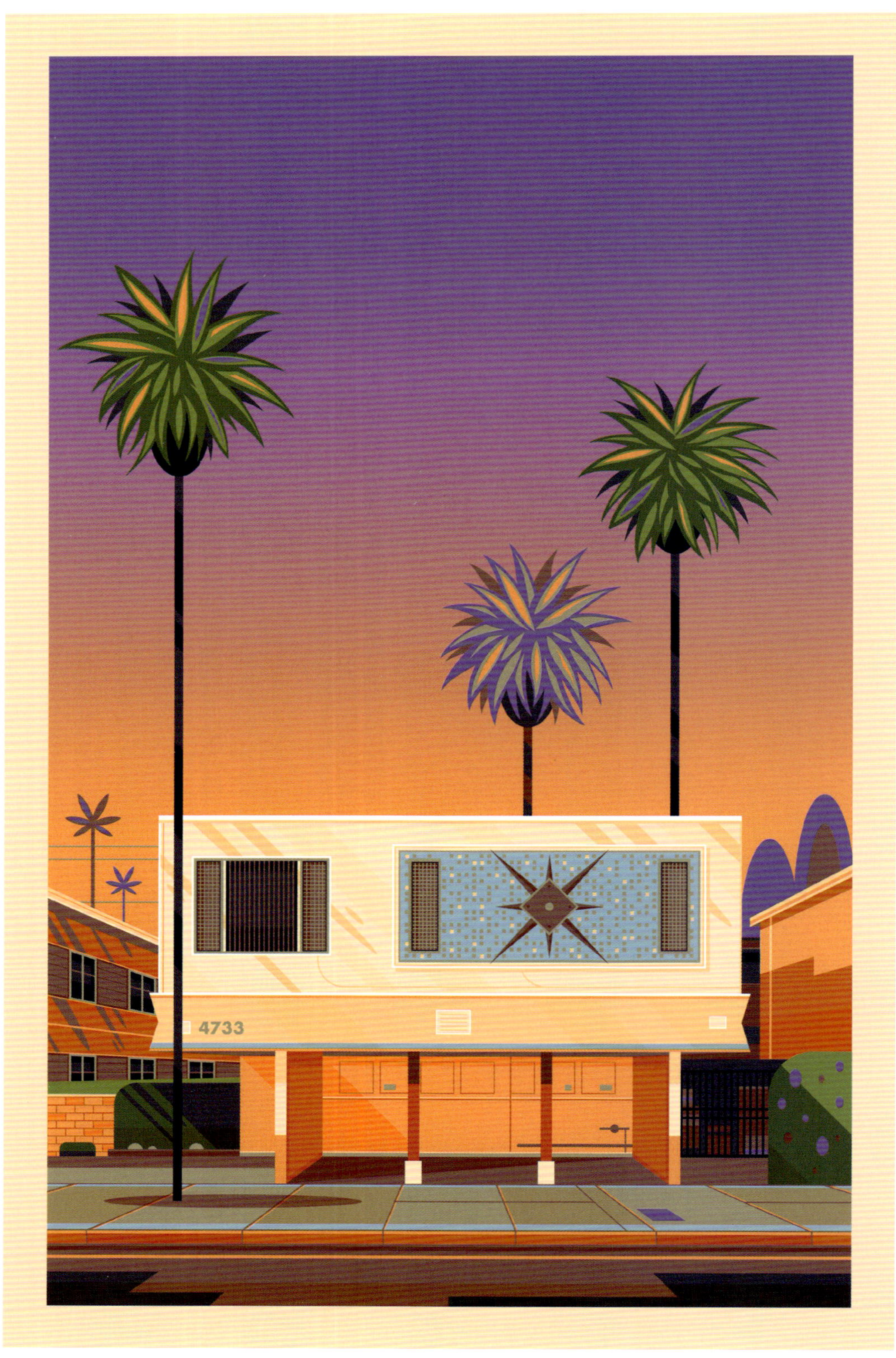


ABOVE

*Dingbat House on Beverly*
Limited Edition
2022

ACROSS

*Dingbat House in Mar Vista*
Limited Edition
2020

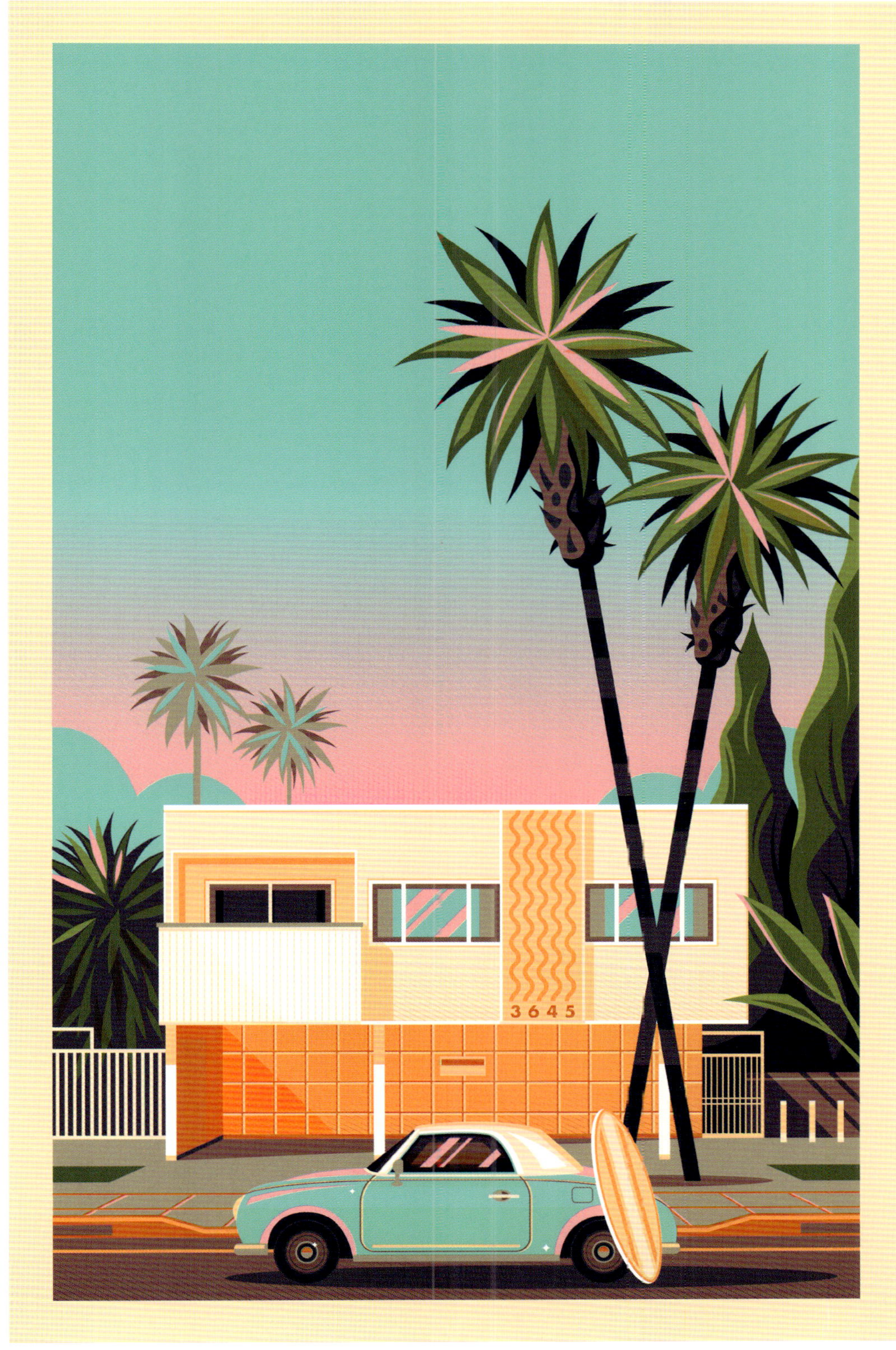
3645

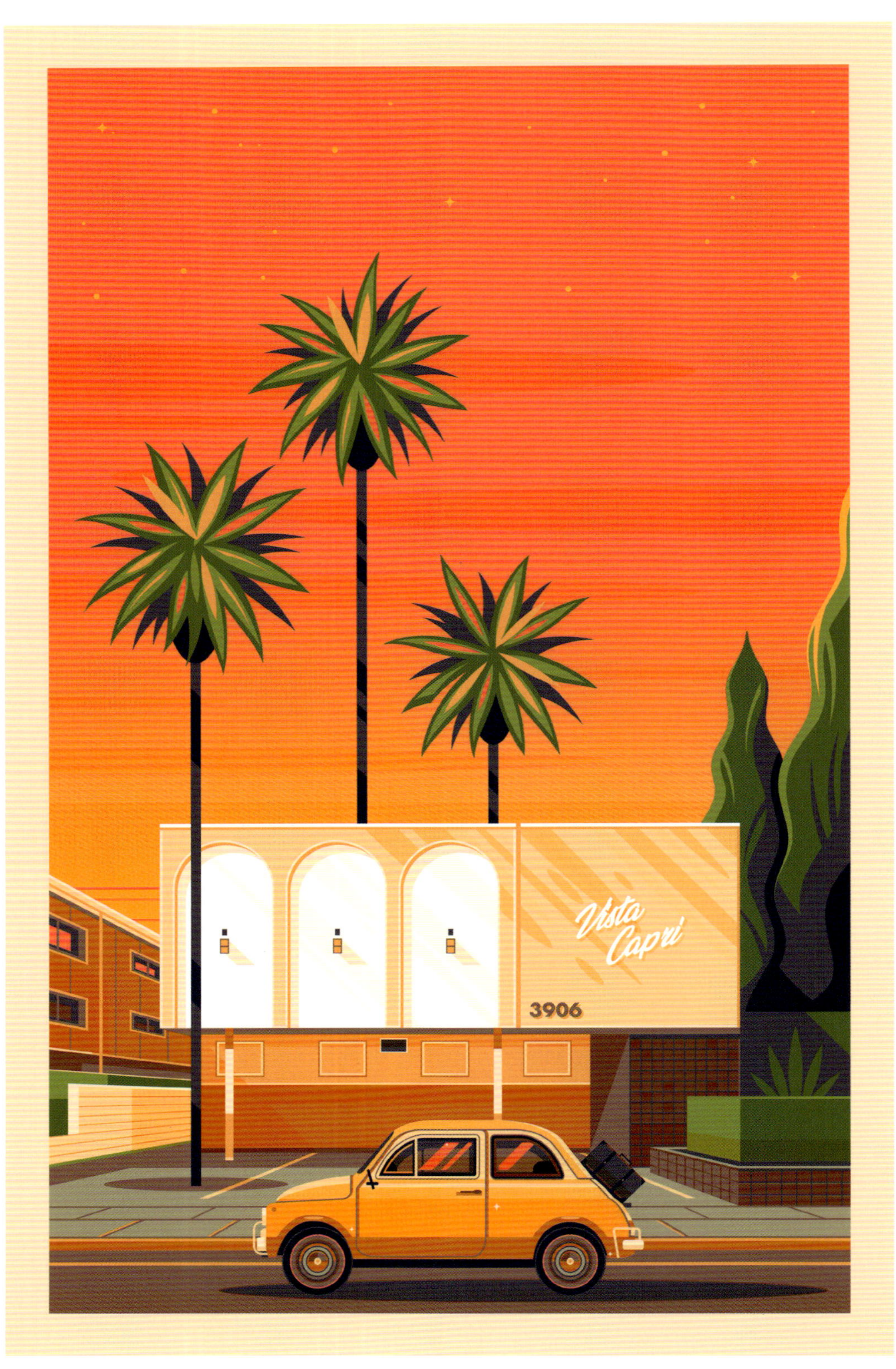


ABOVE

*Dingbat House in Culver City*
Limited Edition
2021

ACROSS

*Dingbat House on Sunset*
Limited Edition
2023

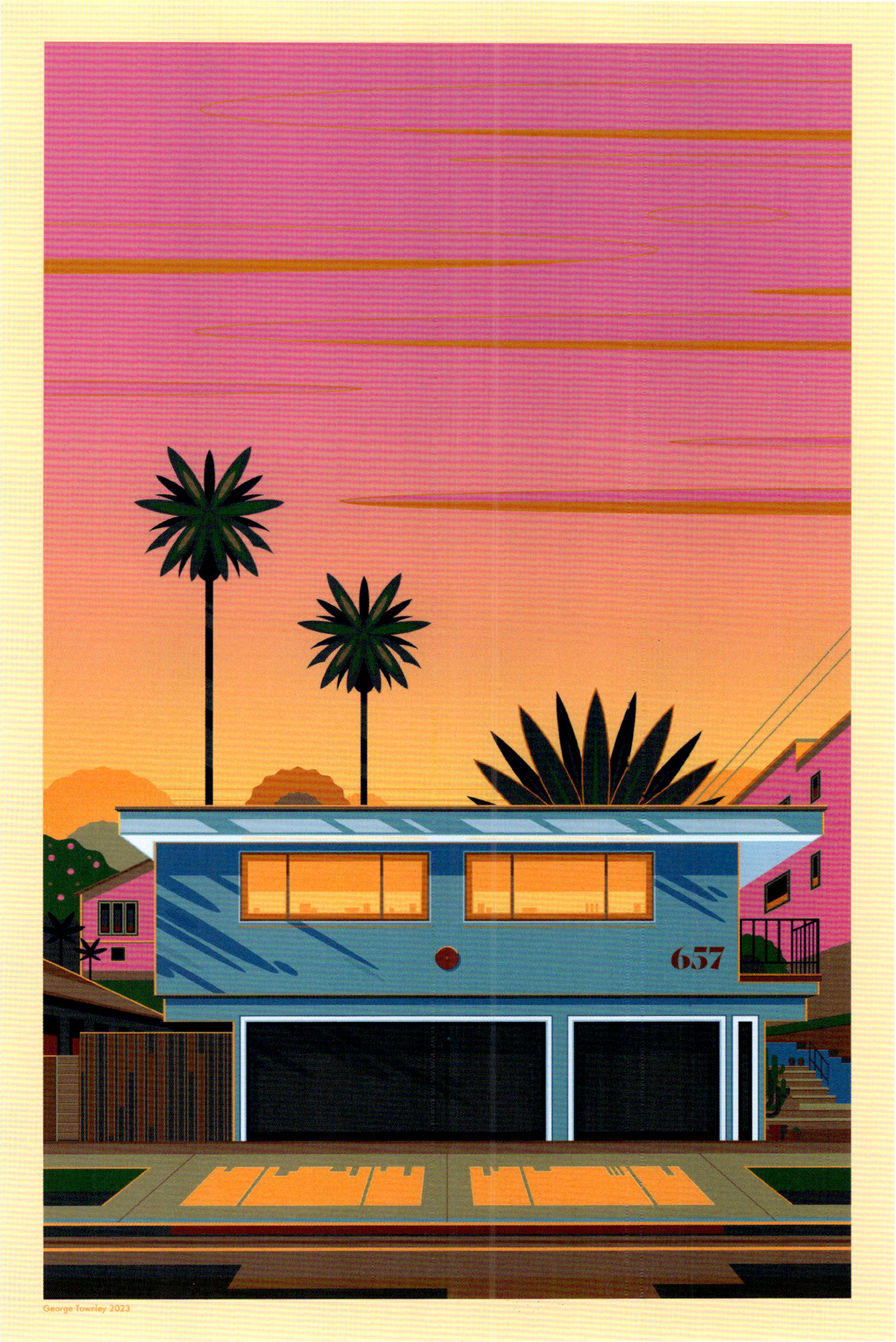

George Townley 2023

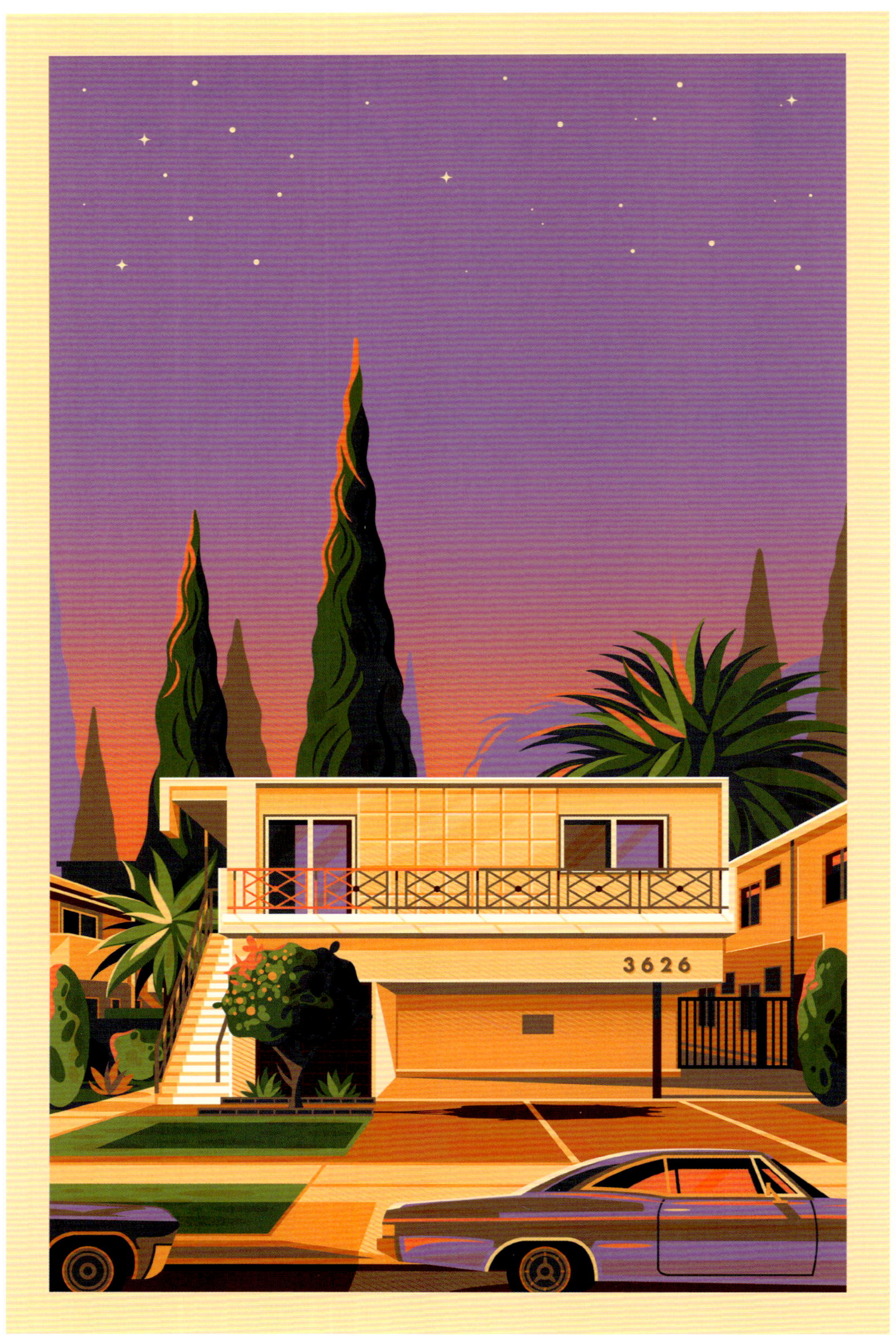


ABOVE

*Dingbat House on Vinton*
Limited Edition
2019

ACROSS

*Dingbat House on Keystone*
Limited Edition
2020

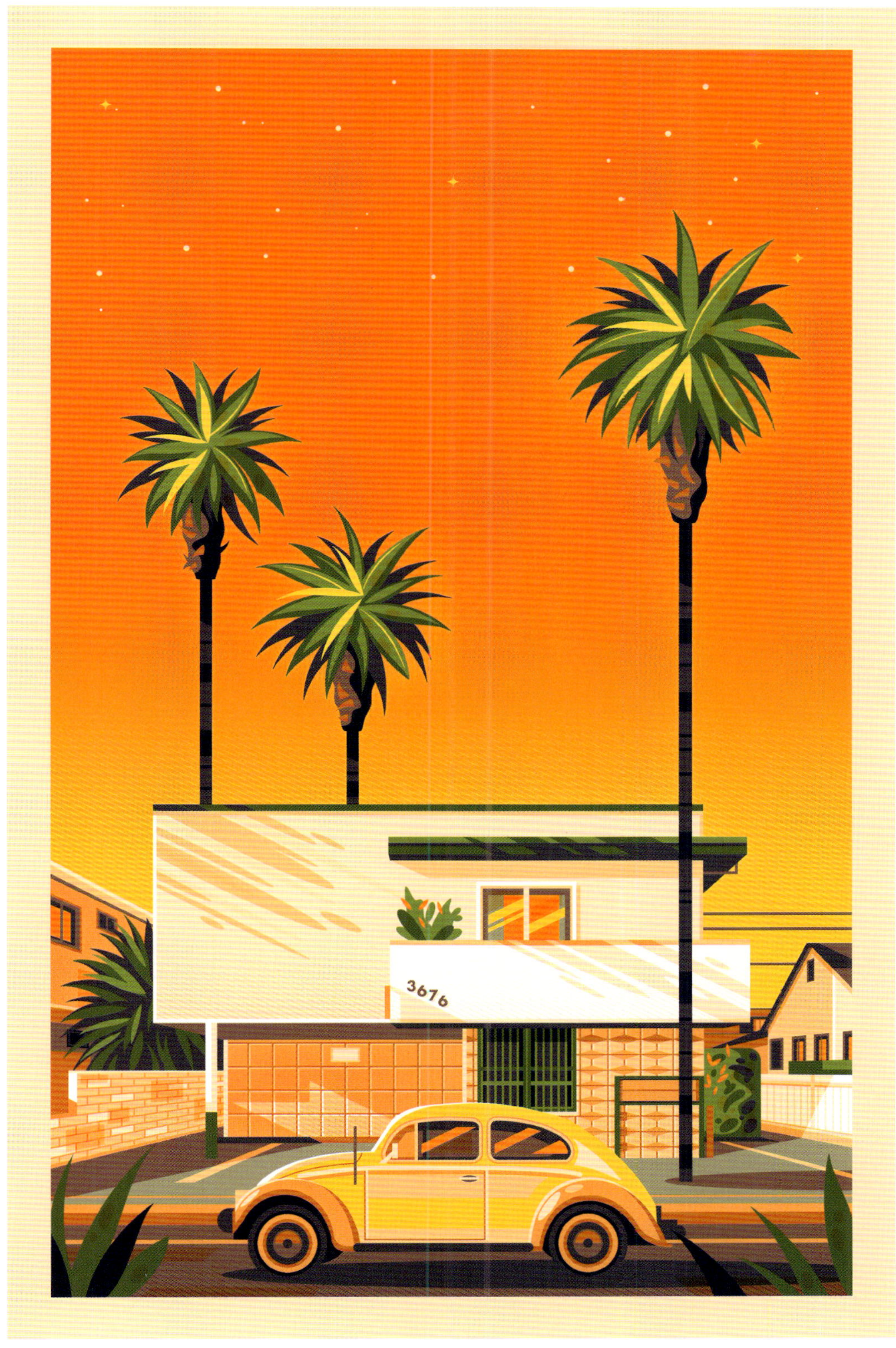
3676

**Once you get past the cheeky name**, this apartment perfectly encapsulates everything I love about dingbat houses: the clean, simple design, the playful cursive typography, and the midcentury modern-inspired symbol on the facade. And with a name like that, it's no wonder this building has become such an inside joke among locals.

Fun fact: the owner of this building also owns the "Chee-Zee" apartments just around the corner. A commitment to amusingly named dingbat houses is definitely niche, but I respect it.

ACROSS

*Crapi Apartments*
Limited Edition
2024

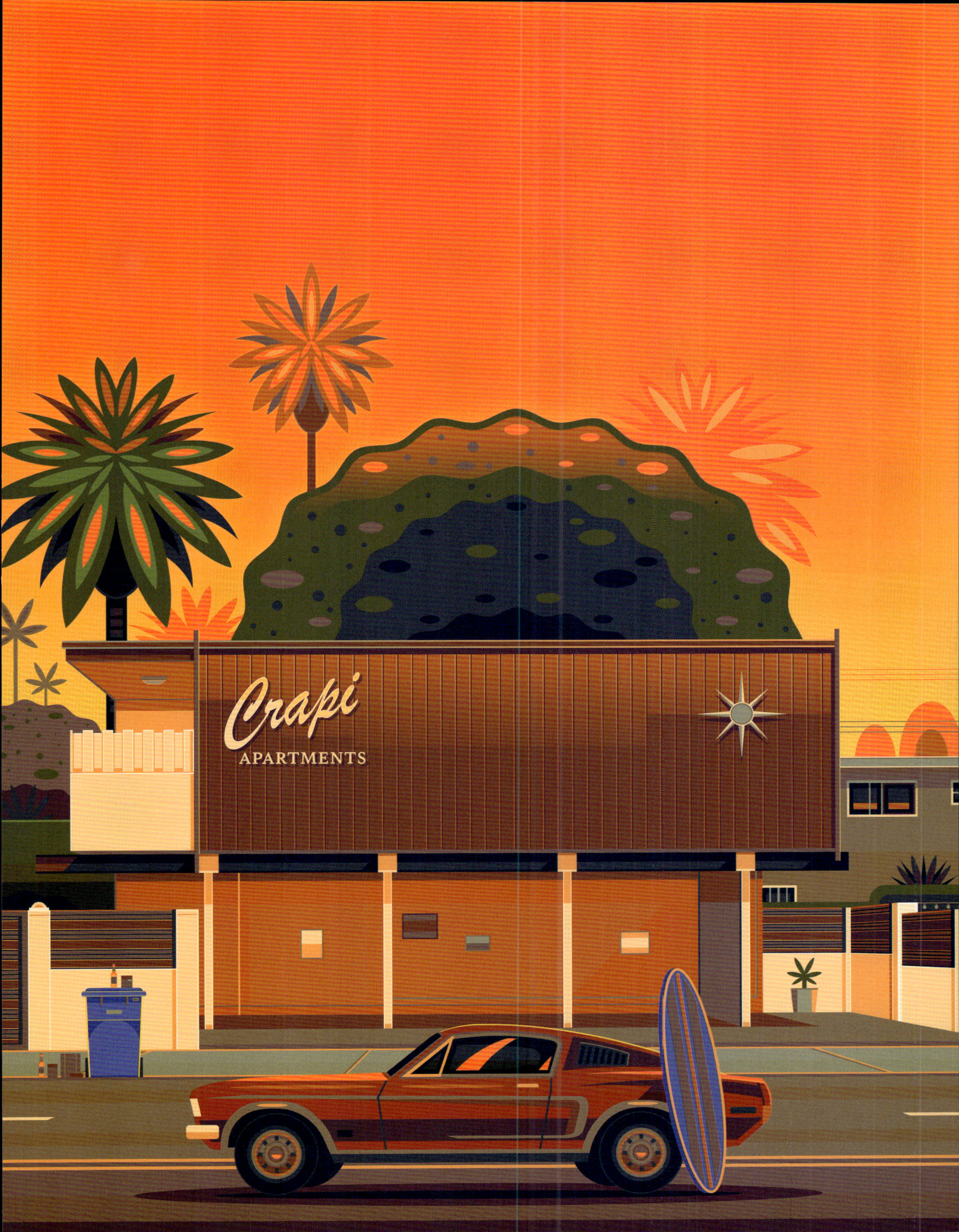
Crapi
APARTMENTS

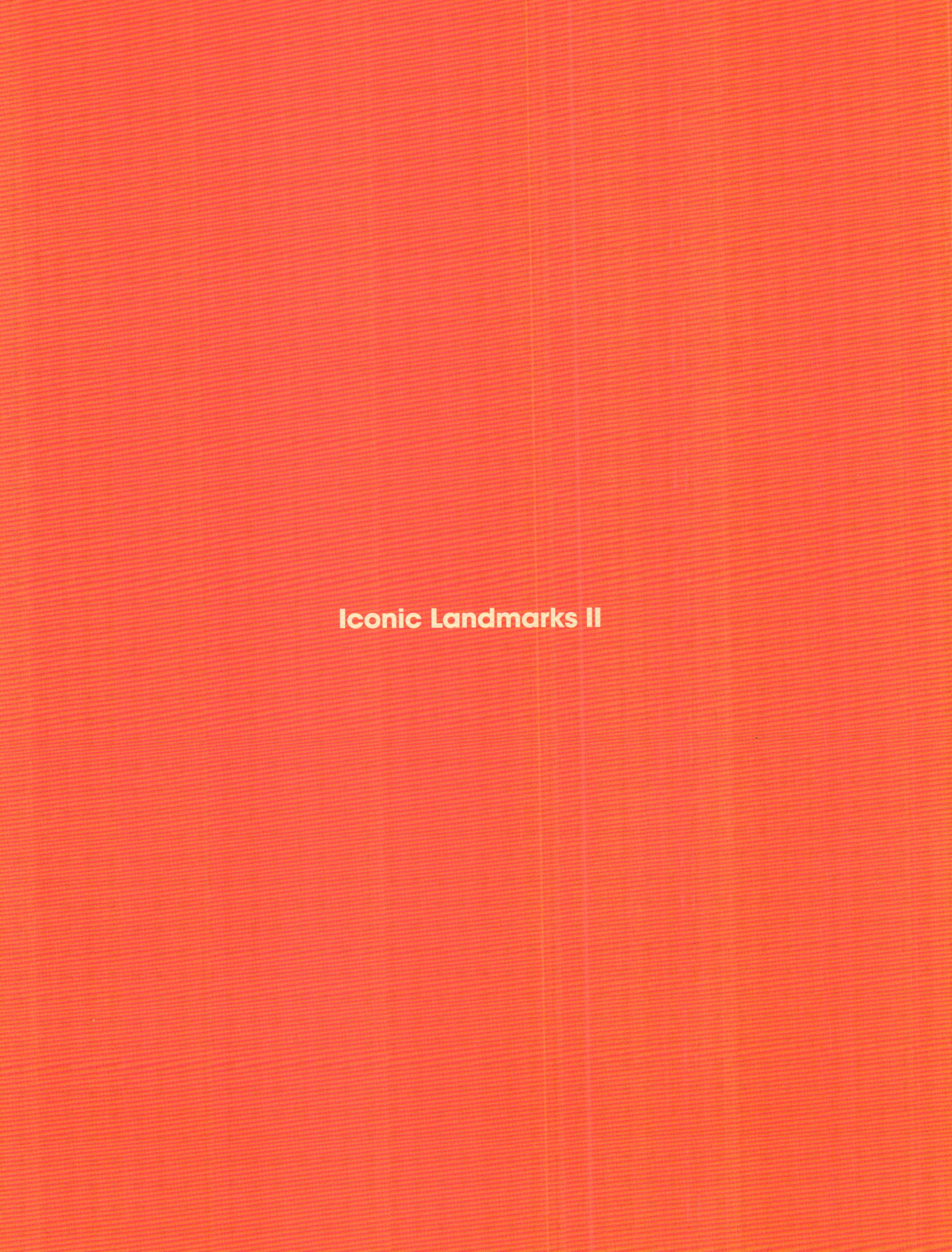

Iconic Landmarks II

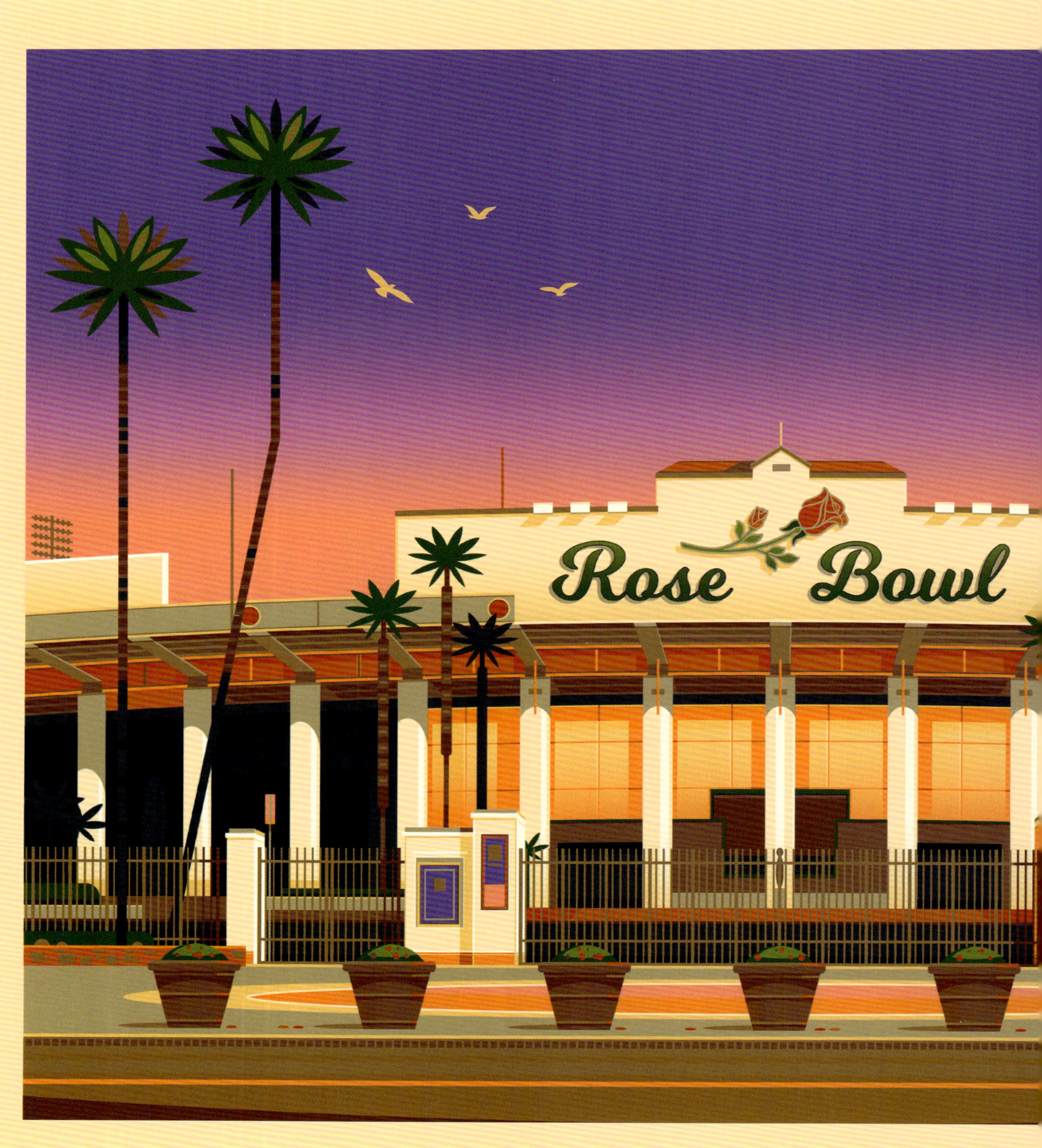
Rose Bowl

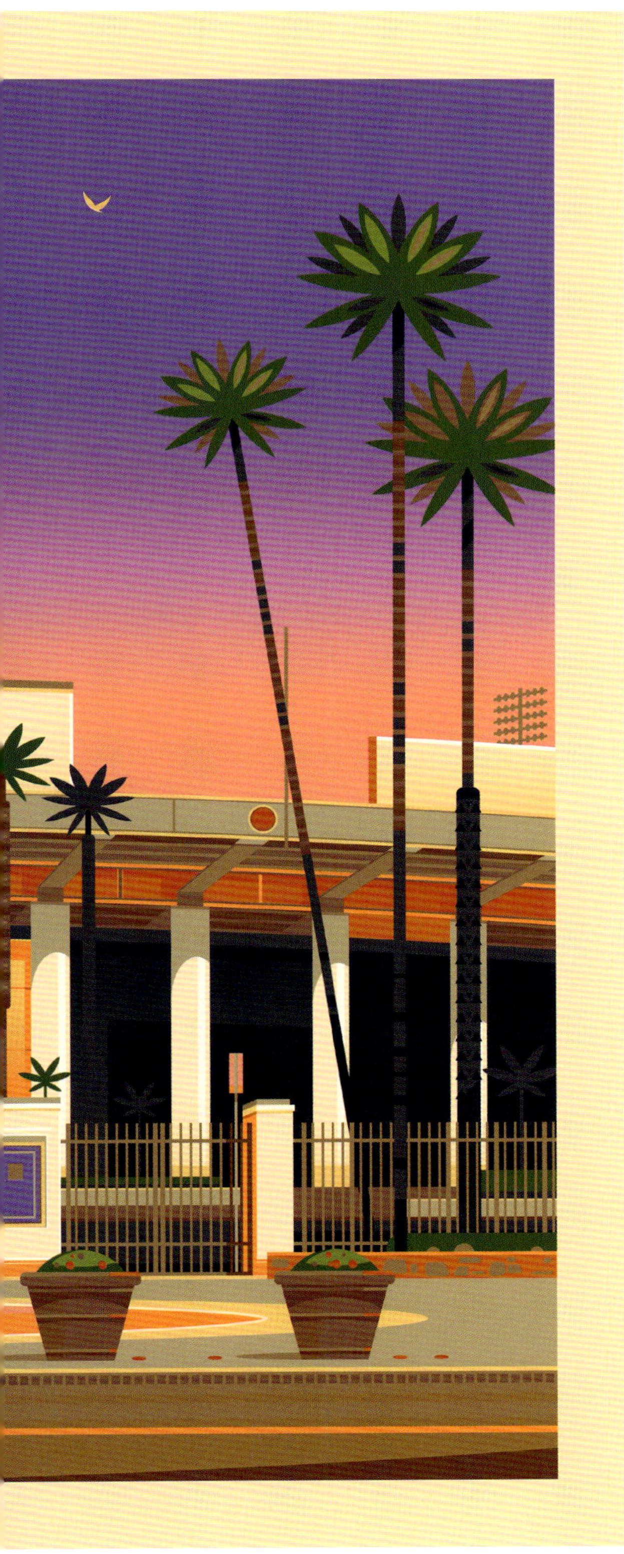

# ROSE BOWL STADIUM

| ADDRESS | ARCHITECT(S) | YEAR |
|---|---|---|
| 1001 Rose Bowl Dr.<br>Pasadena, CA<br>91103 | Myron Hunt | 1922 |



ACROSS

*Rose Bowl Stadium*
Open Edition
2023

# SANTA MONICA PIER

| ADDRESS | ARCHITECT(S) | YEAR |
|---|---|---|
| 200 Santa Monica Pier<br>Santa Monica, CA<br>90401 | Charles I. D. Looff | 1916 |



**The first day of my first ever visit to Los Angeles** ended with a sunset at this pier. I always recommend anyone visiting LA for the first time make time to experience a West Coast sunset. Once you look past the crowds of people doing the same thing, you're rewarded with a view that feels entirely your own.

Funnily enough, Santa Monica Pier is also home to one of my favourite food spots in the city. Right at the entrance you'll find a place called "Pier Burger," and it very quickly became a favourite of mine. Locals are usually surprised when I mention it as one of my go-to burger spots, likely because there are so many other well-known options around. But I think nostalgia just makes everything taste better.

GATEFOLD

*Santa Monica Pier*
Limited Edition
2022

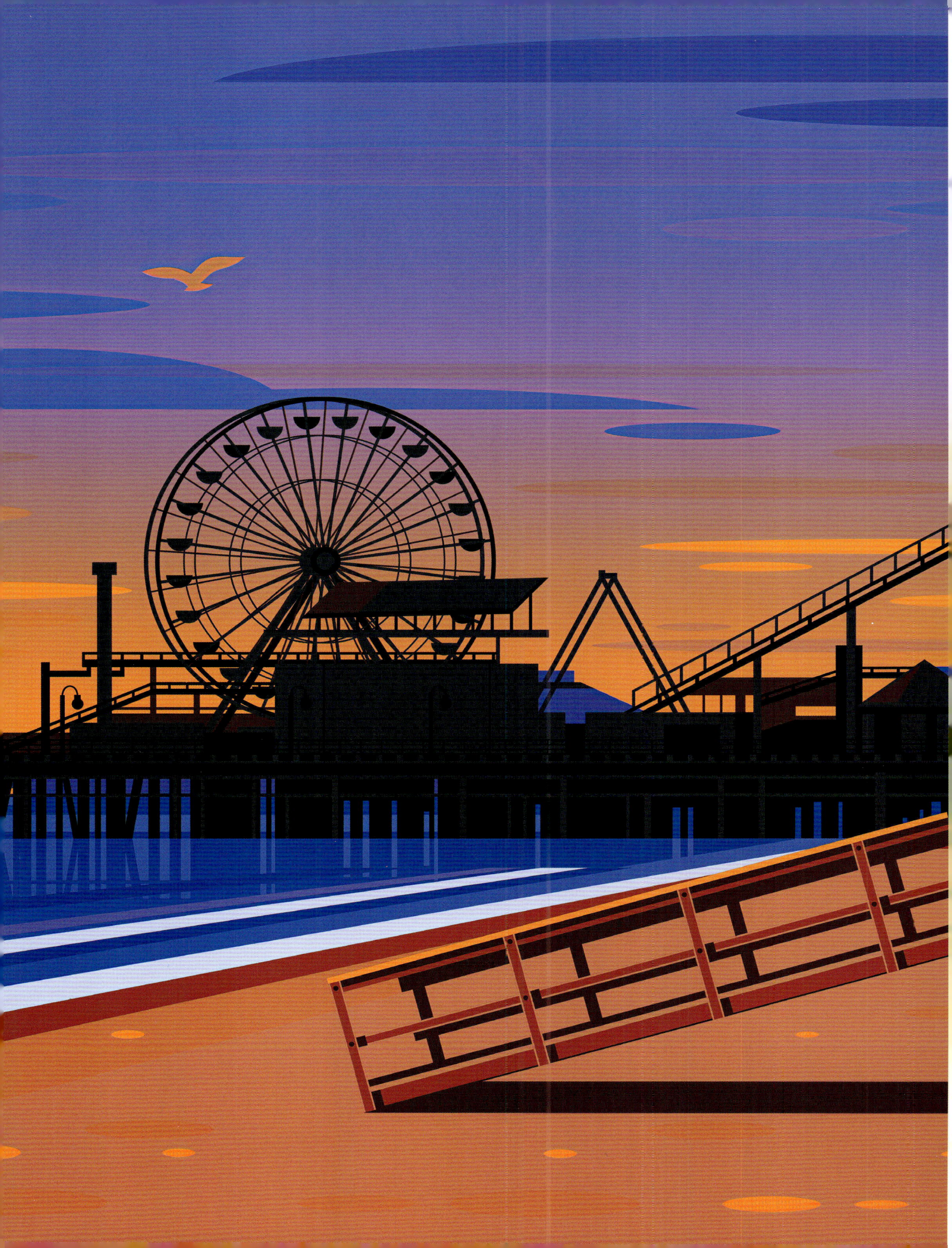

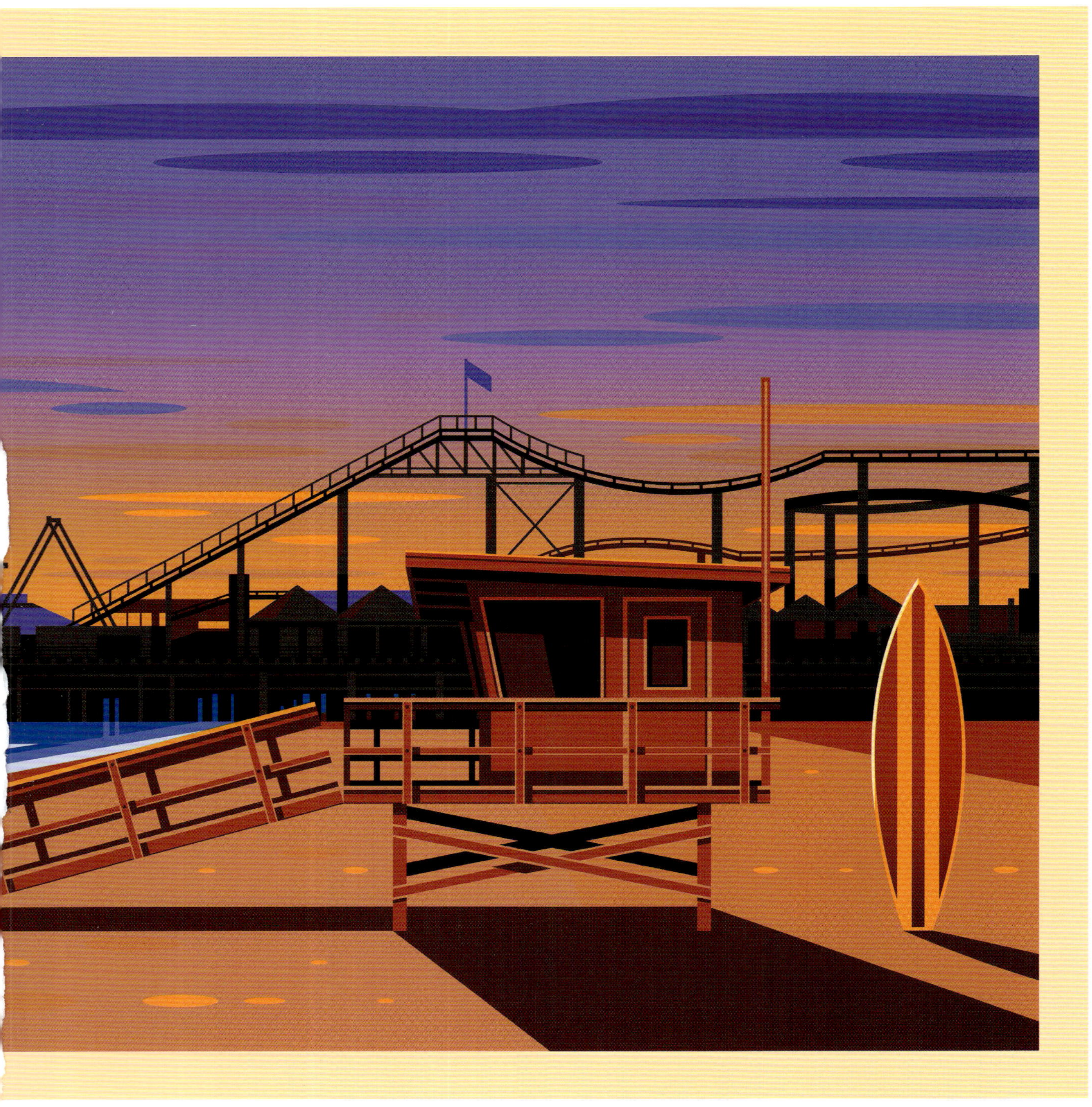

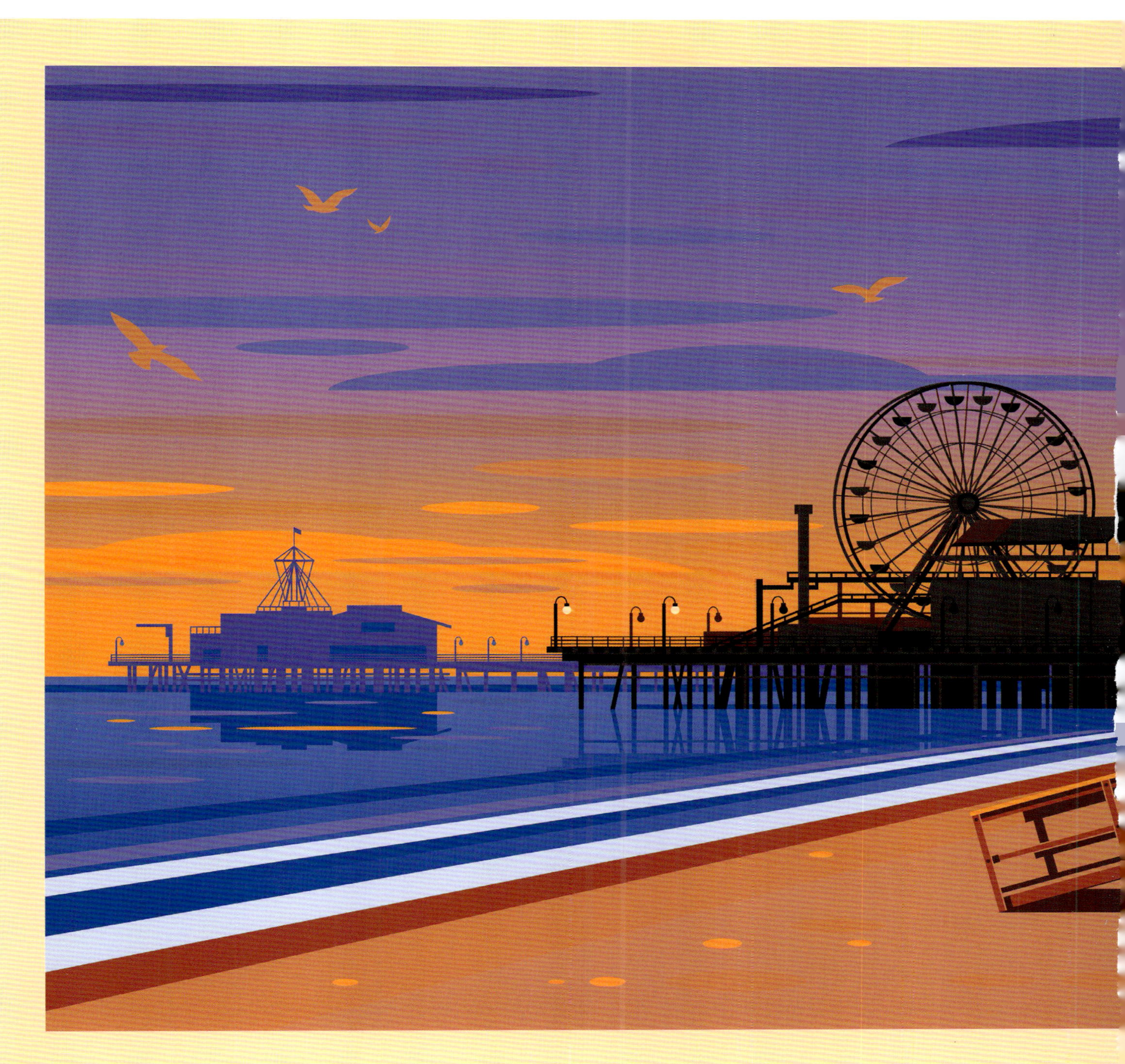

# CAPITOL RECORDS BUILDING

ADDRESS
1750 Vine St.
Los Angeles, CA
90028

ARCHITECT(S)
Louis Naidorf

YEAR
1956



**The Capitol Records Building is instantly recognisable** with its distinctive design that mimics a stack of records on a turntable. It's not just a pretty building, it's steeped in musical history, housing the offices of some of the world's most famous record labels.

Fun fact: When completed, it became the world's first circular office building.

Another fun fact: The light atop the tower blinks "Hollywood" in Morse code, a charming nod to the city it calls home.

And another fun fact: The building's design was a happy accident. The architect claimed he wasn't aiming to make it look like a stack of records, but the resemblance became an unforgettable hallmark.

ACROSS

*Capitol Records (Orange Sunset)*
Limited Edition
2019

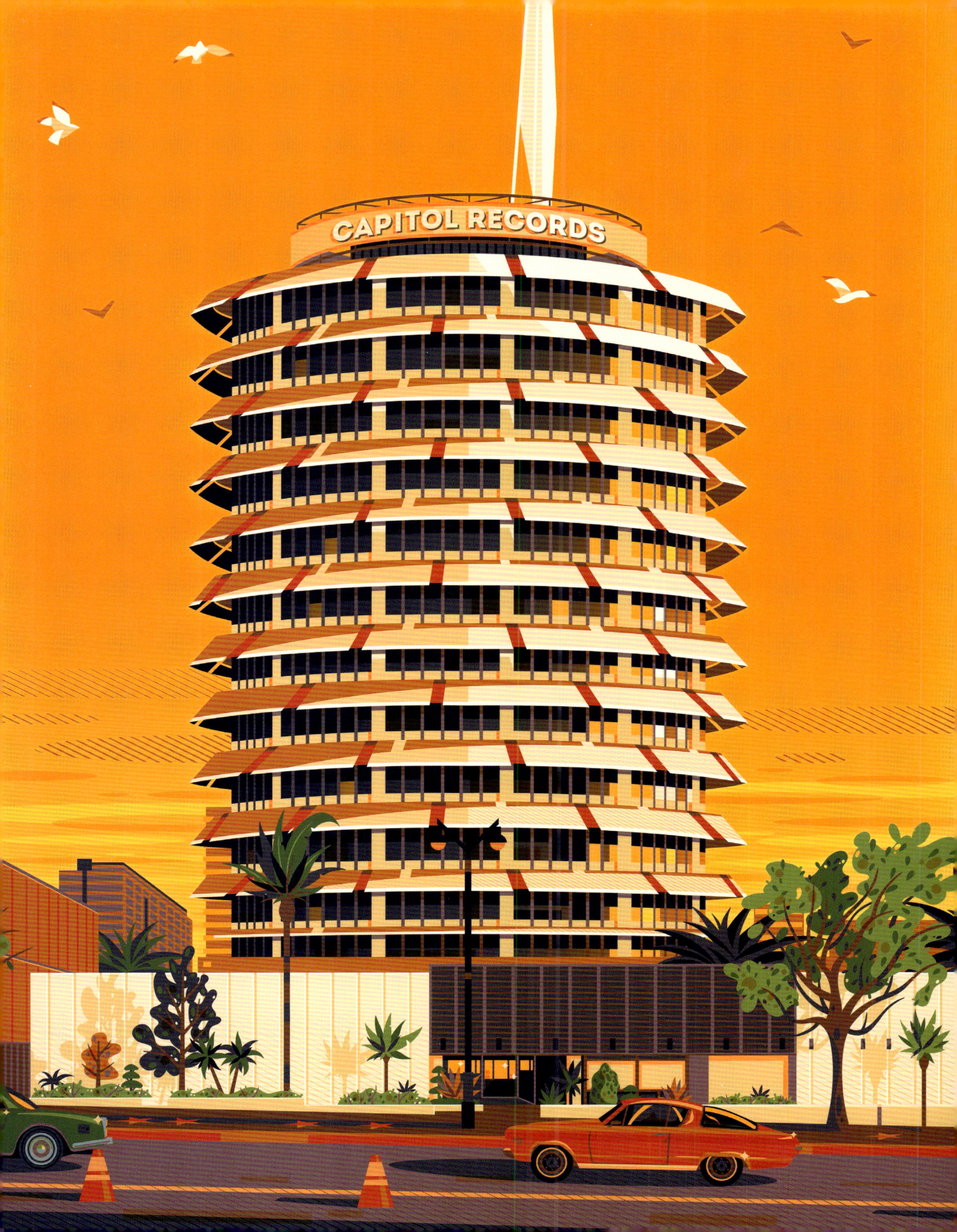
CAPITOL RECORDS

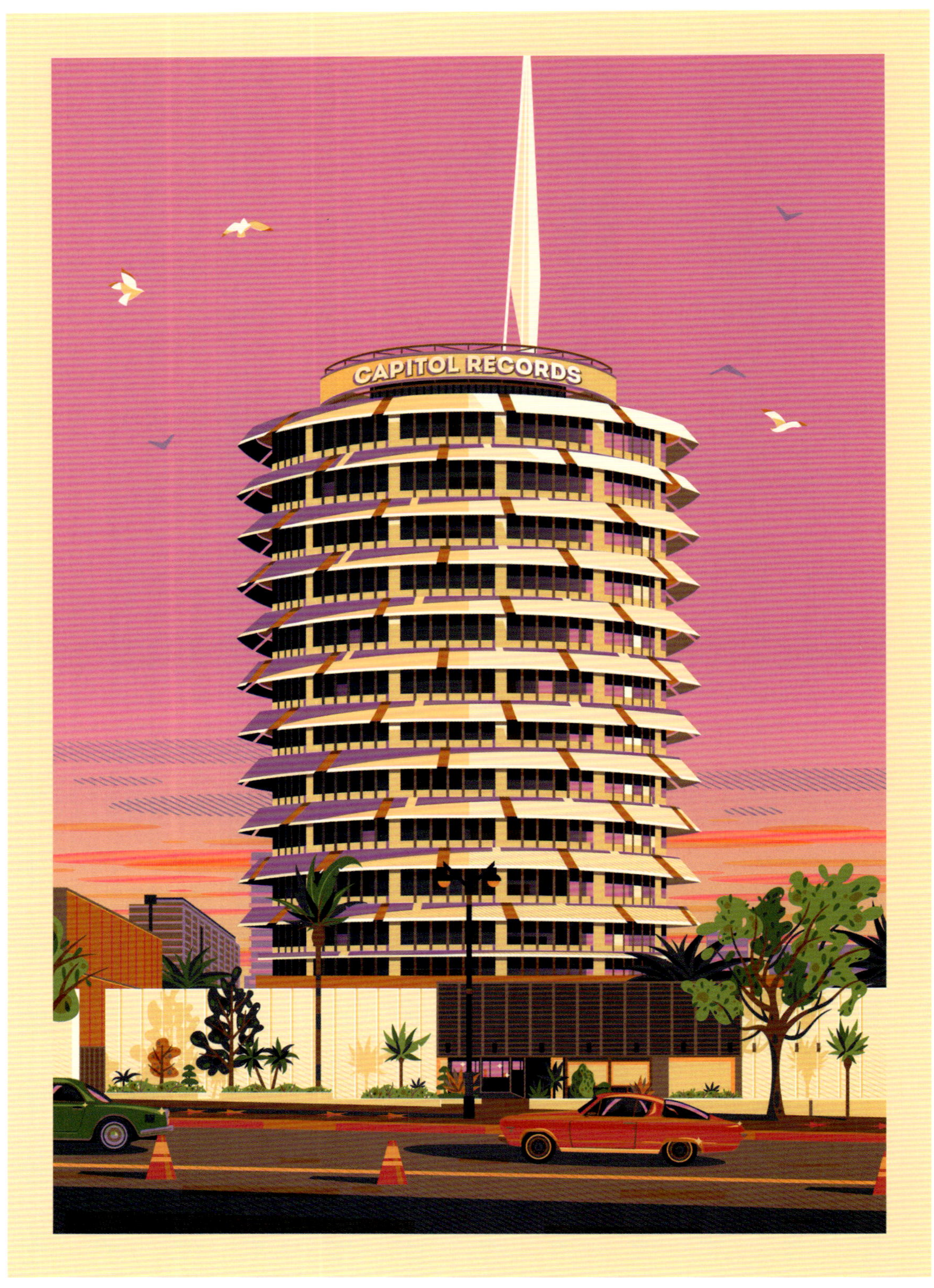


ABOVE

*Capitol Records (Purple Sunset)*
Open Edition
2019

ACROSS

*Capitol Records*

Open Edition
2019

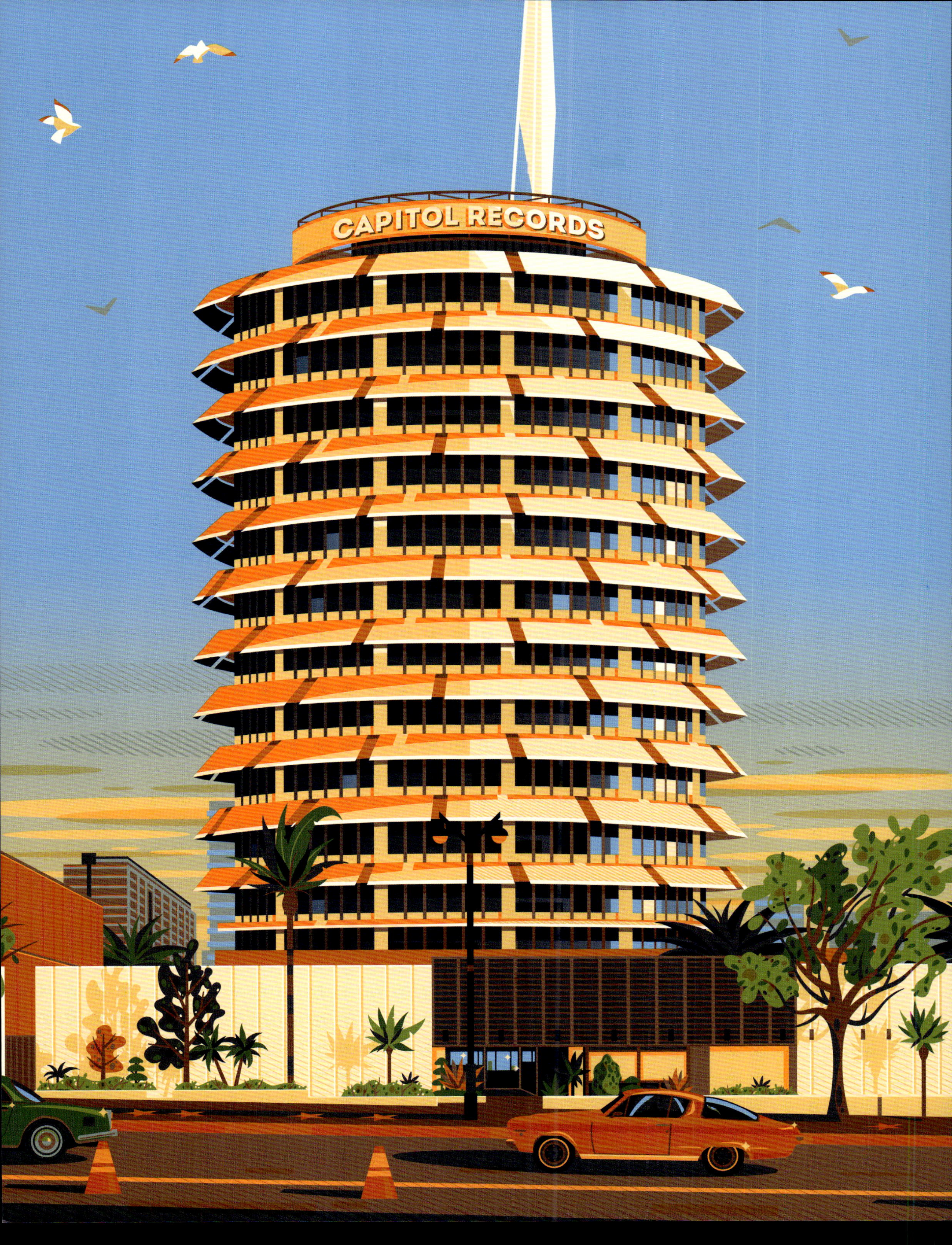
CAPITOL RECORDS

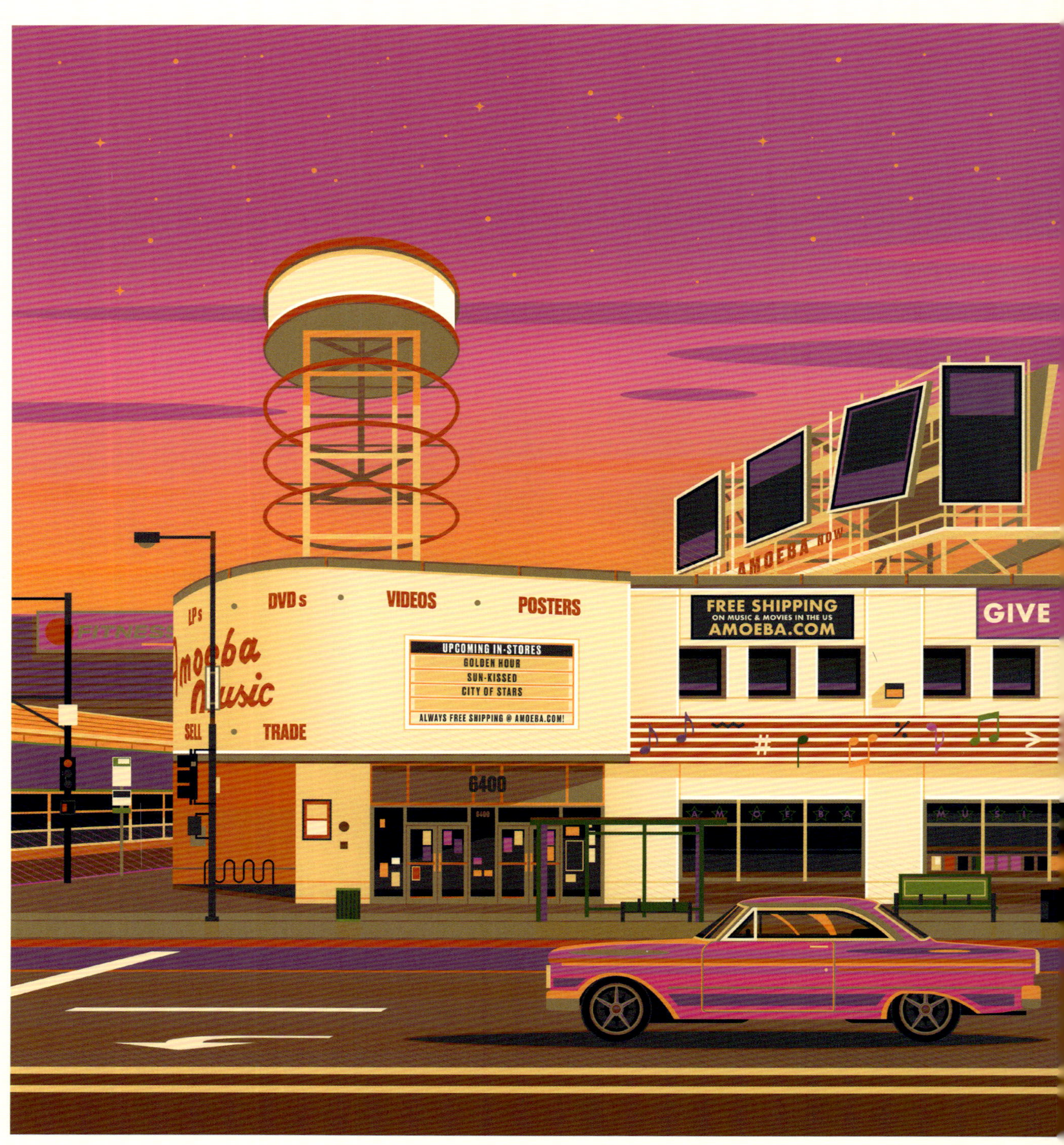
LPs
DVDs
VIDEOS
POSTERS
Amoeba Music
SELL
TRADE
UPCOMING IN-STORES
GOLDEN HOUR
SUN-KISSED
CITY OF STARS
ALWAYS FREE SHIPPING @ AMOEBA.COM!
FREE SHIPPING
ON MUSIC & MOVIES IN THE US
AMOEBA.COM
GIVE
AMOEBA NOW
6400
A M O E B A

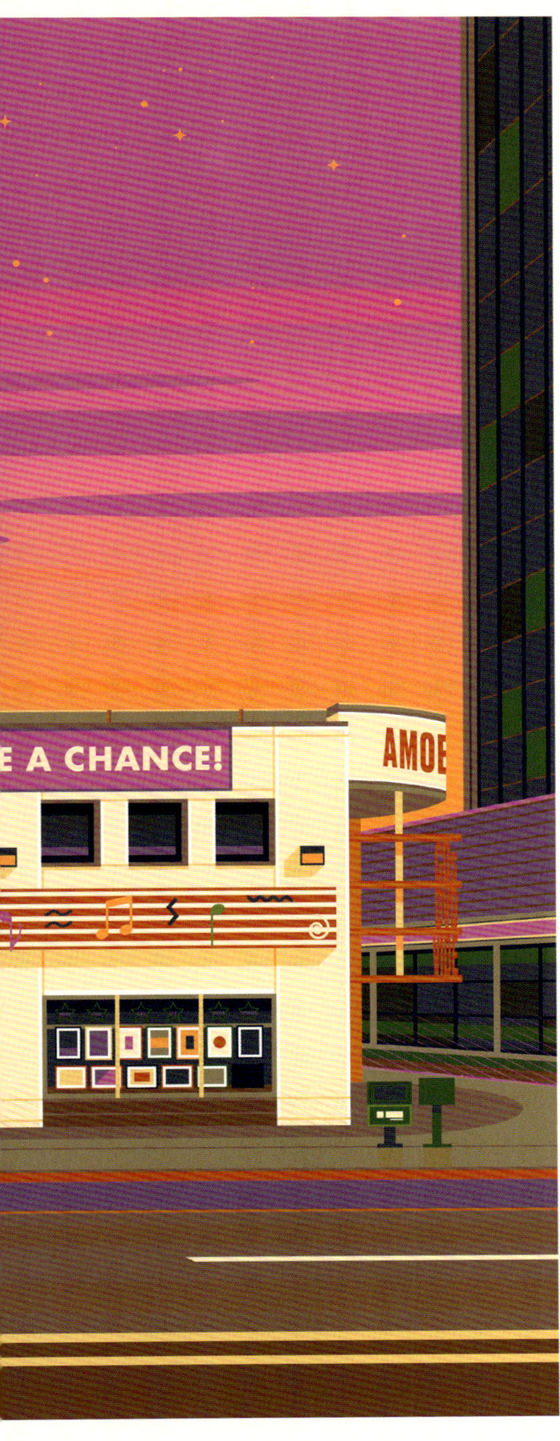


# AMOEBA MUSIC

| ADDRESS | ARCHITECT(S) | YEAR |
| --- | --- | --- |
| 6400 Sunset Blvd.<br>Los Angeles, CA<br>90028 | N/A | 1980 |



ACROSS

*Amoeba Music*
Open Edition
2021

# THE WILTERN

| ADDRESS | ARCHITECT(S) | YEAR |
|---|---|---|
| 3790 Wilshire Blvd.<br>Los Angeles, CA<br>90010 | Stiles Clements,<br>G. Albert Lansburgh | 1931 |



**My rendition of The Wiltern** was a late addition to my fifth annual art show. I nearly didn't finish it in time, but after a few late nights I got it completed the day of the deadline.

I'm thrilled that it came to fruition as the very first day I shared it online, the owner of The Wiltern reached out to express his love for the print. He even requested custom pieces for himself, his family, and his friends, offering VIP treatment at a show of my choice in return.

It makes me wonder how many other failed projects of mine would have had similar results if given a second chance.

ACROSS

*The Wiltern*
Limited Edition
2024

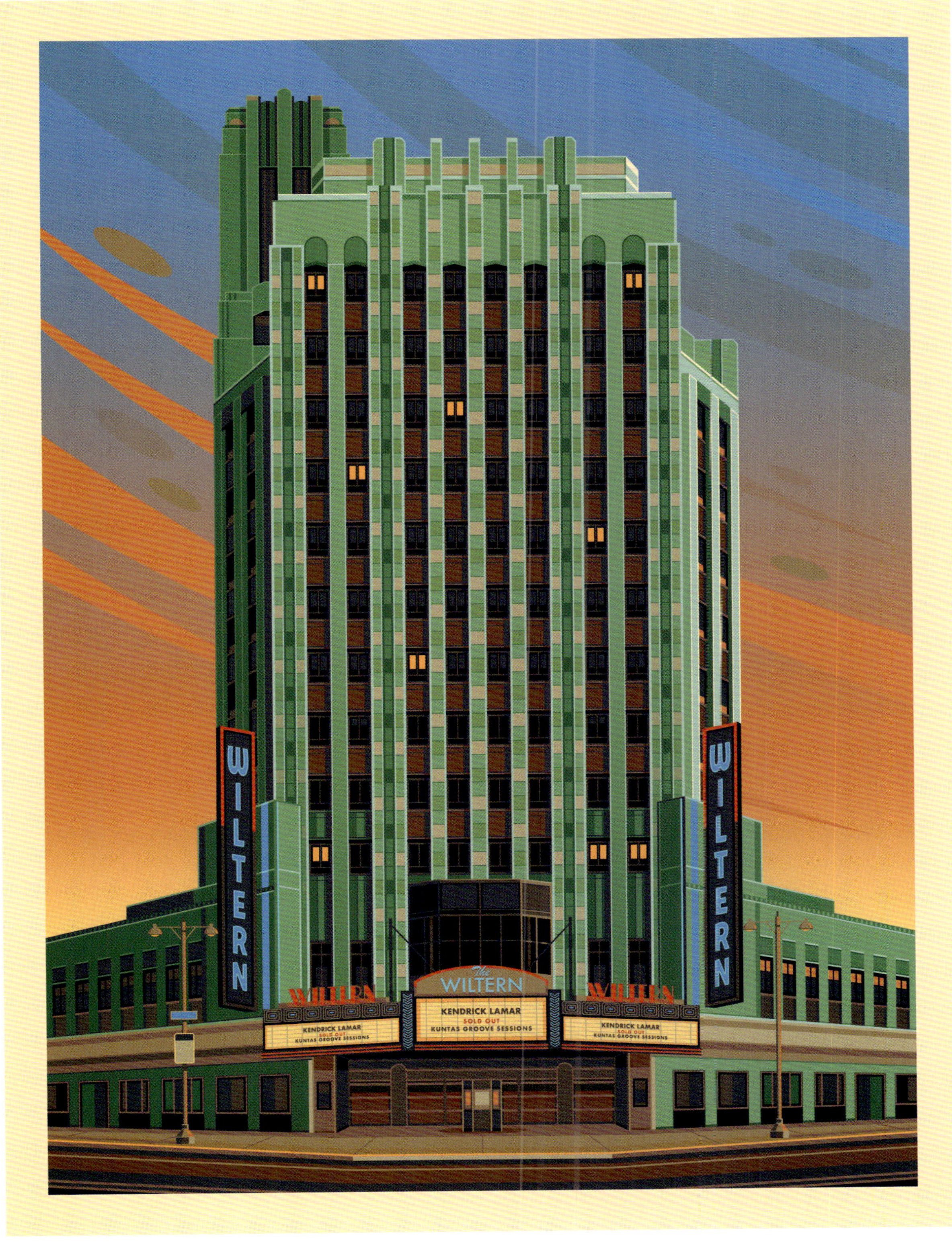
WILTERN
The WILTERN
KENDRICK LAMAR
SOLD OUT
KUNTAS GROOVE SESSIONS
WILTERN

# ROYCE HALL

| ADDRESS | ARCHITECT(S) | YEAR |
|---|---|---|
| 340 Royce Dr.<br>Los Angeles, CA<br>90095 | Allison & Allison | 1929 |



ACROSS

*Royce Hall*
Open Edition
2023

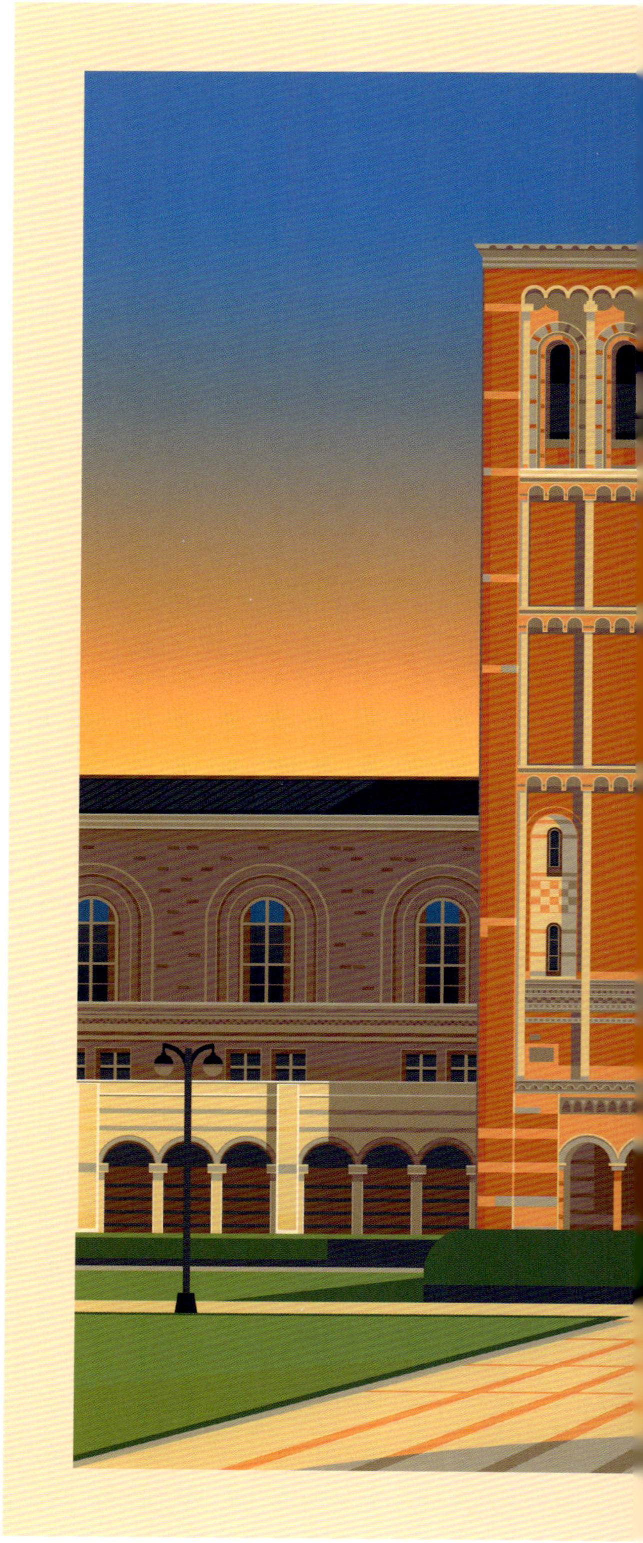

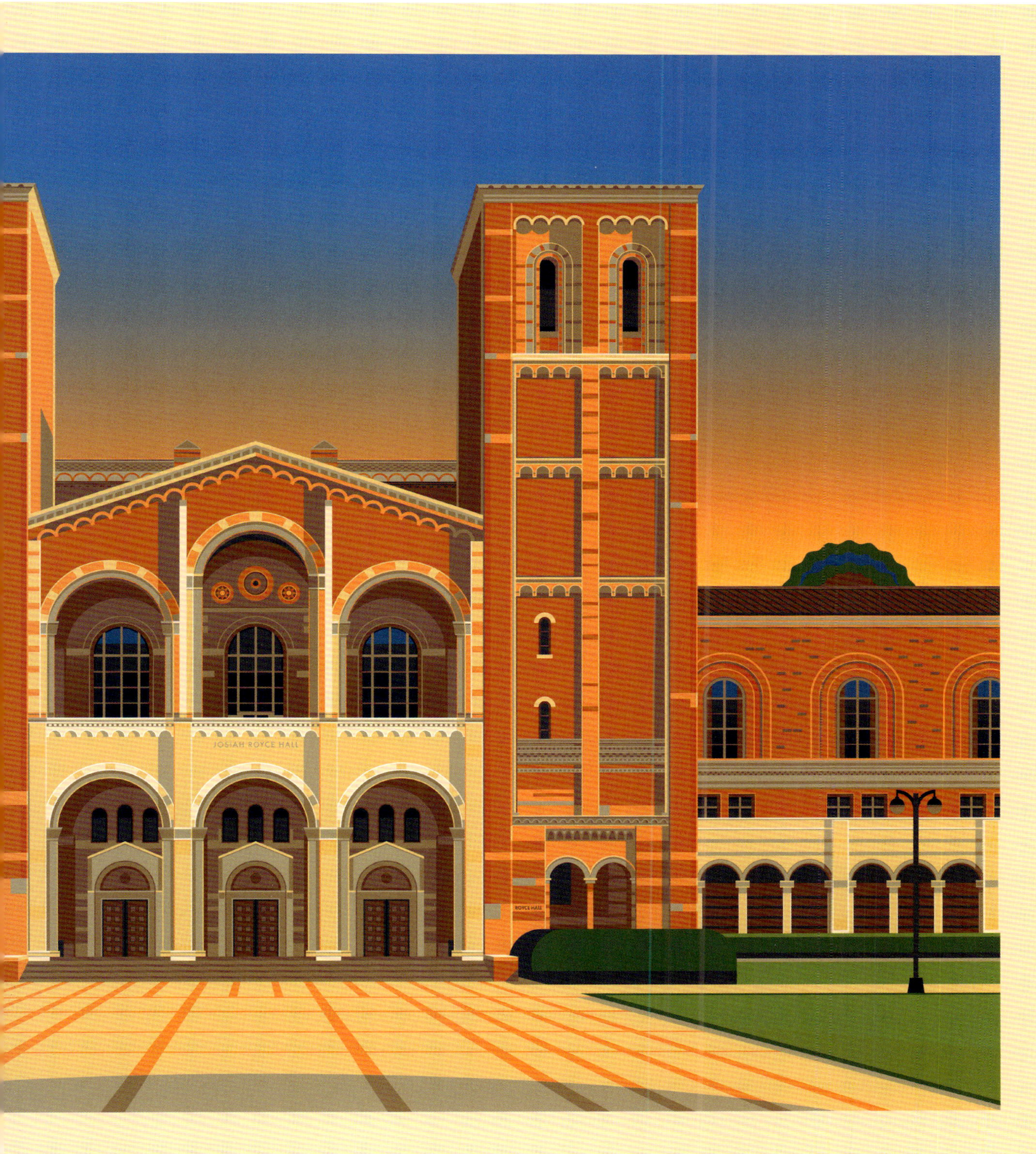
JOSIAH ROYCE HALL
ROYCE HALL

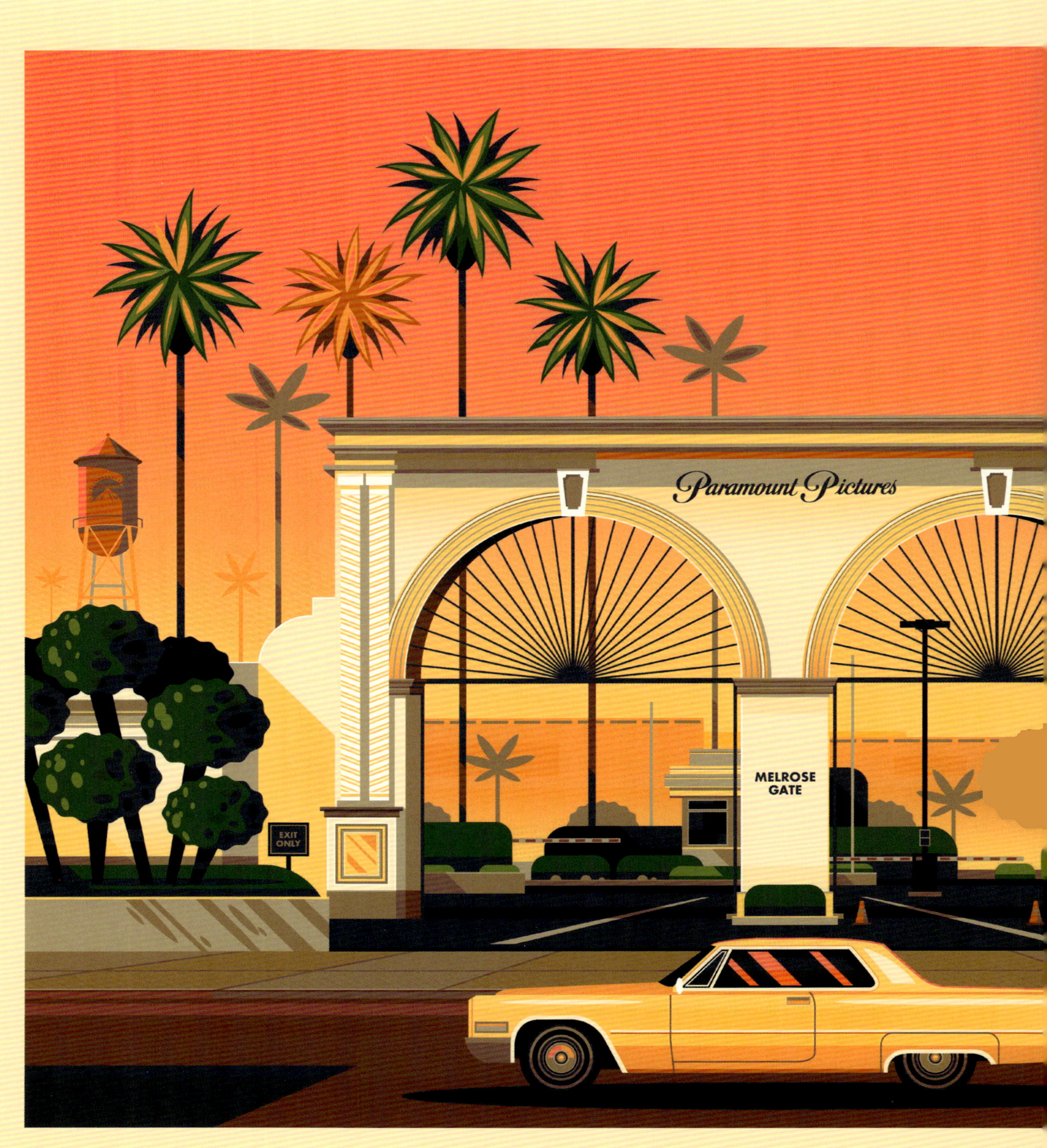
Paramount Pictures
MELROSE GATE
EXIT ONLY

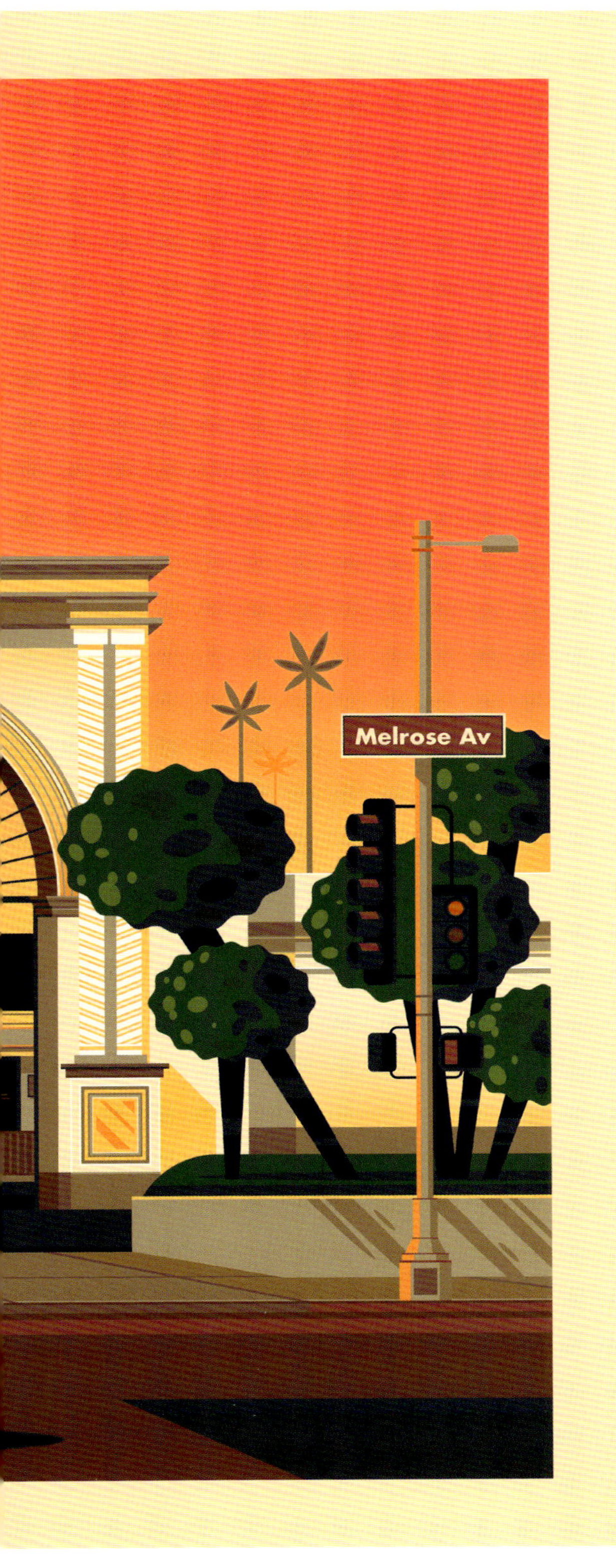


# PARAMOUNT PICTURES GATE

| ADDRESS | ARCHITECT(S) | YEAR |
|---|---|---|
| 5515 Melrose Ave.<br>Los Angeles, CA<br>90038 | N/A | 1926 |



ACROSS

*Paramount Pictures Gate*
Limited Edition
2022

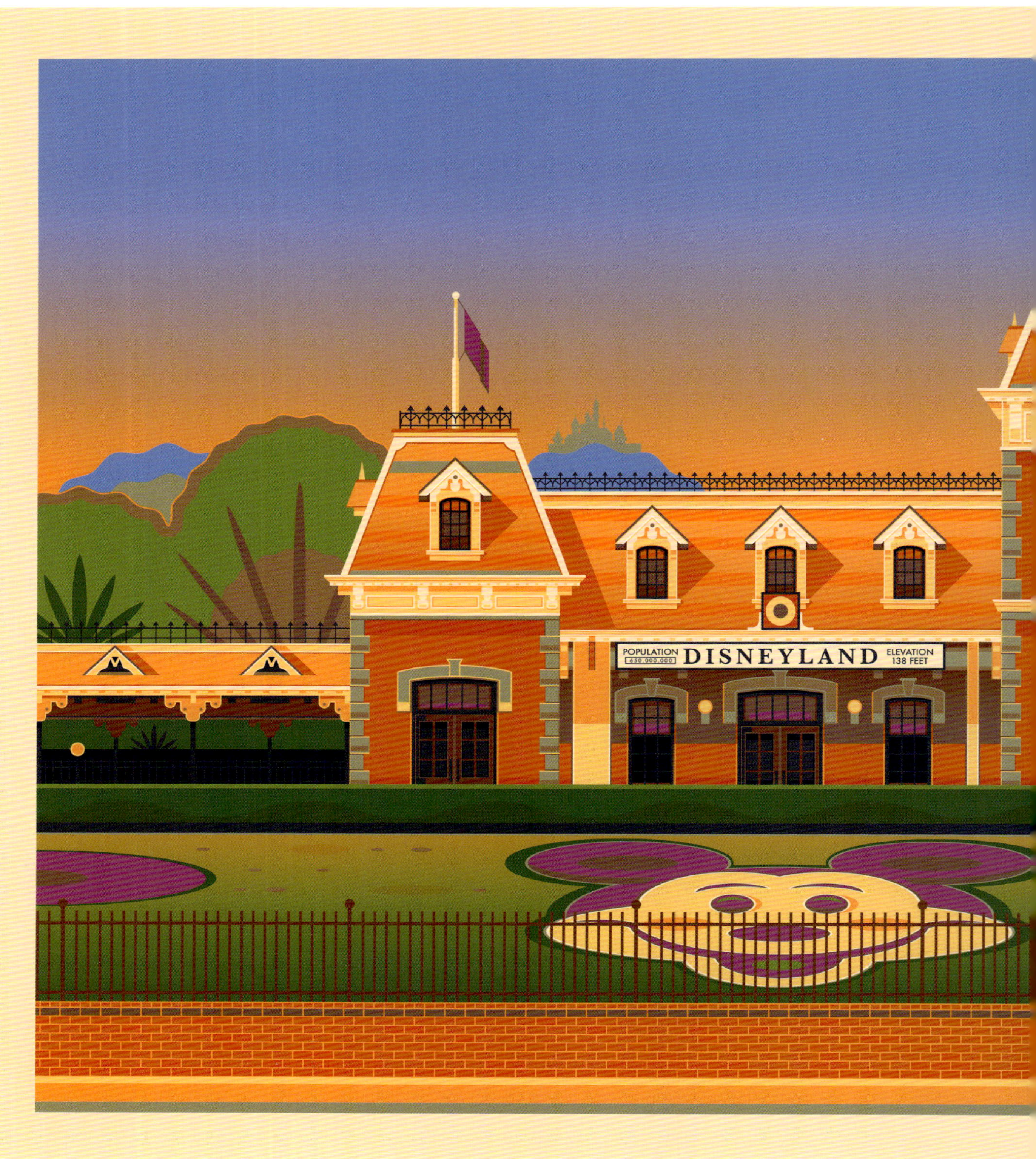
POPULATION 650,000,000
DISNEYLAND
ELEVATION 138 FEET

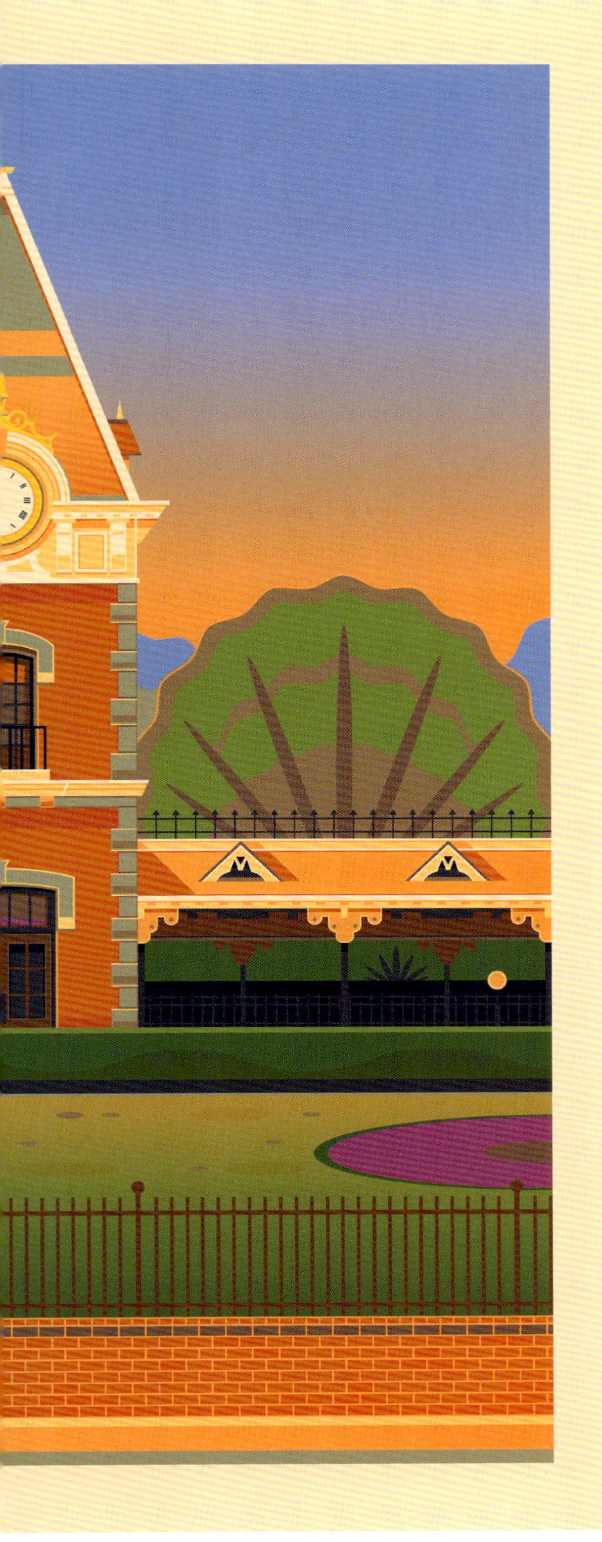

# DISNEYLAND PARK

| ADDRESS | ARCHITECT(S) | YEAR |
|---|---|---|
| Disneyland Park<br>Anaheim, CA<br>92802 | Disney Imagineering | 1955 |



ACROSS

*Disneyland Entrance*
Open Edition
2023

# THE GEORGIAN HOTEL

| ADDRESS | ARCHITECT(S) | YEAR |
|---|---|---|
| 1415 Ocean Ave.<br>Santa Monica, CA<br>90401 | M. Eugene Durfee | 1931 |



**The Georgian Hotel in Santa Monica** is a true Art Deco gem. Its bold turquoise facade and elegant design harken back to Hollywood's golden age, making it a favourite spot for both locals and tourists alike.

Funny story: When I shared this print on Instagram, I mentioned in the caption that the hotel is often referred to as "the most haunted hotel in America." The hotel's own account was quick to jump into the comments, firmly denying the rumour and assuring me there's no supernatural activity—which, let's be honest, is exactly what a haunted hotel *would* say.

ACROSS

*The Georgian Hotel*
Limited Edition
2021

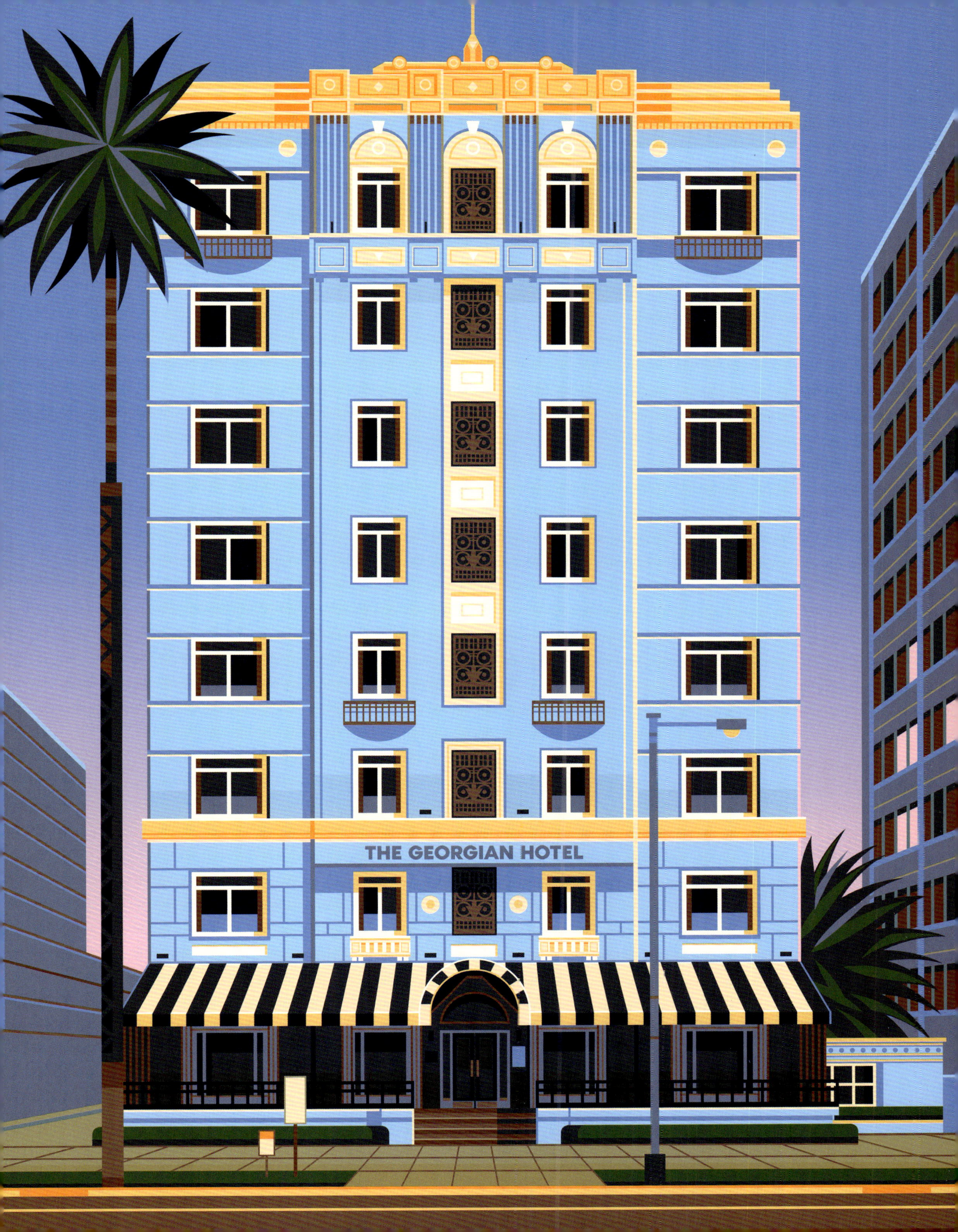
THE GEORGIAN HOTEL

# THE BEVERLY HILLS HOTEL

| ADDRESS | ARCHITECT(S) | YEAR |
|---|---|---|
| 9641 Sunset Blvd.<br>Beverly Hills, CA<br>90210 | Elmer Grey | 1912 |



ACROSS

*The Beverly Hills Hotel*
Limited Edition
2024

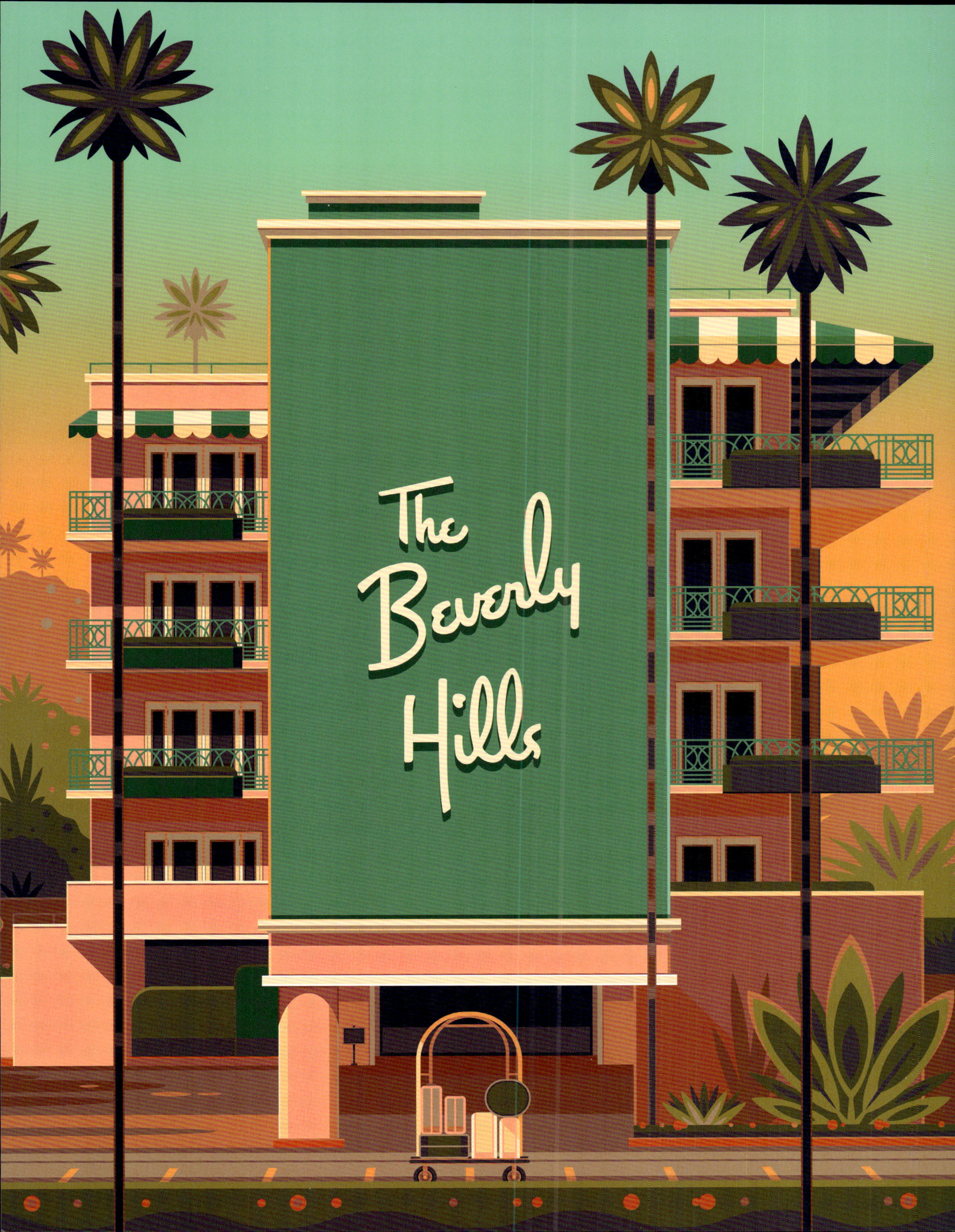
The Beverly Hills

# SAFARI INN

ADDRESS
1911 W Olive Ave.
Burbank, CA
91506

ARCHITECT(S)
Beausoleil Architects
(Remodeled)

YEAR
1955



ACROSS

*Safari Inn*
Limited Edition
2023

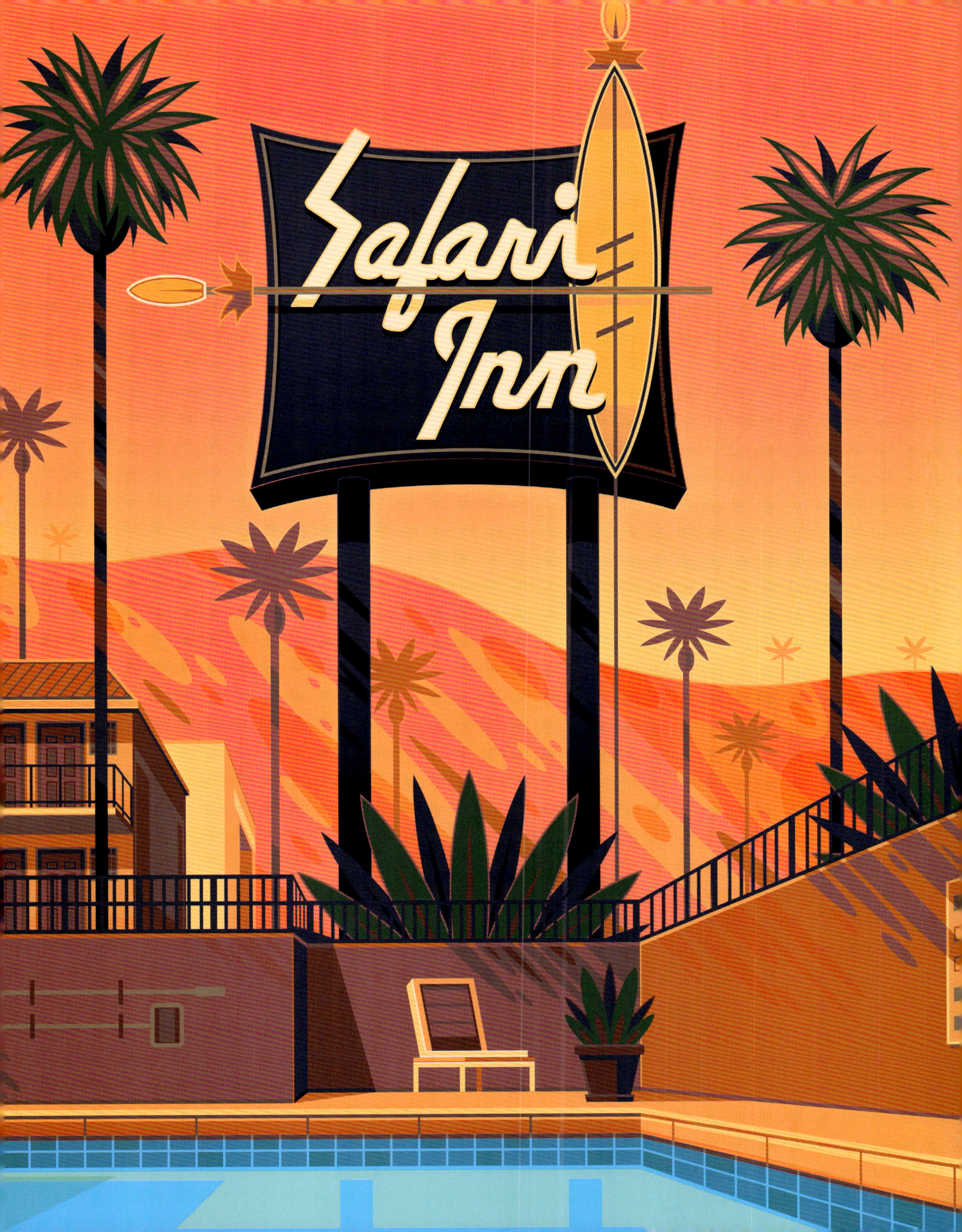
Safari
Inn

# PARKER CENTER

| ADDRESS | ARCHITECT(S) | YEAR |
|---|---|---|
| 100 W 1st St.<br>Los Angeles, CA<br>90012 | Welton Becket<br>J. E. Stanton | 1955 |



ACROSS

*Parker Center (Detail)*
Open Edition
2018

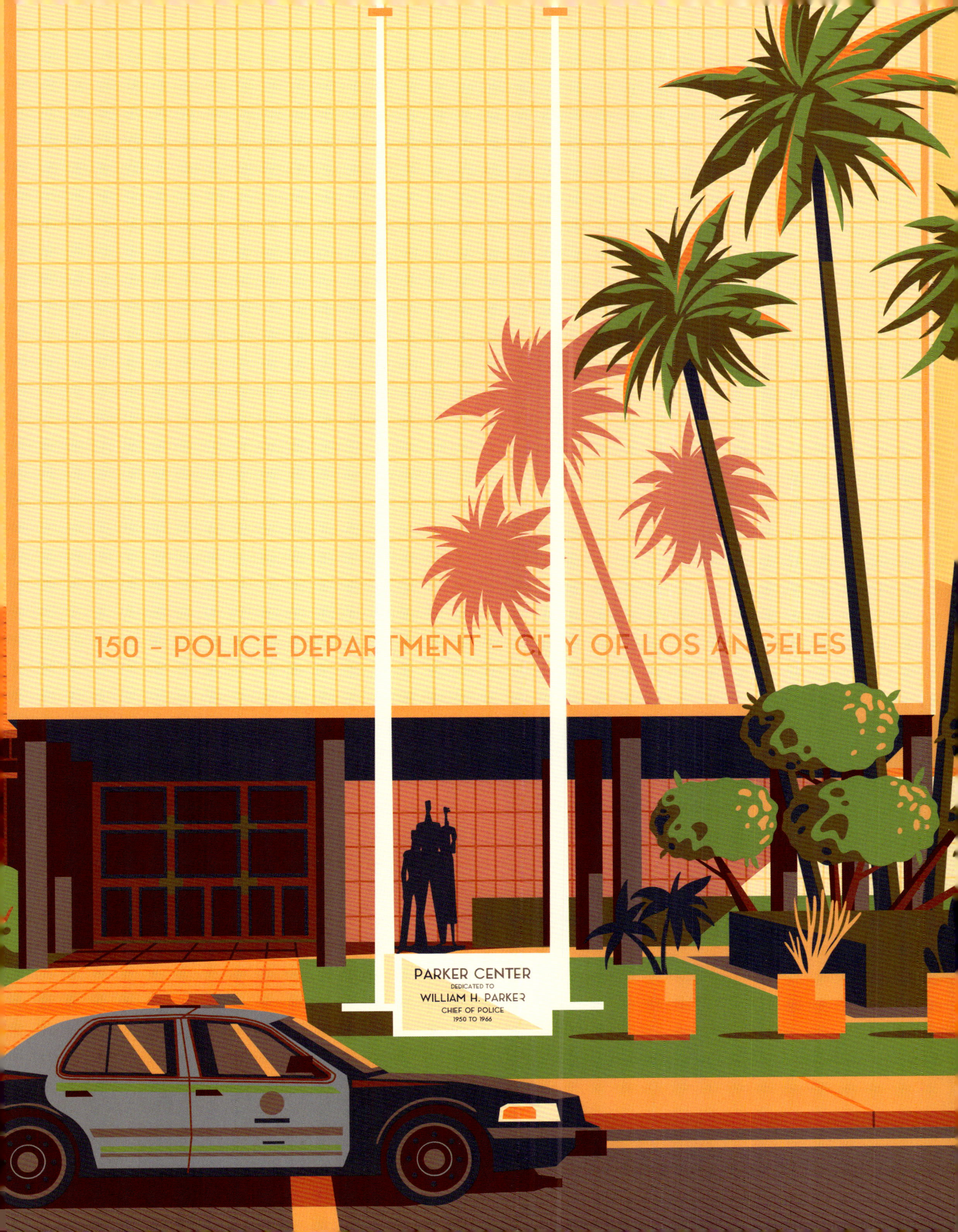
PARKER CENTER
DEDICATED TO
WILLIAM H. PARKER
CHIEF OF POLICE
1950 TO 1966

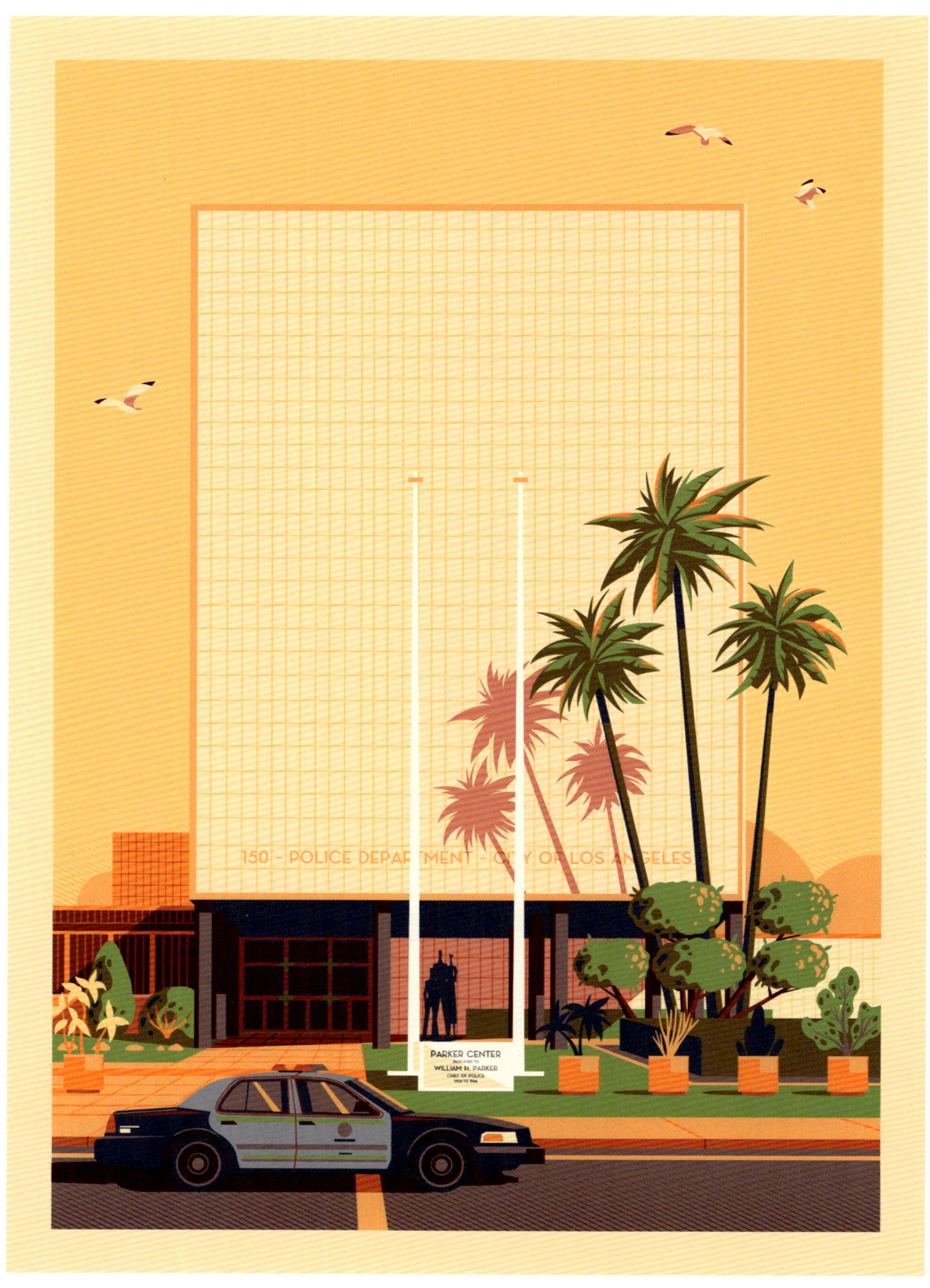


ABOVE

*Parker Center*

Open Edition
2018

ACROSS

*Parker Center (Sunset)*
Limited Edition
2018

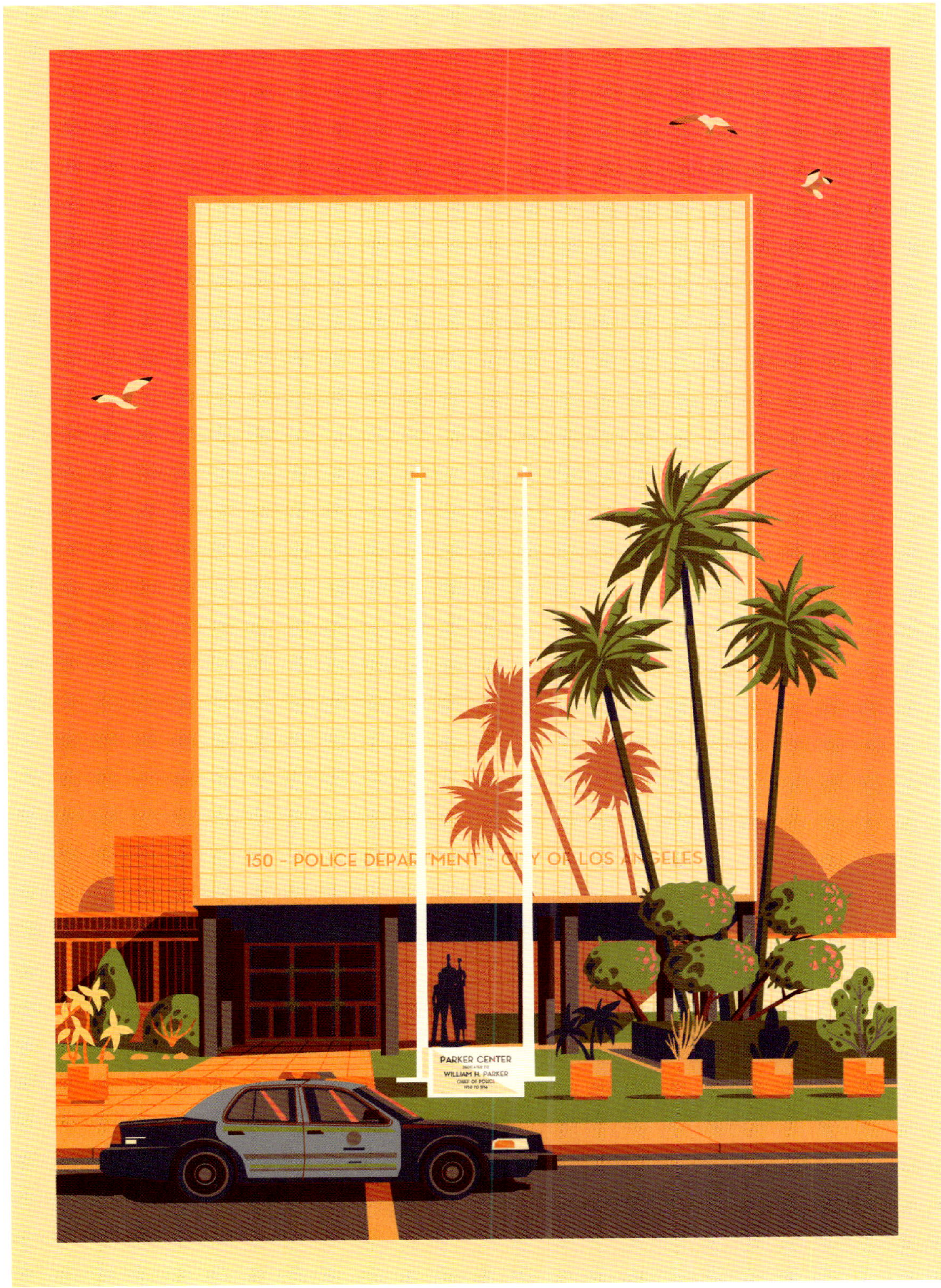
PARKER CENTER
WILLIAM H. PARKER

# SIXTH STREET BRIDGE

| ADDRESS | ARCHITECT(S) | YEAR |
| --- | --- | --- |
| E 6th St.<br>Los Angeles, CA<br>90013 | Merrill Butler, Louis L. Huot,<br>Louis Blume | 1932 |



ACROSS

*Sixth Street Bridge*
Open Edition
2018

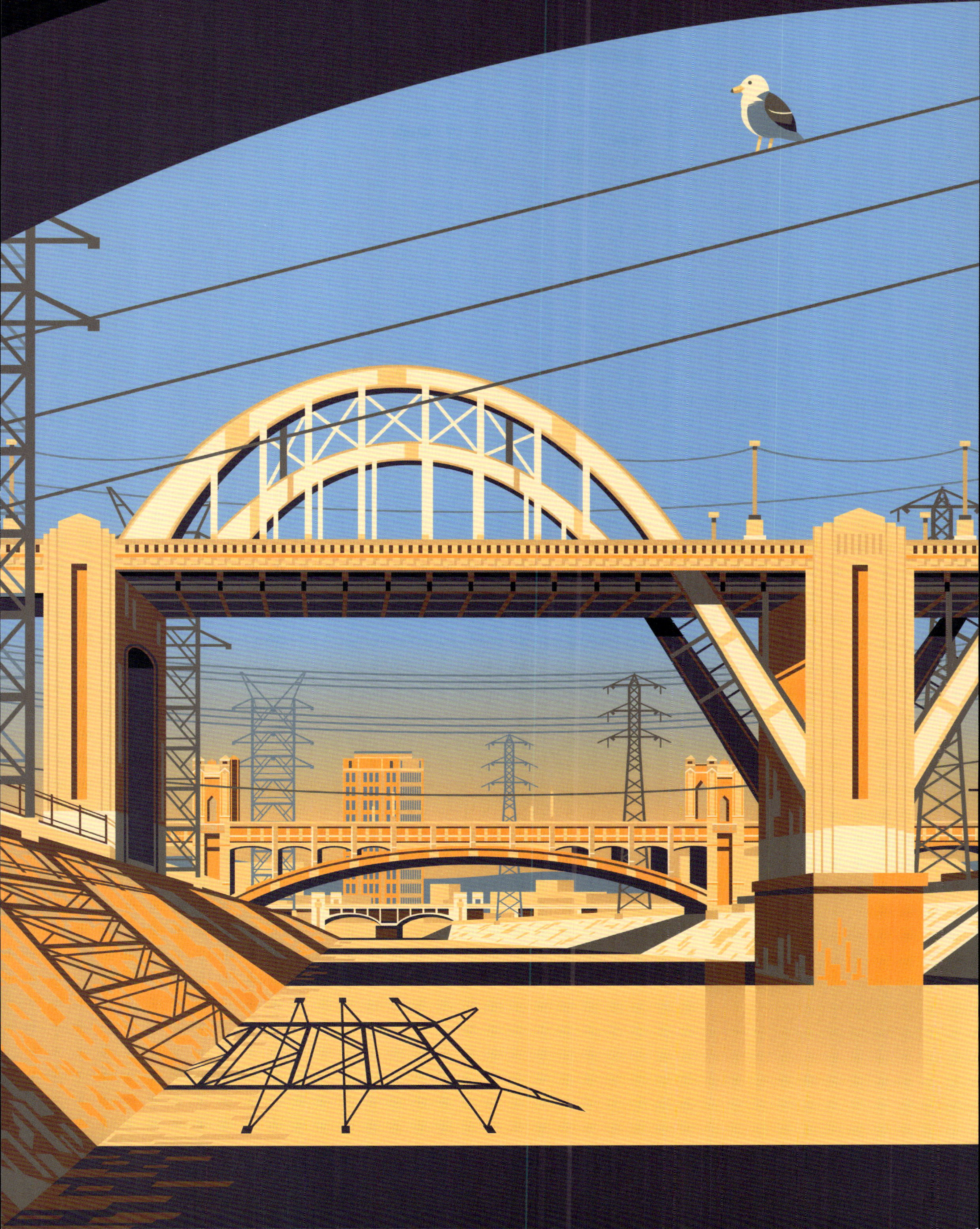

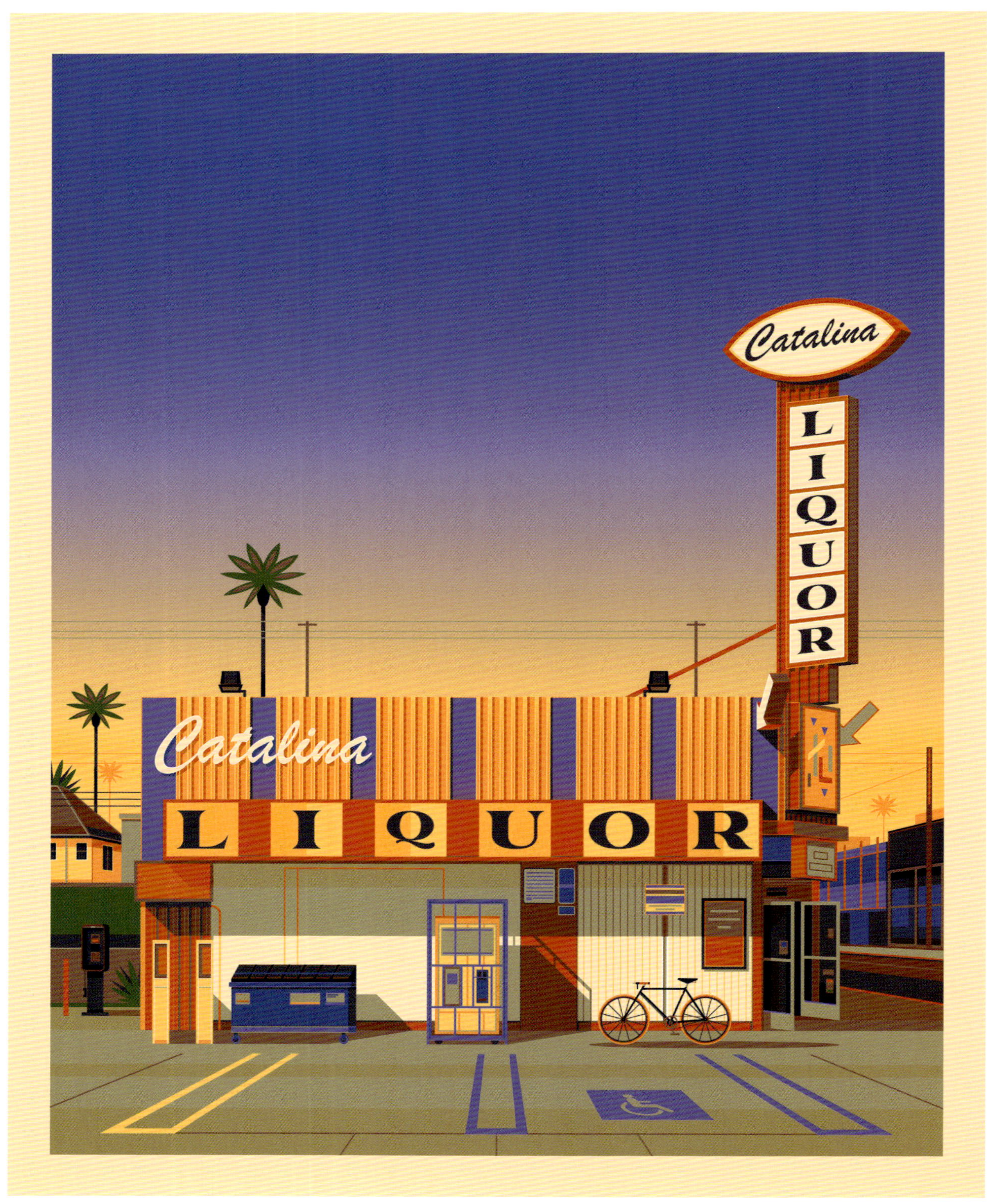


ABOVE

*Catalina Liquor*

Open Edition
2023

ACROSS

*Catalina Liquor (Sunset)*
Limited Edition
2023

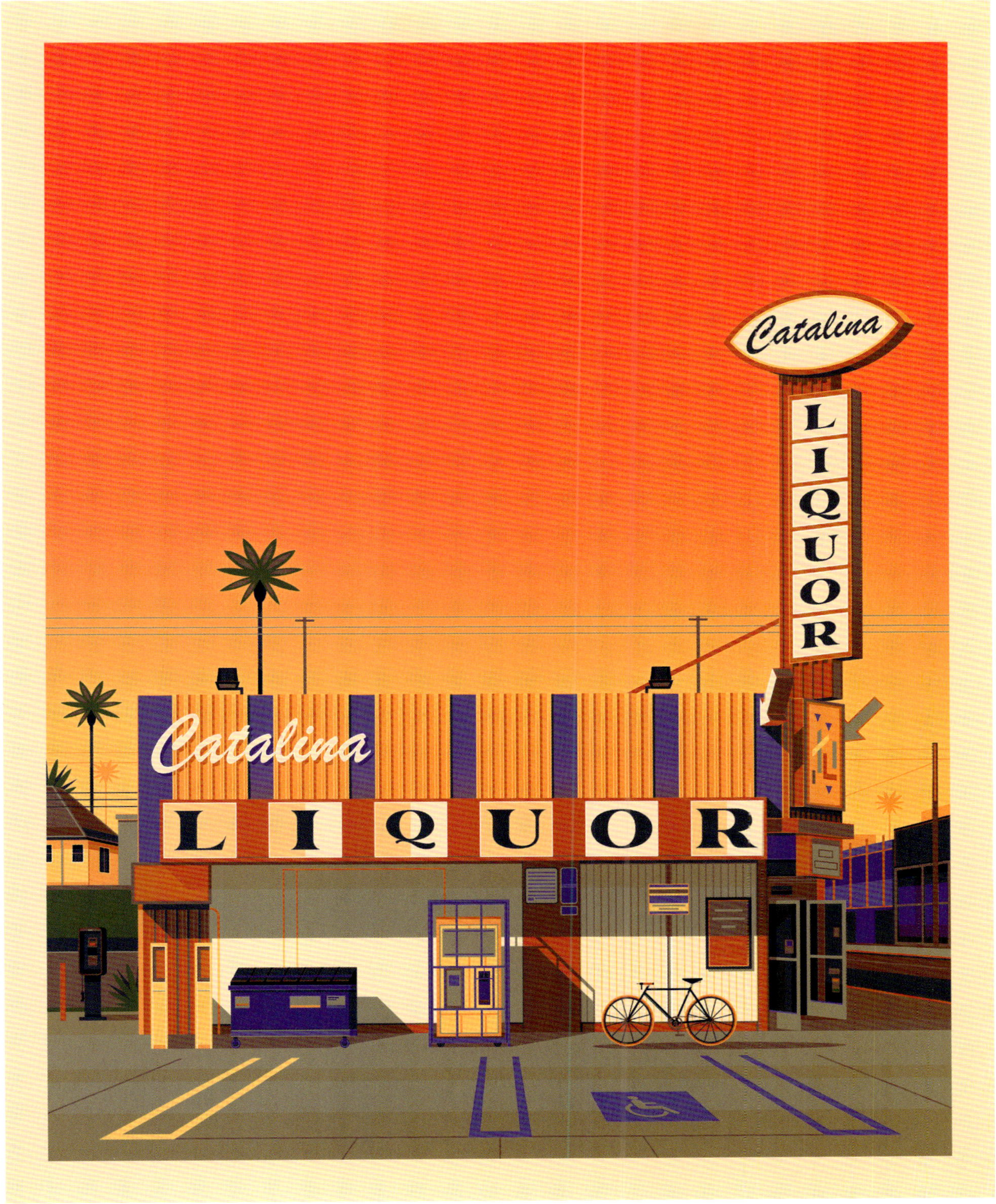

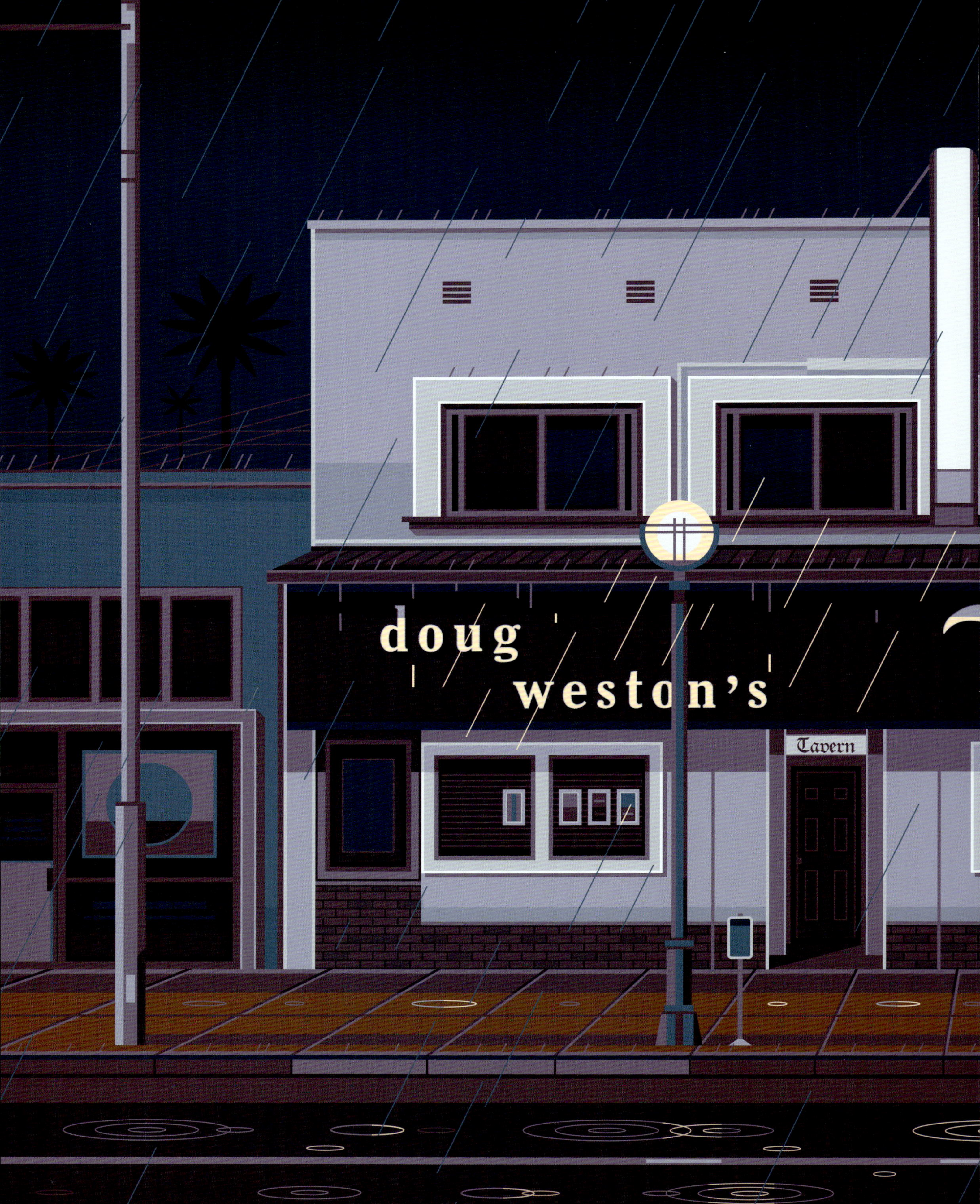
doug
weston's
Tavern

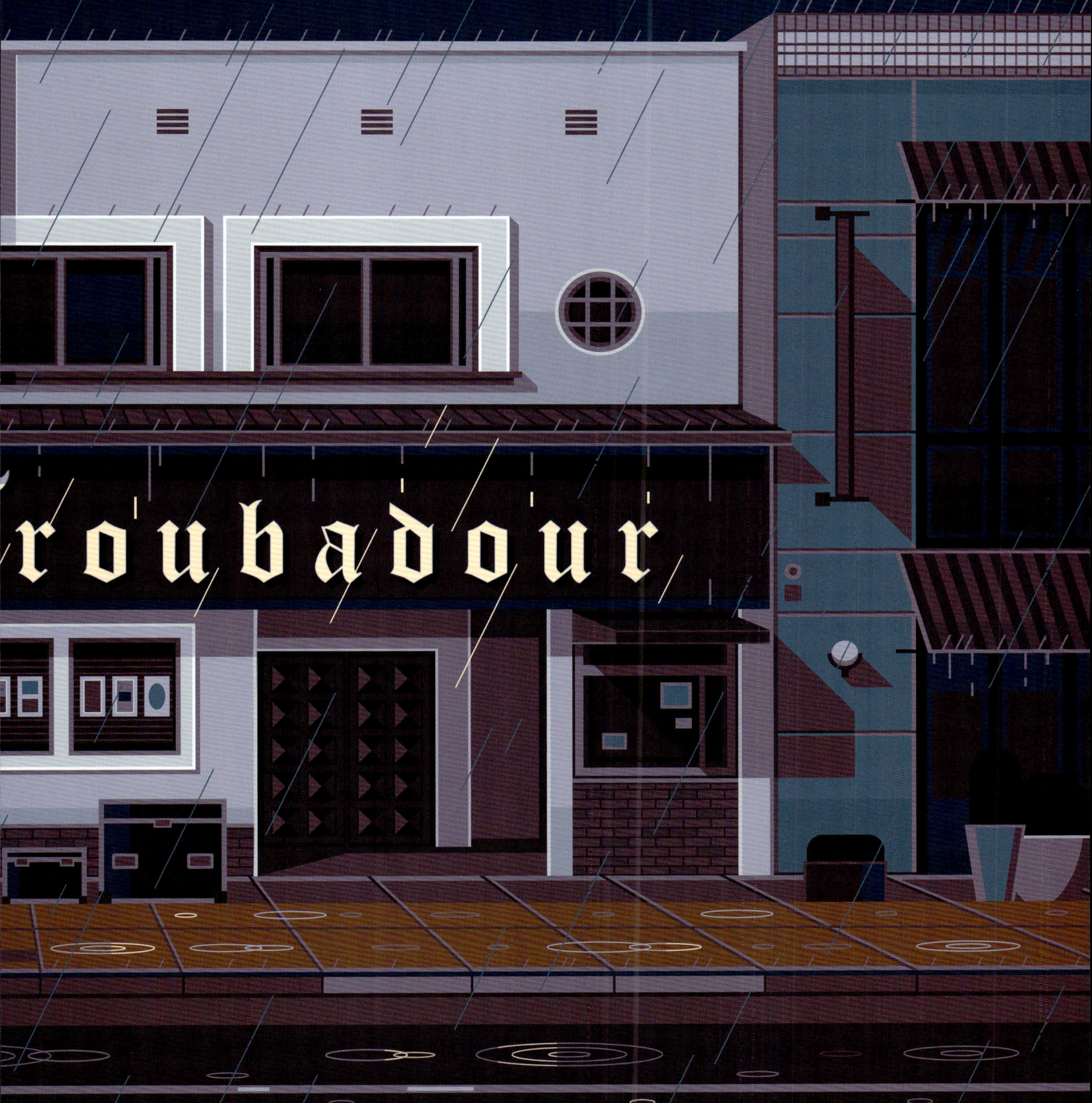
roubadour

# DOUG WESTON'S TROUBADOUR

| ADDRESS | ARCHITECT(S) | YEAR |
|---|---|---|
| 9081 N Santa Monica Blvd.<br>West Hollywood, CA<br>90069 | N/A | 1957 |



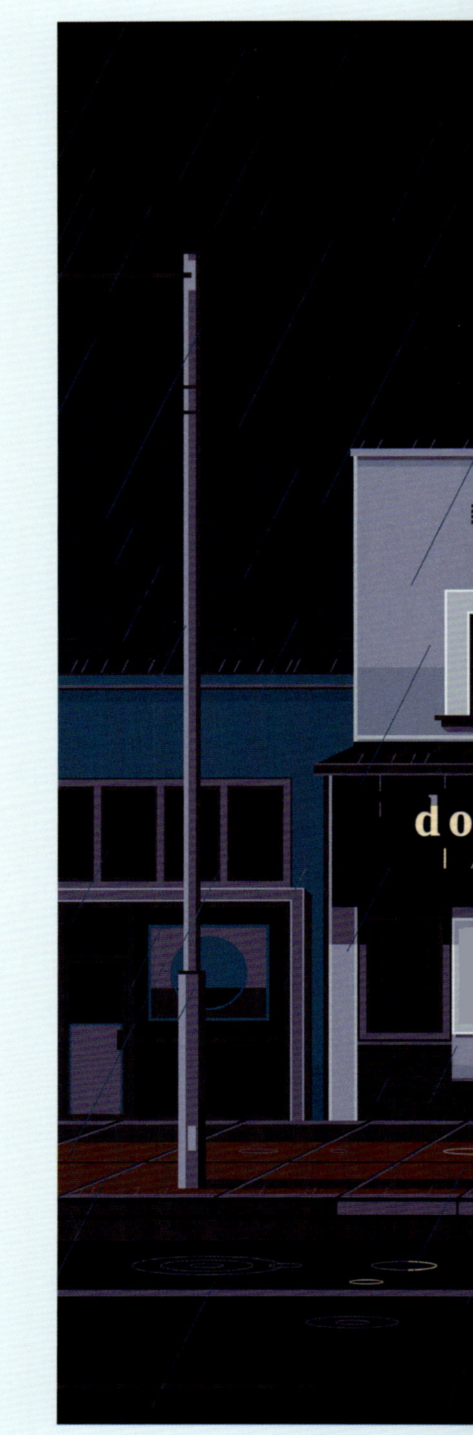

**You can't talk about the Troubadour without** delving into the wild, untamed rock and roll culture that defined the Sunset Strip in the 1970s and '80s, a chaotic, almost lawless era where anything seemed possible, and excess was the norm.

The venue, which was initially opened by Doug Weston in the '50s, played a part in kickstarting so many of the careers of your favourite artists. It was here that acts like Elton John, James Taylor, and The Eagles found their footing, performing on its legendary stage before launching into global fame. Its small, unassuming space gave fans the rare opportunity to witness musical history up close, cementing the Troubadour's status as a rock and roll icon worthy of standing alongside the stars it helped create.

ACROSS

*Troubadour*
Limited Edition
2023

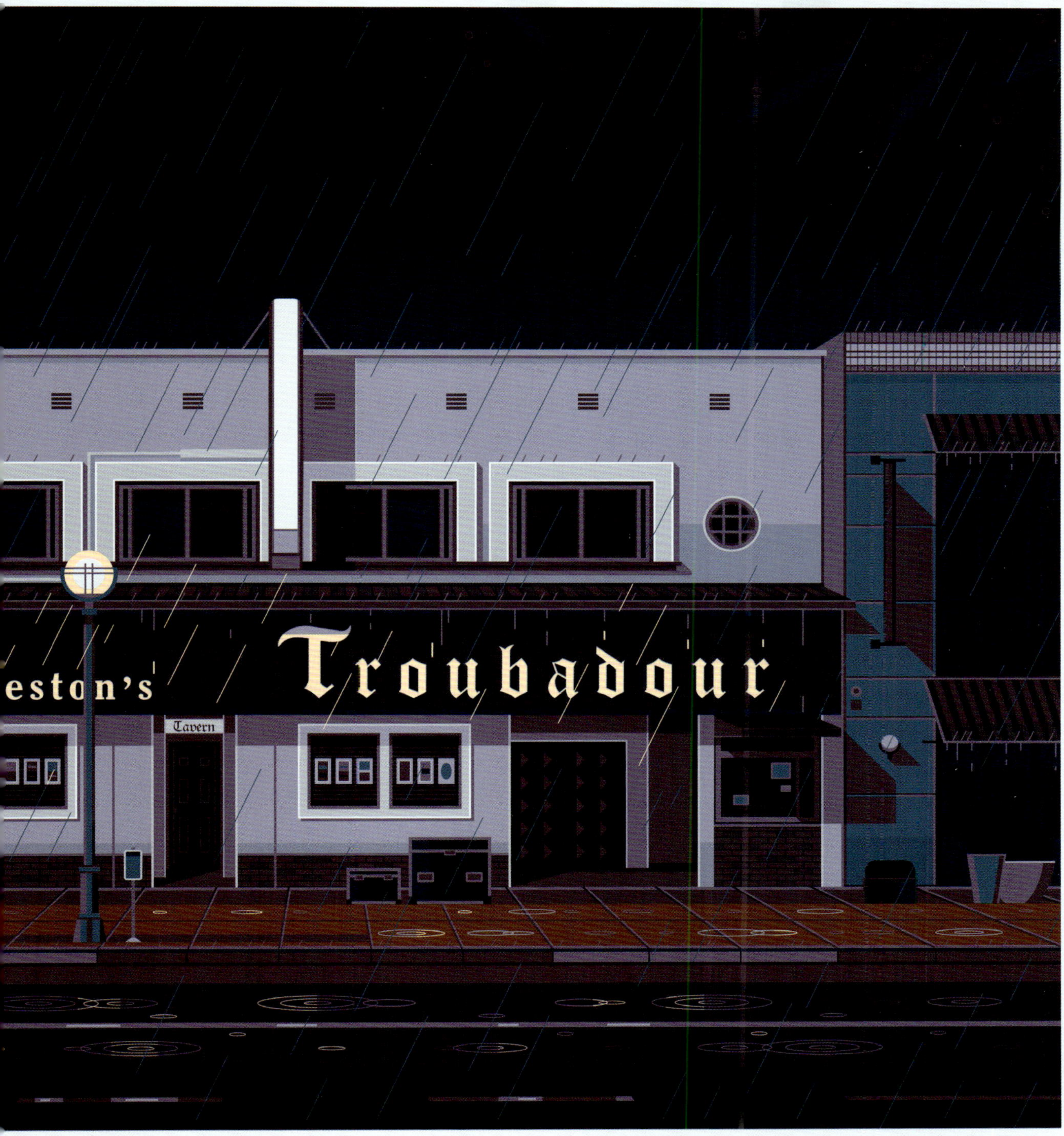

# THE VIPER ROOM

| ADDRESS | ARCHITECT(S) | YEAR |
| --- | --- | --- |
| 8852 Sunset Blvd.<br>West Hollywood, CA<br>90069 | N/A | 1993 |



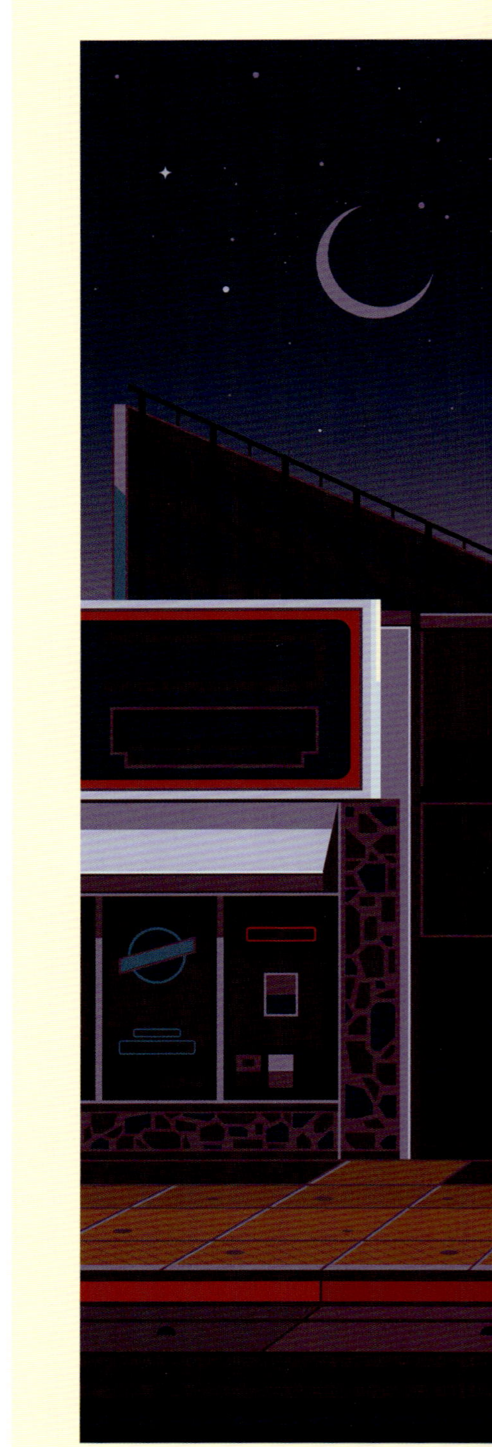

**The Viper Room holds a special connection for me.** Though I've never been inside for a show, it's forever linked to the tragic passing of River Phoenix, one of my favourite actors. Although River passed away before I was even born, his incredible body of work continues to keep his legacy alive for new generations, including myself.

I wanted this artwork to be a quiet tribute to him. The sign includes a subtle nod to his band, "Aleka's Attic", a detail that only a few eagle-eyed fans have spotted when talking about this piece.

ACROSS

*The Viper Room*
Limited Edition
2022

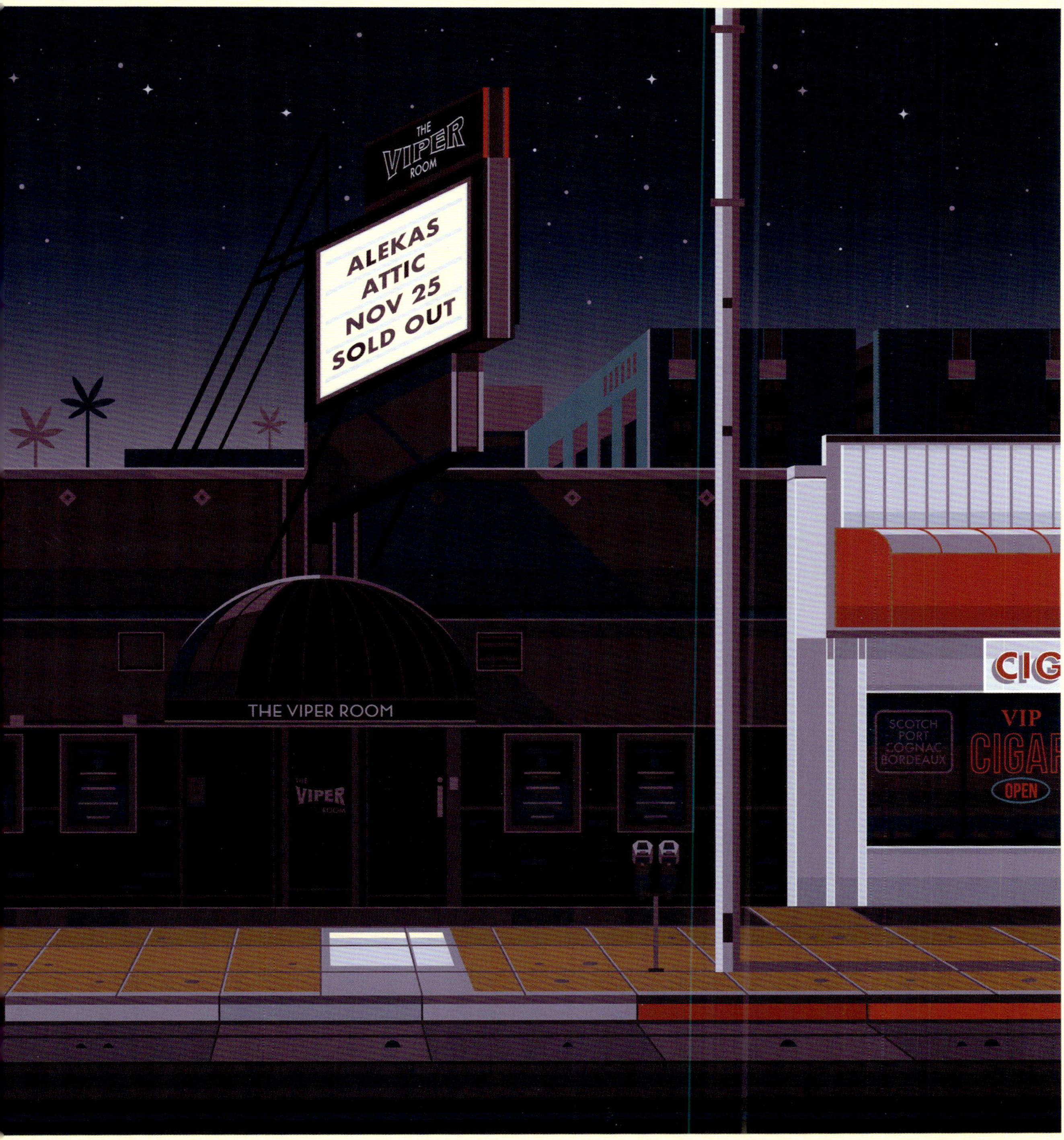

# Iconic Theaters

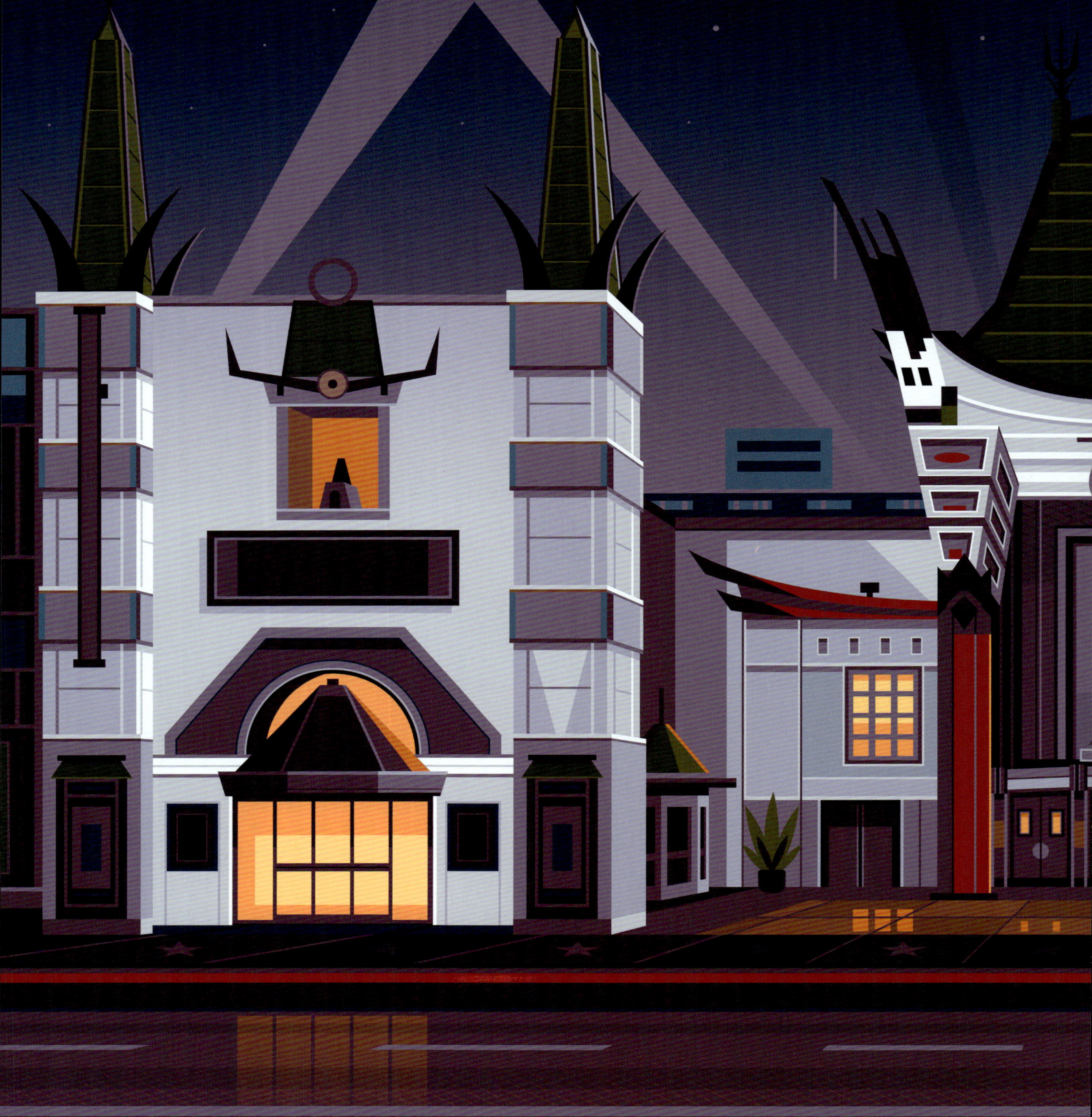

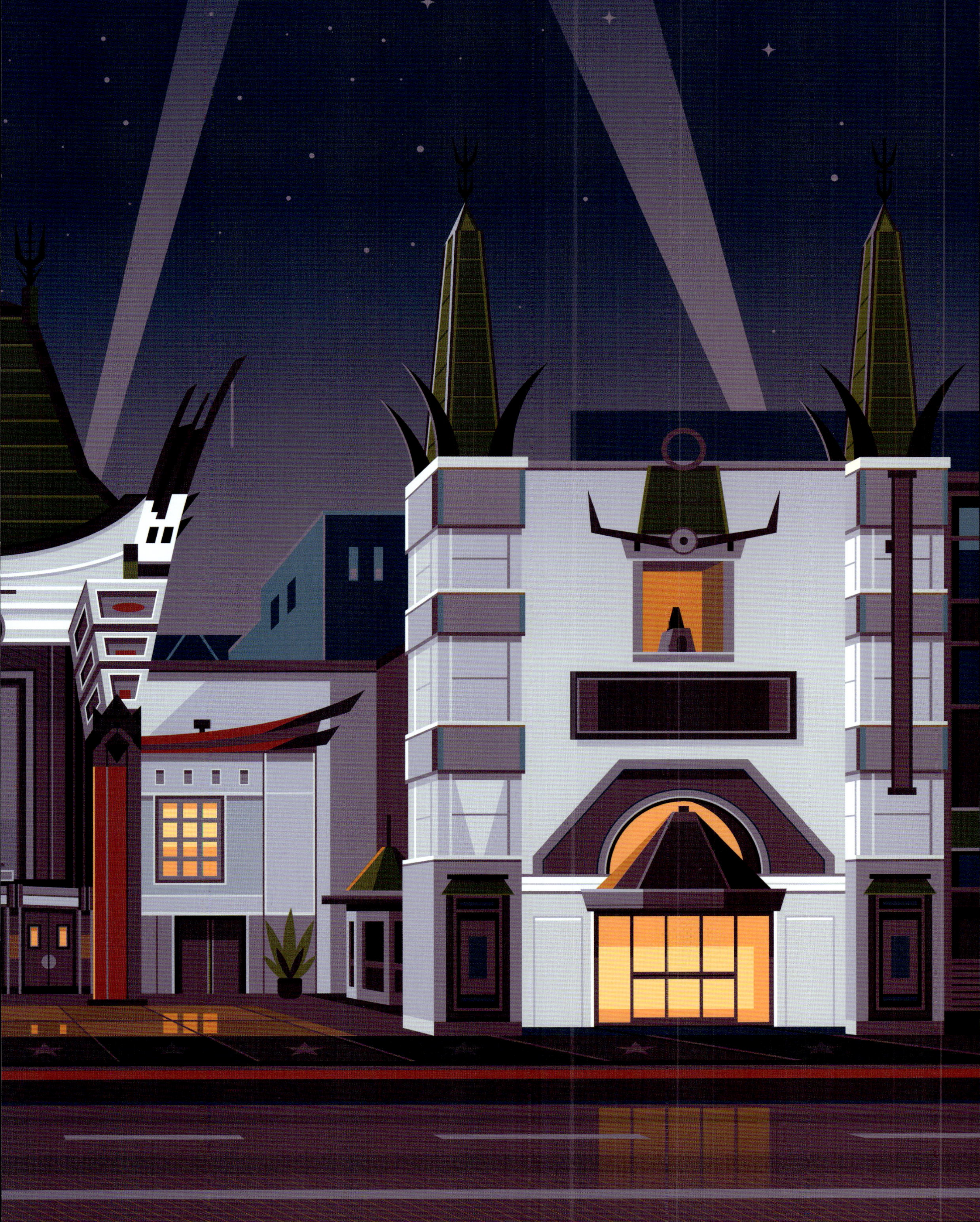

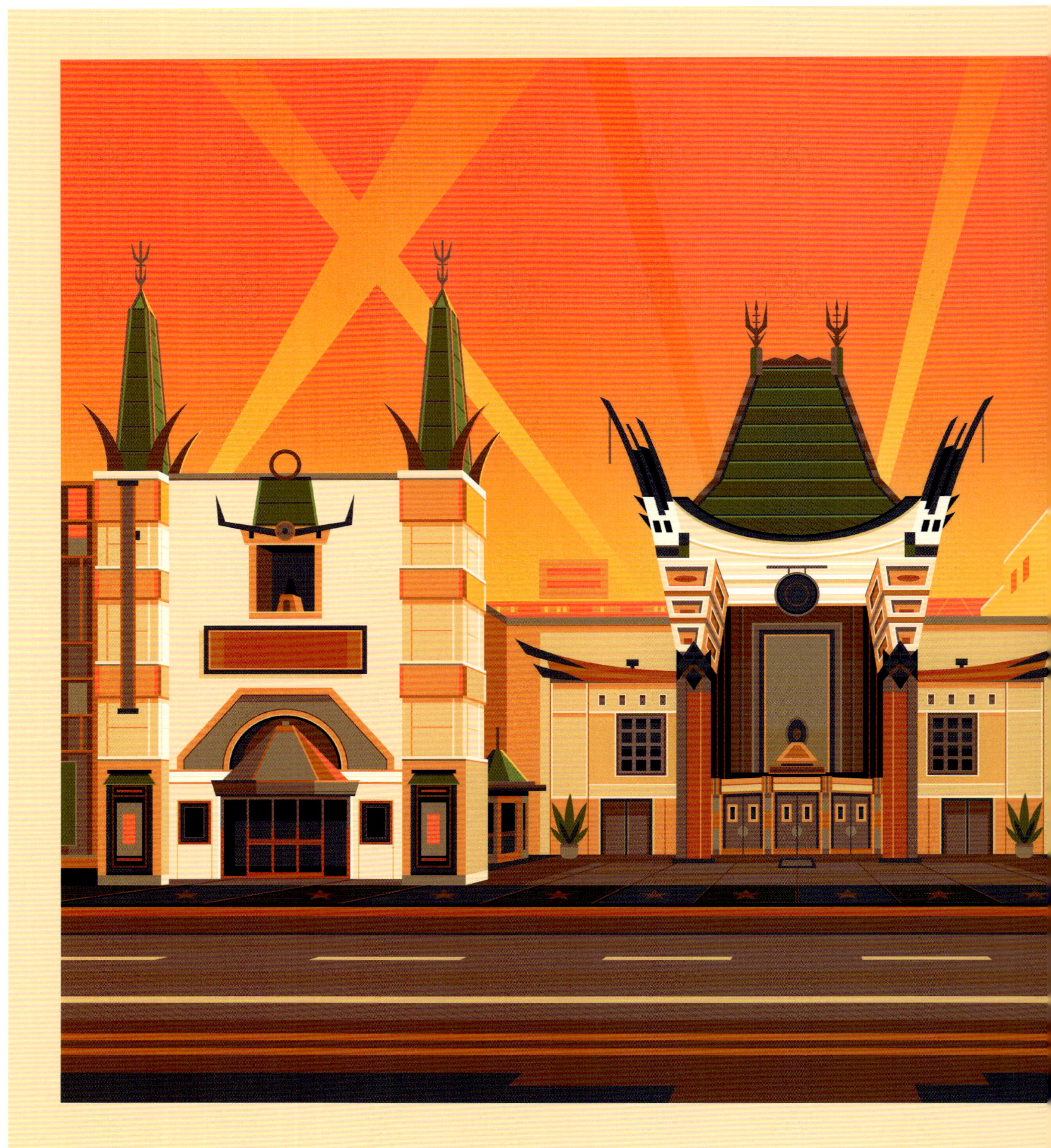

PREVIOUS SPREAD

*Chinese Theatre (Night)*
Limited Edition
2021

ABOVE

*Chinese Theatre*
Open Edition
2021

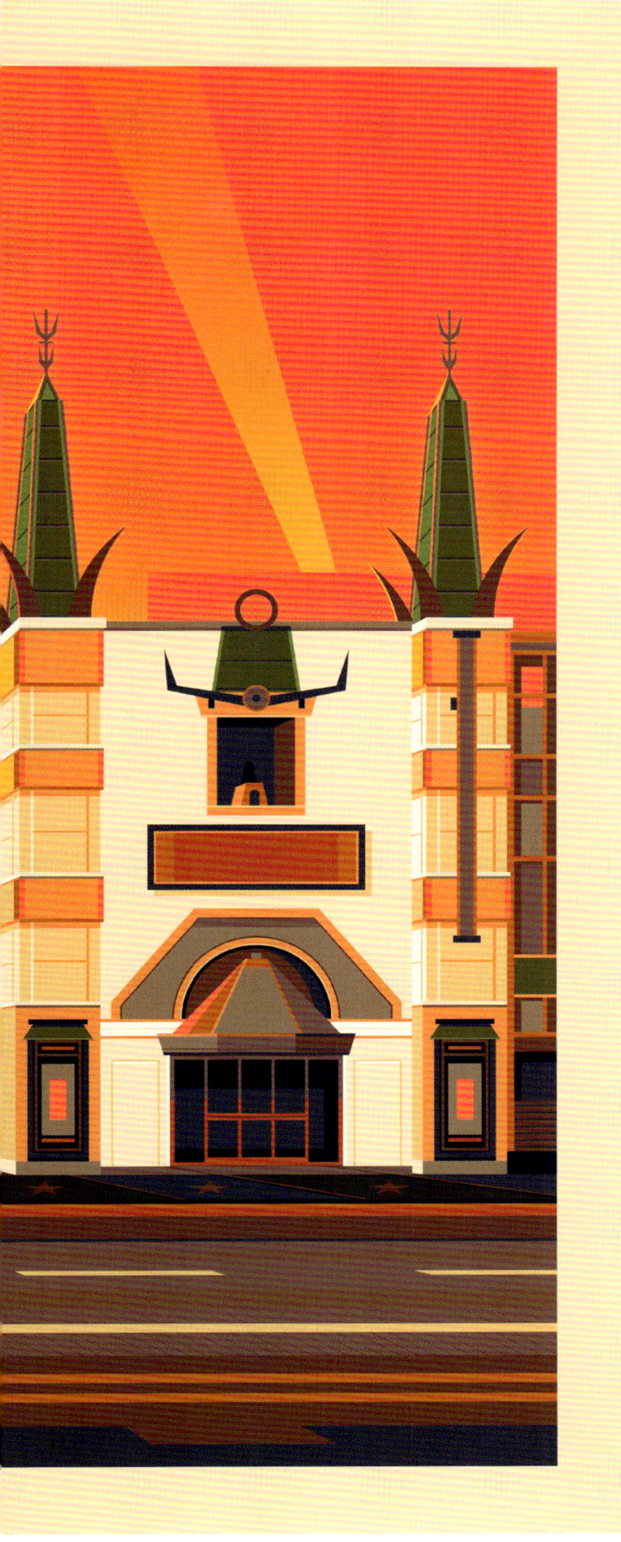

# CHINESE THEATRE

| ADDRESS | ARCHITECT(S) | YEAR |
| --- | --- | --- |
| 6925 Hollywood Blvd.<br>Los Angeles, CA<br>90028 | Meyer & Holler | 1920 |



**I remember this being the place I looked forward to** seeing the most when I arrived in LA for the very first time. I mean it's the Chinese Theatre, it's in the heart of Hollywood, has those famous handprints out front, and has been a part of movie history for as long as anyone can remember. It's the ultimate tourist spot in LA, and I was, after all, a tourist.

While the building itself lived up to the hype, it was my first time truly being away from home, and the chaotic nature of the Walk of Fame very quickly overwhelmed me.

That said, don't let this discourage you from visiting such a historic landmark. There's something magical about seeing the prints of so many legendary movie stars in real life and imagining standing where they once stood. It's an experience that stays with you.

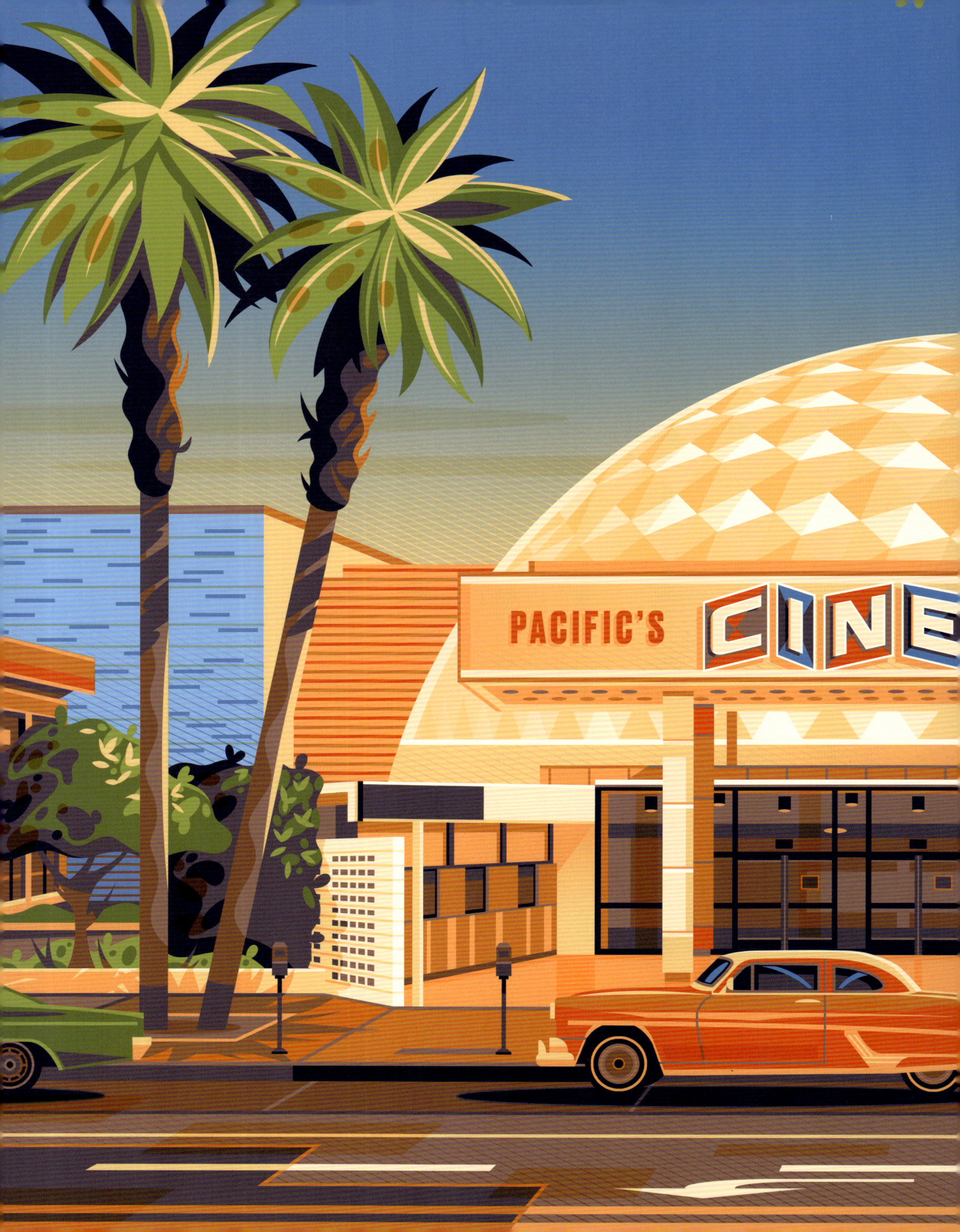
PACIFIC'S
CINE

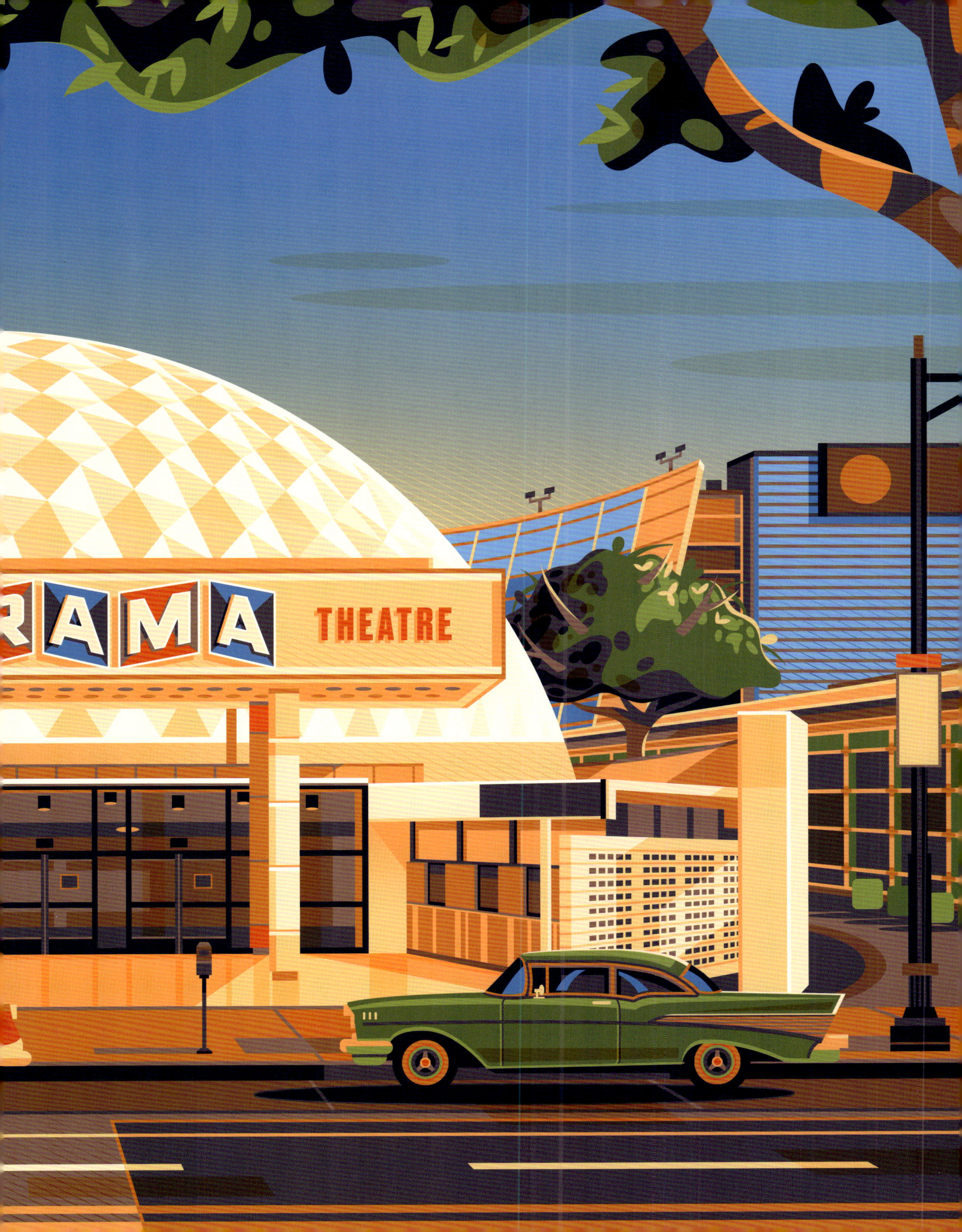
RAMA
THEATRE

# CINERAMA DOME

| ADDRESS | ARCHITECT(S) | YEAR |
|---|---|---|
| 6360 Sunset Blvd.<br>Los Angeles, CA<br>90028 | Welton Becket<br>& Associates | 1963 |

**I'd consider the Cinerama Dome** the most popular illustration I've ever created, and rightfully so. It's one of the most unique cinemas in Los Angeles and absolutely oozes classic Hollywood charm.



This print actually marked a turning point for me. It was the moment I realised I could transition from my job into freelance illustration. While I enjoyed the work and my colleagues, I knew the 9–5 life wasn't for me, so I took the leap. But with that leap came immediate doubt. *What if it didn't work out?* I had just left a comfortable job, and now I had no pay, living in a city with a notoriously high cost of living. The pressure was on.

A few days after making that decision, we released a new variant of my *Cinerama Dome* print in tribute to the theatre after it closed its doors for the last time, and the response was overwhelming. Any doubts I had disappeared, and I was more inspired than ever to chase this new path.

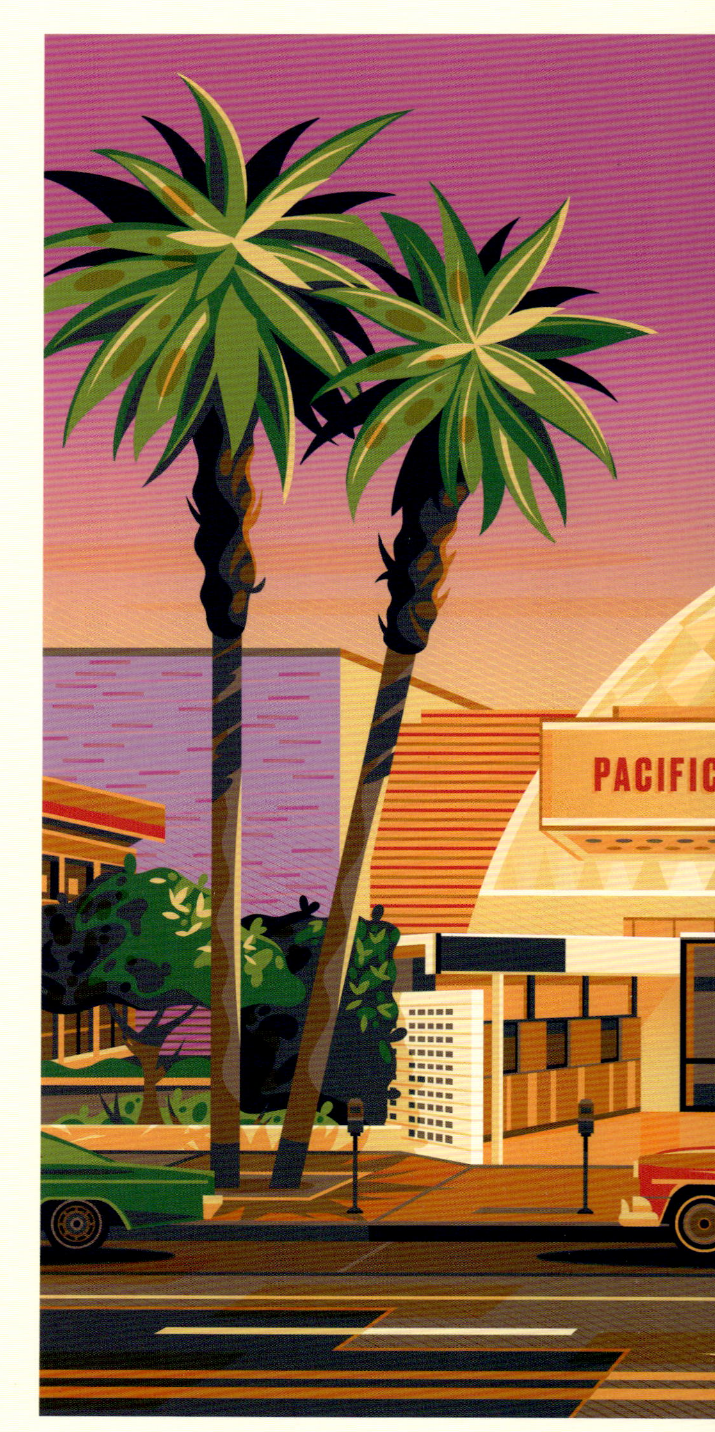

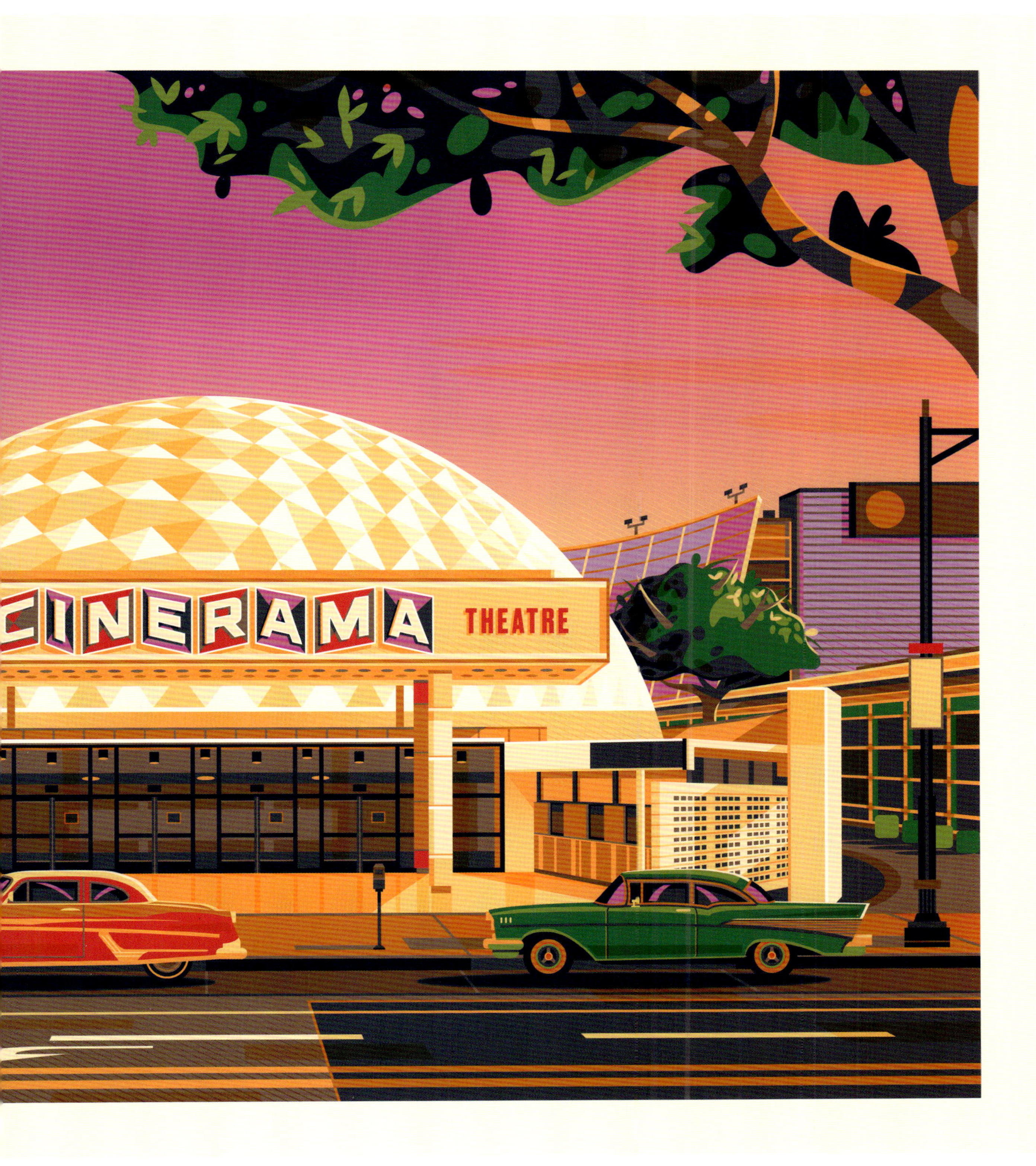




PREVIOUS SPREAD

*Cinerama Dome*

Open Edition
2019

ABOVE

*Cinerama Dome (Purple Sunset)*

Limited Edition
2019

NEXT SPREAD

*Cinerama Dome (Night)*

Timed Edition
2019

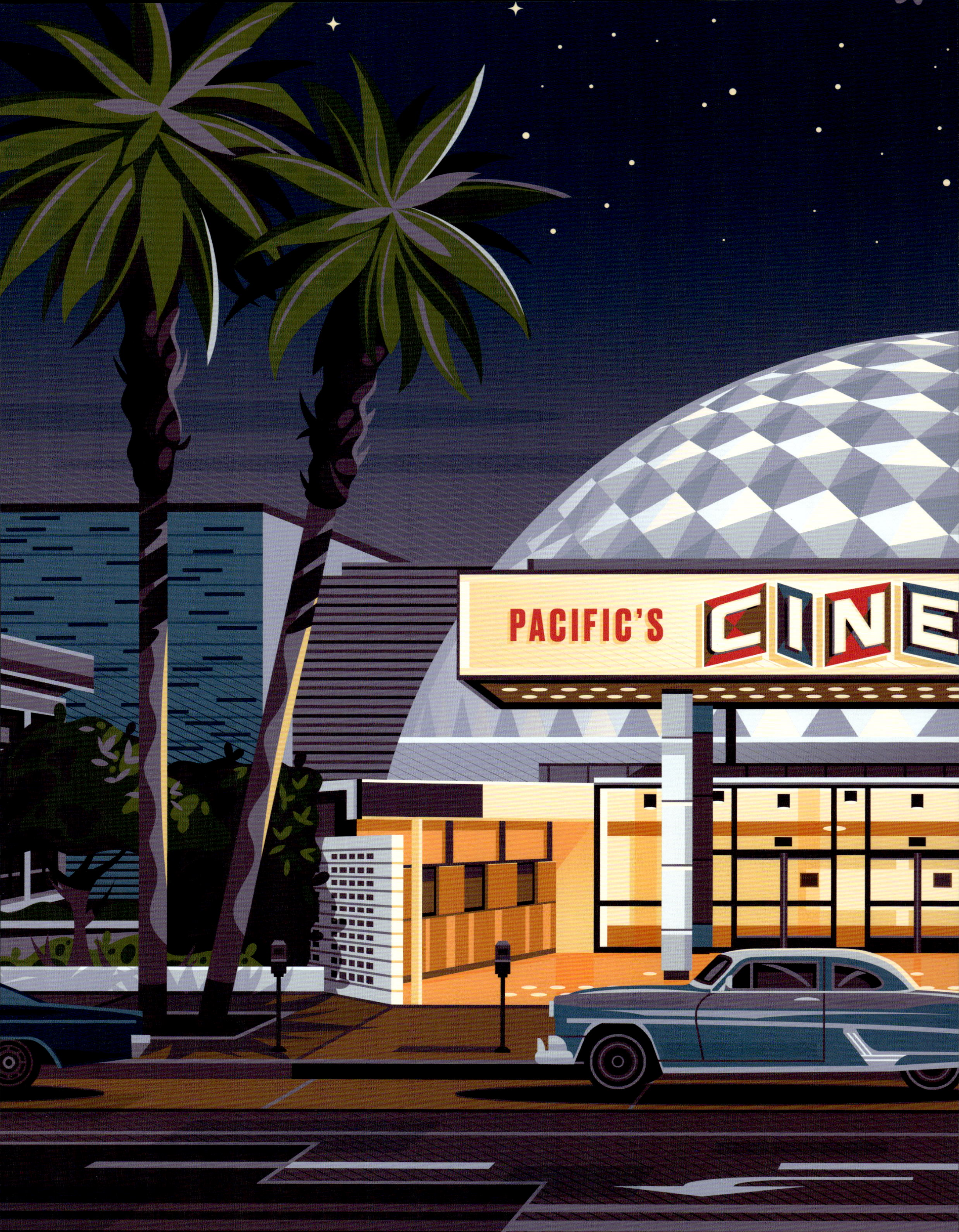
PACIFIC'S
CINE

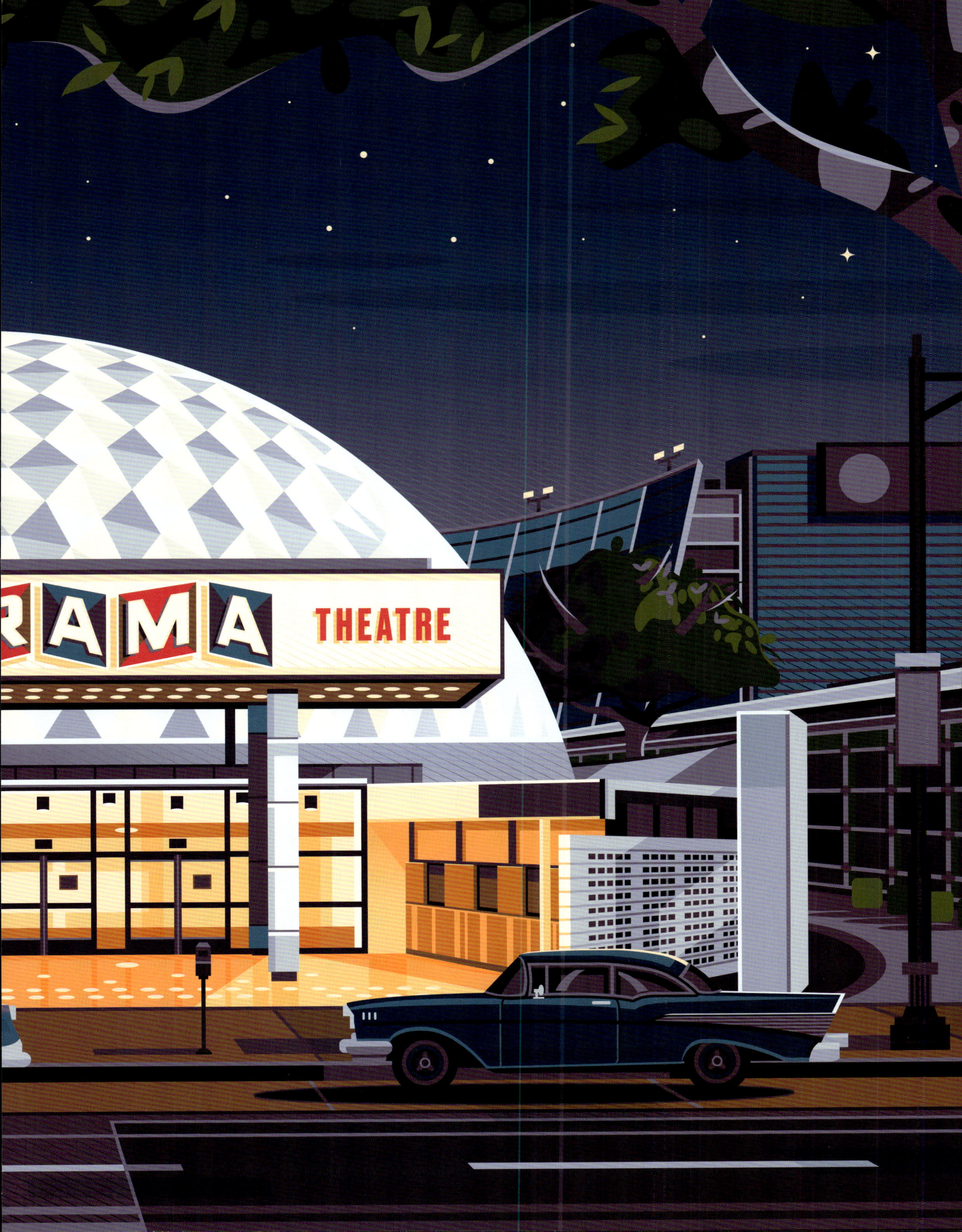
RAMA
THEATRE

# NEW BEVERLY CINEMA

ADDRESS
7165 Beverly Blvd.
Los Angeles, CA
90036

ARCHITECT(S)
John P. Edwards,
Warren Frazier Overpeck

YEAR
1929

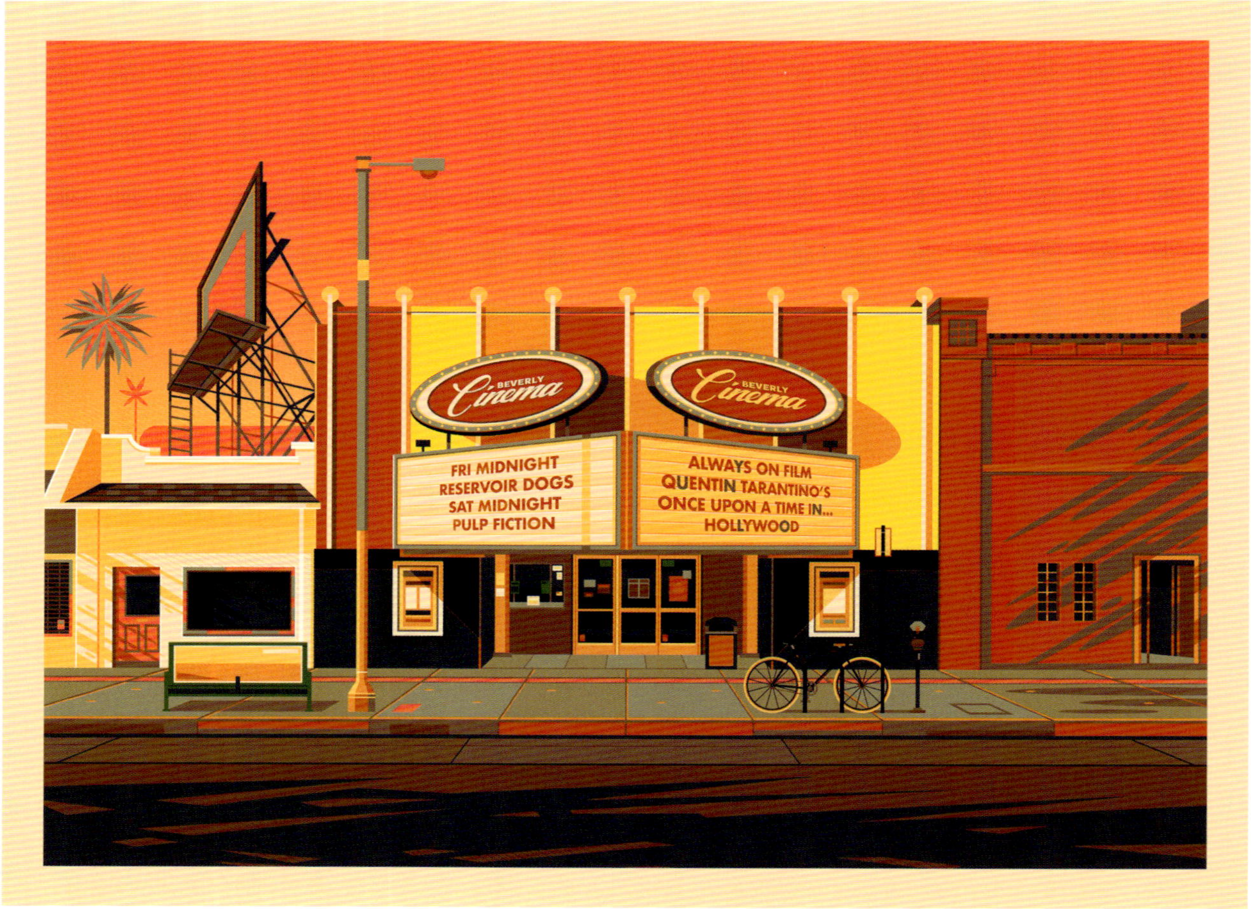

ABOVE
*New Beverly Cinema (Sunset)*
Limited Edition
2021

ACROSS
*New Beverly Cinema*
Open Edition
2021

NEXT SPREAD
*New Beverly Cinema (Night)*
Limited Edition
2021

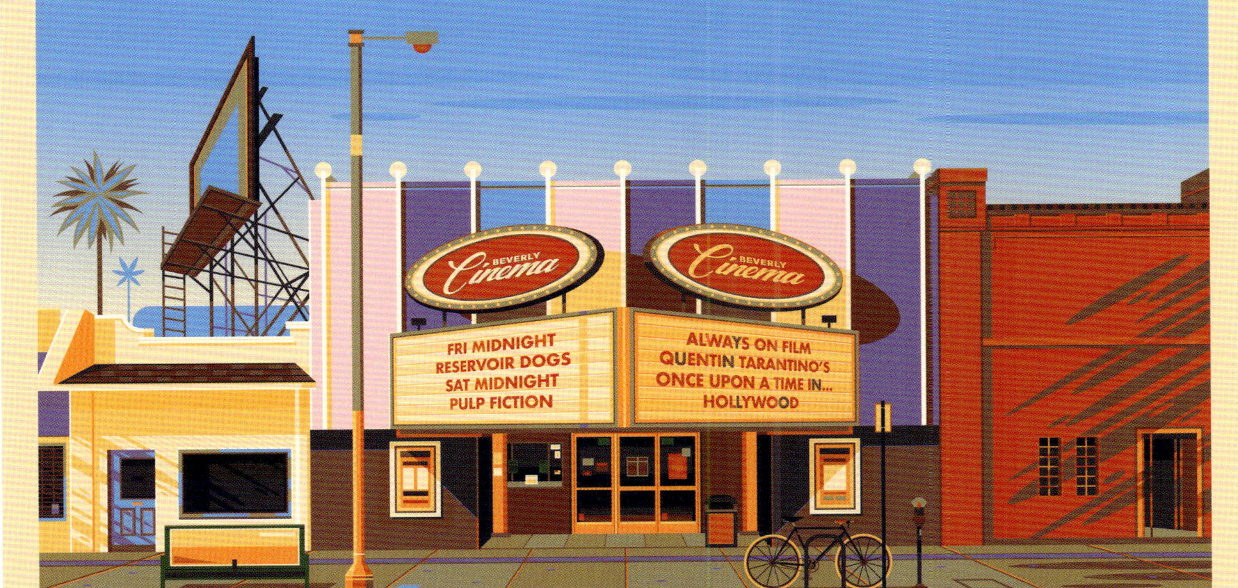
BEVERLY
Cinema
BEVERLY
Cinema
FRI MIDNIGHT
RESERVOIR DOGS
SAT MIDNIGHT
PULP FICTION
ALWAYS ON FILM
QUENTIN TARANTINO'S
ONCE UPON A TIME IN...
HOLLYWOOD

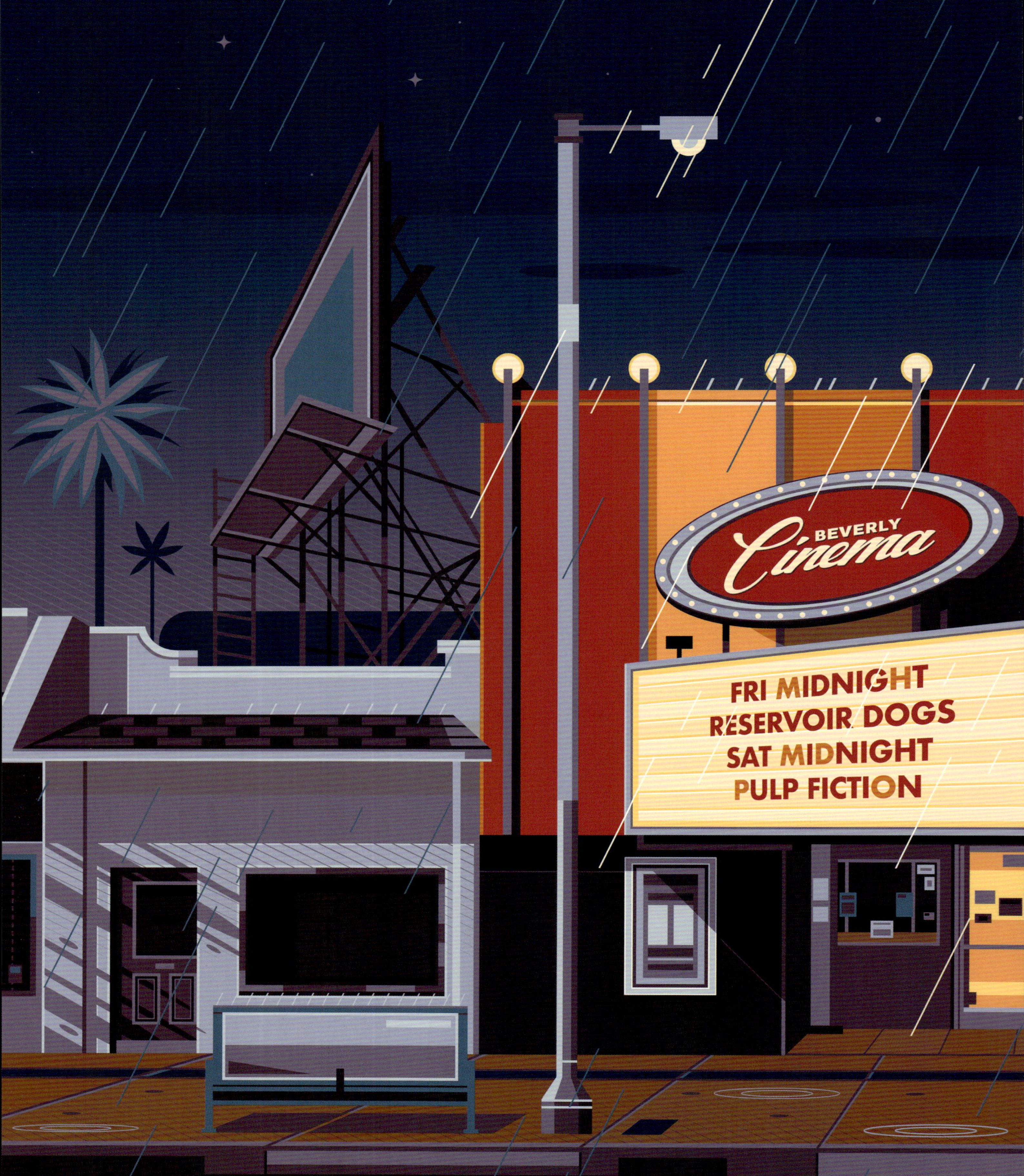
BEVERLY
Cinema
FRI MIDNIGHT
RESERVOIR DOGS
SAT MIDNIGHT
PULP FICTION

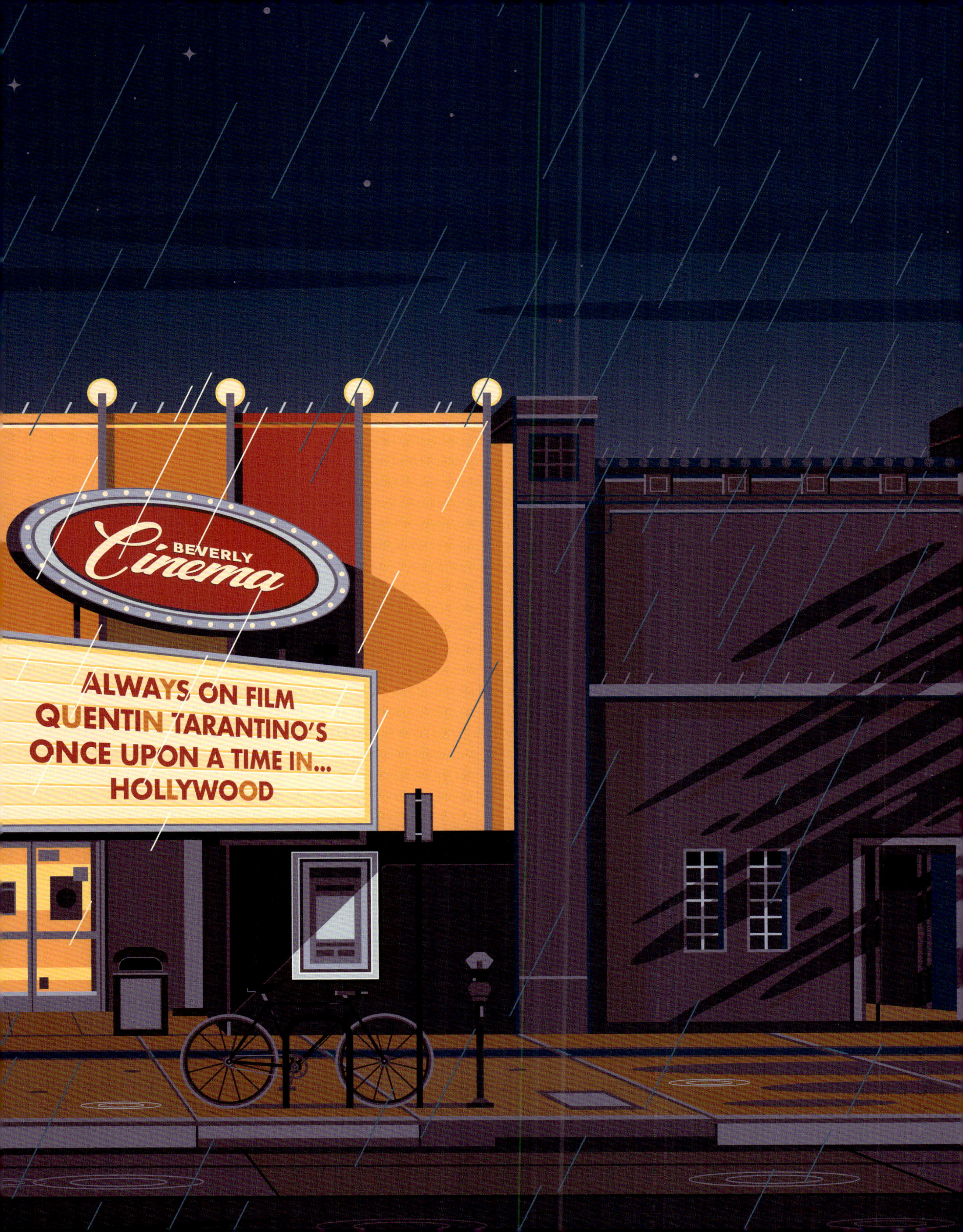
BEVERLY
Cinema
ALWAYS ON FILM
QUENTIN TARANTINO'S
ONCE UPON A TIME IN...
HOLLYWOOD

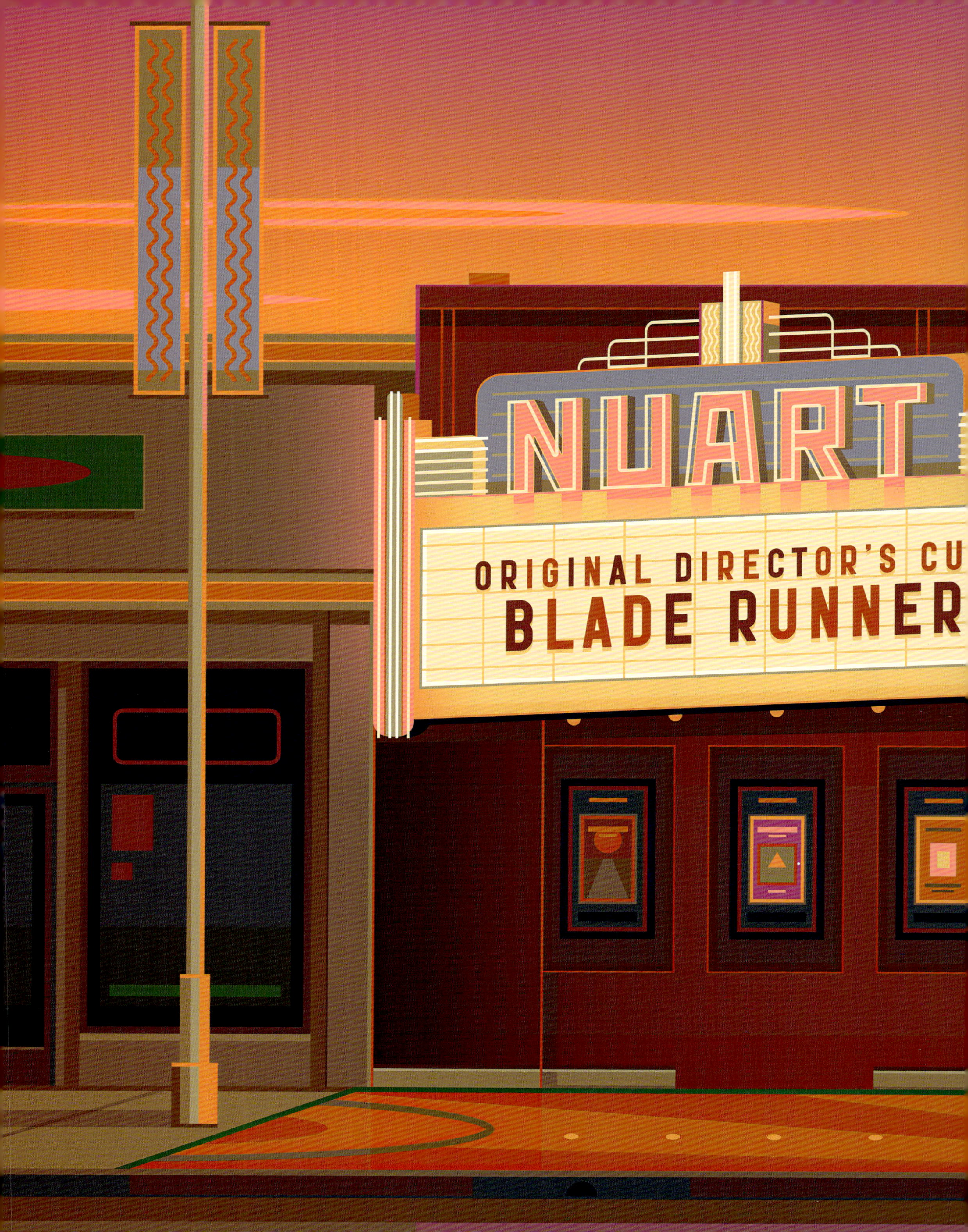
NUART
ORIGINAL DIRECTOR'S CU
BLADE RUNNER

# NUART THEATRE

ADDRESS
11272 Santa Monica Blvd.
Los Angeles, CA
90025

ARCHITECT(S)
N/A

YEAR
1929



**The Nuart Theatre might not have the same fame** as some of its Hollywood counterparts, but since opening in 1929, it has proven its staying power. Over the years, it has cemented itself as a fan favourite, particularly for its legendary midnight screenings of *The Rocky Horror Picture Show*, a tradition it's upheld since the early 1970s. It's one of the few places in Los Angeles where you can experience films in a setting that echoes the city's golden age of cinema, with an authentic, intimate vibe that modern cinemas just can't replicate.

This was another instance of wanting to make use of the longer dimensions to capture the intricate details, from its classic architecture to the vibrant neon signs, bringing out the unique charm of this local gem.

GATEFOLD

*Nuart Theatre*
Limited Edition
2024

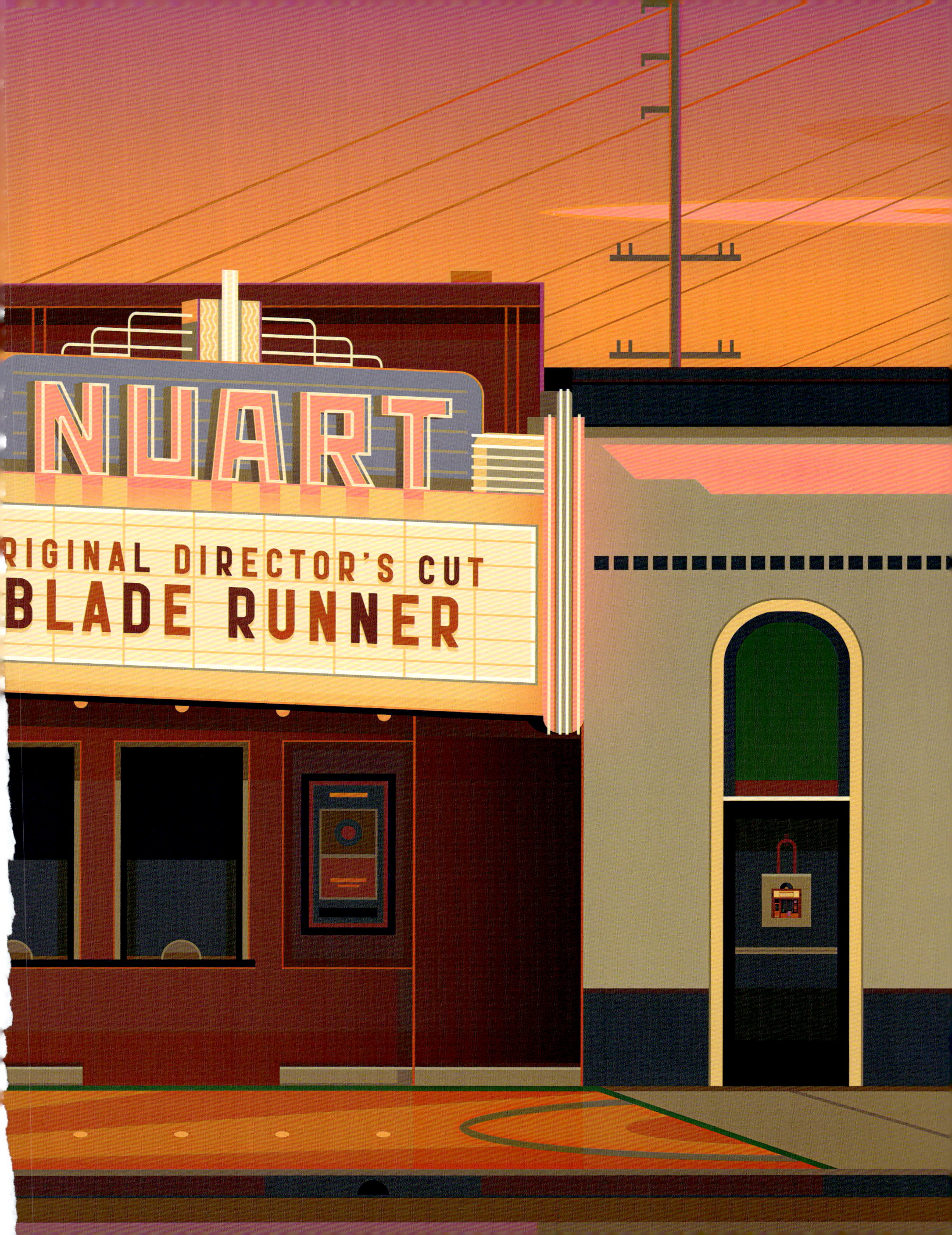
NUART
RIGINAL DIRECTOR'S CUT
BLADE RUNNER

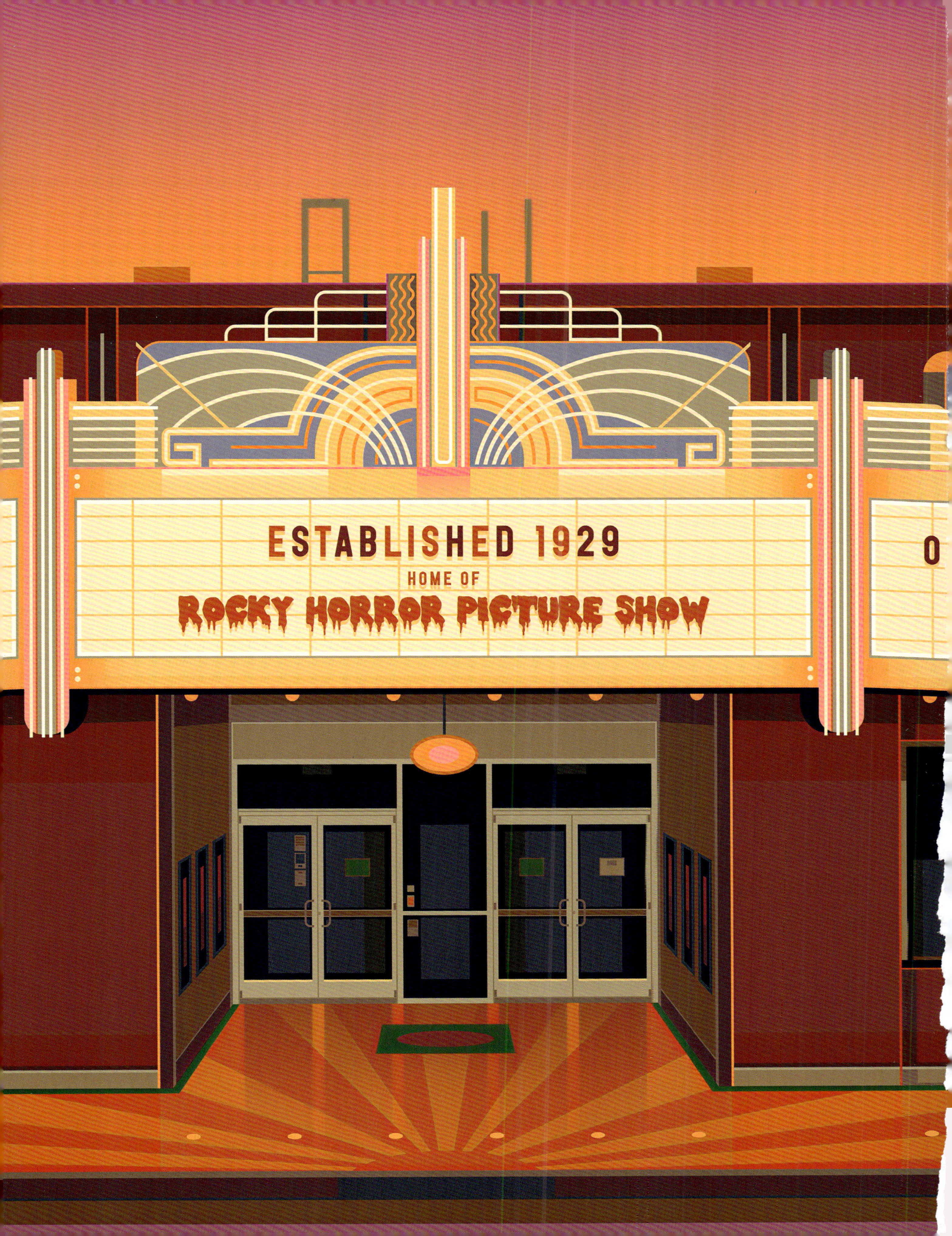
ESTABLISHED 1929
HOME OF
ROCKY HORROR PICTURE SHOW

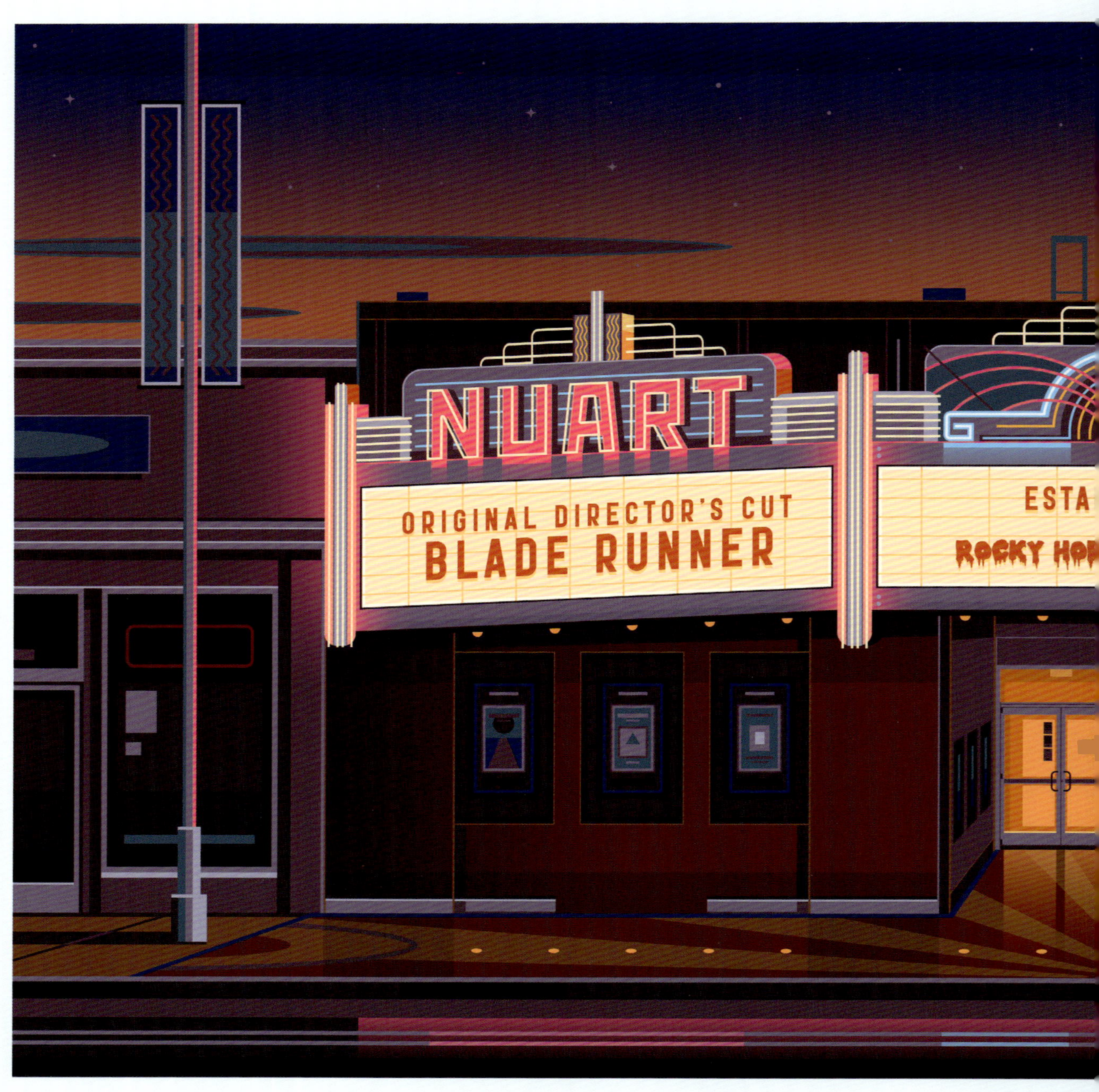


ABOVE

*Nuart Theatre (Night)*
Limited Edition
2024

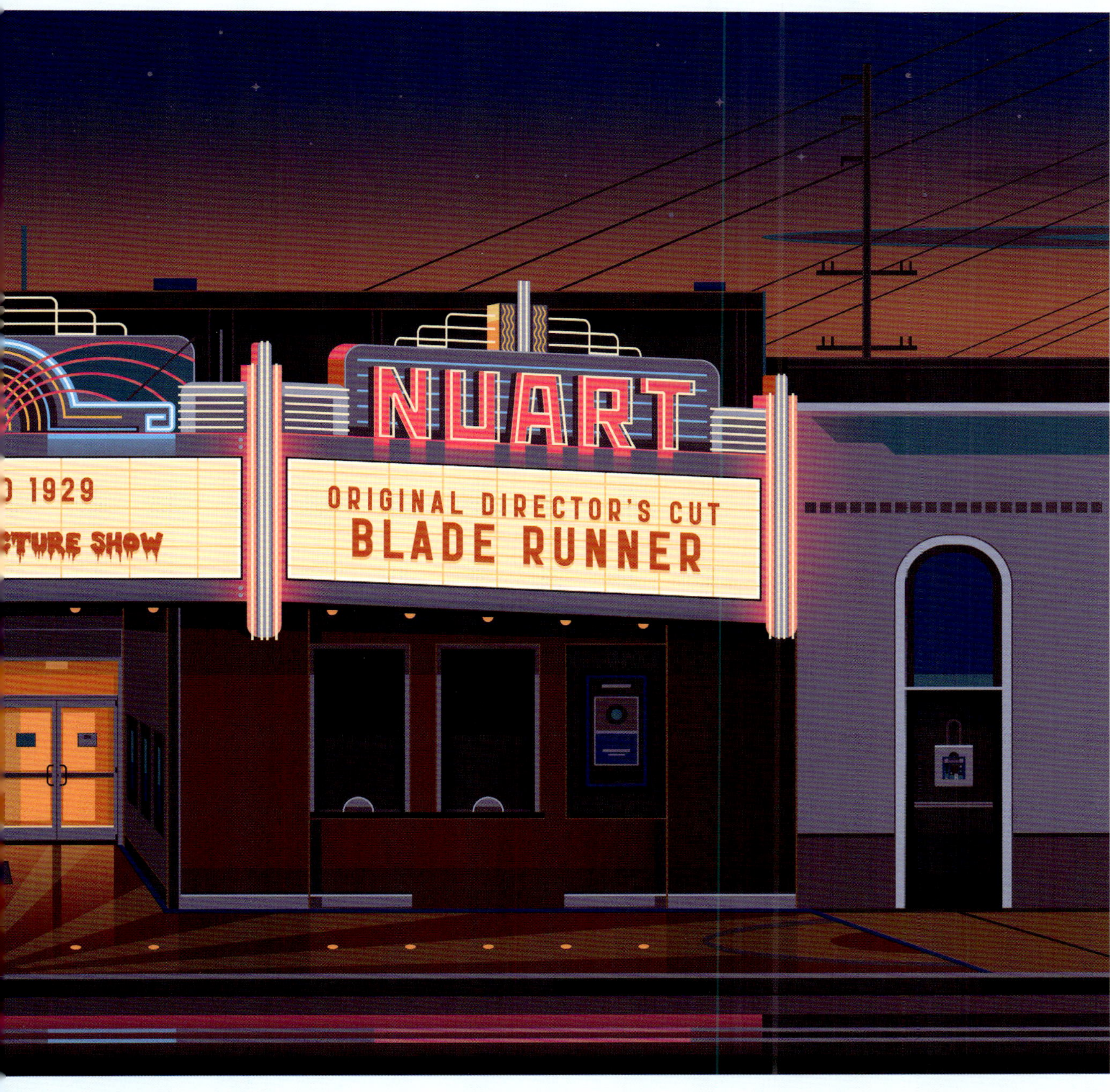

NUART
) 1929
CTURE SHOW
ORIGINAL DIRECTOR'S CUT
BLADE RUNNER

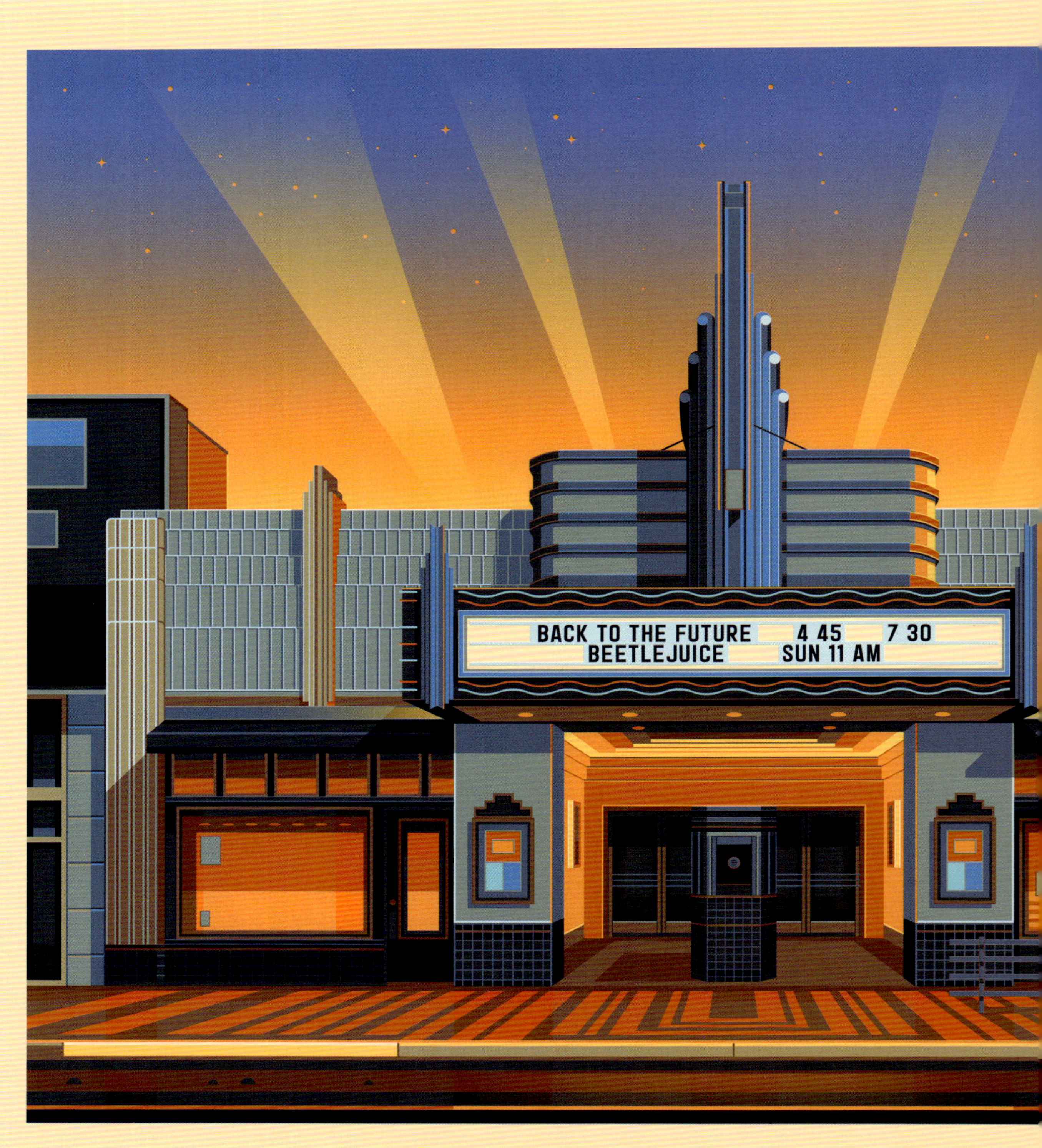
BACK TO THE FUTURE 4 45 7 30
BEETLEJUICE SUN 11 AM

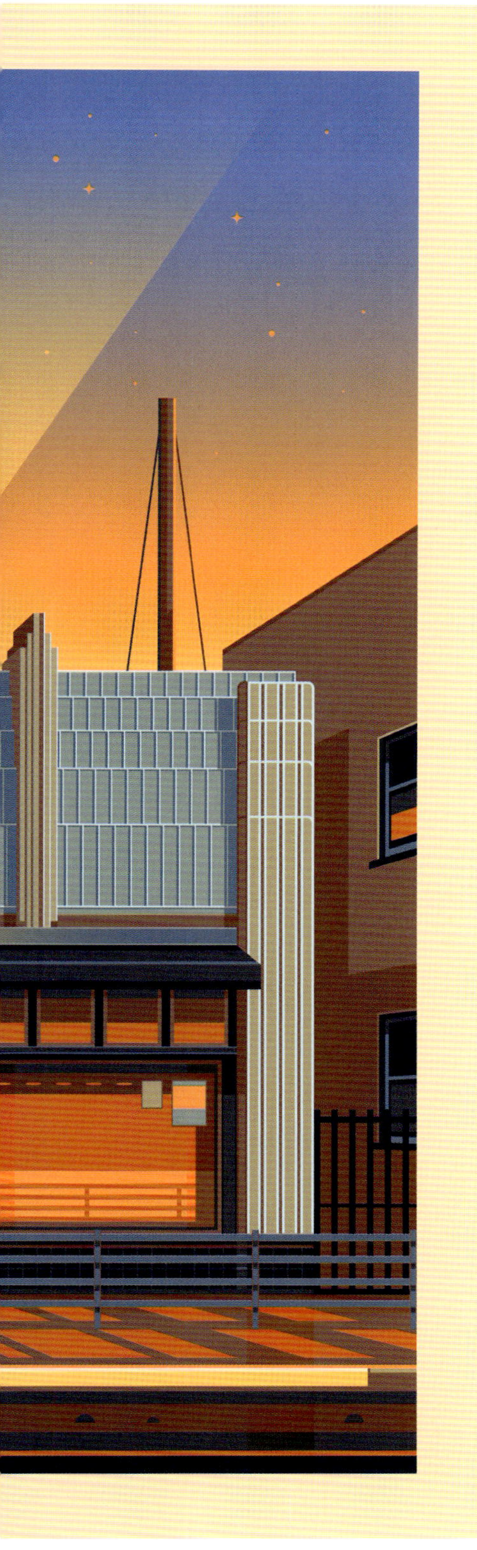

# ART THEATRE OF LONG BEACH

| ADDRESS | ARCHITECT(S) | YEAR |
|---|---|---|
| 2025 E 4th St.<br>Long Beach, CA<br>90814 | N/A | 1924 |



ACROSS

*Art Theatre of Long Beach*
Limited Edition
2024

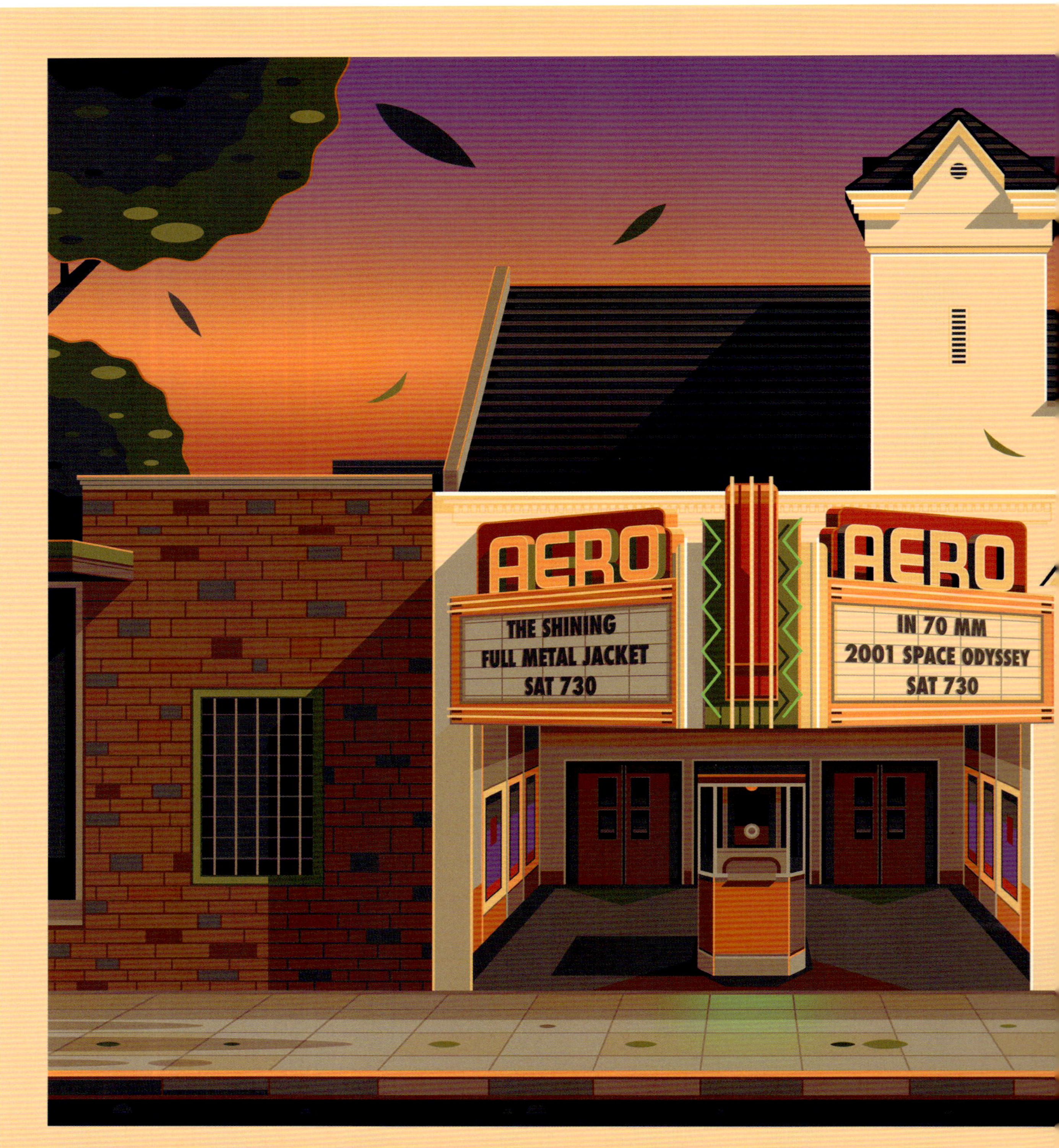
AERO
THE SHINING
FULL METAL JACKET
SAT 730
AERO
IN 70 MM
2001 SPACE ODYSSEY
SAT 730

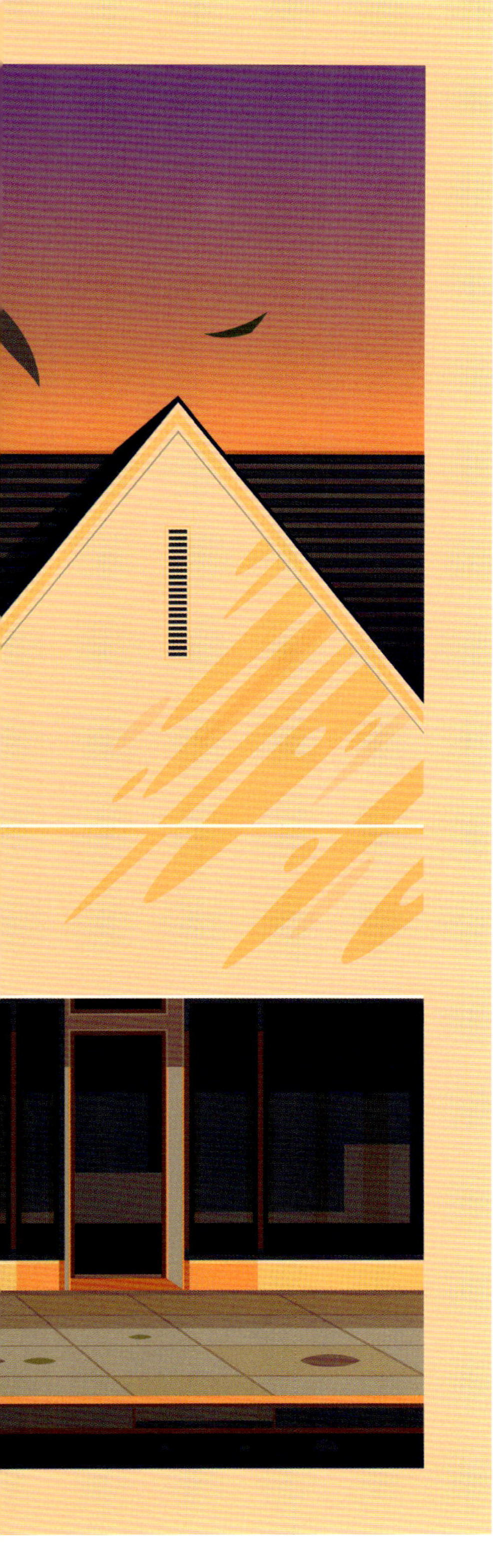

# AERO THEATRE

| ADDRESS | ARCHITECT(S) | YEAR |
| --- | --- | --- |
| 1328 Montana Ave.<br>Santa Monica, CA<br>90403 | N/A | 1940 |



ACROSS

*Aero Theatre*
Limited Edition
2023

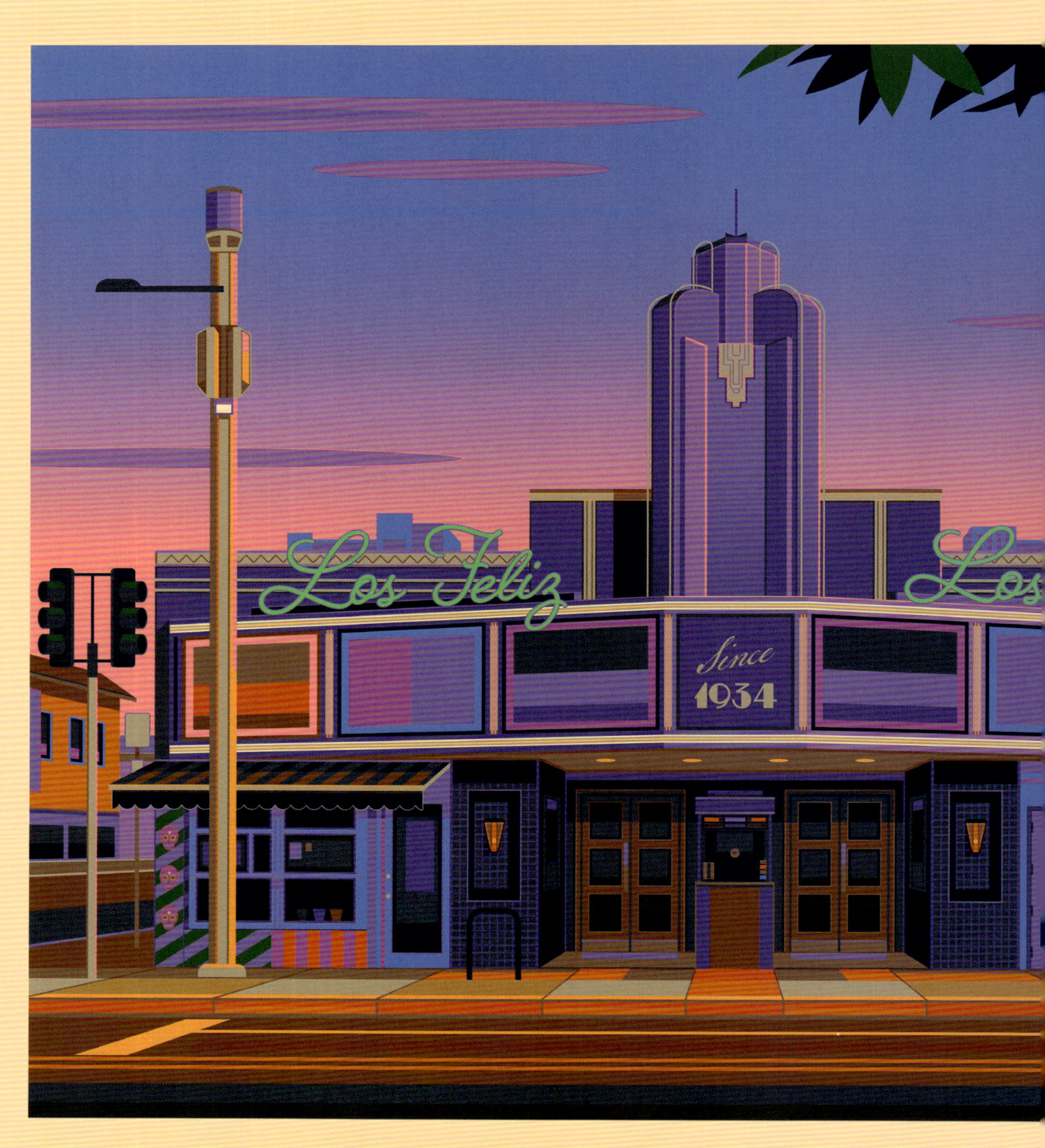
Los Feliz
Since
1934
Los

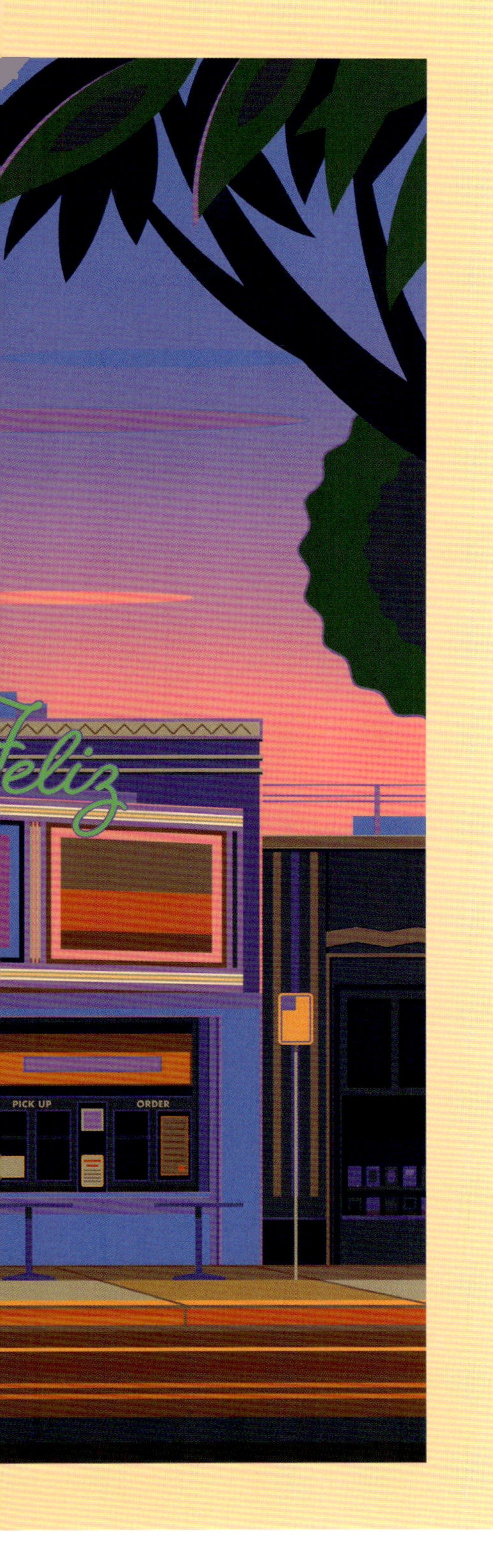


# LOS FELIZ THEATRE

| ADDRESS | ARCHITECT(S) | YEAR |
|---|---|---|
| 1822 N Vermont Ave.<br>Los Angeles, CA<br>90027 | Clifford A. Balch | 1935 |



ACROSS

*Los Feliz Theatre*
Limited Edition
2023

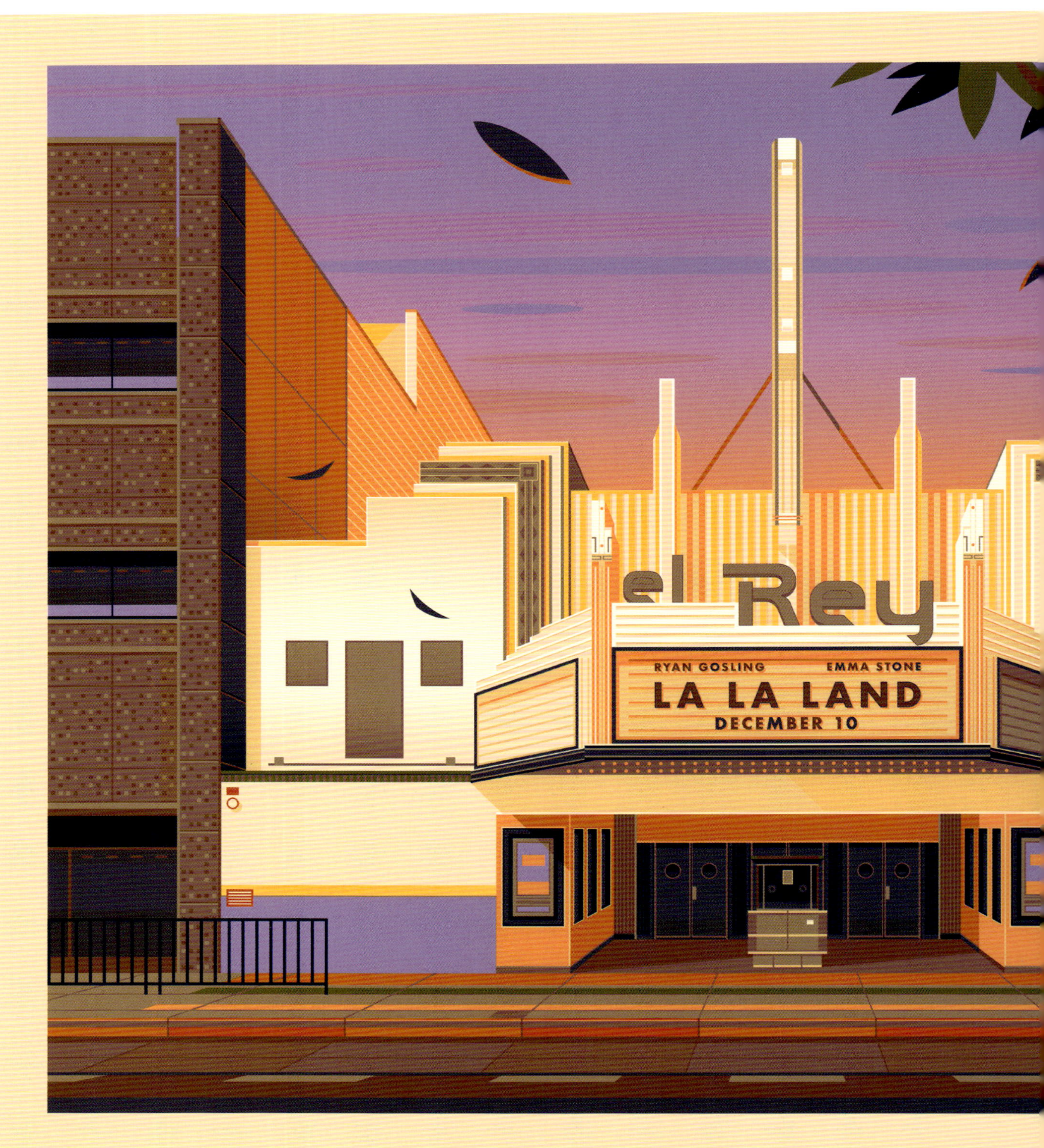
el Rey
RYAN GOSLING
EMMA STONE
LA LA LAND
DECEMBER 10

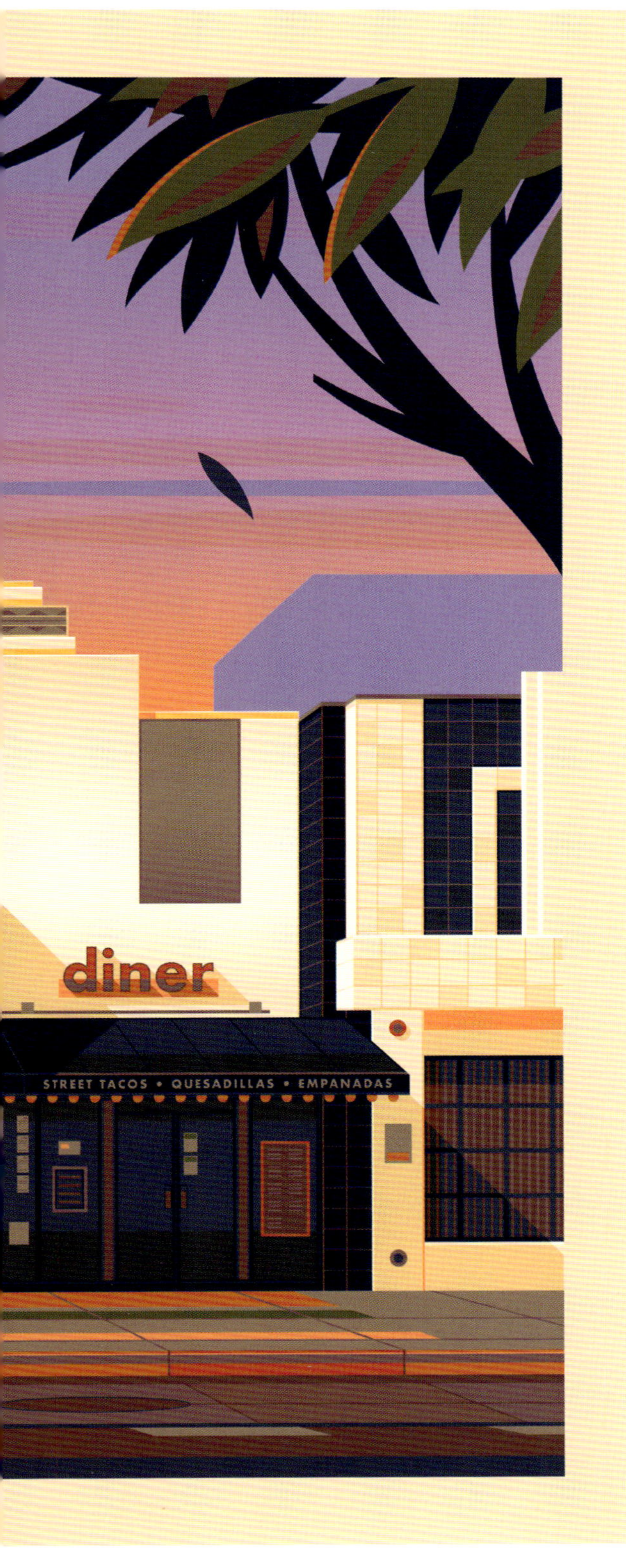


# EL REY THEATRE

| ADDRESS | ARCHITECT(S) | YEAR |
|---|---|---|
| 5515 Wilshire Blvd.<br>Los Angeles, CA<br>90036 | Clifford A. Balch | 1936 |



ACROSS

*El Rey Theatre*
Limited Edition
2021

# LOS ANGELES THEATRE

ADDRESS
615 S Broadway
Los Angeles, CA
90014

ARCHITECT(S)
S. Charles Lee
S. Tilden Norton

YEAR
1931



**The Los Angeles Theatre, with its stunning French Baroque** facade and luxurious interior, is a perfect example of a style unique to LA, blending European elegance with Hollywood flair. These theatres were not just places to watch films; they were experiences in themselves, built to reflect the grandeur of the golden age of cinema.

Downtown Los Angeles is home to an incredible collection of historic theatres. Unfortunately, many of these gems have either closed their doors or are now primarily used for private events, largely due to changing times and the evolution of entertainment venues.

It's a shame that so many of these iconic spaces are being lost to time, as they played such a vital role in Hollywood's story. For example, the Los Angeles Theatre is famously tied to the premiere of Charlie Chaplin's *City Lights* in 1931. It's said that Chaplin contributed to its completion to ensure the theatre was ready for his film's debut, a claim that, while debated, helps add to the legend.

Thankfully, like so much of Los Angeles, these theatres continue to live on through the big screen. Their cultural significance make them a favourite filming location, preserving their legacy for new generations to admire.

ACROSS

*Los Angeles Theatre (Detail)*
Limited Edition
2023

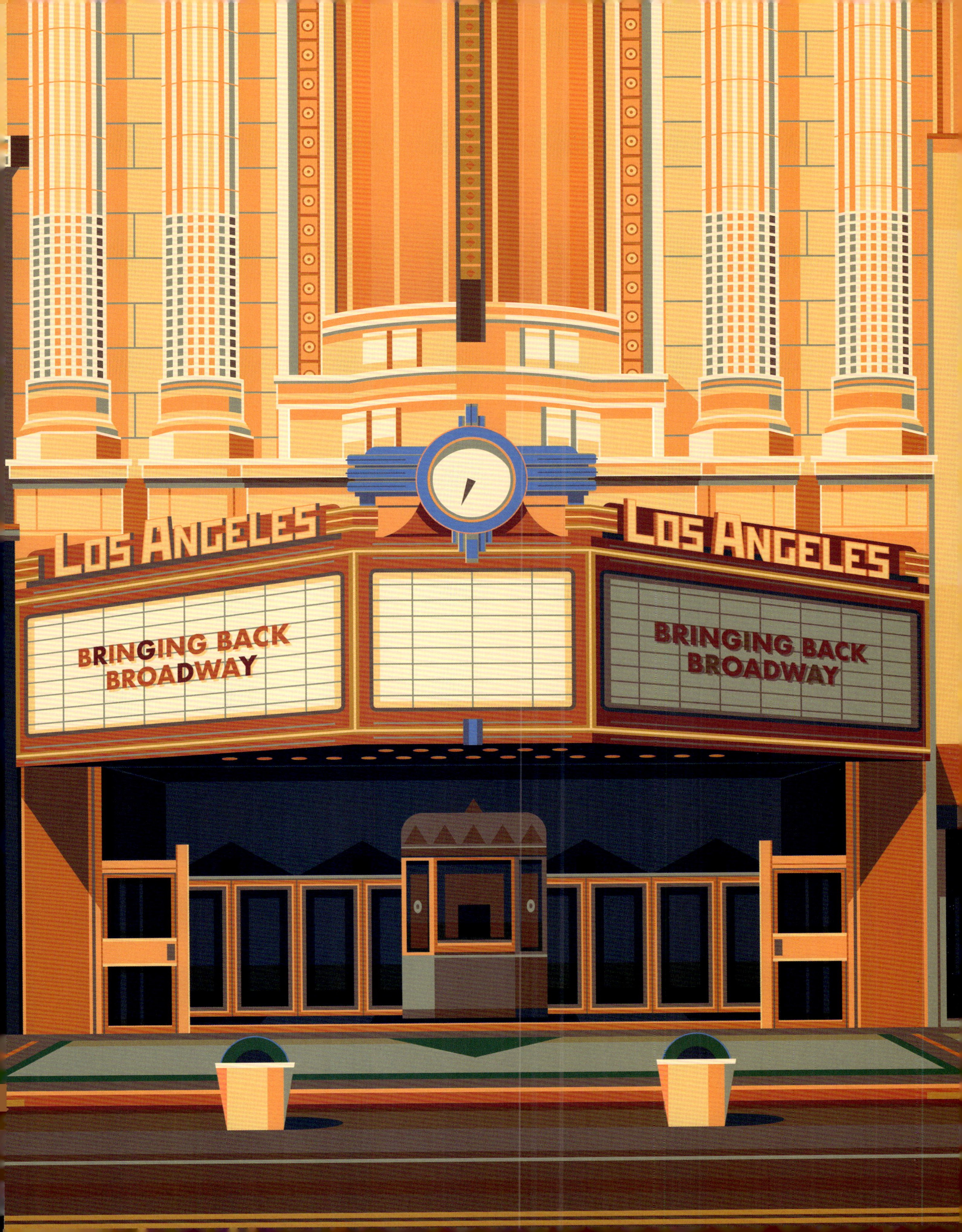
LOS ANGELES
BRINGING BACK BROADWAY
LOS ANGELES
BRINGING BACK BROADWAY

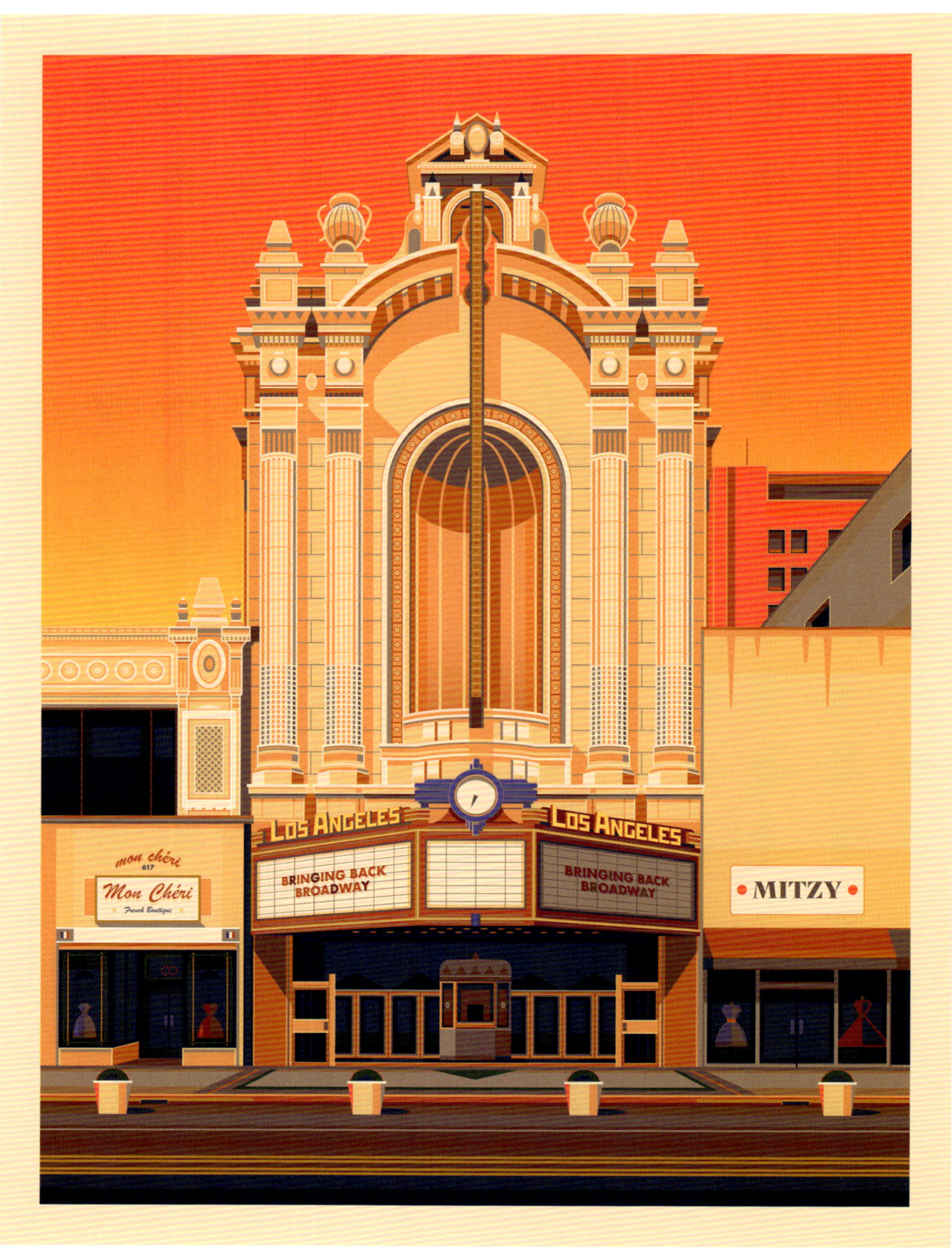


ABOVE

*Los Angeles Theatre (Sunset)*
Limited Edition
2023

ACROSS

*Los Angeles Theatre*

Limited Edition
2023

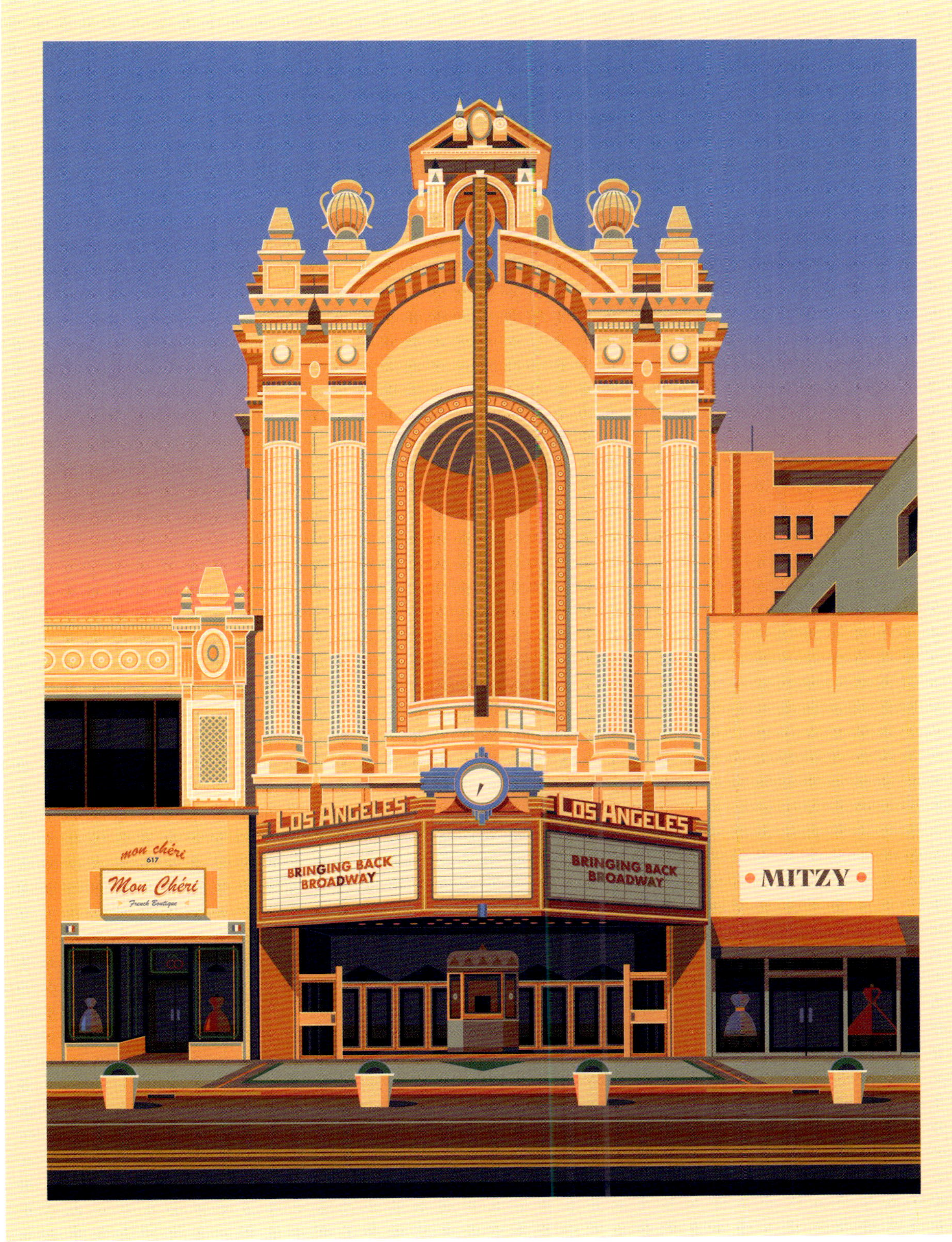
LOS ANGELES
BRINGING BACK BROADWAY
LOS ANGELES
BRINGING BACK BROADWAY
mon chéri
617
Mon Chéri
French Boutique
MITZY

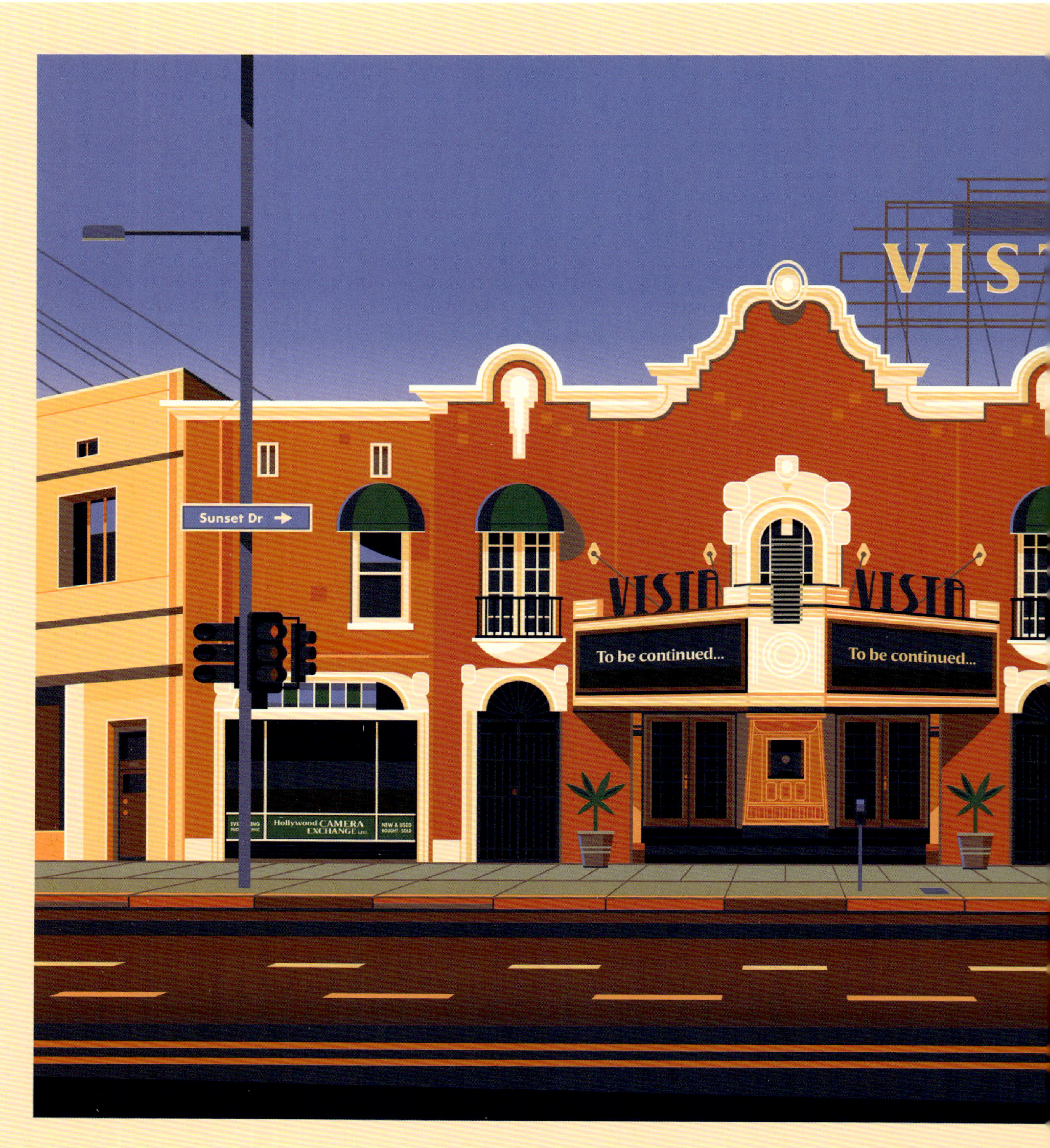
VIST
Sunset Dr
VISTA
VISTA
To be continued...
To be continued...
Hollywood CAMERA EXCHANGE

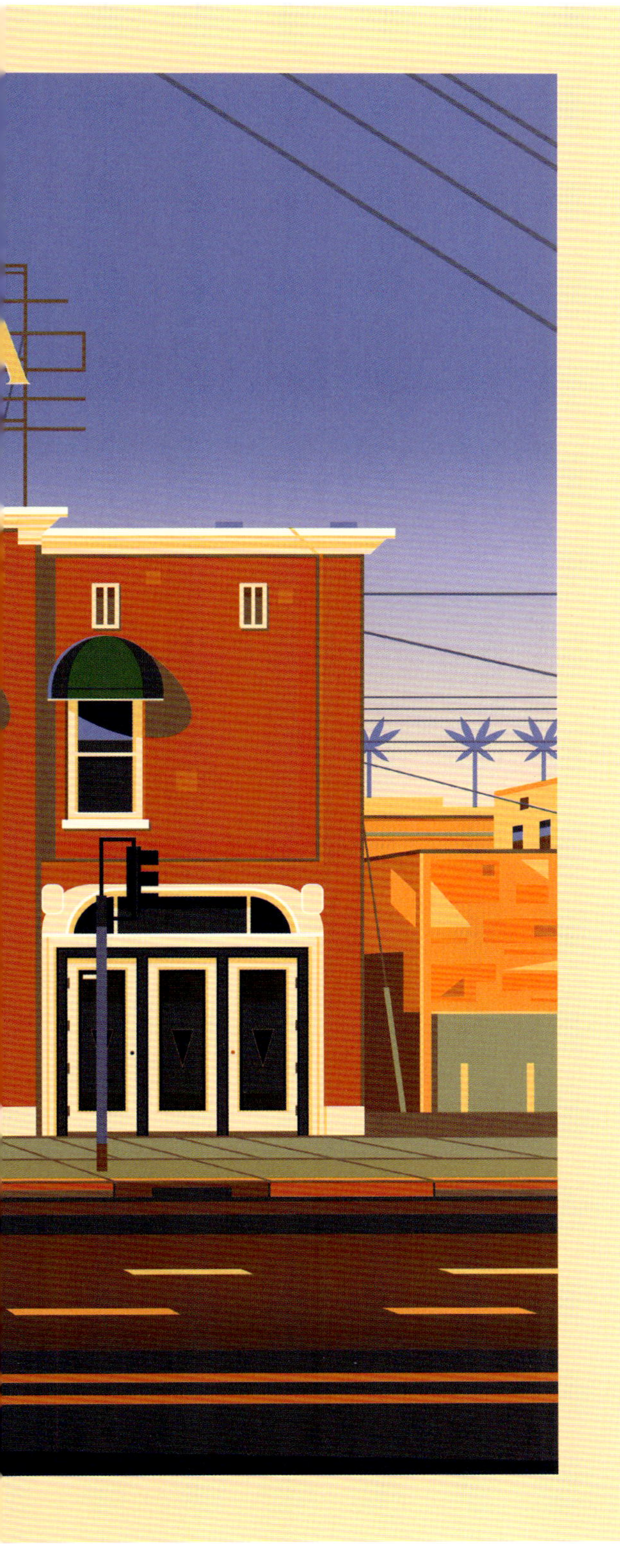

# VISTA THEATRE

| ADDRESS | ARCHITECT(S) | YEAR |
|---|---|---|
| 4473 Sunset Dr.<br>Los Angeles, CA<br>90027 | Lewis A. Smith | 1923 |



ACROSS

*Vista Theatre*

Limited Edition
2021

NEXT SPREAD

*Vista Theatre (Sunset)*
Limited Edition
2021

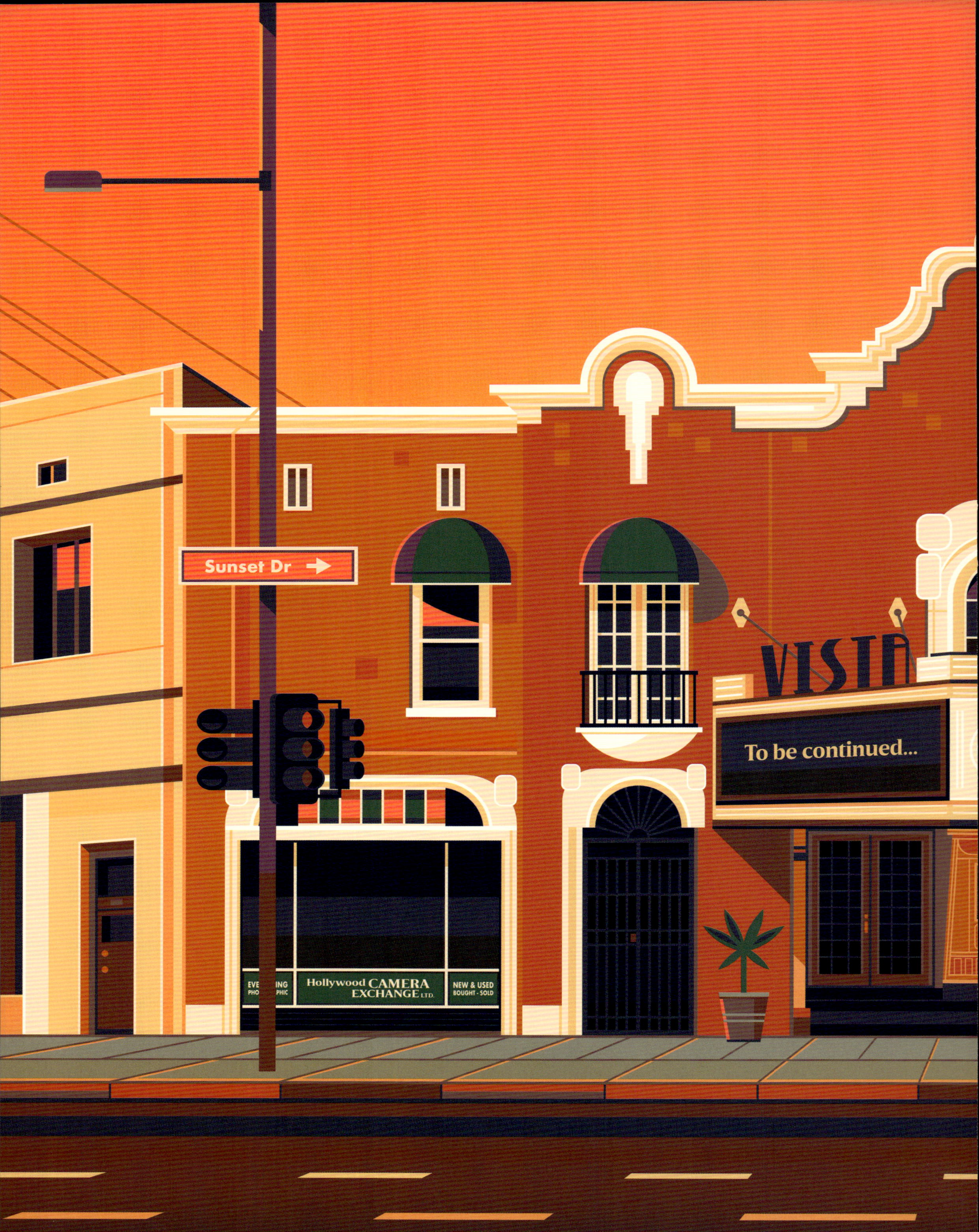
Sunset Dr
VISTA
To be continued...
Hollywood CAMERA EXCHANGE LTD.
NEW & USED
BOUGHT - SOLD

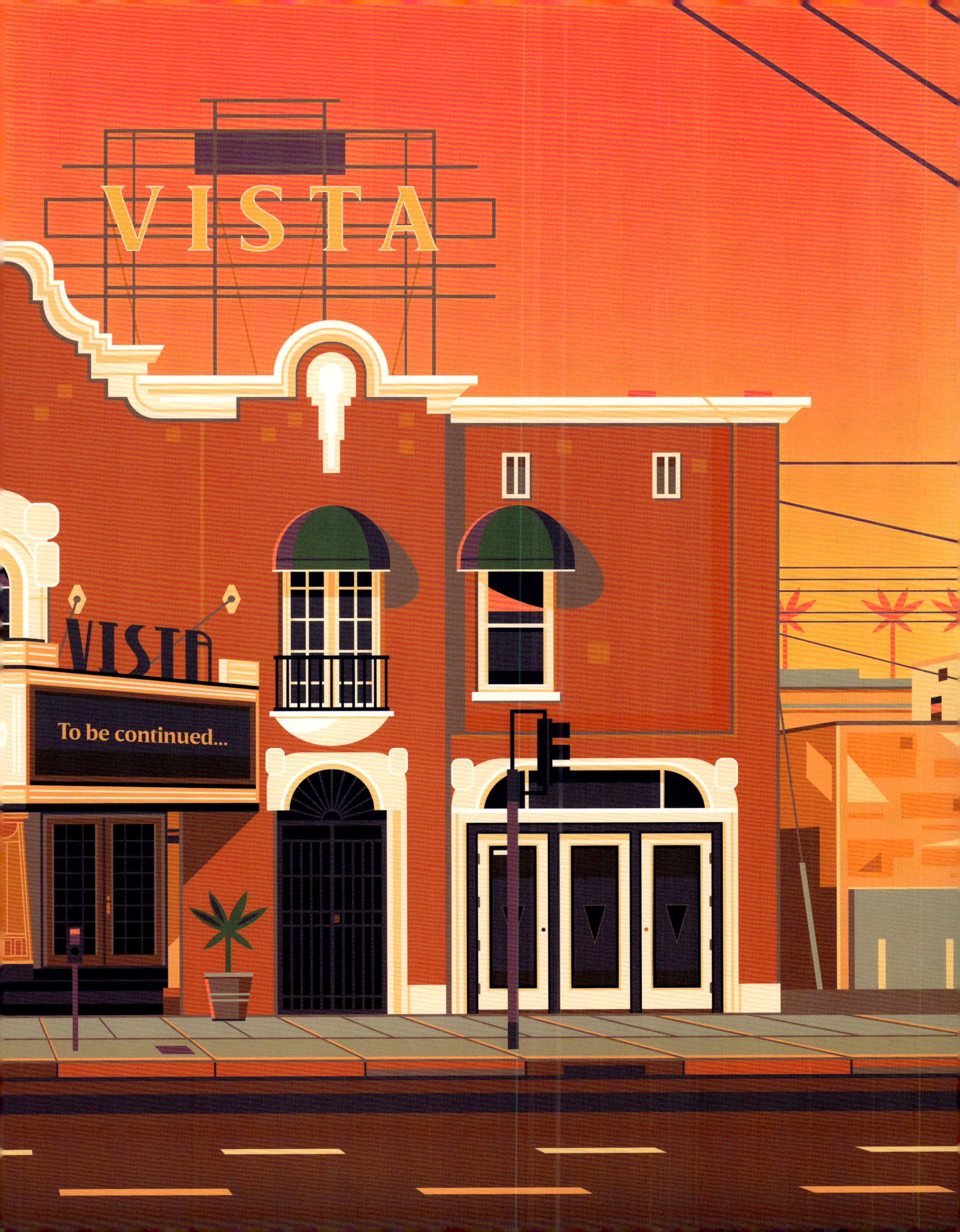
VISTA
VISTA
To be continued...

Detour: Palm Springs

# TWIN PALMS ESTATE

ADDRESS
1145 E Vía Colusa
Palm Springs, CA
92262

ARCHITECT(S)
E. Stewart Williams

YEAR
1947



**The Twin Palms Estate** is best known as Frank Sinatra's Palm Springs getaway. It's a beautifully designed mid-century modern home, complete with a piano-shaped pool, endless palm trees, and stunning views of the mountains. It's the most "Palm Springs" home you could ask for.

After posting my rendition online, I decided to take a shot in the dark and put it out into the world that I'd love to visit the house. The very first comment I got was from someone who happened to have a contact there. They connected me with the company that manages events at the estate and arranged a private tour for the next time I was in Palm Springs. Walking through the house felt like stepping back into the 1950s.

It was a nice little reminder that if you want something, put it out into the world, you never know what might happen.

ACROSS
*Twin Palms Estate (Night)*
Limited Edition
2023

NEXT SPREAD
*Twin Palms Estate*
Limited Edition
2023

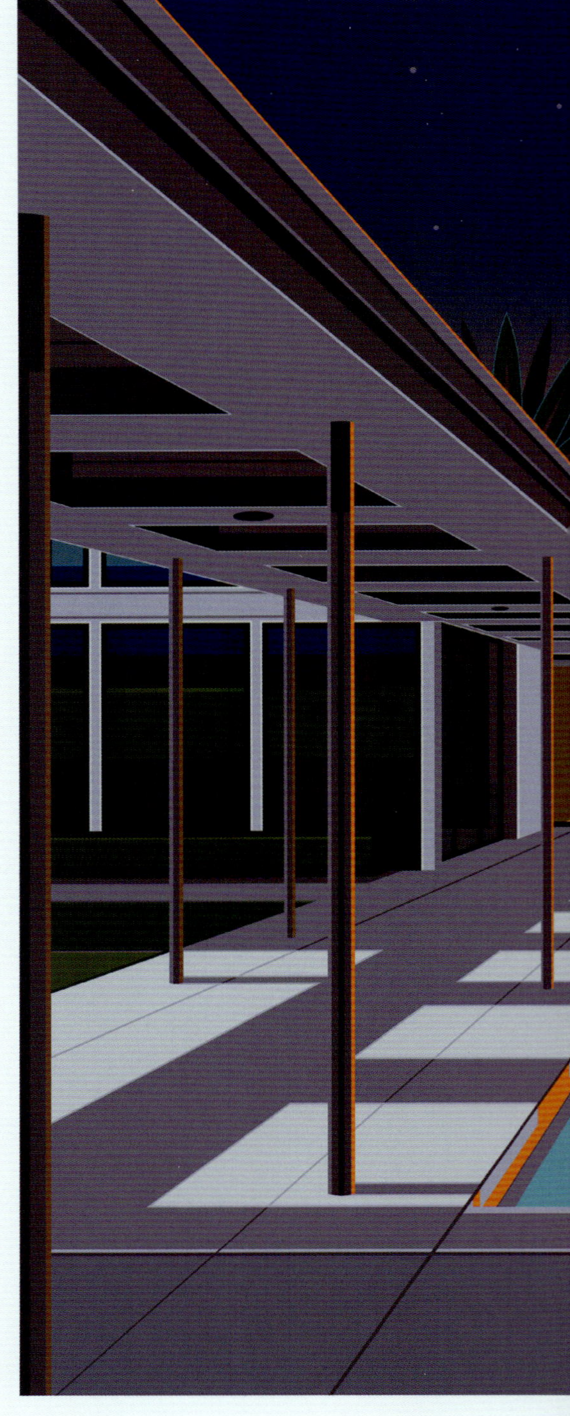

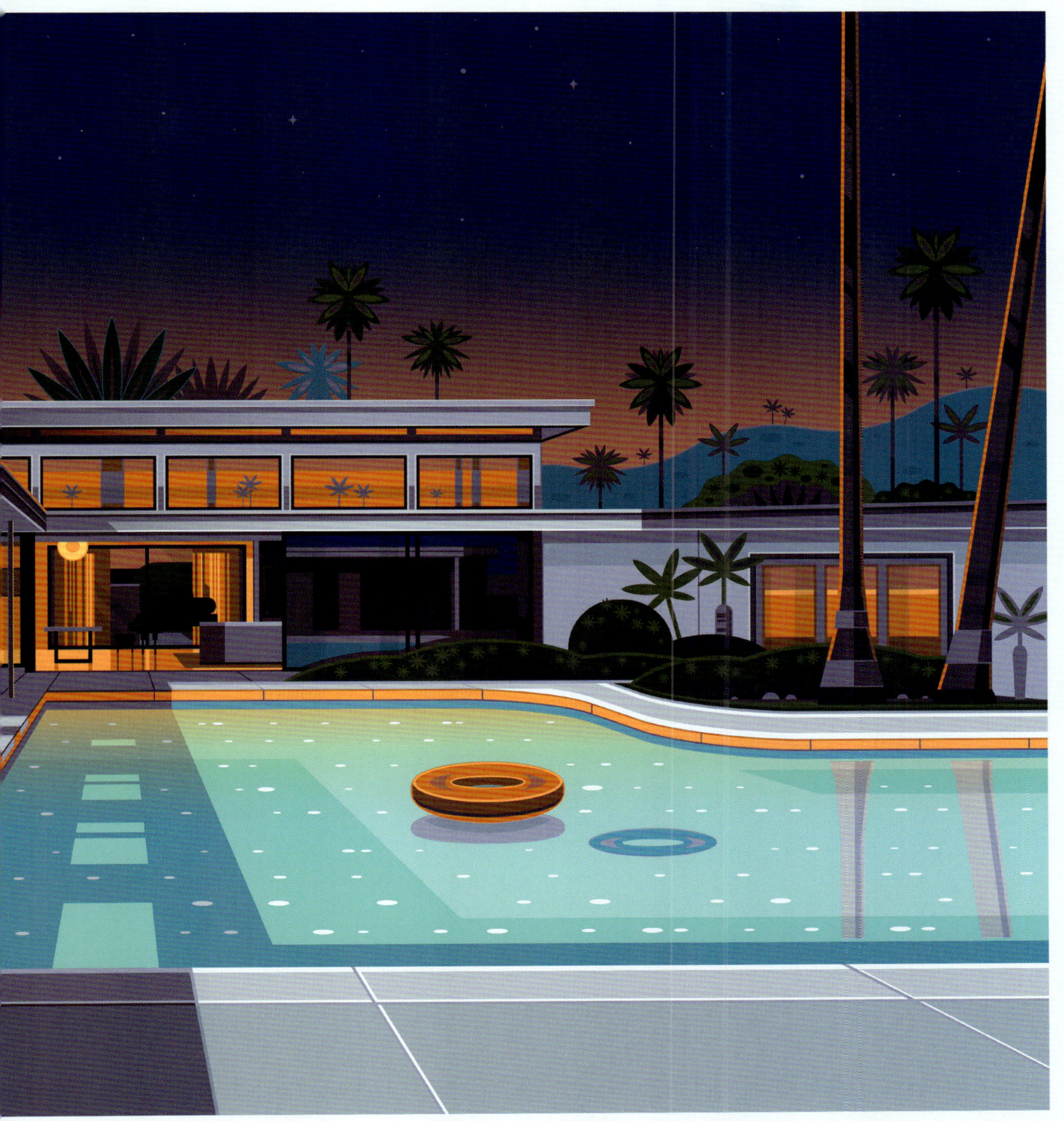

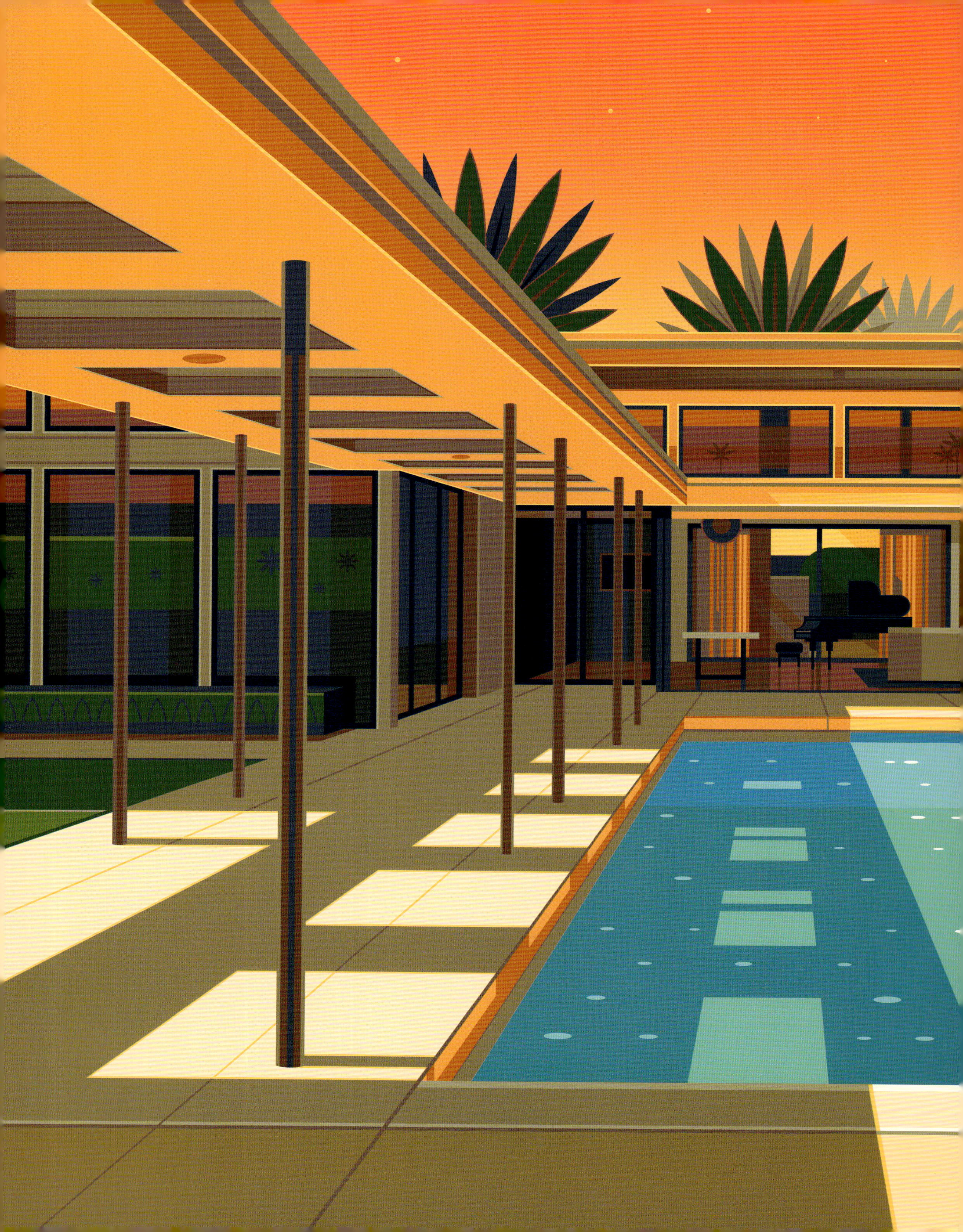

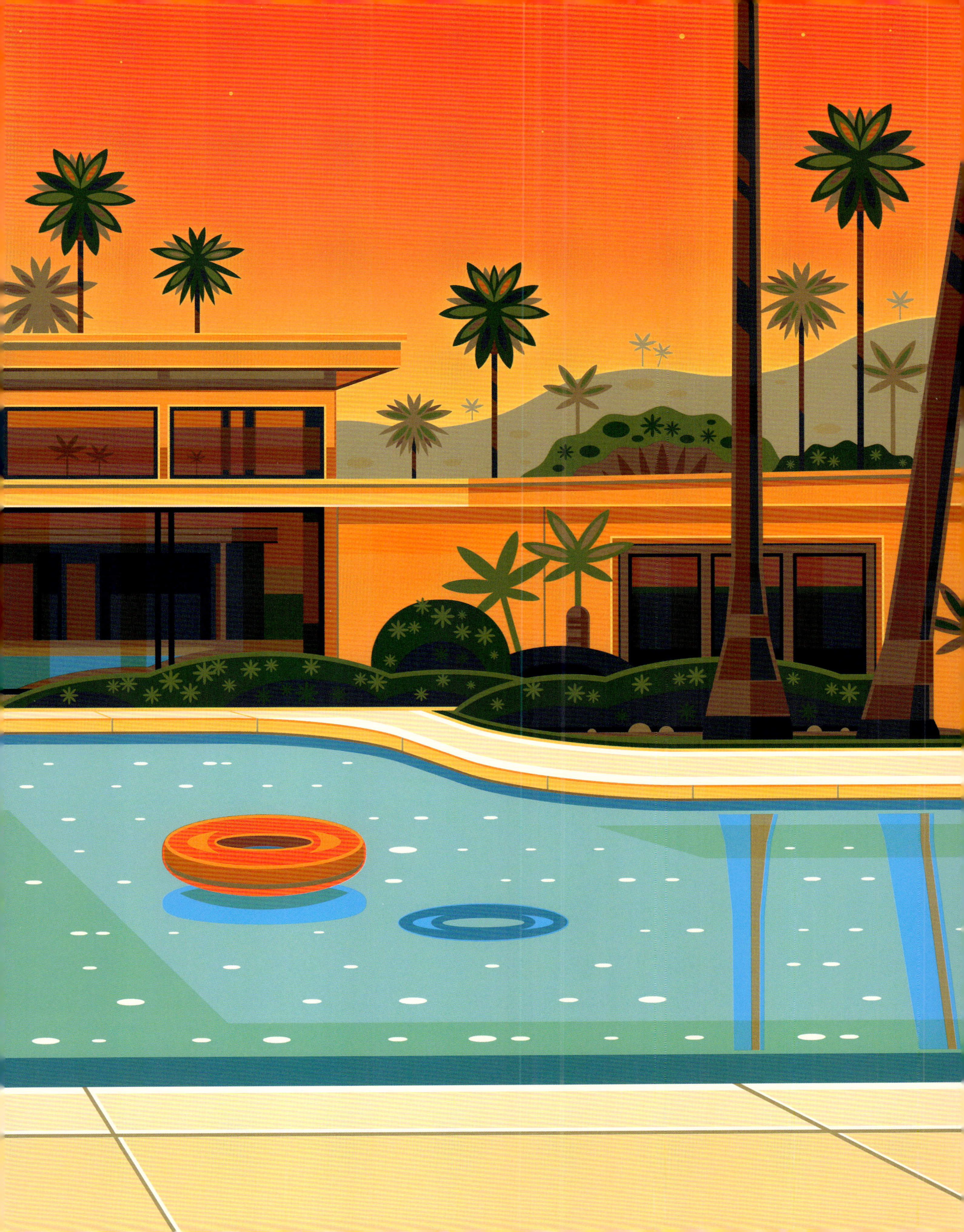

# PARK IMPERIAL SOUTH

| ADDRESS | ARCHITECT(S) | YEAR |
|---|---|---|
| Palm Springs, CA 92264 | William Cody | 1960 |



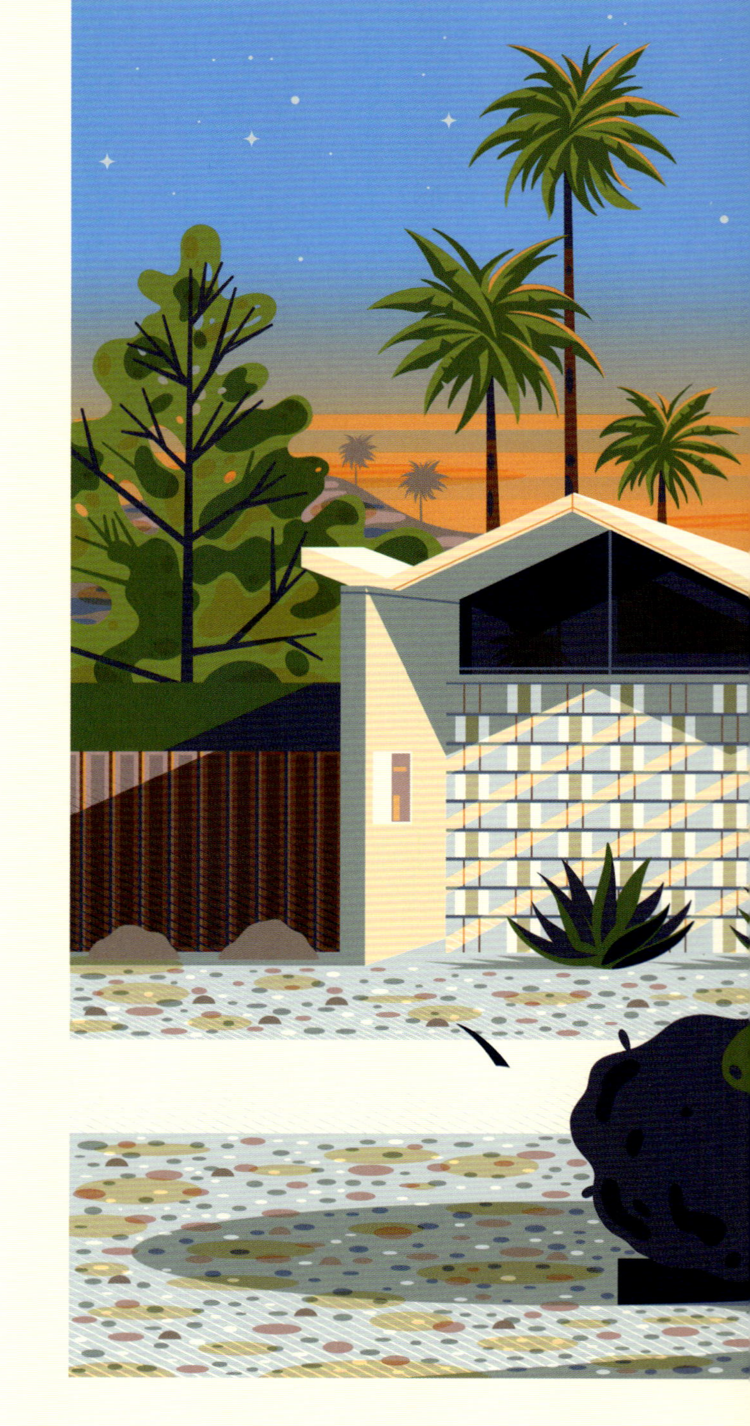

ACROSS

*Park Imperial South*
Open Edition
2018

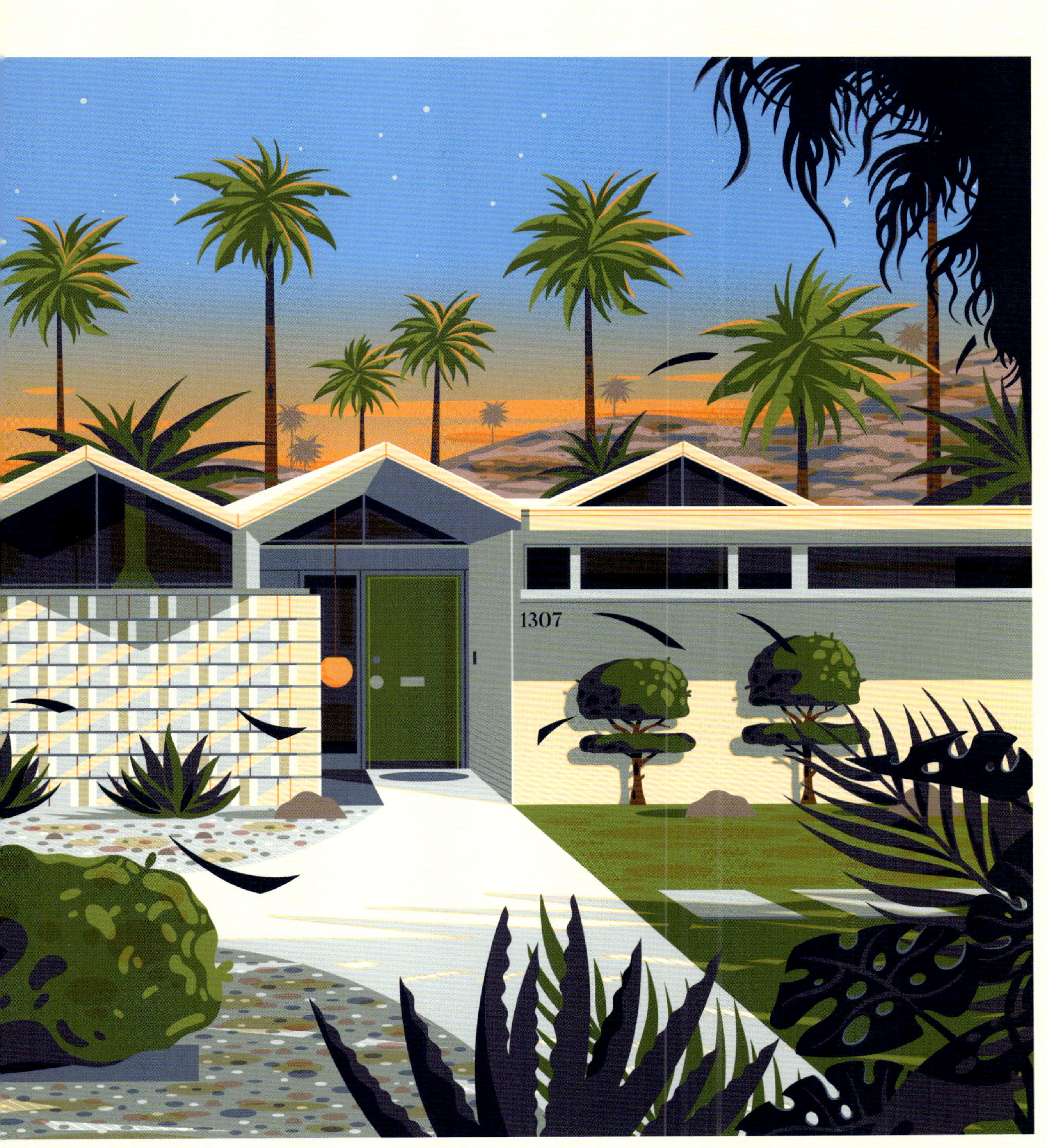
1307

# ALEXANDER HOMES

| ADDRESS | ARCHITECT(S) | YEAR |
|---|---|---|
| Palm Springs, CA | William Krisel | 1957 |

**Although not an iconic landmark itself**, this style of architecture is worth mentioning as it defines Palm Springs, a popular detour just a couple hours away from Los Angeles. Known for its midcentury modern charm, Palm Springs offers a completely different pace and serves as a relaxing escape from LA's hustle and bustle while still delivering a rich connection to Southern California's design history.



This particular home is an Alexander House, part of a development designed by architects like William Krisel, who played a pivotal role in shaping Palm Springs' unique identity. The Alexanders were instrumental in bringing mid-century modern design to the mainstream during the 1950s and '60s, creating stylish yet affordable homes that have become a defining feature of the area.

If you make it out there, I highly recommend renting a bicycle and cycling around the Las Palmas neighbourhood. There are so many beautiful homes to admire, and it's easy to see why Palm Springs continues to be a haven for architecture lovers and vacationers alike.

GATEFOLD

*Alexander Home*
Open Edition
2023

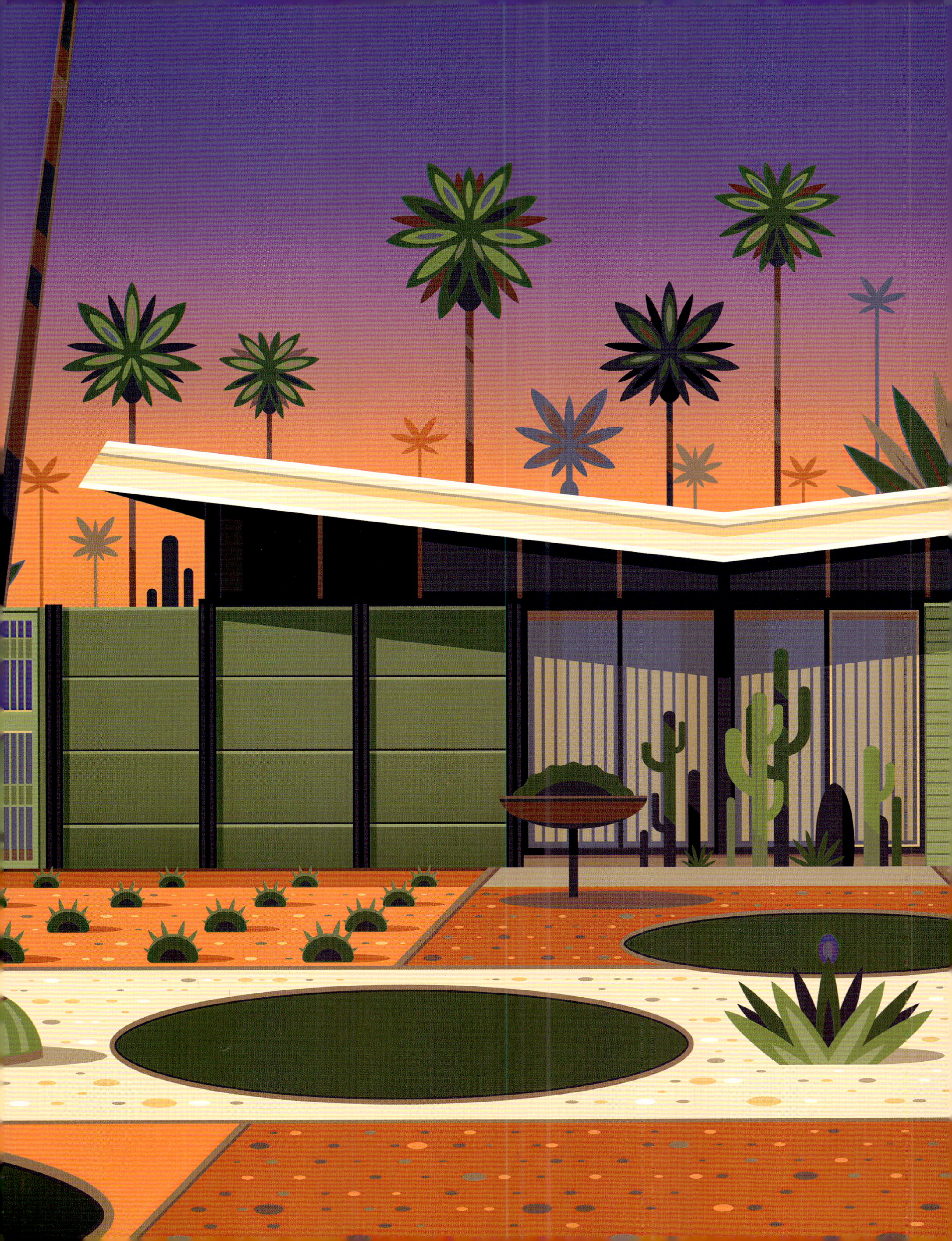

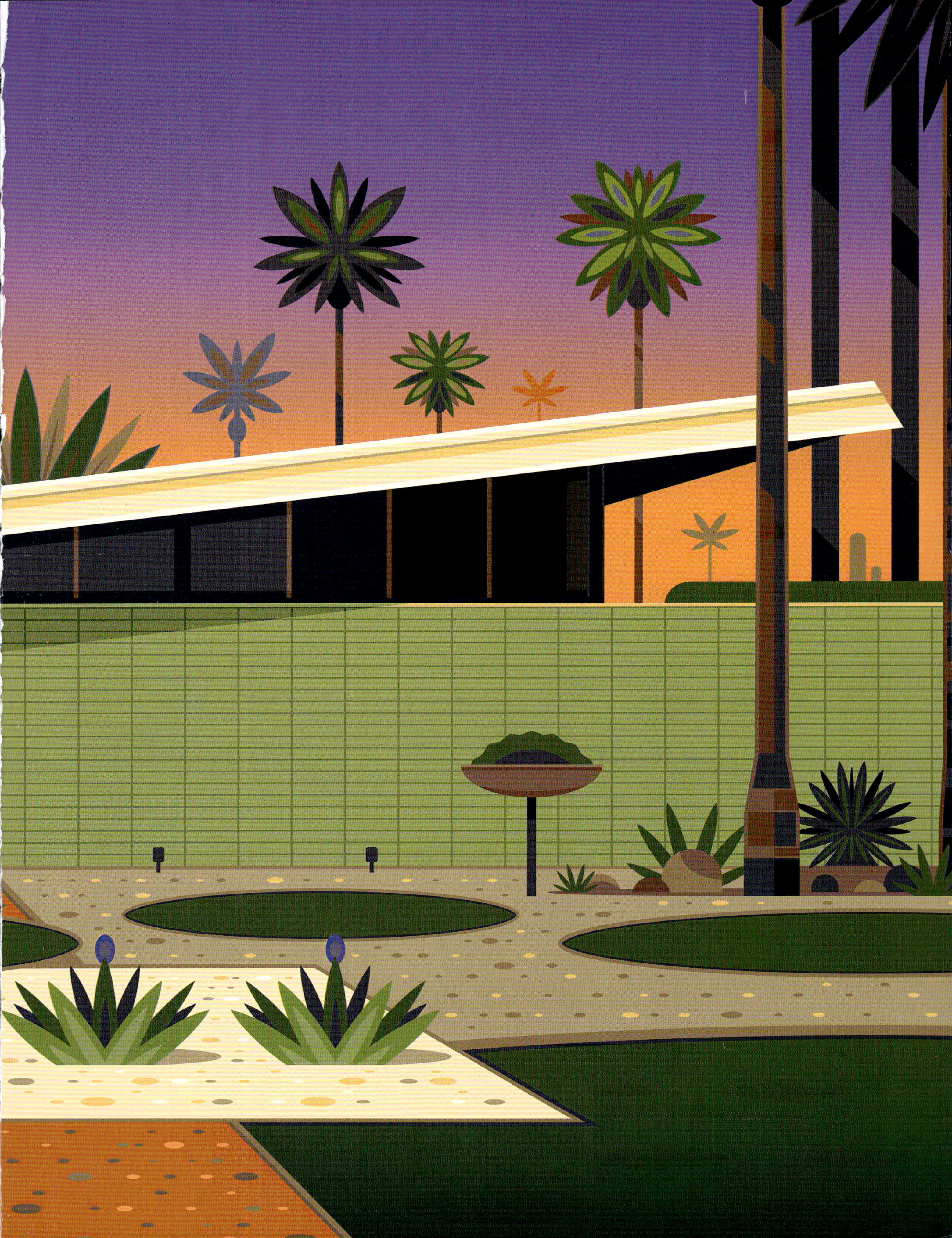

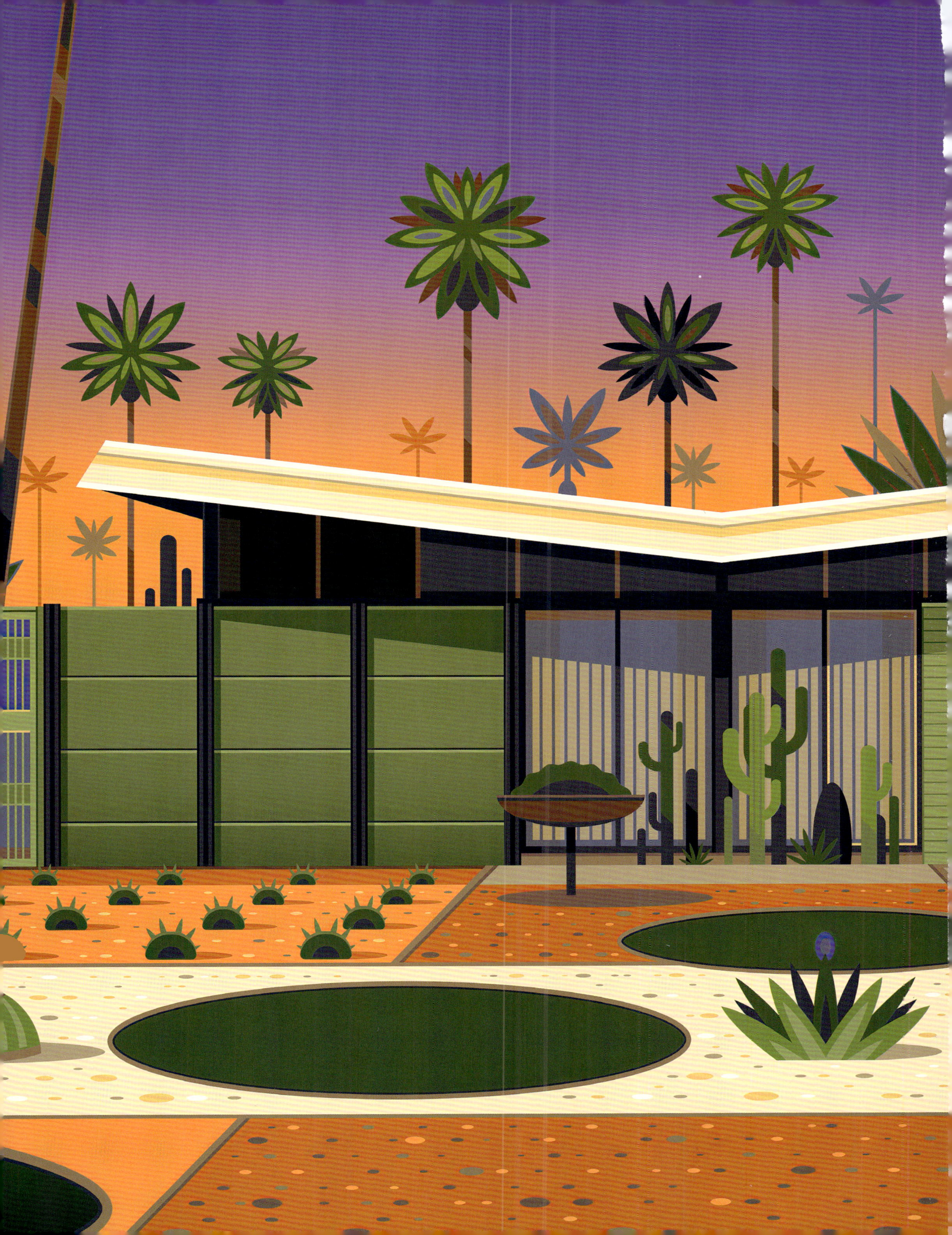

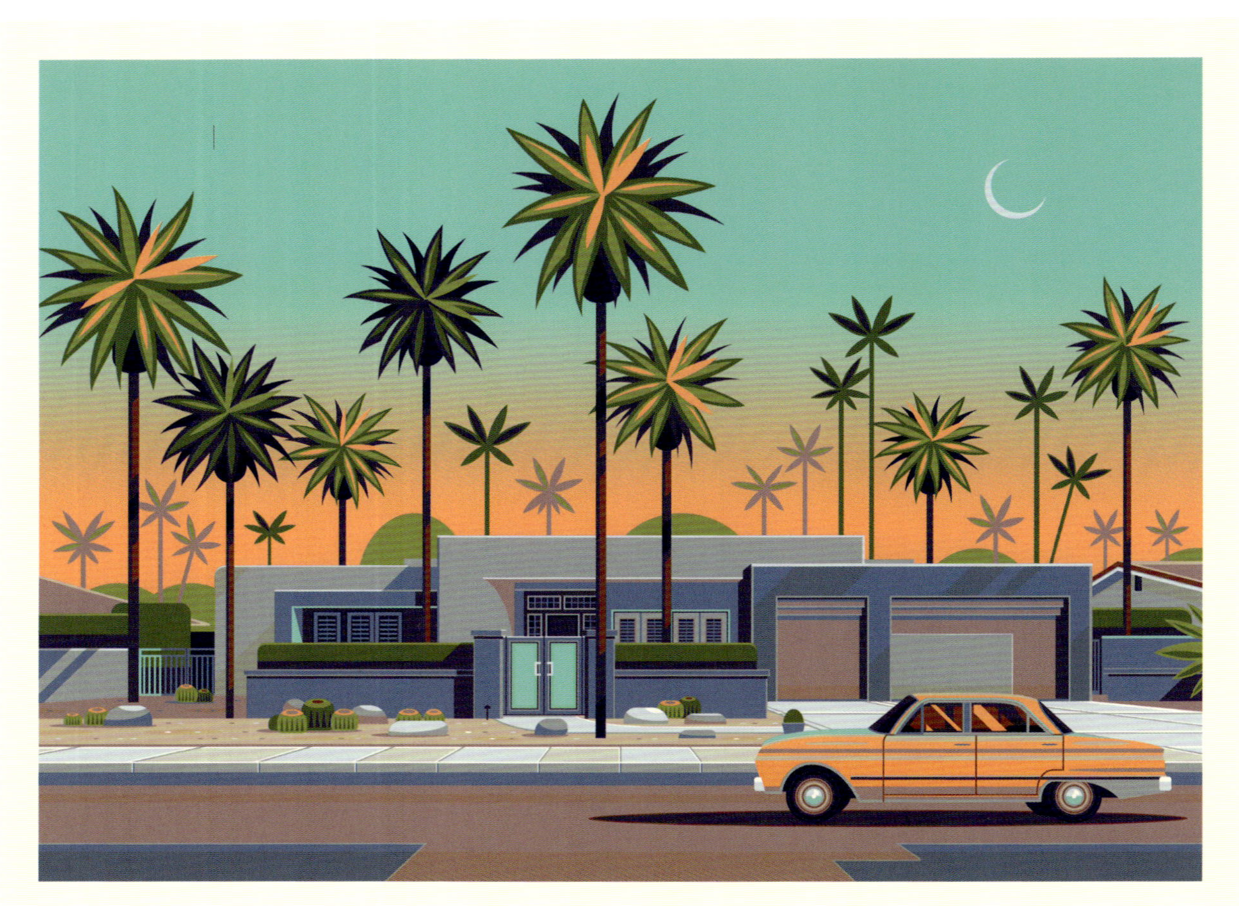

ABOVE

*House on Caliente*
Limited Edition
2021

ACROSS

*House on Via Vadera*
Limited Edition
2020

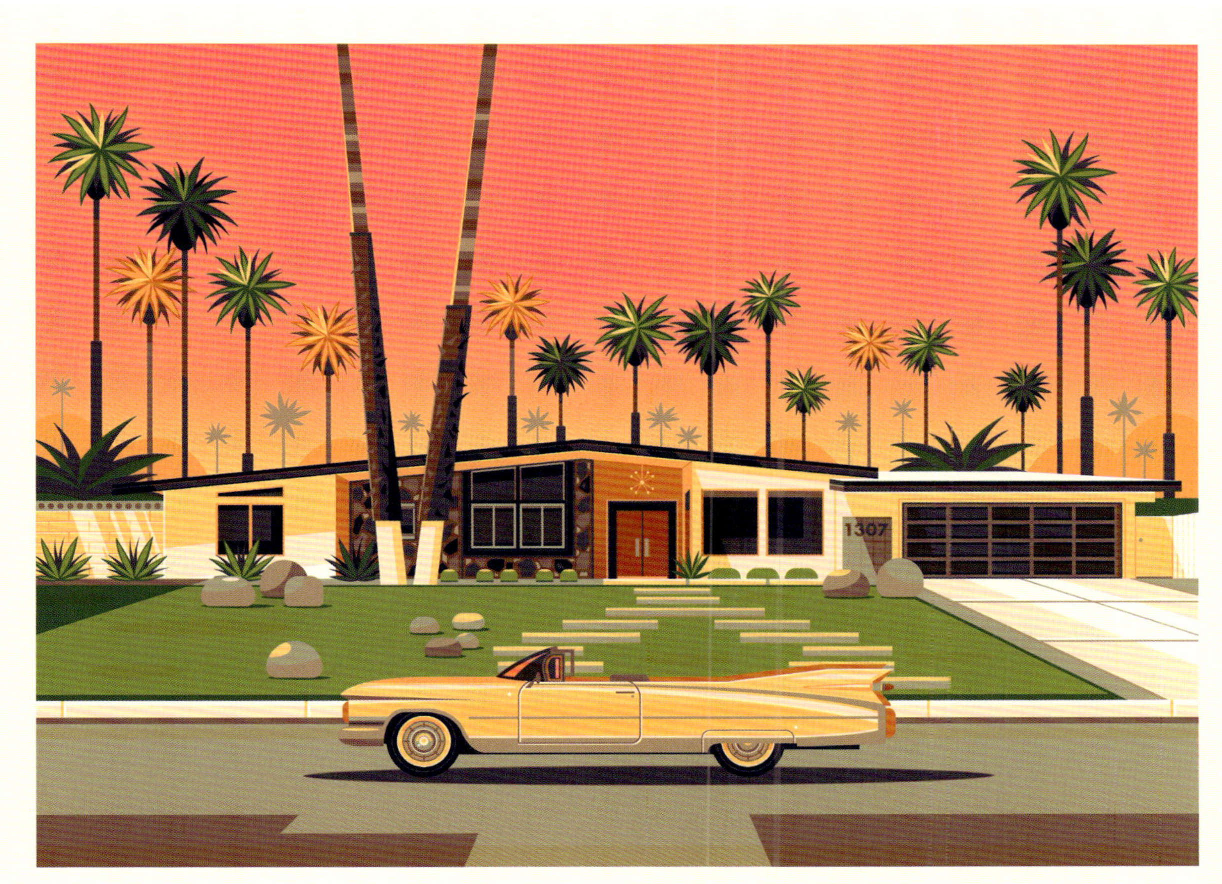
1307

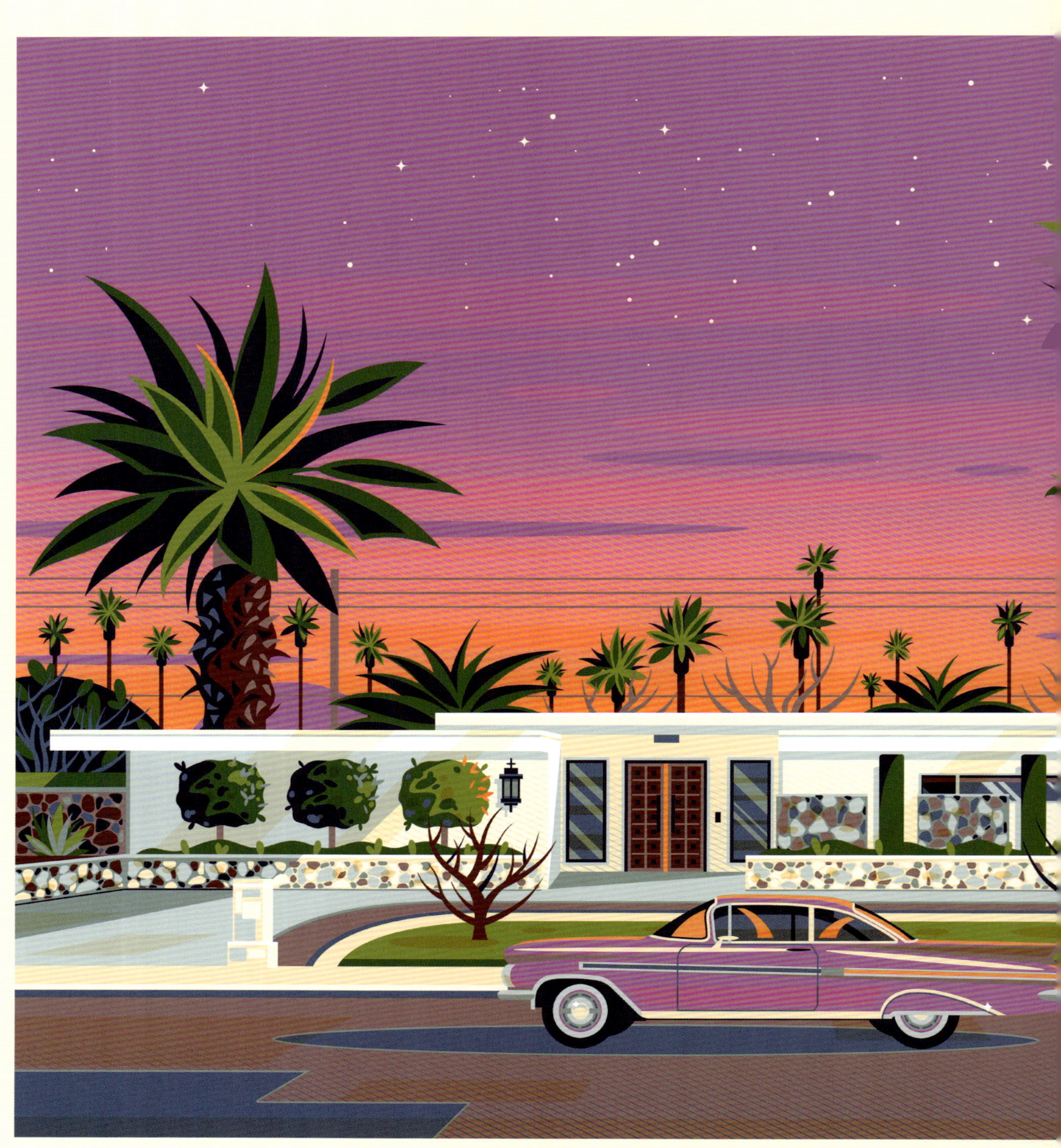

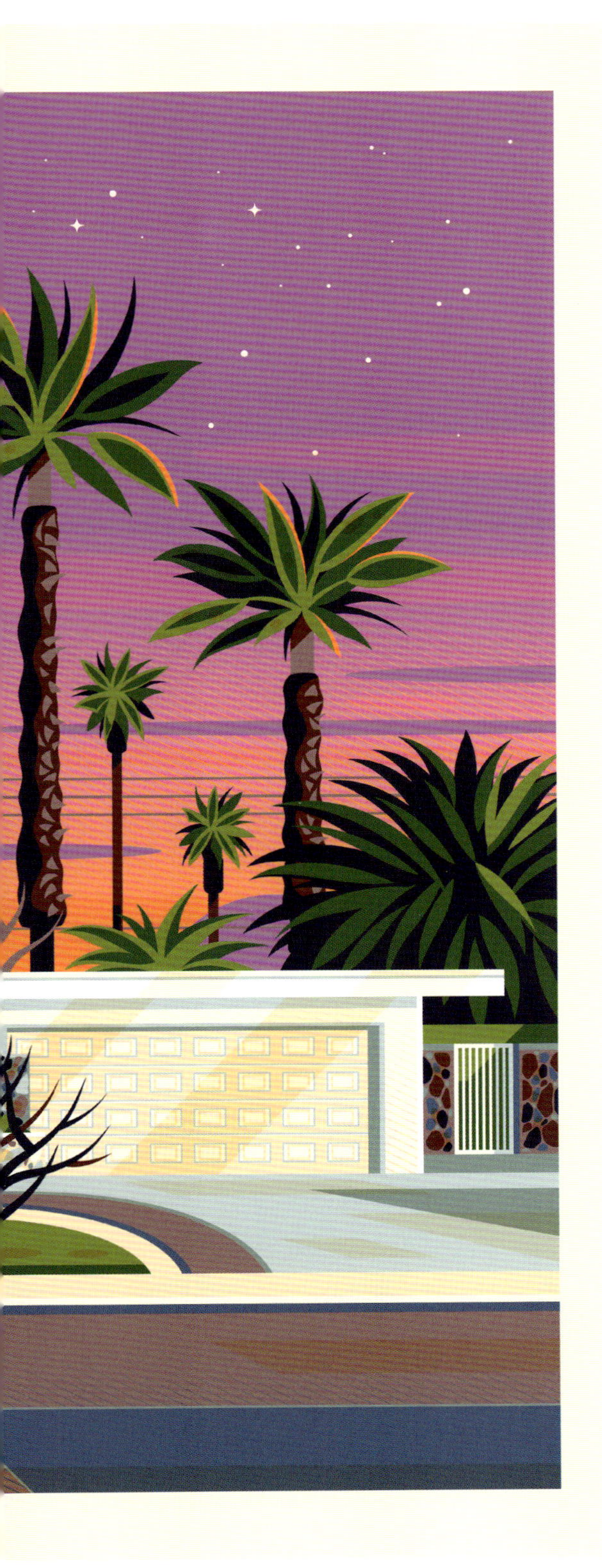



ACROSS

*Palm Springs at Dusk*
Limited Edition
2020

NEXT SPREAD

*Moonlight Over Las Palmas*
Limited Edition
2023

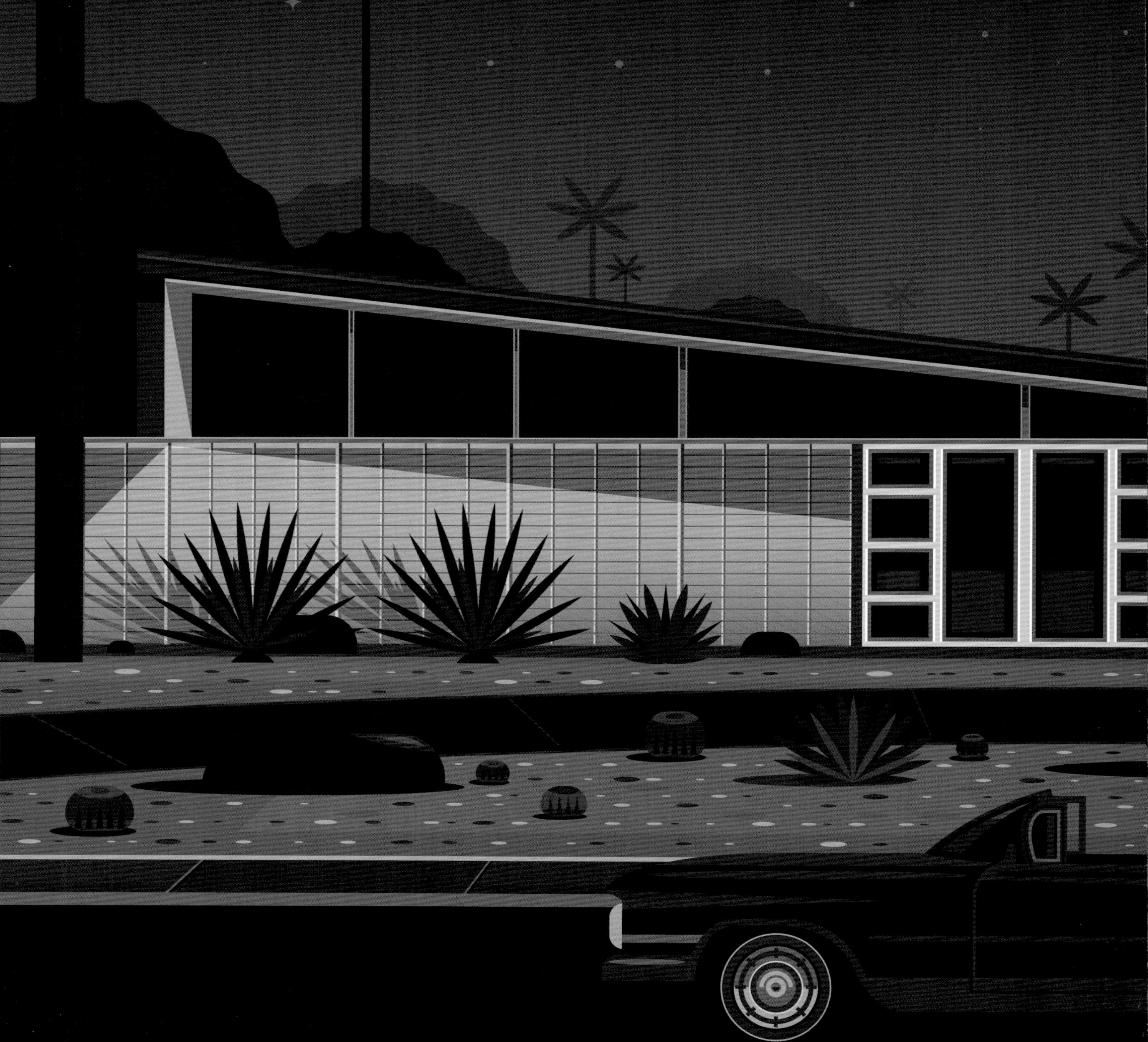

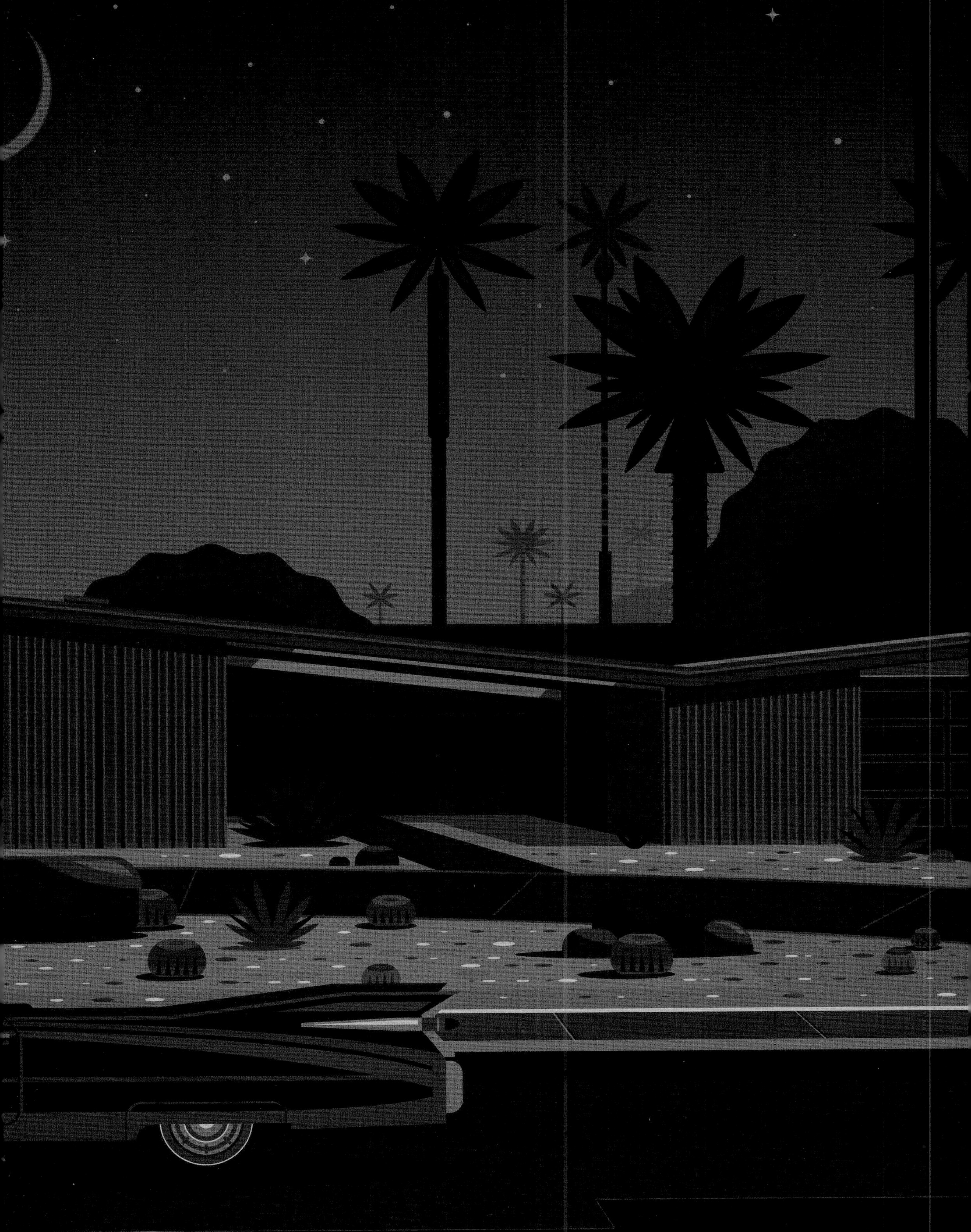

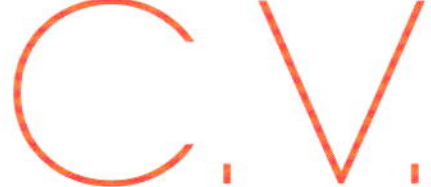


BORN
1996

EDUCATION
University of Central Lancashire
2014–2017

**2024**

*City of Stars—The Art of George Townley,*
Gallery1988, Los Angeles, CA



**2023**

*After Hours—The Art of George Townley,*
Gallery1988, Los Angeles, CA

**2022**

*Sunflower—The Art of George Townley,*
Gallery1988, Los Angeles, CA

**2021**

*Sun-Kissed—The Art of George Townley,*
Gallery1988, Los Angeles, CA
*Frank Lloyd Wright: Timeless,*
Spoke Art, Taliesin West, Scottsdale, AZ

**2020**

*Golden Hour—The Art of George Townley,*
Gallery1988, Los Angeles, CA

*Frank Lloyd Wright: Timeless,*
Spoke Art, San Francisco, CA
*Franchise Three,*
Gallery1988, Los Angeles, CA

**2019**

*LA Local—Inspired by Los Angeles,*
Gallery1988, Los Angeles, CA
*Miyazaki—An Art Show Tribute,*
Spoke Art, Honolulu, HI
*Frank Lloyd Wright: Timeless,*
Spoke Art x Taliesin West, Scottsdale, AZ
*Frank Lloyd Wright: Timeless,*
Spoke Art x Hashimoto Contemporary, New York City, NY
*Frank Lloyd Wright: Timeless,*
Spoke Art x Taliesin, Spring Green, WI

**2018**



*O Coen, Where Art Thou?,*
Spoke Art, New York City, NY
*Miyazaki—An Art Show Tribute,*
Spoke Art, Los Angeles, CA
*30x30—Celebrating the Films of 1988,*
London, England

**2017**

*Miyazaki—An Art Show Tribute,*
Spoke Art, San Francisco, CA
*In Dreams—David Lynch Tribute,*
Spoke Art, New York City, NY
*D&AD New Blood 2017,*
London, England
*Miyazaki—An Art Show Tribute,*
Spoke Art, Portland, OR
*Bad Dads—Wes Anderson Tribute,*
Spoke Art, New York City, NY

# BIOGRAPHY

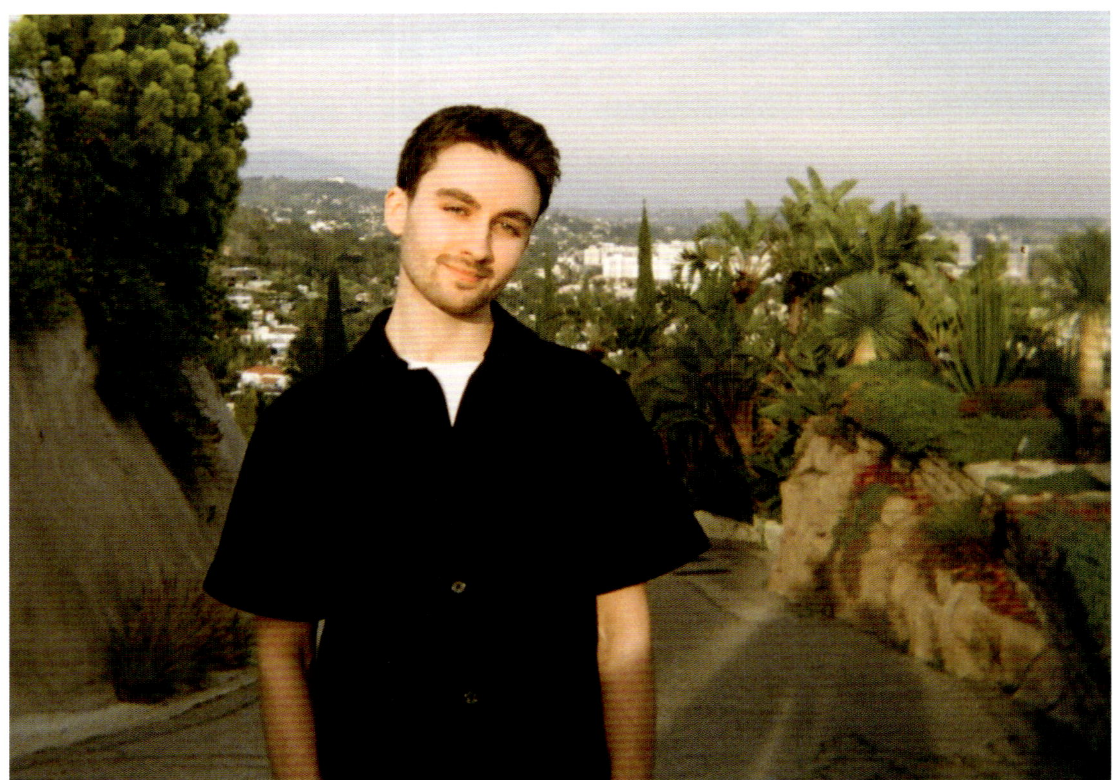



**George Townley is an illustrator and designer based in London** with a passion for capturing architecture and the spirit of Los Angeles. Growing up in Northern England, surrounded by grey and dreary surroundings, George turned to art as a means of escape, finding joy and inspiration in bringing these vibrant worlds to life.

This passion blossomed during a study abroad program in San Marcos, California, where the sunny, laid-back environment of Southern California completely transformed his style. This experience ignited a lifelong fascination with Americana and the unique charm of Los Angeles, which has since become a defining feature of his work. Through his art, George hopes to spark nostalgia and inspire others to find their own way to escape and dream.

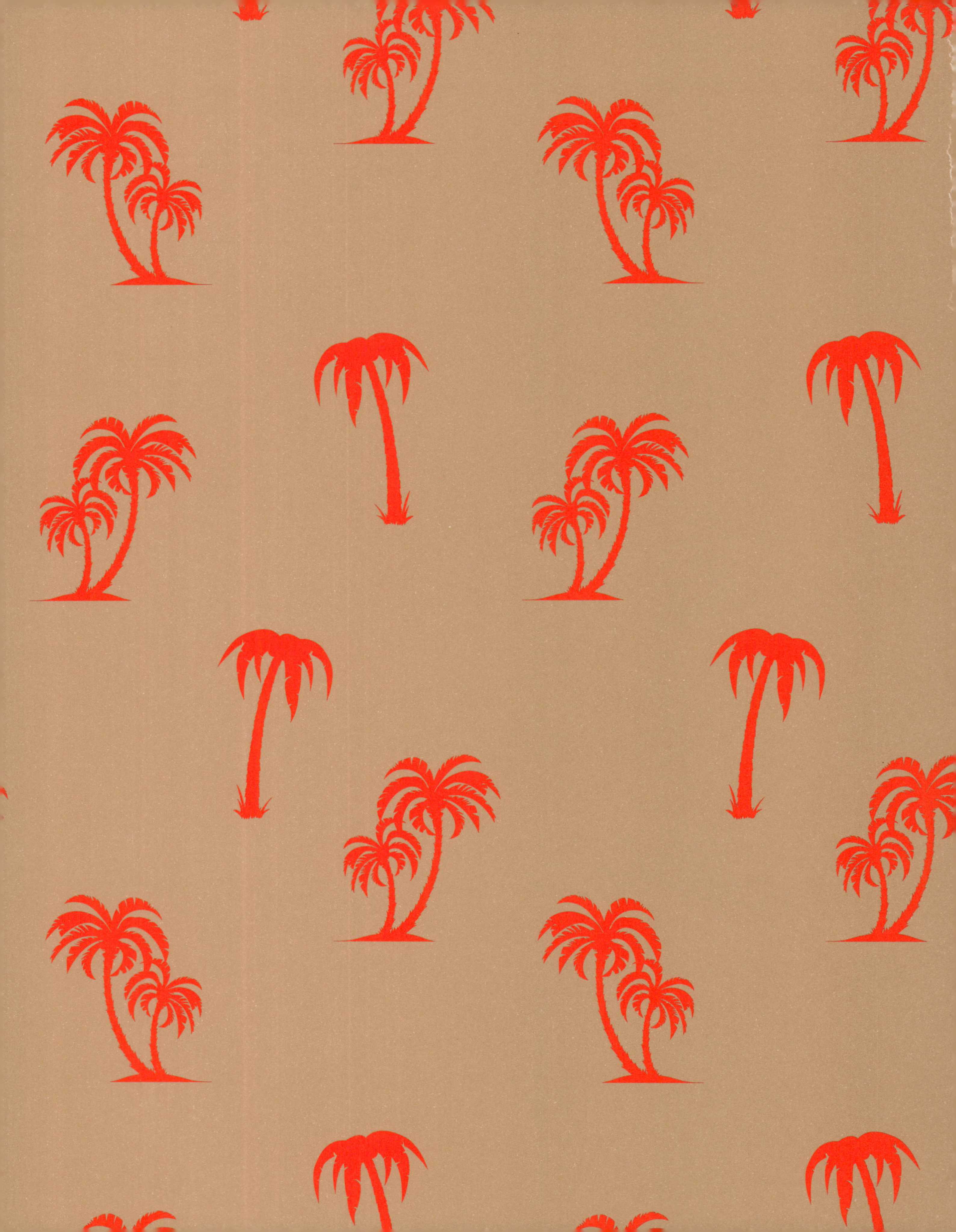